GUMSHOE CITY

WORDS BY:

WINSTON GAMBRO

PICTURES BY:

MICHAEL LEE HARRIS

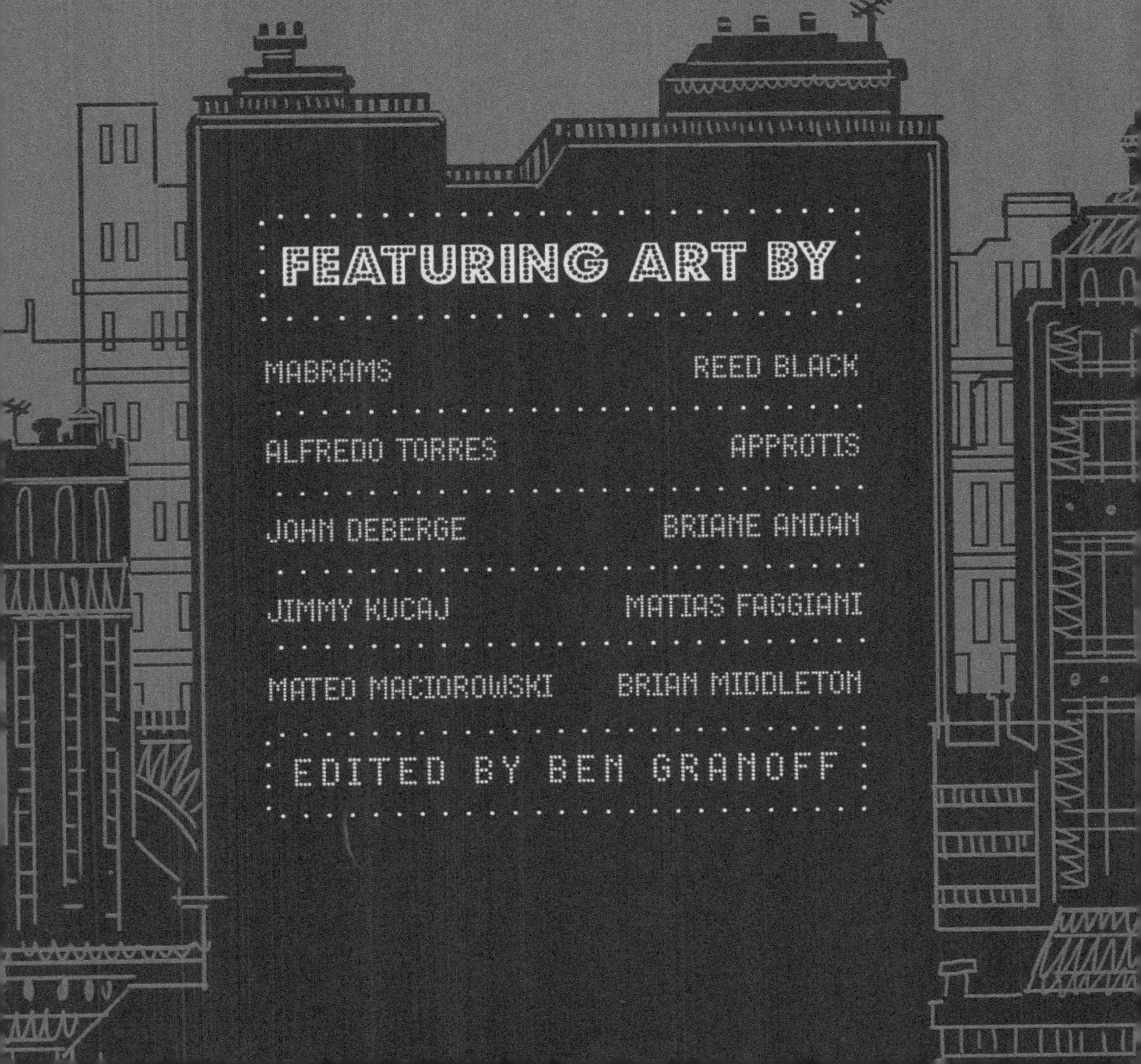

FEATURING ART BY

MABRAMS

REED BLACK

ALFREDO TORRES

APPROTIS

JOHN DEBERGE

BRIANE ANDAN

JIMMY KUCAJ

MATIAS FAGGIANI

MATEO MACIOROWSKI

BRIAN MIDDLETON

EDITED BY BEN GRANOFF

Published by Markosia Enterprises, PO BOX 3477, Barnet, Hertfordshire, EN5 9HN.
FIRST PRINTING, February 2024. Harry Markos, Director.
ISBN 978-1-916968-24-0

FOR **MARKOSIA ENTERPRISES** LTD

HARRY MARKOS
PUBLISHER & MANAGING PARTNER

GM JORDAN
SPECIAL PROJECTS CO-ORDINATOR

ANDY BRIGGS
CREATIVE CONSULTANT

IAN SHARMAN
EDITOR IN CHIEF

www.markosia.com

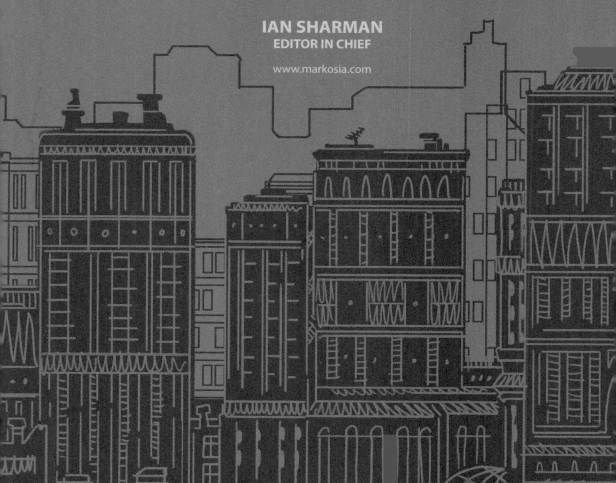

THE CASE OF
THE ONGOING BEEF

CHAPTER 1

THE DEAD DAME IN THE DOMICILE

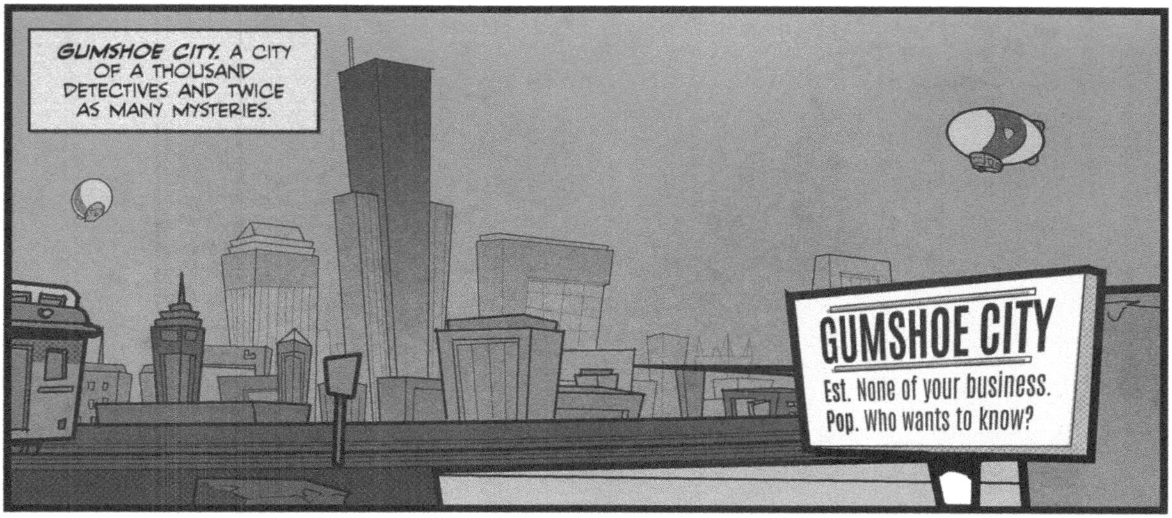
GUMSHOE CITY. A CITY OF A THOUSAND DETECTIVES AND TWICE AS MANY MYSTERIES.
GUMSHOE CITY
Est. None of your business.
Pop. Who wants to know?

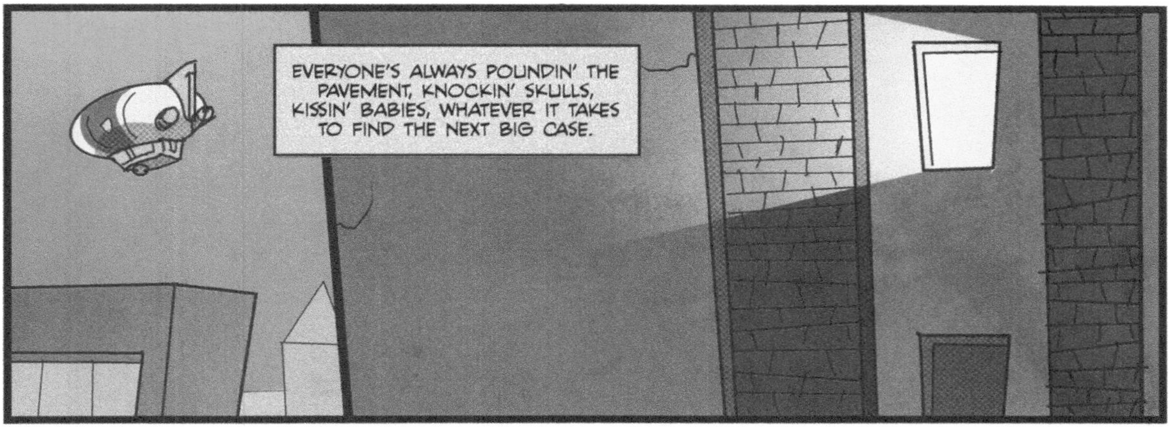
EVERYONE'S ALWAYS POUNDIN' THE PAVEMENT, KNOCKIN' SKULLS, KISSIN' BABIES, WHATEVER IT TAKES TO FIND THE NEXT BIG CASE.

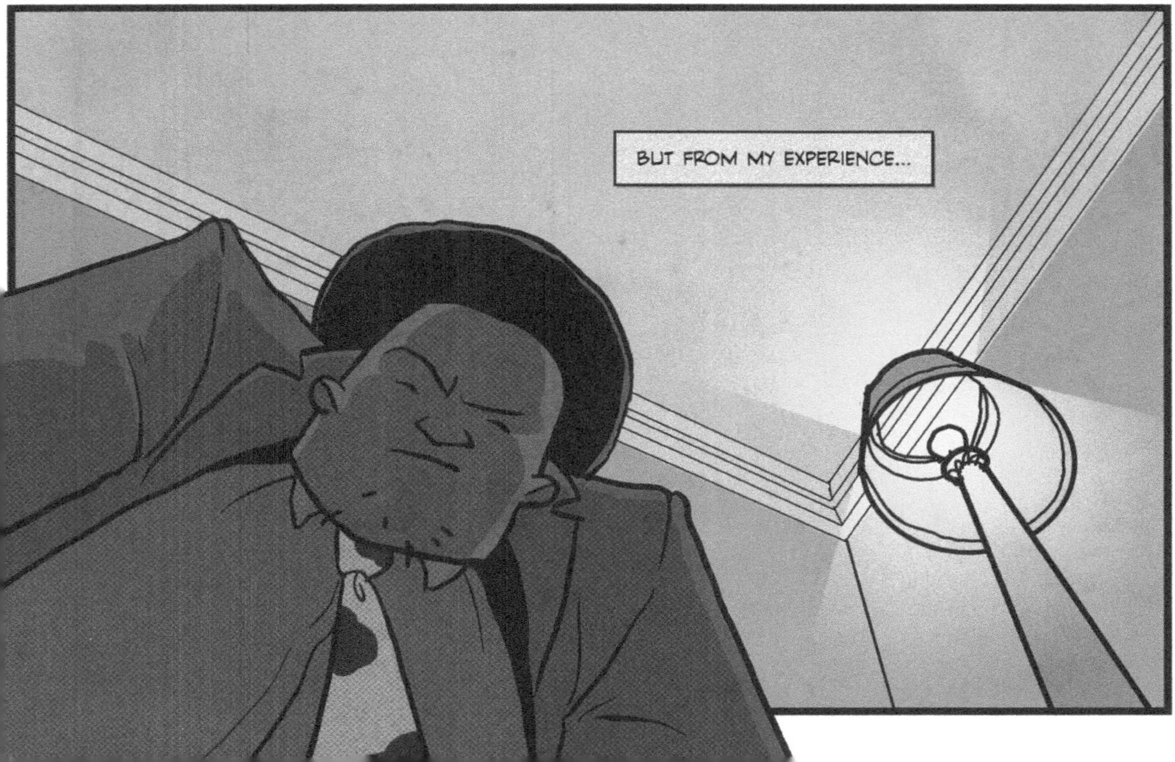
BUT FROM MY EXPERIENCE...

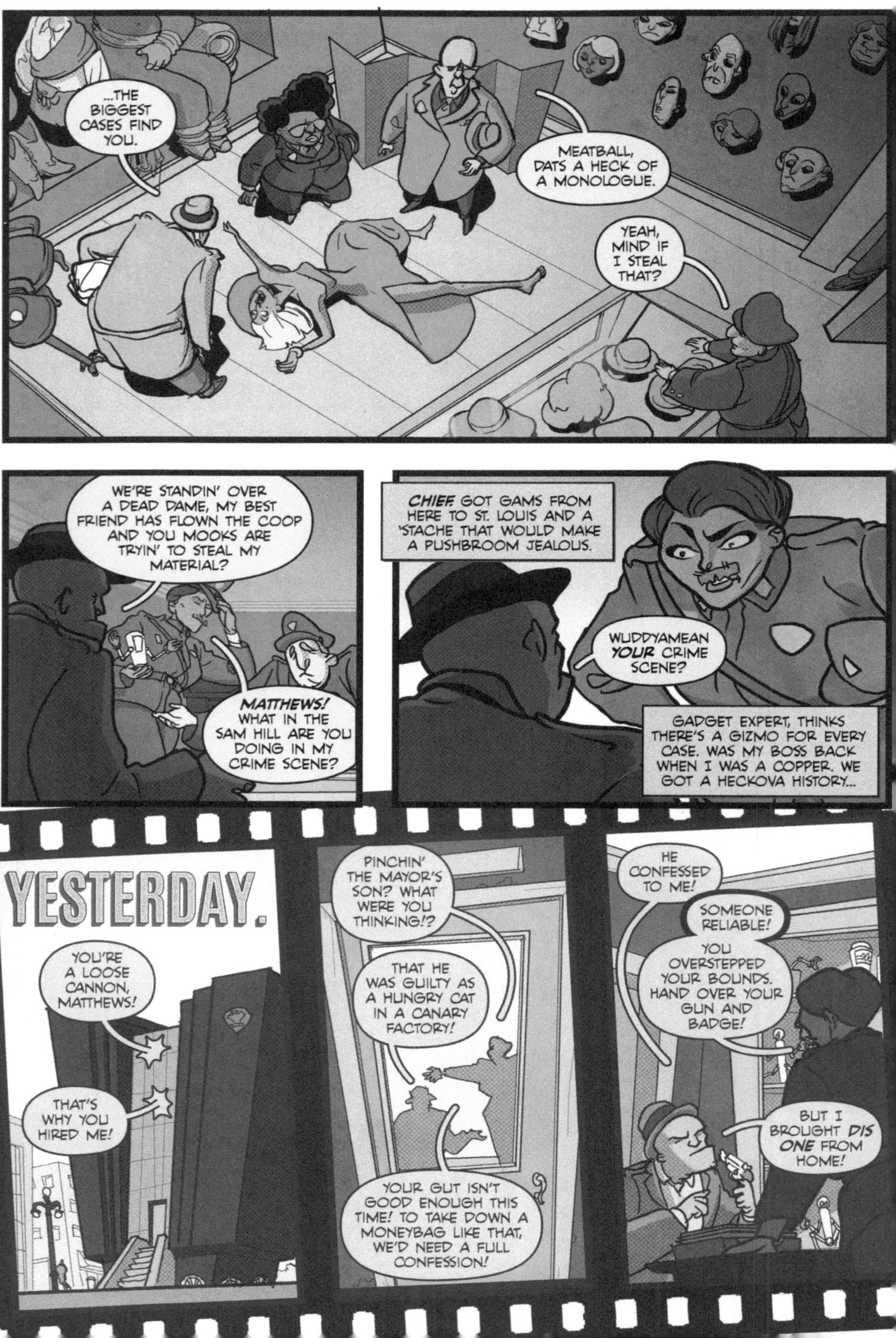
...THE BIGGEST CASES FIND YOU.
MEATBALL, DATS A HECK OF A MONOLOGUE.
YEAH, MIND IF I STEAL THAT?
WE'RE STANDIN' OVER A DEAD DAME, MY BEST FRIEND HAS FLOWN THE COOP AND YOU MOOKS ARE TRYIN' TO STEAL MY MATERIAL?
MATTHEWS! WHAT IN THE SAM HILL ARE YOU DOING IN MY CRIME SCENE?
CHIEF. GOT GAMS FROM HERE TO ST. LOUIS AND A 'STACHE THAT WOULD MAKE A PUSHBROOM JEALOUS.
WUDDYAMEAN YOUR CRIME SCENE?
GADGET EXPERT, THINKS THERE'S A GIZMO FOR EVERY CASE. WAS MY BOSS BACK WHEN I WAS A COPPER. WE GOT A HECKOVA HISTORY...
YESTERDAY.
YOU'RE A LOOSE CANNON, MATTHEWS!
THAT'S WHY YOU HIRED ME!
PINCHIN' THE MAYOR'S SON? WHAT WERE YOU THINKING!?
THAT HE WAS GUILTY AS A HUNGRY CAT IN A CANARY FACTORY!
YOUR GUT ISN'T GOOD ENOUGH THIS TIME! TO TAKE DOWN A MONEYBAG LIKE THAT, WE'D NEED A FULL CONFESSION!
HE CONFESSED TO ME!
SOMEONE RELIABLE!
YOU OVERSTEPPED YOUR BOUNDS. HAND OVER YOUR GUN AND BADGE!
BUT I BROUGHT DIS ONE FROM HOME!

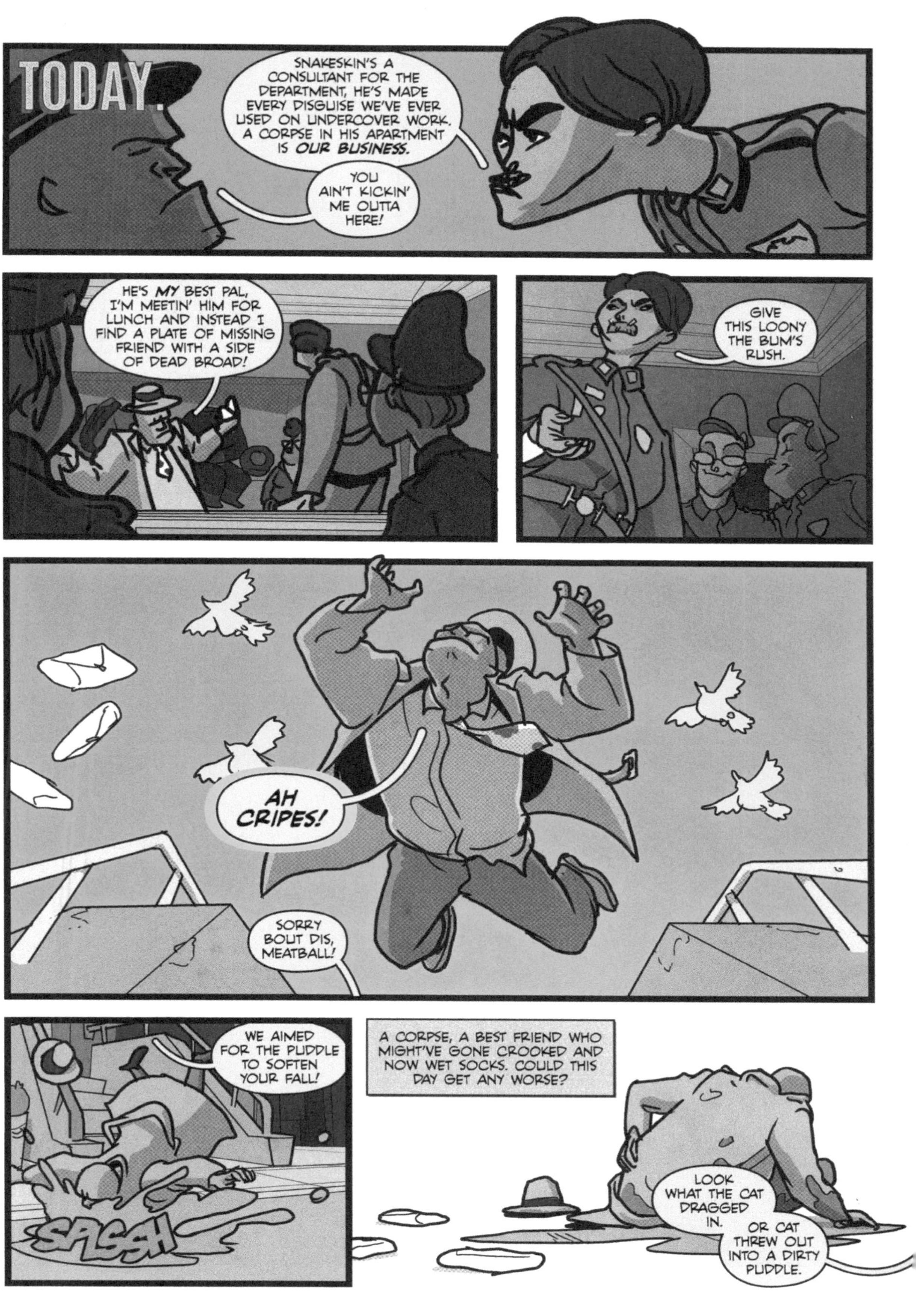
TODAY.
SNAKESKIN'S A CONSULTANT FOR THE DEPARTMENT, HE'S MADE EVERY DISGUISE WE'VE EVER USED ON UNDERCOVER WORK. A CORPSE IN HIS APARTMENT IS OUR BUSINESS.
YOU AIN'T KICKIN' ME OUTTA HERE!
HE'S MY BEST PAL, I'M MEETIN' HIM FOR LUNCH AND INSTEAD I FIND A PLATE OF MISSING FRIEND WITH A SIDE OF DEAD BROAD!
GIVE THIS LOONY THE BUM'S RUSH.
AH CRIPES!
SORRY BOUT DIS, MEATBALL!
WE AIMED FOR THE PUDDLE TO SOFTEN YOUR FALL!
SPLSSH
A CORPSE, A BEST FRIEND WHO MIGHT'VE GONE CROOKED AND NOW WET SOCKS. COULD THIS DAY GET ANY WORSE?
LOOK WHAT THE CAT DRAGGED IN.
OR CAT THREW OUT INTO A DIRTY PUDDLE.

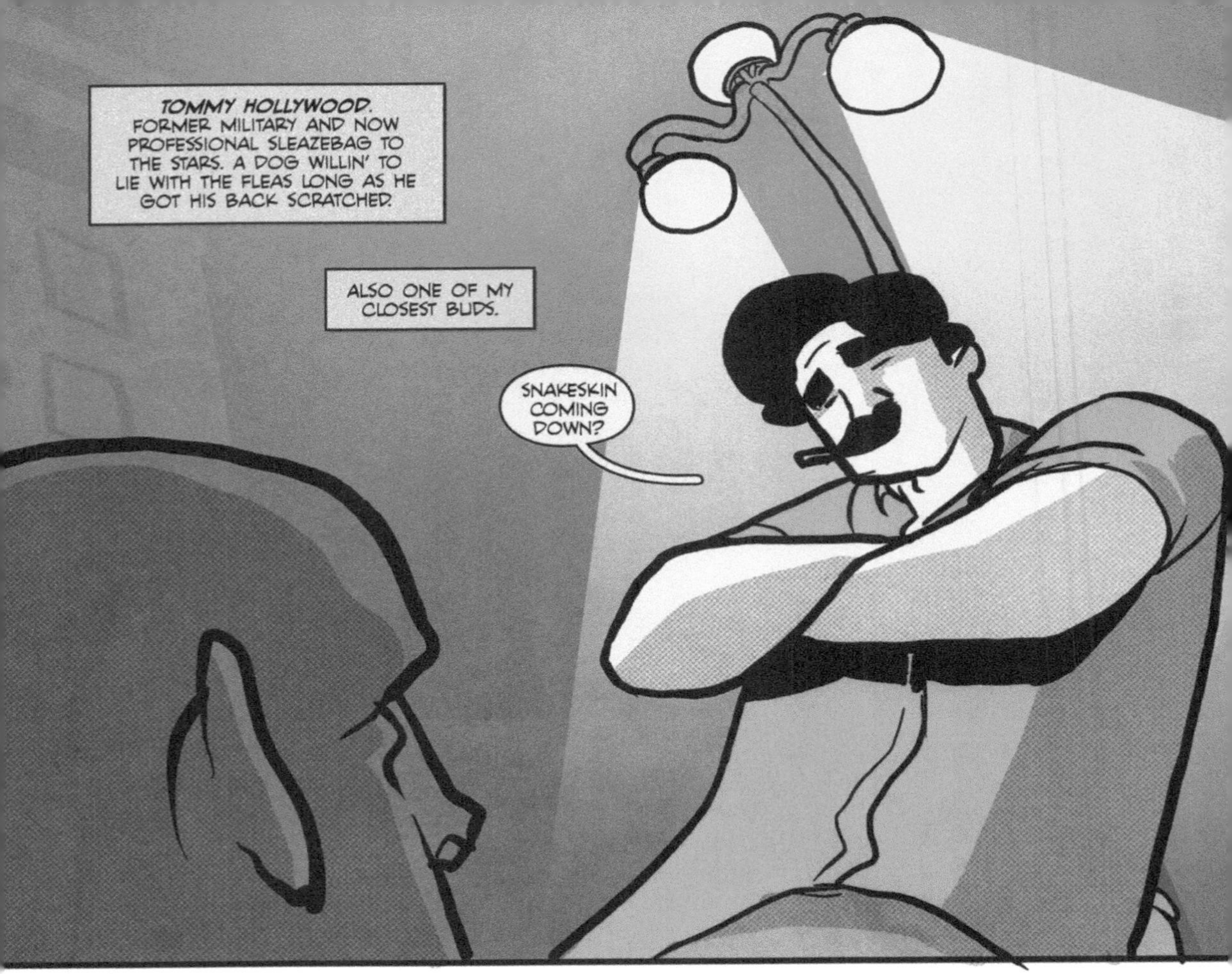
TOMMY HOLLYWOOD. FORMER MILITARY AND NOW PROFESSIONAL SLEAZEBAG TO THE STARS. A DOG WILLIN' TO LIE WITH THE FLEAS LONG AS HE GOT HIS BACK SCRATCHED.
ALSO ONE OF MY CLOSEST BUDS.
SNAKESKIN COMING DOWN?
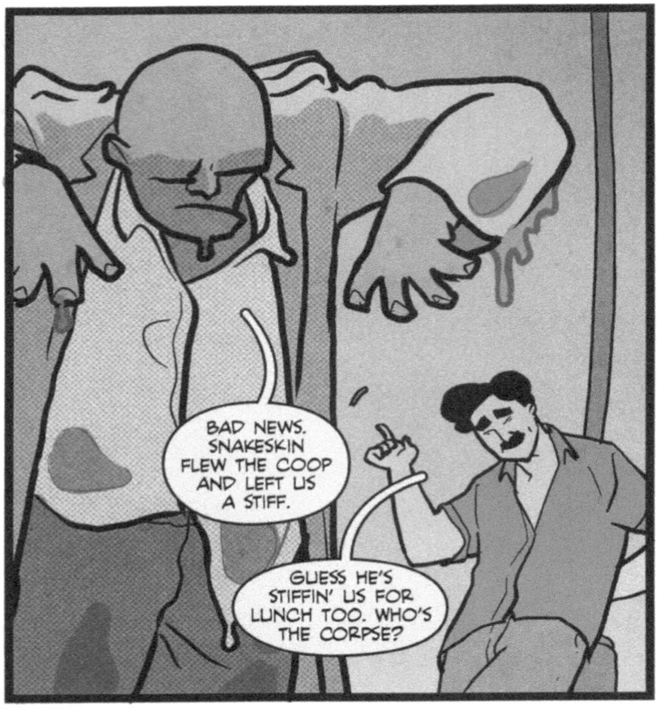
BAD NEWS. SNAKESKIN FLEW THE COOP AND LEFT US A STIFF.
GUESS HE'S STIFFIN' US FOR LUNCH TOO. WHO'S THE CORPSE?
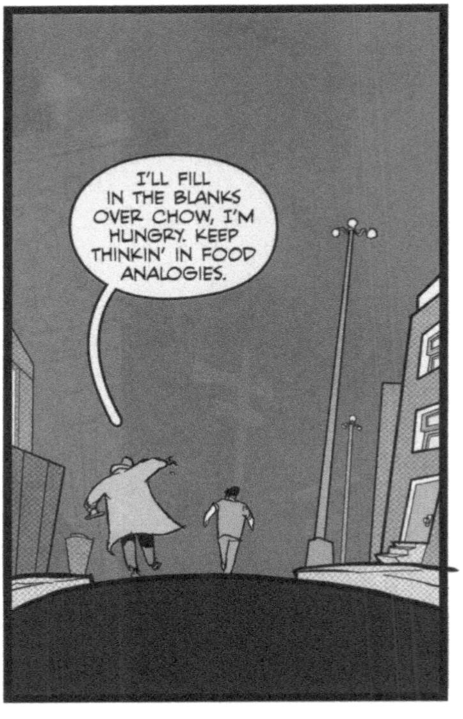
I'LL FILL IN THE BLANKS OVER CHOW, I'M HUNGRY. KEEP THINKIN' IN FOOD ANALOGIES.

CHAPTER 2
Last Supper

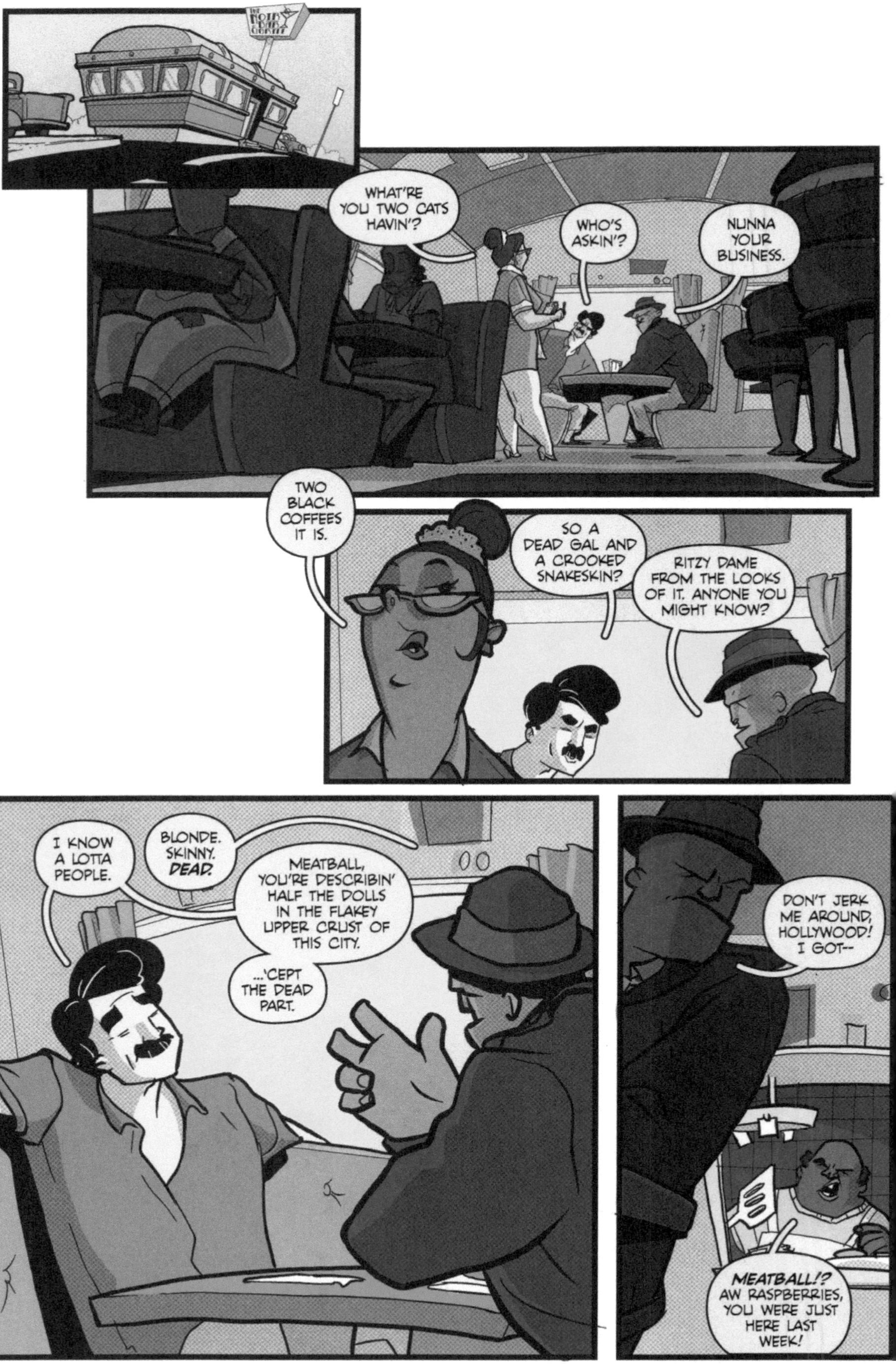
WHAT'RE YOU TWO CATS HAVIN'?
WHO'S ASKIN'?
NUNNA YOUR BUSINESS.
TWO BLACK COFFEES IT IS.
SO A DEAD GAL AND A CROOKED SNAKESKIN?
RITZY DAME FROM THE LOOKS OF IT. ANYONE YOU MIGHT KNOW?
I KNOW A LOTTA PEOPLE.
BLONDE. SKINNY. ***DEAD.***
MEATBALL, YOU'RE DESCRIBIN' HALF THE DOLLS IN THE FLAKEY UPPER CRUST OF THIS CITY.
...'CEPT THE DEAD PART.
DON'T JERK ME AROUND, HOLLYWOOD! I GOT--
MEATBALL!? AW RASPBERRIES, YOU WERE JUST HERE LAST WEEK!

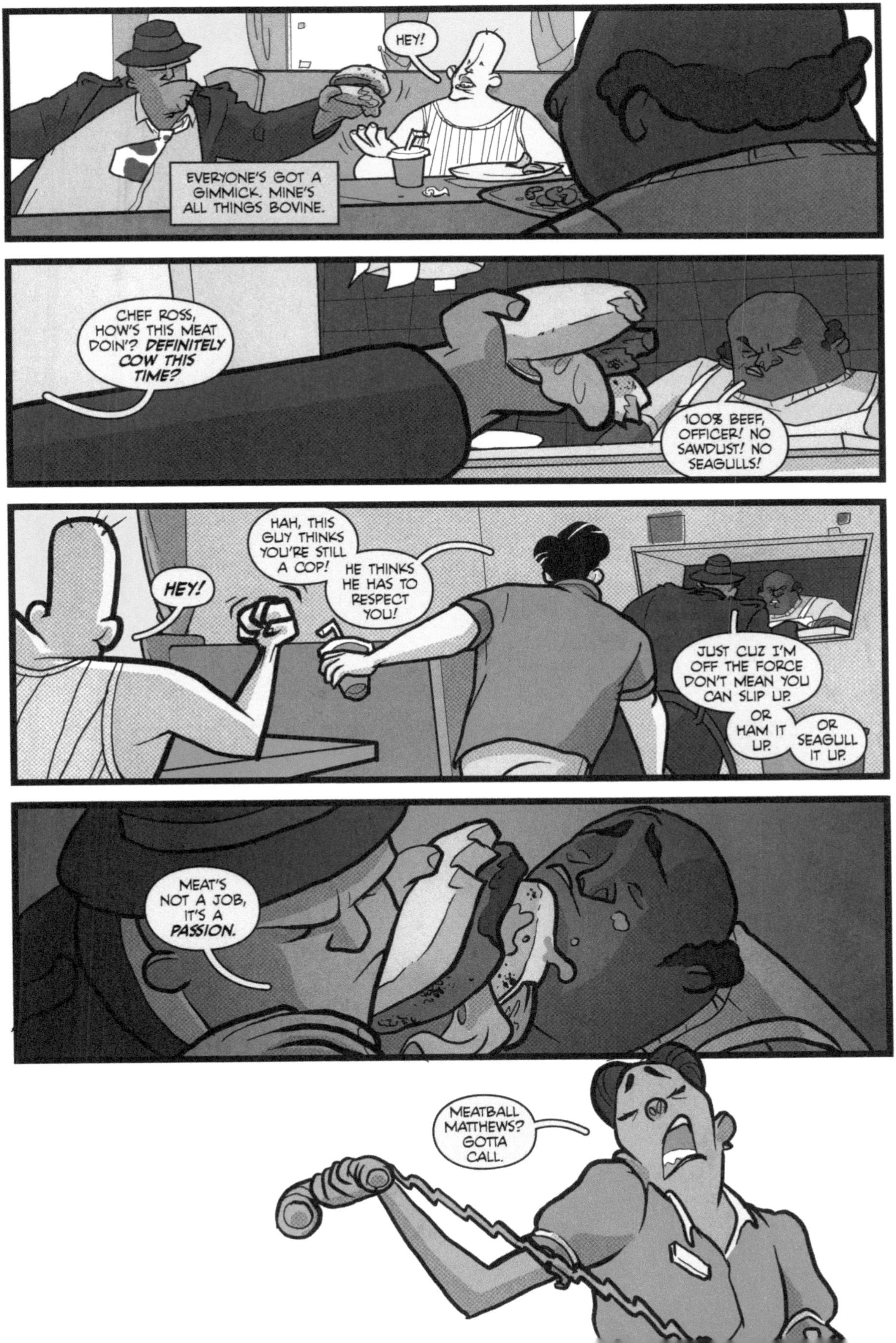
HEY!
EVERYONE'S GOT A GIMMICK. MINE'S ALL THINGS BOVINE.
CHEF ROSS, HOW'S THIS MEAT DOIN'? DEFINITELY COW THIS TIME?
100% BEEF, OFFICER! NO SAWDUST! NO SEAGULLS!
HEY!
HAH, THIS GUY THINKS YOU'RE STILL A COP!
HE THINKS HE HAS TO RESPECT YOU!
JUST CUZ I'M OFF THE FORCE DON'T MEAN YOU CAN SLIP UP.
OR HAM IT UP.
OR SEAGULL IT UP.
MEAT'S NOT A JOB, IT'S A PASSION.
MEATBALL MATTHEWS? GOTTA CALL.

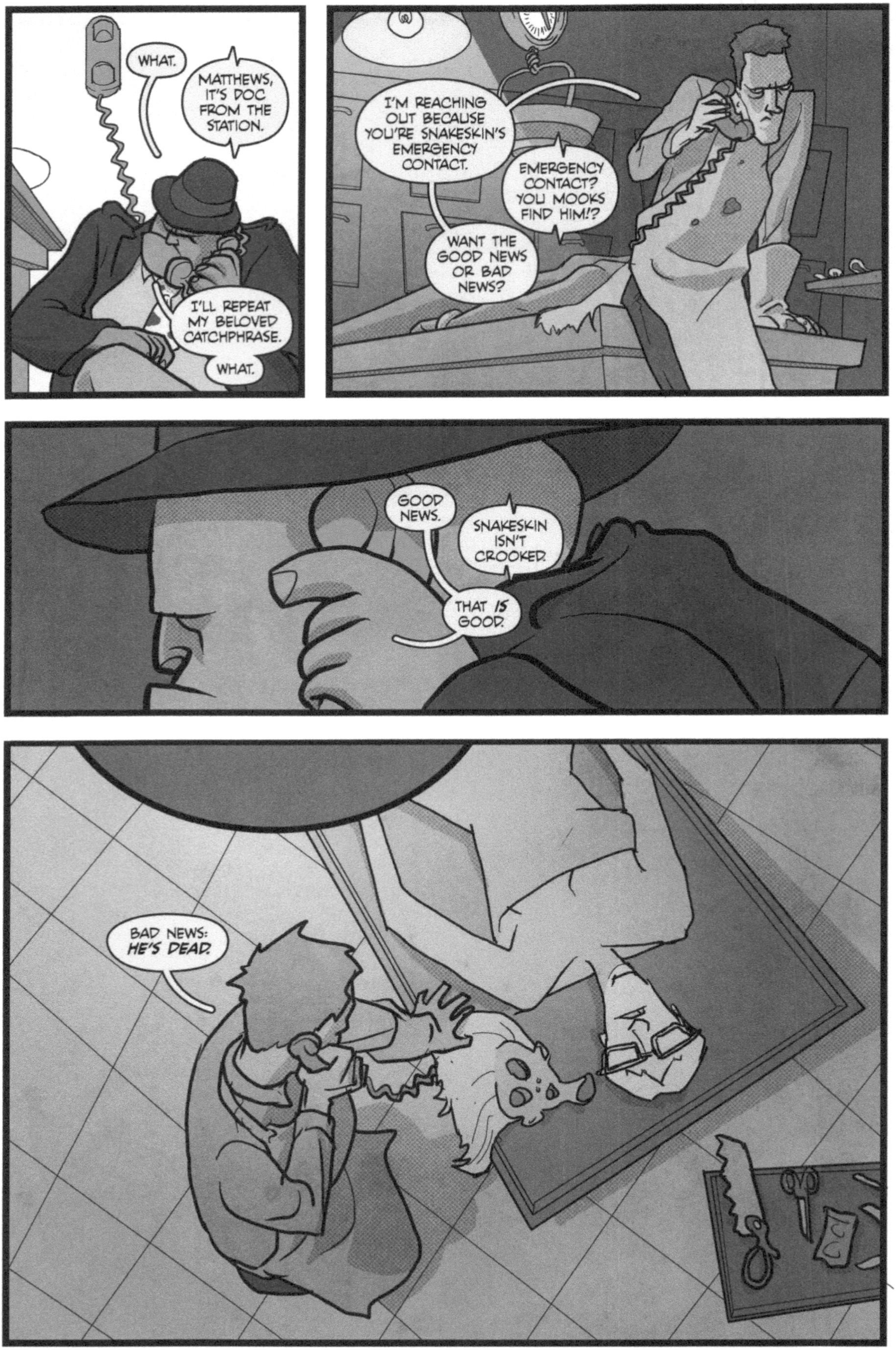
WHAT.
MATTHEWS, IT'S DOC FROM THE STATION.
I'LL REPEAT MY BELOVED CATCHPHRASE.
WHAT.
I'M REACHING OUT BECAUSE YOU'RE SNAKESKIN'S EMERGENCY CONTACT.
EMERGENCY CONTACT? YOU MOOKS FIND HIM!?
WANT THE GOOD NEWS OR BAD NEWS?
GOOD NEWS.
SNAKESKIN ISN'T CROOKED.
THAT *IS* GOOD.
BAD NEWS: ***HE'S DEAD.***

CHAPTER 3

IT HAPPENED AT THE DOCKS!

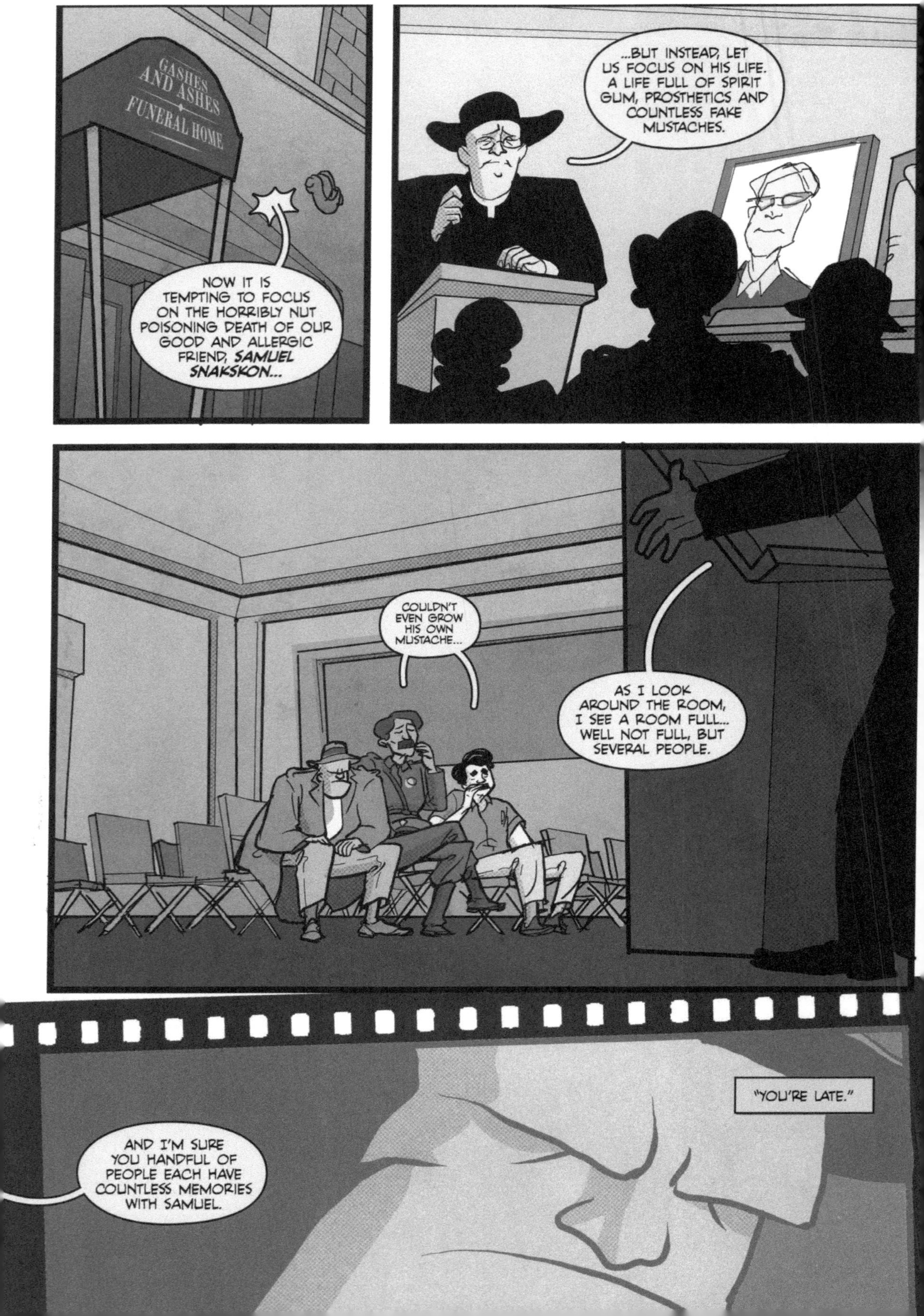
GASHES AND ASHES FUNERAL HOME
NOW IT IS TEMPTING TO FOCUS ON THE HORRIBLY NUT POISONING DEATH OF OUR GOOD AND ALLERGIC FRIEND, SAMUEL SNAKSKON...
...BUT INSTEAD, LET US FOCUS ON HIS LIFE. A LIFE FULL OF SPIRIT GUM, PROSTHETICS AND COUNTLESS FAKE MUSTACHES.
COULDN'T EVEN GROW HIS OWN MUSTACHE...
AS I LOOK AROUND THE ROOM, I SEE A ROOM FULL... WELL NOT FULL, BUT SEVERAL PEOPLE.
"YOU'RE LATE."
AND I'M SURE YOU HANDFUL OF PEOPLE EACH HAVE COUNTLESS MEMORIES WITH SAMUEL.

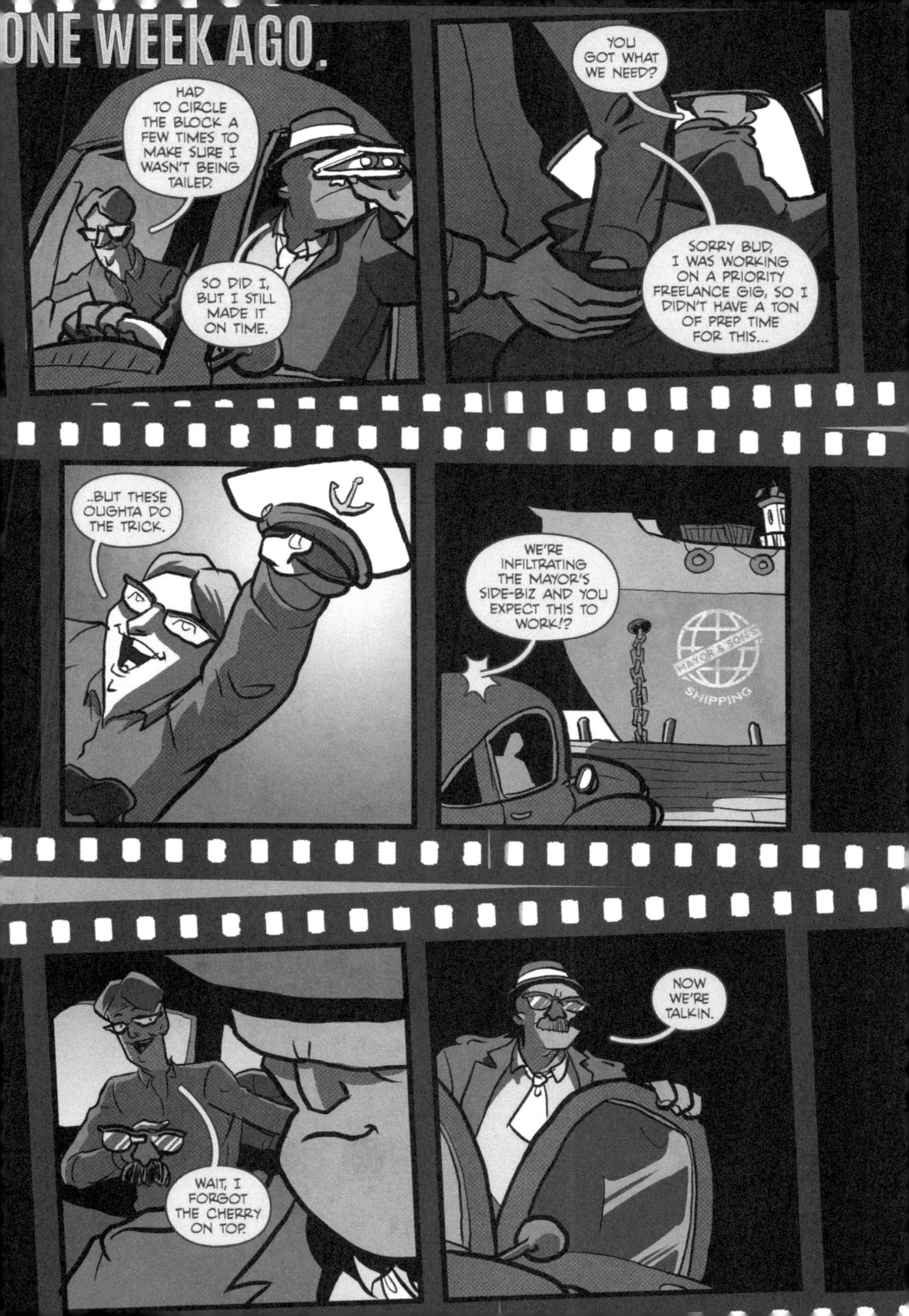
ONE WEEK AGO.
HAD TO CIRCLE THE BLOCK A FEW TIMES TO MAKE SURE I WASN'T BEING TAILED.
SO DID I, BUT I STILL MADE IT ON TIME.
YOU GOT WHAT WE NEED?
SORRY BUD, I WAS WORKING ON A PRIORITY FREELANCE GIG, SO I DIDN'T HAVE A TON OF PREP TIME FOR THIS...
..BUT THESE OUGHTA DO THE TRICK.
WE'RE INFILTRATING THE MAYOR'S SIDE-BIZ AND YOU EXPECT THIS TO WORK!?
MAYOR & SON'S
SHIPPING
WAIT, I FORGOT THE CHERRY ON TOP.
NOW WE'RE TALKIN.

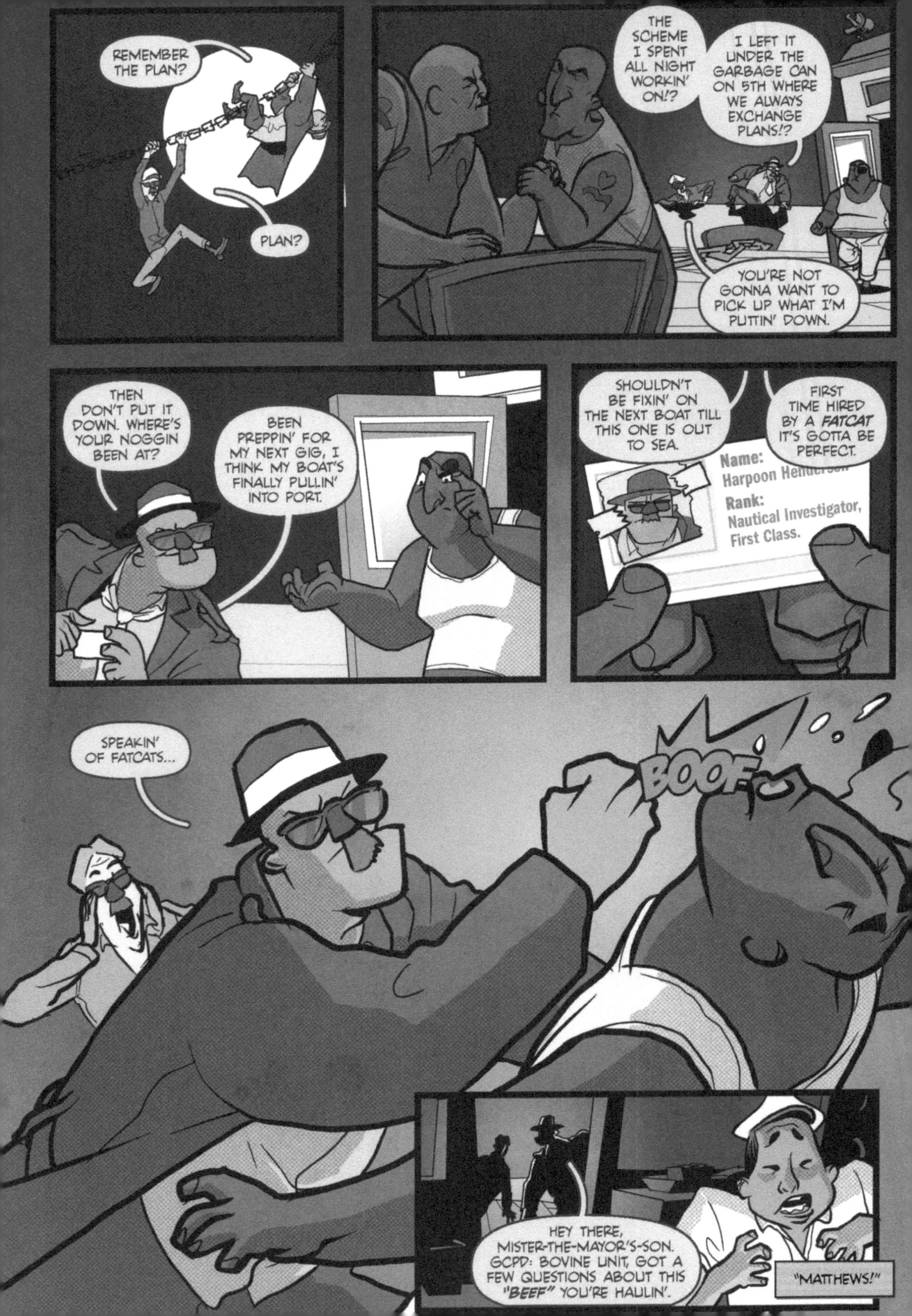
REMEMBER THE PLAN?
PLAN?
THE SCHEME I SPENT ALL NIGHT WORKIN' ON!?
I LEFT IT UNDER THE GARBAGE CAN ON 5TH WHERE WE ALWAYS EXCHANGE PLANS!?
YOU'RE NOT GONNA WANT TO PICK UP WHAT I'M PUTTIN' DOWN.
THEN DON'T PUT IT DOWN. WHERE'S YOUR NOGGIN BEEN AT?
BEEN PREPPIN' FOR MY NEXT GIG, I THINK MY BOAT'S FINALLY PULLIN' INTO PORT.
SHOULDN'T BE FIXIN' ON THE NEXT BOAT TILL THIS ONE IS OUT TO SEA.
FIRST TIME HIRED BY A FATCAT IT'S GOTTA BE PERFECT.
Name: Harpoon Henderson
Rank: Nautical Investigator, First Class.
SPEAKIN' OF FATCATS...
BOOF
HEY THERE, MISTER-THE-MAYOR'S-SON. GCPD: BOVINE UNIT, GOT A FEW QUESTIONS ABOUT THIS "BEEF" YOU'RE HAULIN'.
"MATTHEWS!"

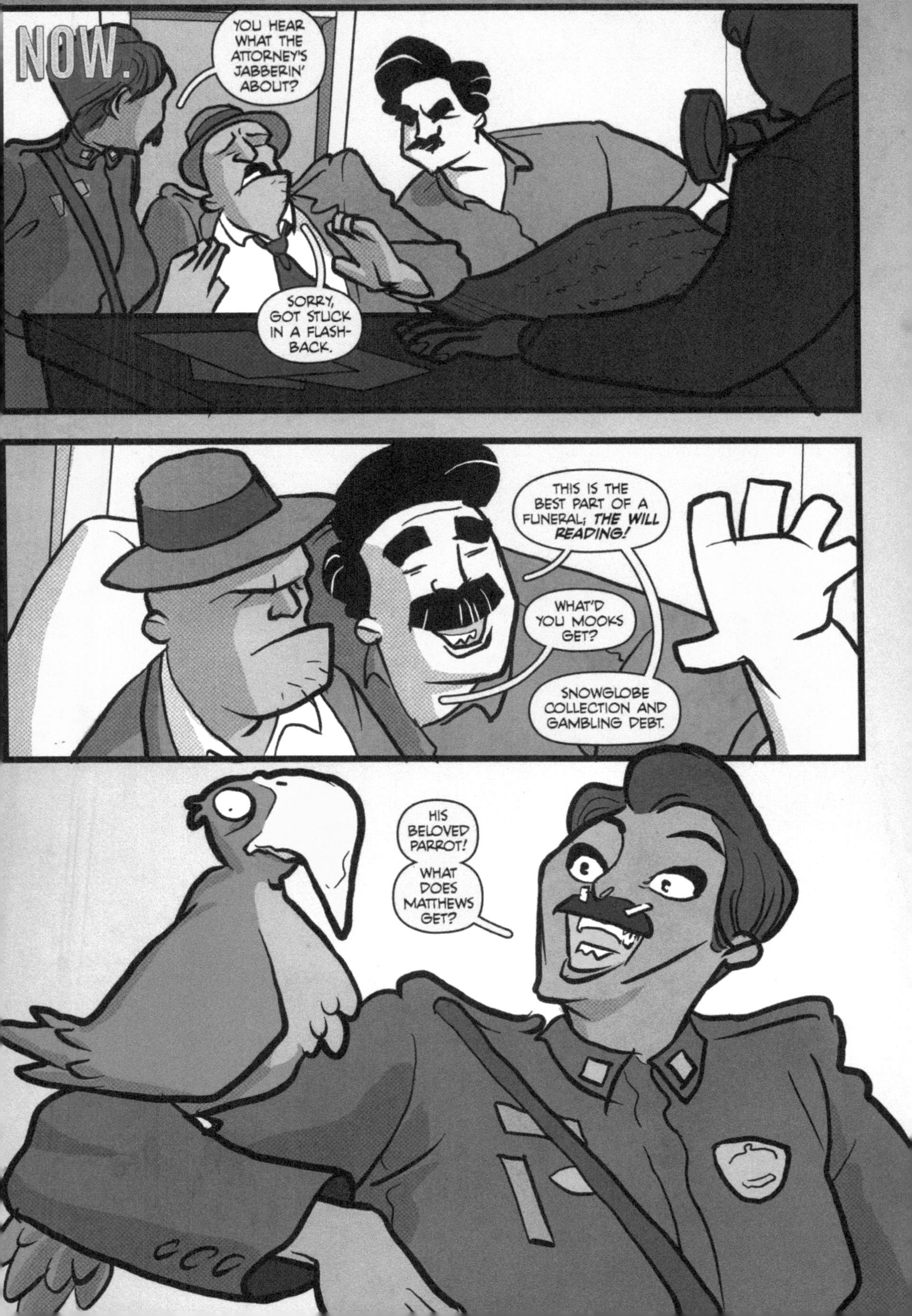
NOW.
YOU HEAR WHAT THE ATTORNEY'S JABBERIN' ABOUT?
SORRY, GOT STUCK IN A FLASH-BACK.
THIS IS THE BEST PART OF A FUNERAL; *THE WILL READING!*
WHAT'D YOU MOOKS GET?
SNOWGLOBE COLLECTION AND GAMBLING DEBT.
HIS BELOVED PARROT!
WHAT DOES MATTHEWS GET?

CHAPTER 4
WITH FRIENDS LIKE THESE...

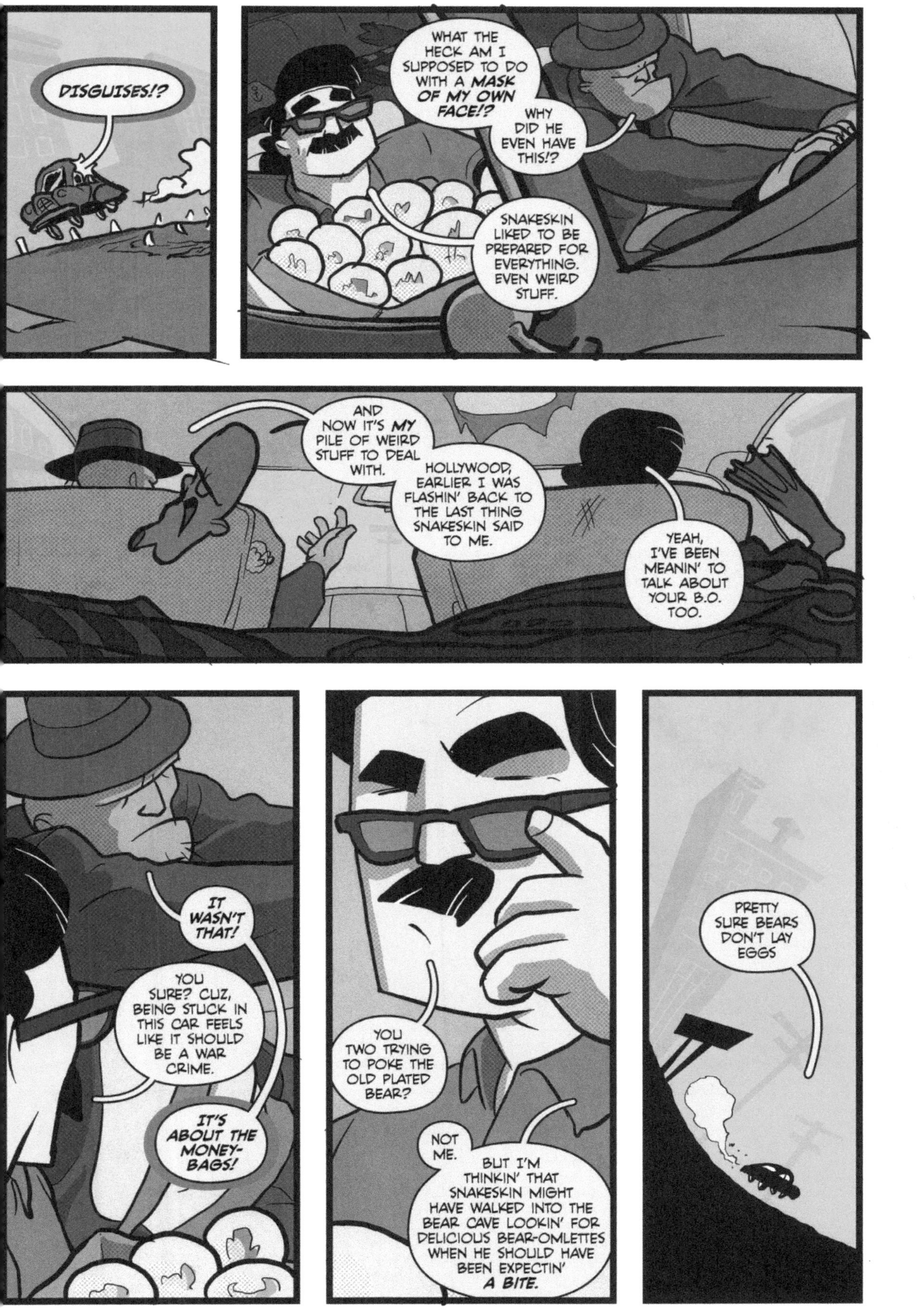
DISGUISES!?
WHAT THE HECK AM I SUPPOSED TO DO WITH A MASK OF MY OWN FACE!?
WHY DID HE EVEN HAVE THIS!?
SNAKESKIN LIKED TO BE PREPARED FOR EVERYTHING. EVEN WEIRD STUFF.
AND NOW IT'S MY PILE OF WEIRD STUFF TO DEAL WITH.
HOLLYWOOD, EARLIER I WAS FLASHIN' BACK TO THE LAST THING SNAKESKIN SAID TO ME.
YEAH, I'VE BEEN MEANIN' TO TALK ABOUT YOUR B.O. TOO.
IT WASN'T THAT!
YOU SURE? CUZ, BEING STUCK IN THIS CAR FEELS LIKE IT SHOULD BE A WAR CRIME.
IT'S ABOUT THE MONEY-BAGS!
YOU TWO TRYING TO POKE THE OLD PLATED BEAR?
NOT ME.
BUT I'M THINKIN' THAT SNAKESKIN MIGHT HAVE WALKED INTO THE BEAR CAVE LOOKIN' FOR DELICIOUS BEAR-OMLETTES WHEN HE SHOULD HAVE BEEN EXPECTIN' A BITE.
PRETTY SURE BEARS DON'T LAY EGGS

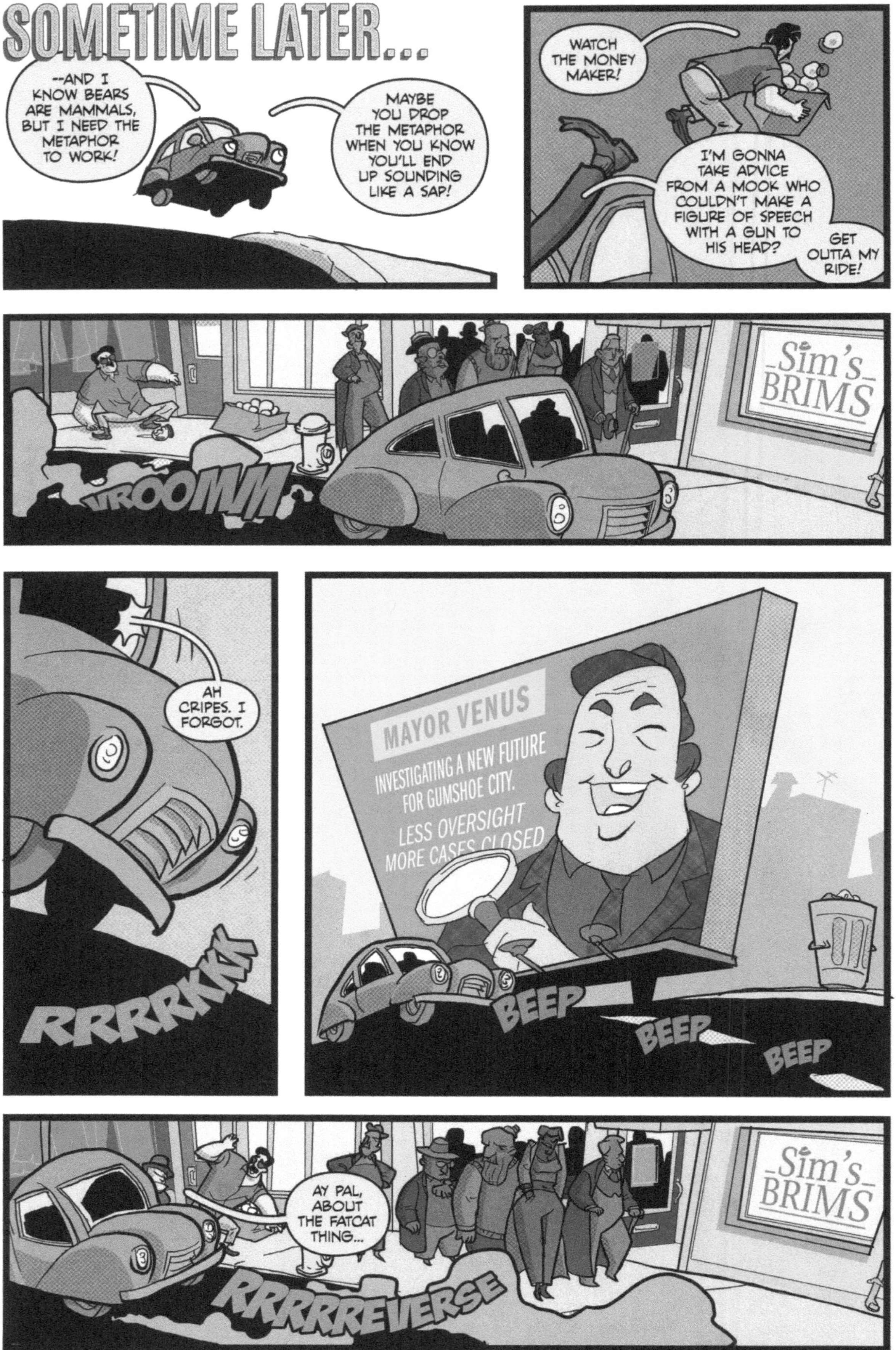
SOMETIME LATER...
--AND I KNOW BEARS ARE MAMMALS, BUT I NEED THE METAPHOR TO WORK!
MAYBE YOU DROP THE METAPHOR WHEN YOU KNOW YOU'LL END UP SOUNDING LIKE A SAP!
WATCH THE MONEY MAKER!
I'M GONNA TAKE ADVICE FROM A MOOK WHO COULDN'T MAKE A FIGURE OF SPEECH WITH A GUN TO HIS HEAD?
GET OUTTA MY RIDE!
Sim's BRIMS
VROOMM
AH CRIPES. I FORGOT.
RRRRKKK
MAYOR VENUS
INVESTIGATING A NEW FUTURE FOR GUMSHOE CITY.
LESS OVERSIGHT
MORE CASES CLOSED
BEEP
BEEP
BEEP
AY PAL, ABOUT THE FATCAT THING...
Sim's BRIMS
RRRRREVERSE

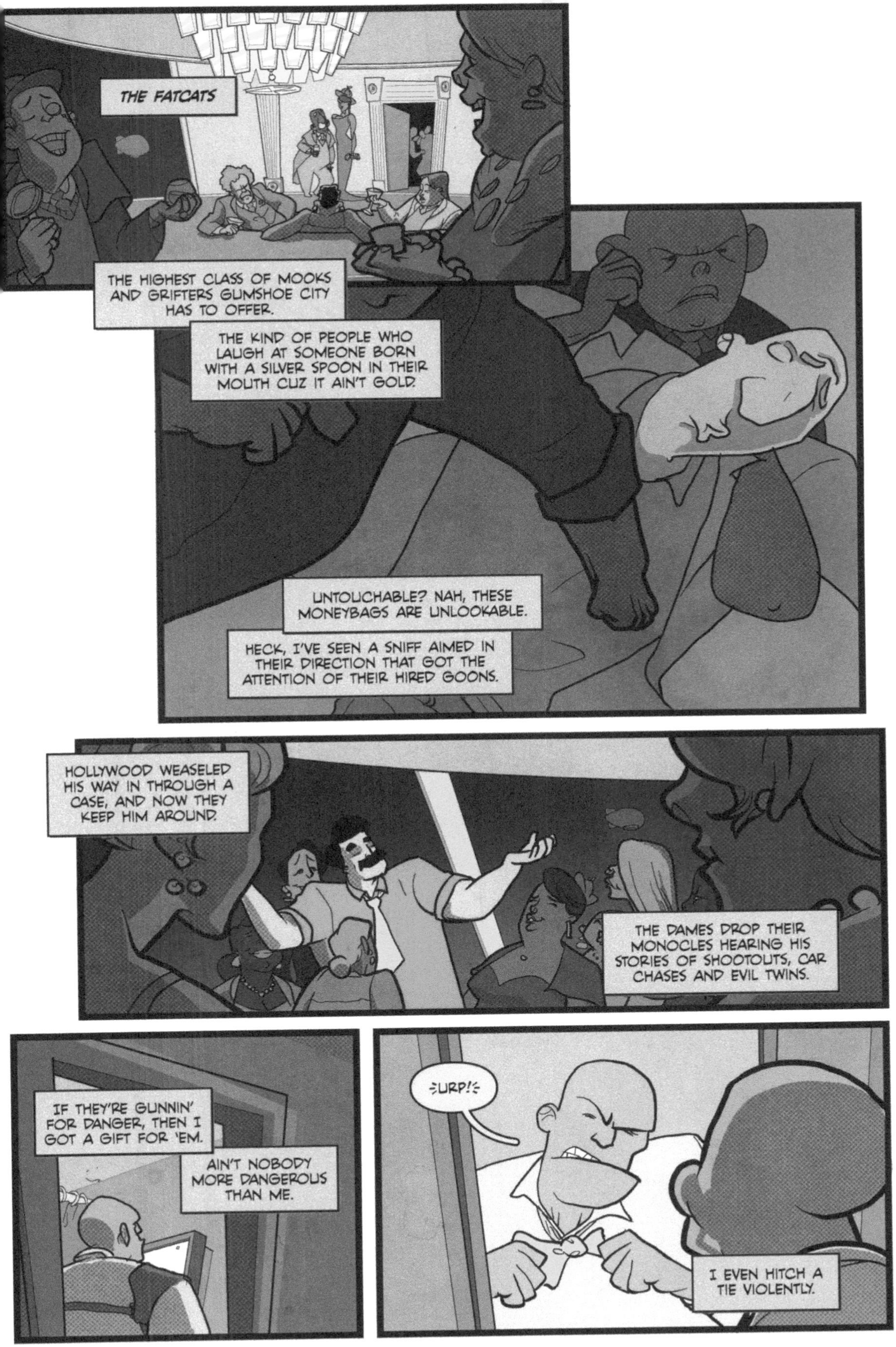
THE FATCATS
THE HIGHEST CLASS OF MOOKS AND GRIFTERS GUMSHOE CITY HAS TO OFFER.
THE KIND OF PEOPLE WHO LAUGH AT SOMEONE BORN WITH A SILVER SPOON IN THEIR MOUTH CUZ IT AIN'T GOLD.
UNTOUCHABLE? NAH, THESE MONEYBAGS ARE UNLOOKABLE.
HECK, I'VE SEEN A SNIFF AIMED IN THEIR DIRECTION THAT GOT THE ATTENTION OF THEIR HIRED GOONS.
HOLLYWOOD WEASELED HIS WAY IN THROUGH A CASE, AND NOW THEY KEEP HIM AROUND.
THE DAMES DROP THEIR MONOCLES HEARING HIS STORIES OF SHOOTOUTS, CAR CHASES AND EVIL TWINS.
IF THEY'RE GUNNIN' FOR DANGER, THEN I GOT A GIFT FOR 'EM.
AIN'T NOBODY MORE DANGEROUS THAN ME.
URP!
I EVEN HITCH A TIE VIOLENTLY.

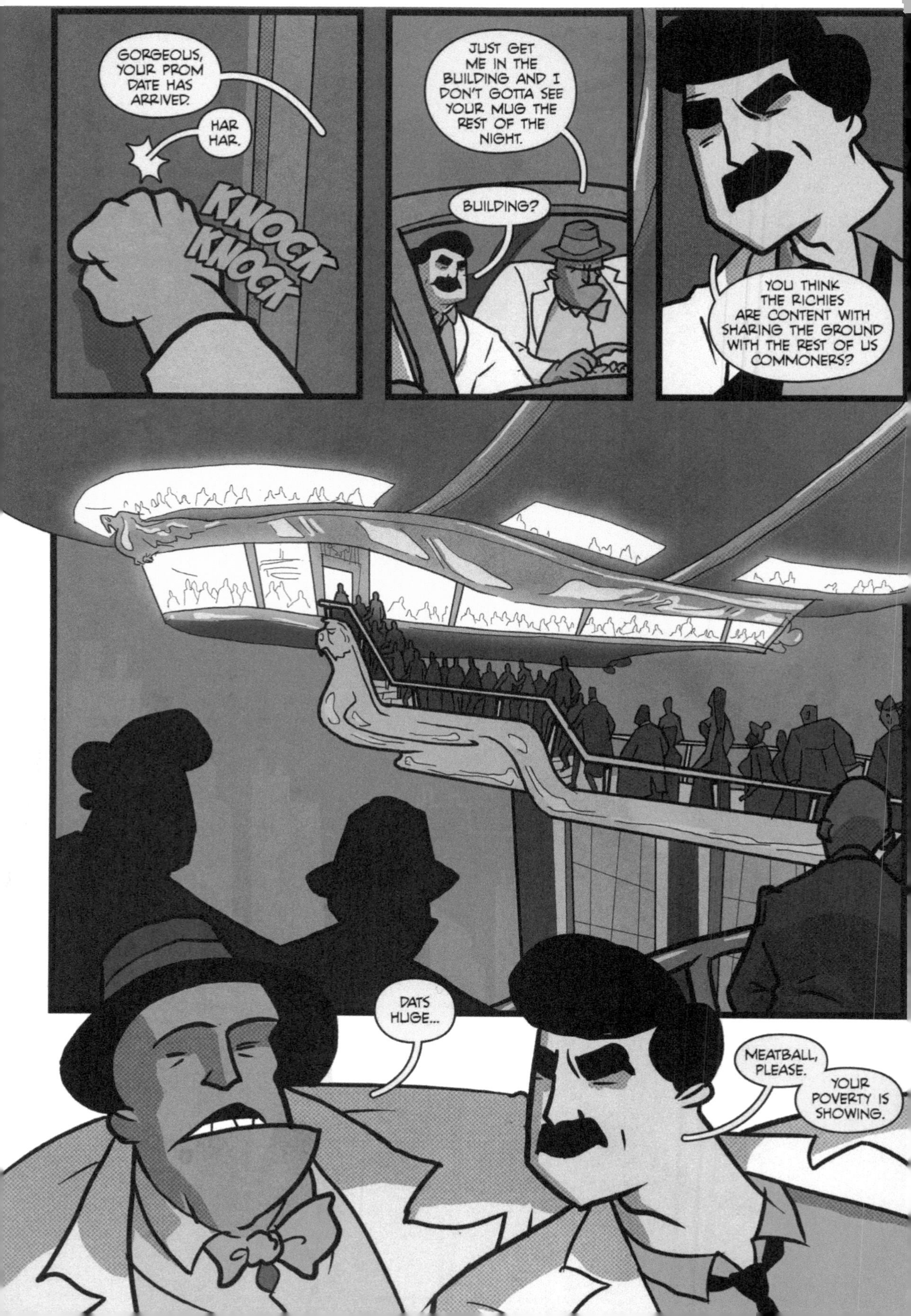
GORGEOUS, YOUR PROM DATE HAS ARRIVED.
HAR HAR.
KNOCK KNOCK
JUST GET ME IN THE BUILDING AND I DON'T GOTTA SEE YOUR MUG THE REST OF THE NIGHT.
BUILDING?
YOU THINK THE RICHIES ARE CONTENT WITH SHARING THE GROUND WITH THE REST OF US COMMONERS?
DATS HUGE...
MEATBALL, PLEASE.
YOUR POVERTY IS SHOWING.

CHAPTER 5 MONEY, CASH, AND OTHER TERRIBLE THING$

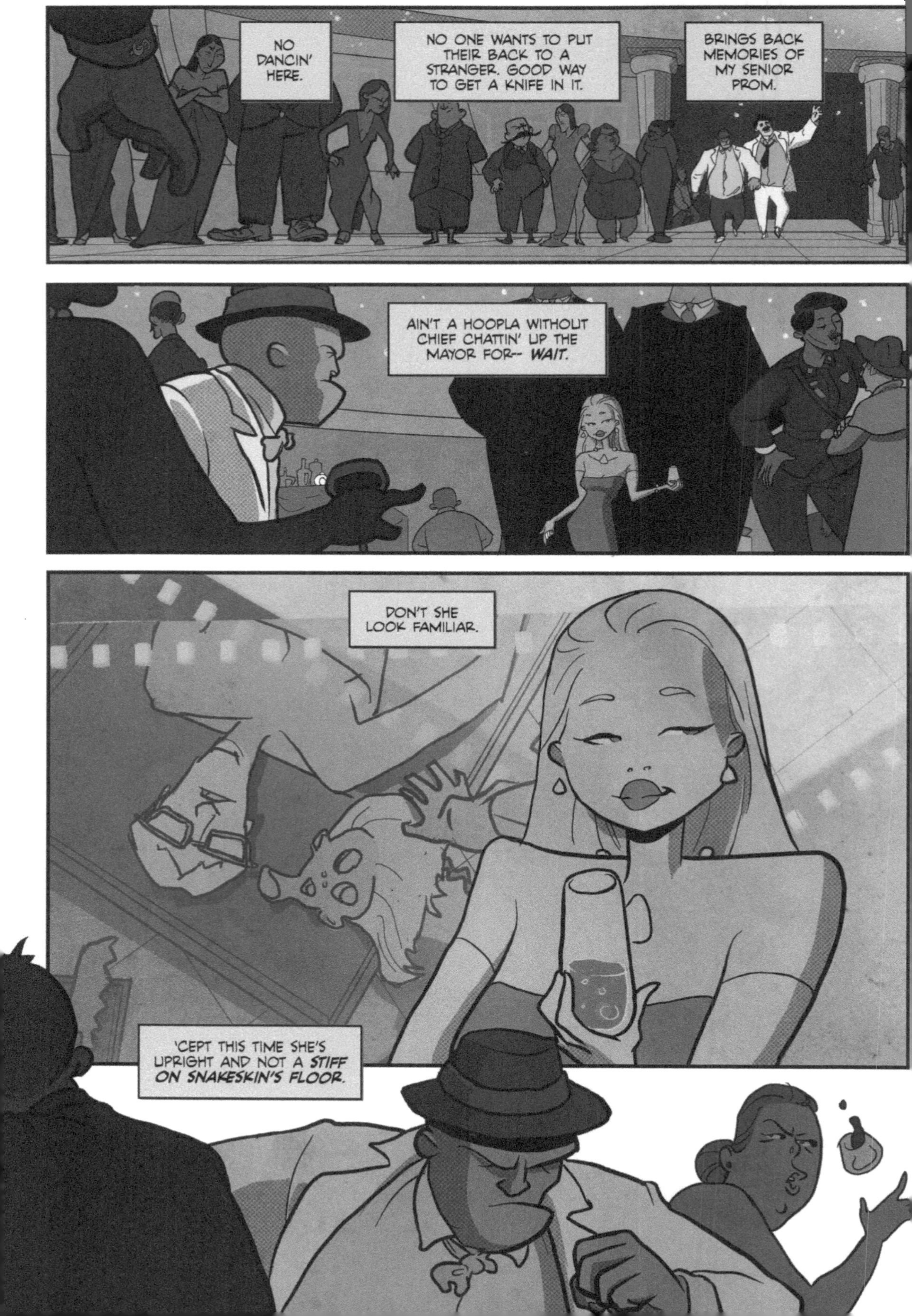
NO DANCIN' HERE.
NO ONE WANTS TO PUT THEIR BACK TO A STRANGER. GOOD WAY TO GET A KNIFE IN IT.
BRINGS BACK MEMORIES OF MY SENIOR PROM.
AIN'T A HOOPLA WITHOUT CHIEF CHATTIN' UP THE MAYOR FOR-- *WAIT.*
DON'T SHE LOOK FAMILIAR.
'CEPT THIS TIME SHE'S UPRIGHT AND NOT A *STIFF ON SNAKESKIN'S FLOOR.*

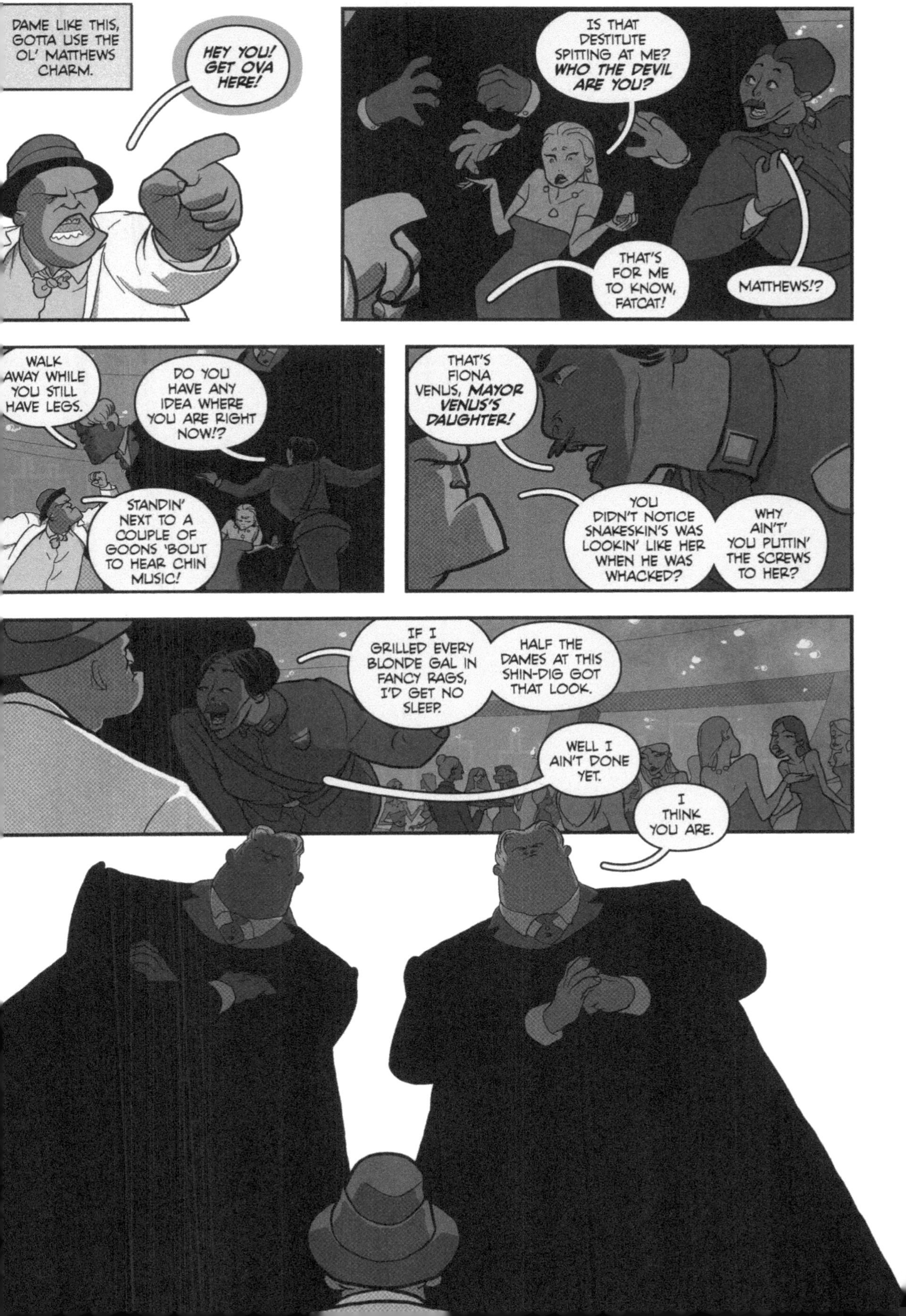
DAME LIKE THIS, GOTTA USE THE OL' MATTHEWS CHARM.
HEY YOU! GET OVA HERE!
IS THAT DESTITUTE SPITTING AT ME? WHO THE DEVIL ARE YOU?
THAT'S FOR ME TO KNOW, FATCAT!
MATTHEWS!?
WALK AWAY WHILE YOU STILL HAVE LEGS.
DO YOU HAVE ANY IDEA WHERE YOU ARE RIGHT NOW!?
STANDIN' NEXT TO A COUPLE OF GOONS 'BOUT TO HEAR CHIN MUSIC!
THAT'S FIONA VENUS, MAYOR VENUS'S DAUGHTER!
YOU DIDN'T NOTICE SNAKESKIN'S WAS LOOKIN' LIKE HER WHEN HE WAS WHACKED?
WHY AIN'T' YOU PUTTIN' THE SCREWS TO HER?
IF I GRILLED EVERY BLONDE GAL IN FANCY RAGS, I'D GET NO SLEEP.
HALF THE DAMES AT THIS SHIN-DIG GOT THAT LOOK.
WELL I AIN'T DONE YET.
I THINK YOU ARE.

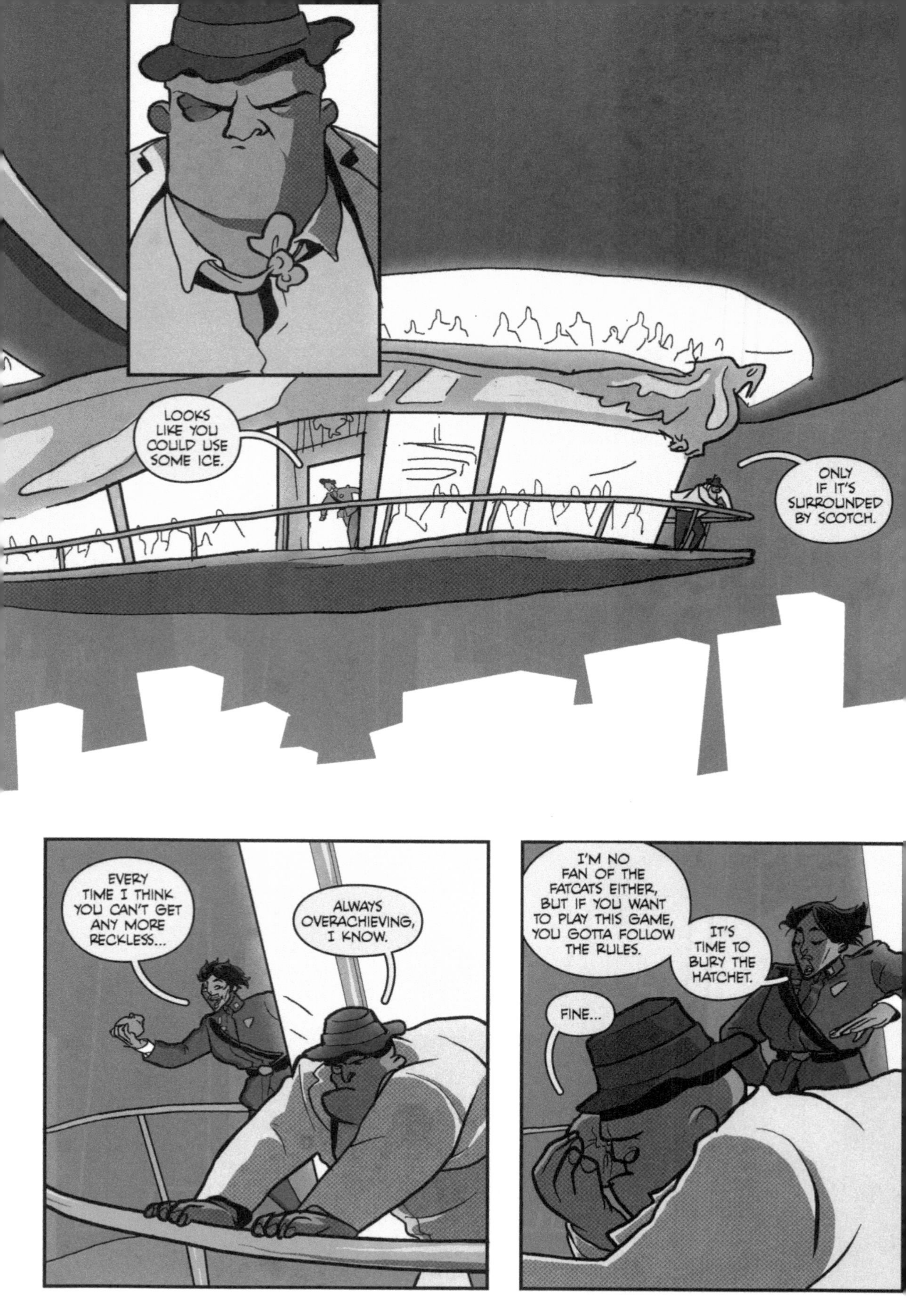
LOOKS LIKE YOU COULD USE SOME ICE.
ONLY IF IT'S SURROUNDED BY SCOTCH.
EVERY TIME I THINK YOU CAN'T GET ANY MORE RECKLESS...
ALWAYS OVERACHIEVING, I KNOW.
I'M NO FAN OF THE FATCATS EITHER, BUT IF YOU WANT TO PLAY THIS GAME, YOU GOTTA FOLLOW THE RULES.
IT'S TIME TO BURY THE HATCHET.
FINE...

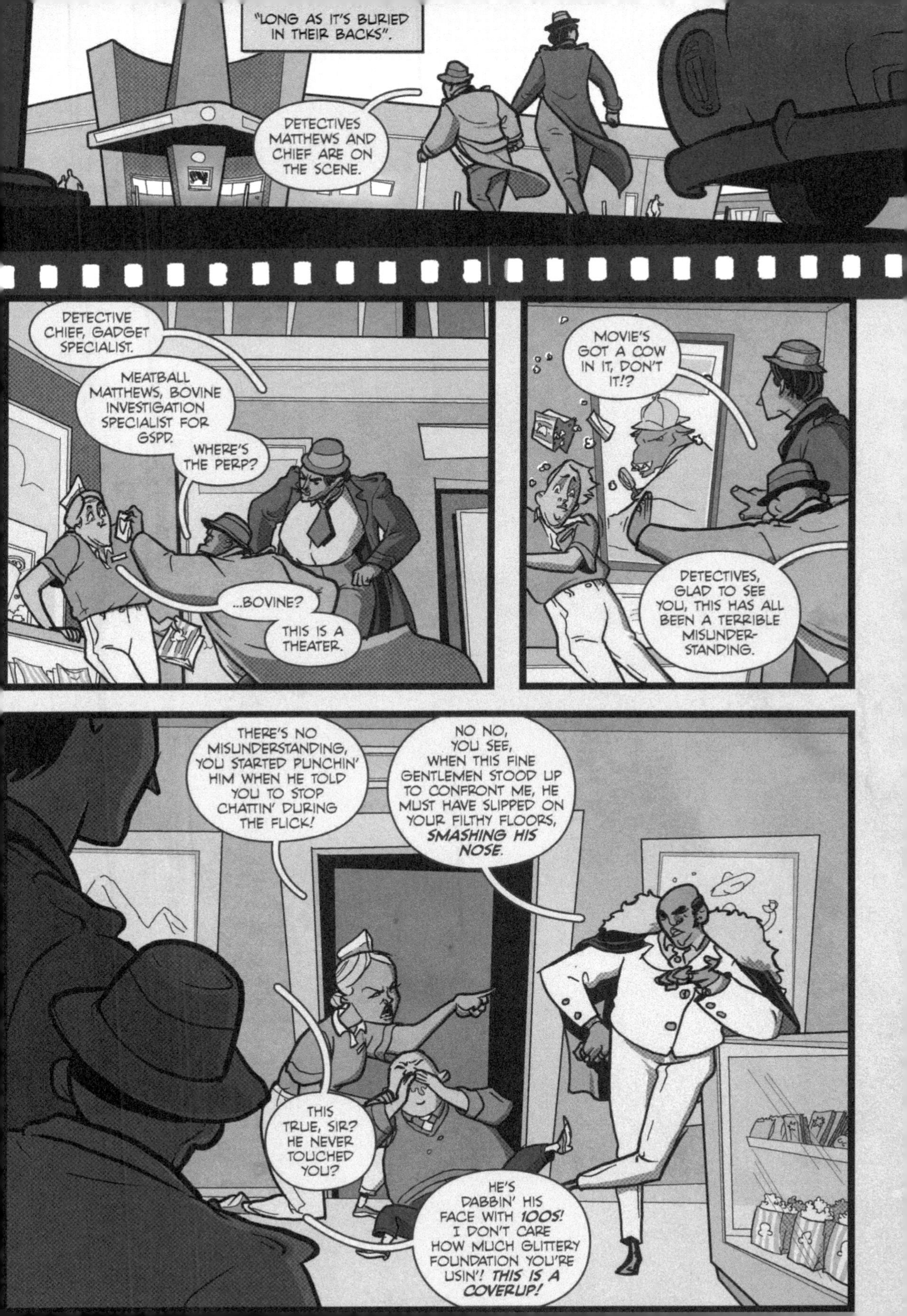

"LONG AS IT'S BURIED IN THEIR BACKS".
DETECTIVES MATTHEWS AND CHIEF ARE ON THE SCENE.
DETECTIVE CHIEF, GADGET SPECIALIST.
MEATBALL MATTHEWS, BOVINE INVESTIGATION SPECIALIST FOR GSPD.
WHERE'S THE PERP?
...BOVINE?
THIS IS A THEATER.
MOVIE'S GOT A COW IN IT, DON'T IT!?
DETECTIVES, GLAD TO SEE YOU, THIS HAS ALL BEEN A TERRIBLE MISUNDER-STANDING.
THERE'S NO MISUNDERSTANDING, YOU STARTED PUNCHIN' HIM WHEN HE TOLD YOU TO STOP CHATTIN' DURING THE FLICK!
NO NO, YOU SEE, WHEN THIS FINE GENTLEMEN STOOD UP TO CONFRONT ME, HE MUST HAVE SLIPPED ON YOUR FILTHY FLOORS, ***SMASHING HIS NOSE***.
THIS TRUE, SIR? HE NEVER TOUCHED YOU?
HE'S DABBIN' HIS FACE WITH ***100S!*** I DON'T CARE HOW MUCH GLITTERY FOUNDATION YOU'RE USIN'! ***THIS IS A COVERUP!***

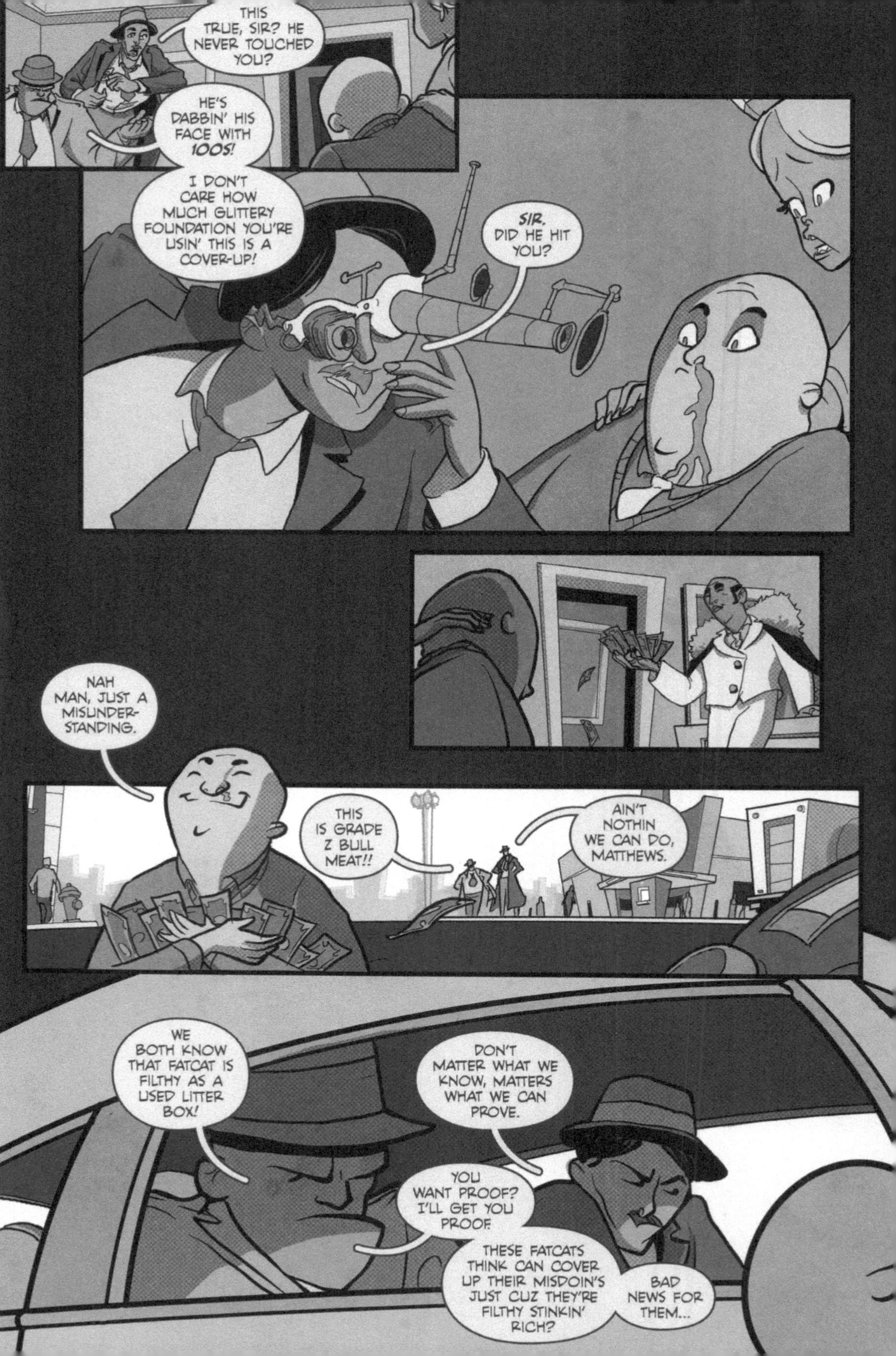
THIS TRUE, SIR? HE NEVER TOUCHED YOU?
HE'S DABBIN' HIS FACE WITH 100S!
I DON'T CARE HOW MUCH GLITTERY FOUNDATION YOU'RE USIN' THIS IS A COVER-UP!
SIR. DID HE HIT YOU?
NAH MAN, JUST A MISUNDER-STANDING.
THIS IS GRADE Z BULL MEAT!!
AIN'T NOTHIN WE CAN DO, MATTHEWS.
WE BOTH KNOW THAT FATCAT IS FILTHY AS A USED LITTER BOX!
DON'T MATTER WHAT WE KNOW, MATTERS WHAT WE CAN PROVE.
YOU WANT PROOF? I'LL GET YOU PROOF.
THESE FATCATS THINK CAN COVER UP THEIR MISDOIN'S JUST CUZ THEY'RE FILTHY STINKIN' RICH?
BAD NEWS FOR THEM...

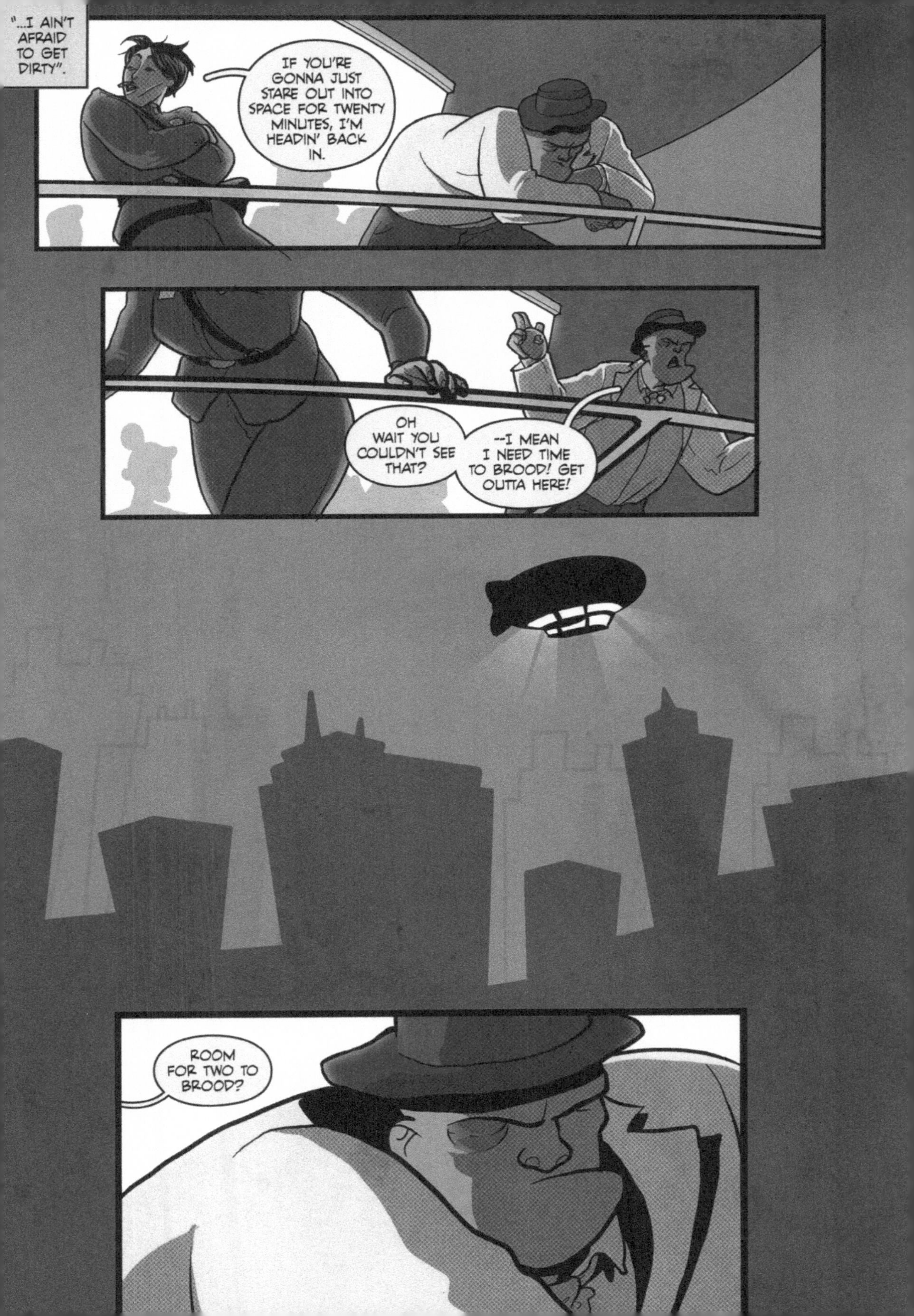
"...I AIN'T AFRAID TO GET DIRTY".
IF YOU'RE GONNA JUST STARE OUT INTO SPACE FOR TWENTY MINUTES, I'M HEADIN' BACK IN.
OH WAIT YOU COULDN'T SEE THAT?
--I MEAN I NEED TIME TO BROOD! GET OUTTA HERE!
ROOM FOR TWO TO BROOD?

Chapter Six
Heartbreakers & Lifetakers

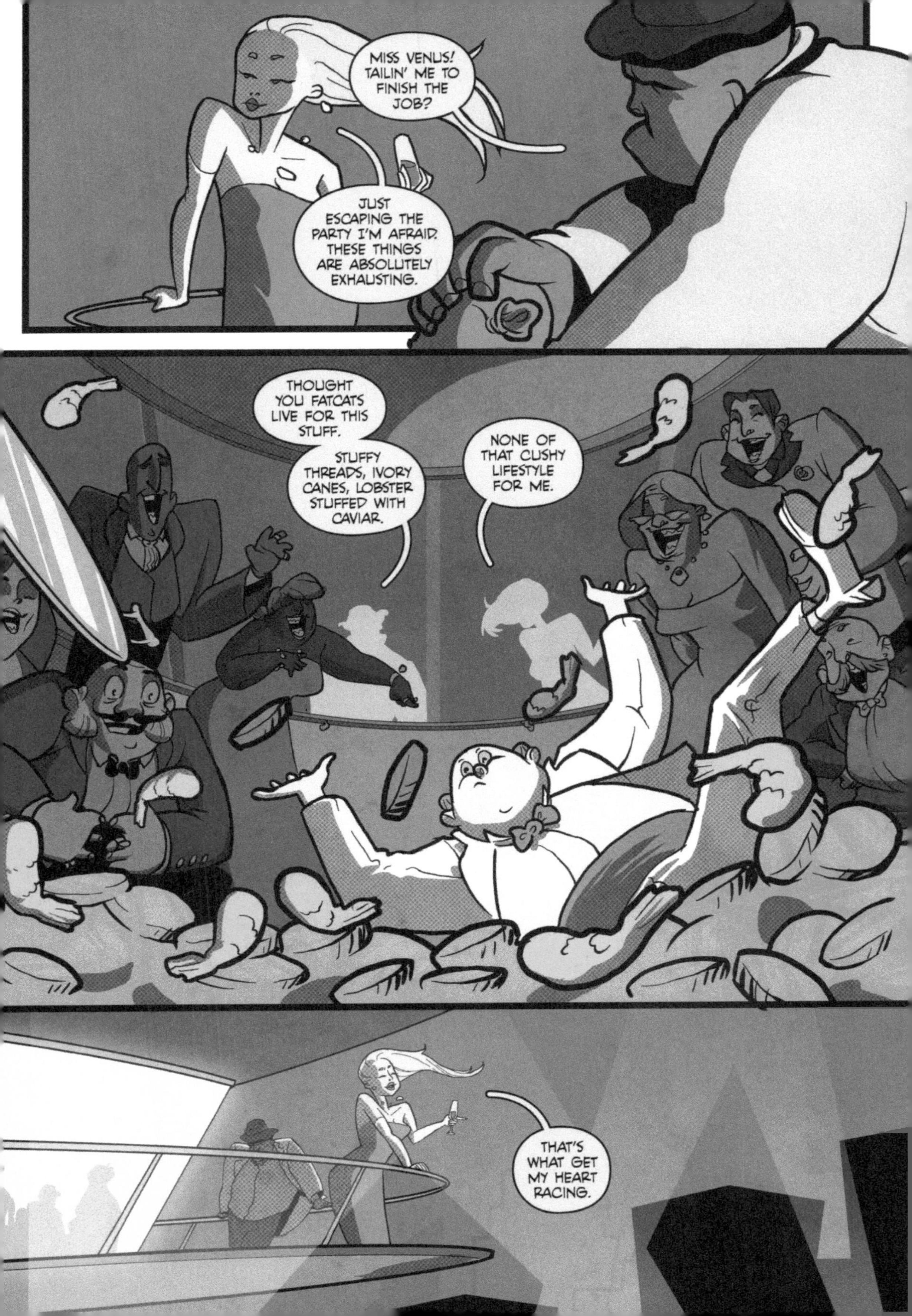
MISS VENUS! TAILIN' ME TO FINISH THE JOB?
JUST ESCAPING THE PARTY I'M AFRAID. THESE THINGS ARE ABSOLUTELY EXHAUSTING.
THOUGHT YOU FATCATS LIVE FOR THIS STUFF.
STUFFY THREADS, IVORY CANES, LOBSTER STUFFED WITH CAVIAR.
NONE OF THAT CUSHY LIFESTYLE FOR ME.
THAT'S WHAT GET MY HEART RACING.

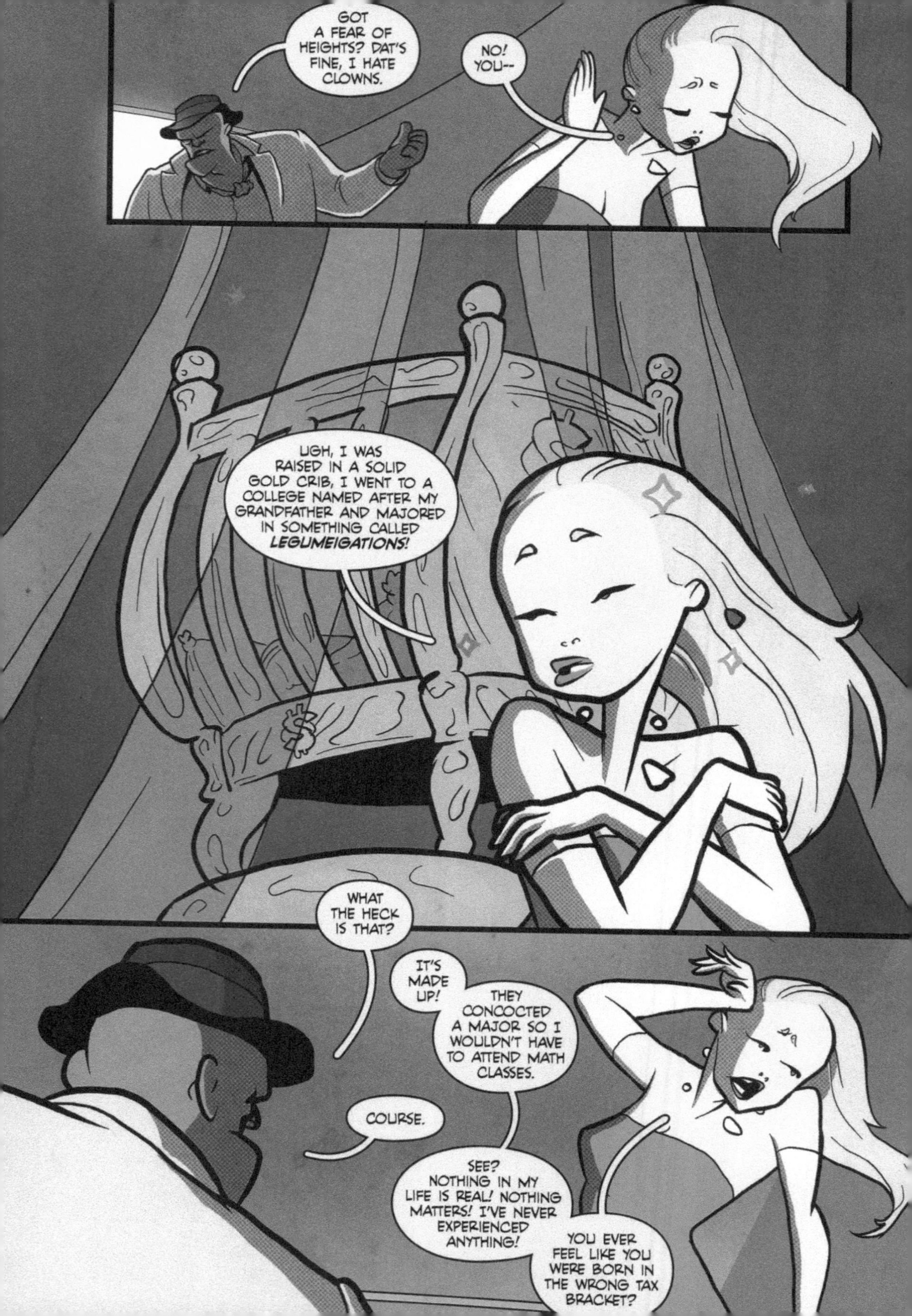
GOT A FEAR OF HEIGHTS? DAT'S FINE, I HATE CLOWNS.
NO! YOU--
UGH, I WAS RAISED IN A SOLID GOLD CRIB, I WENT TO A COLLEGE NAMED AFTER MY GRANDFATHER AND MAJORED IN SOMETHING CALLED *LEGUMEIGATIONS!*
WHAT THE HECK IS THAT?
IT'S MADE UP!
THEY CONCOCTED A MAJOR SO I WOULDN'T HAVE TO ATTEND MATH CLASSES.
COURSE.
SEE? NOTHING IN MY LIFE IS REAL! NOTHING MATTERS! I'VE NEVER EXPERIENCED ANYTHING!
YOU EVER FEEL LIKE YOU WERE BORN IN THE WRONG TAX BRACKET?

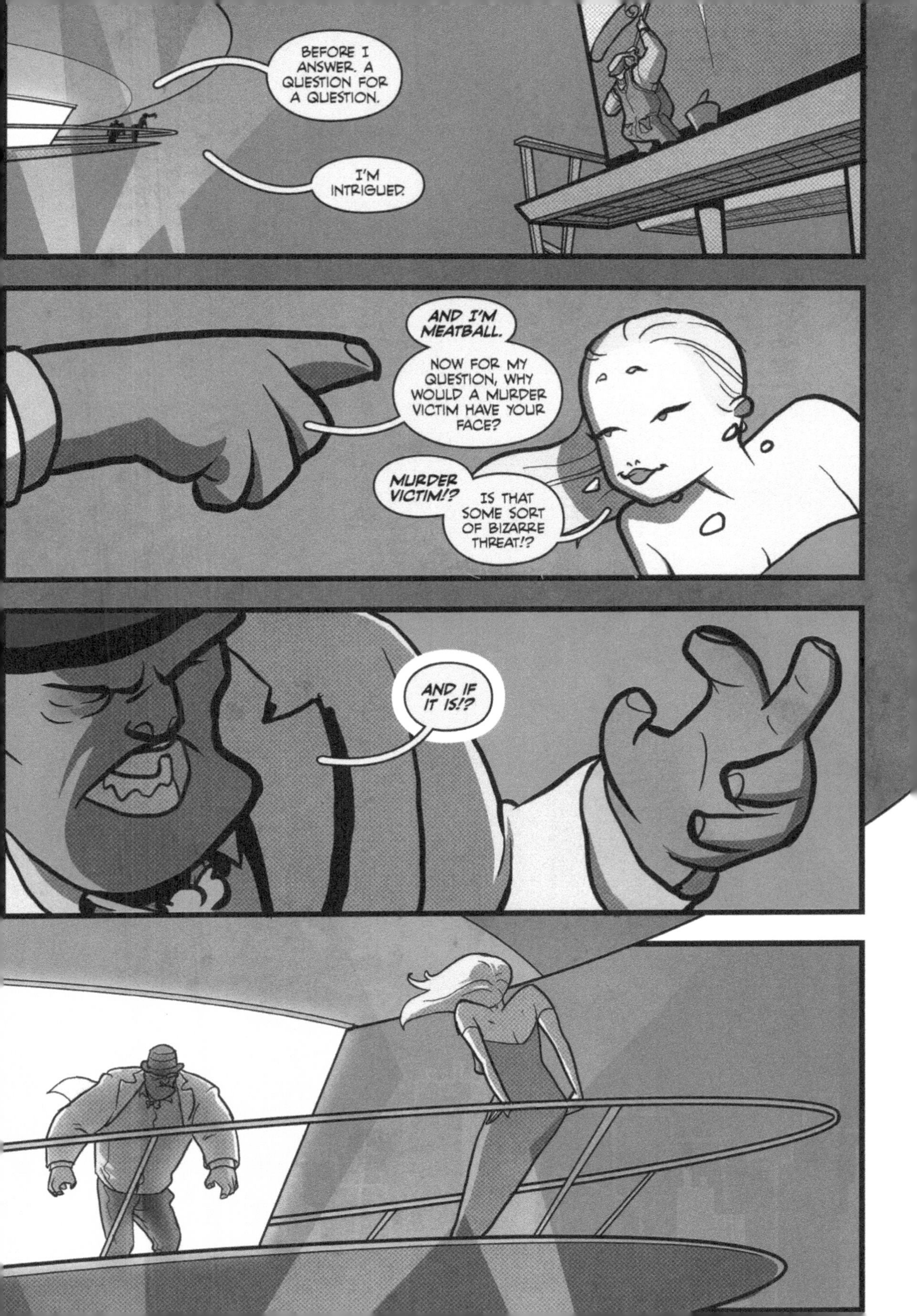
BEFORE I ANSWER. A QUESTION FOR A QUESTION.
I'M INTRIGUED.
AND I'M MEATBALL.
NOW FOR MY QUESTION, WHY WOULD A MURDER VICTIM HAVE YOUR FACE?
MURDER VICTIM!?
IS THAT SOME SORT OF BIZARRE THREAT!?
AND IF IT IS!?

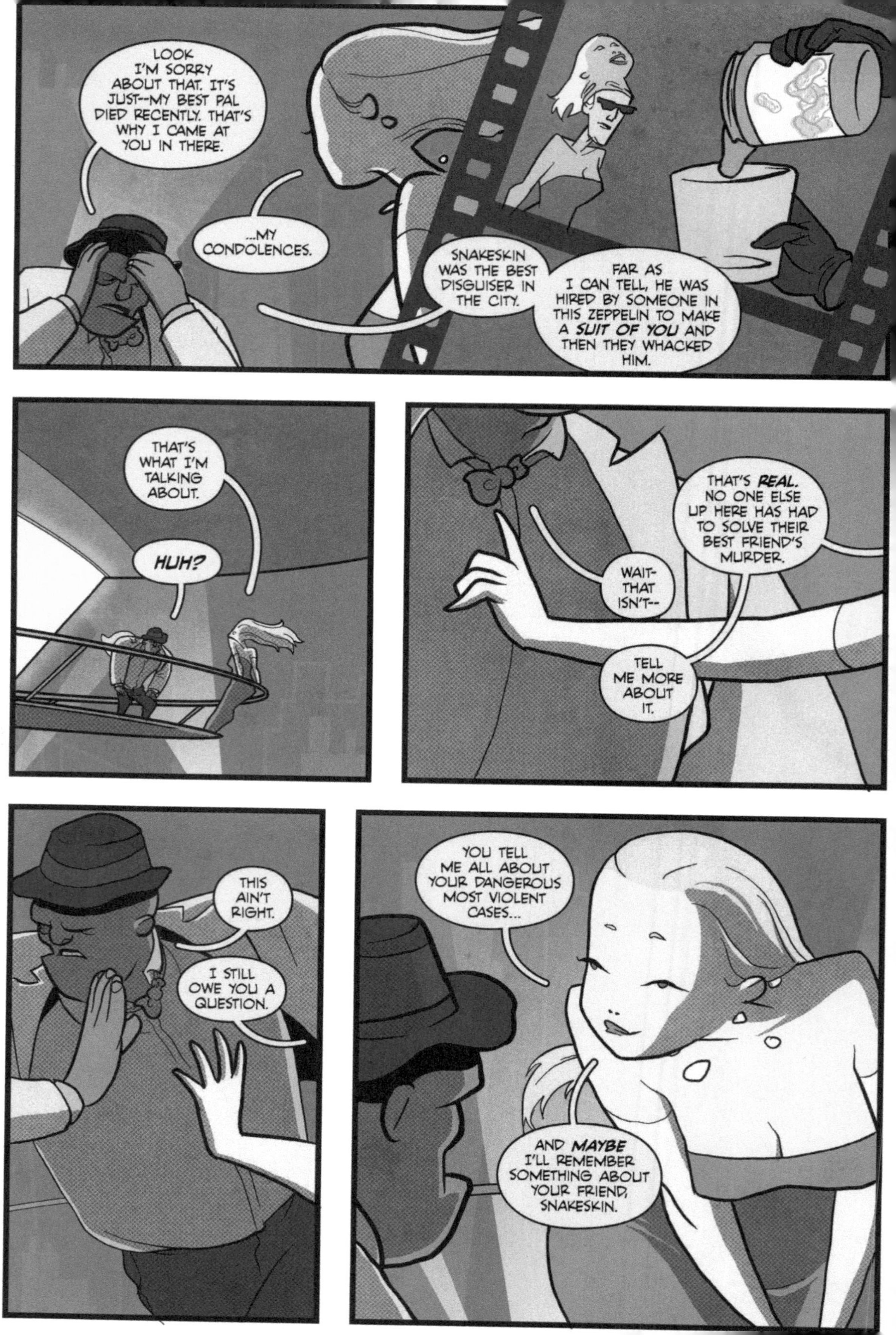
LOOK I'M SORRY ABOUT THAT. IT'S JUST--MY BEST PAL DIED RECENTLY. THAT'S WHY I CAME AT YOU IN THERE.
...MY CONDOLENCES.
SNAKESKIN WAS THE BEST DISGUISER IN THE CITY.
FAR AS I CAN TELL, HE WAS HIRED BY SOMEONE IN THIS ZEPPELIN TO MAKE A *SUIT OF YOU* AND THEN THEY WHACKED HIM.
THAT'S WHAT I'M TALKING ABOUT.
HUH?
THAT'S *REAL.* NO ONE ELSE UP HERE HAS HAD TO SOLVE THEIR BEST FRIEND'S MURDER.
WAIT- THAT ISN'T--
TELL ME MORE ABOUT IT.
THIS AIN'T RIGHT.
I STILL OWE YOU A QUESTION.
YOU TELL ME ALL ABOUT YOUR DANGEROUS MOST VIOLENT CASES...
AND *MAYBE* I'LL REMEMBER SOMETHING ABOUT YOUR FRIEND, SNAKESKIN.

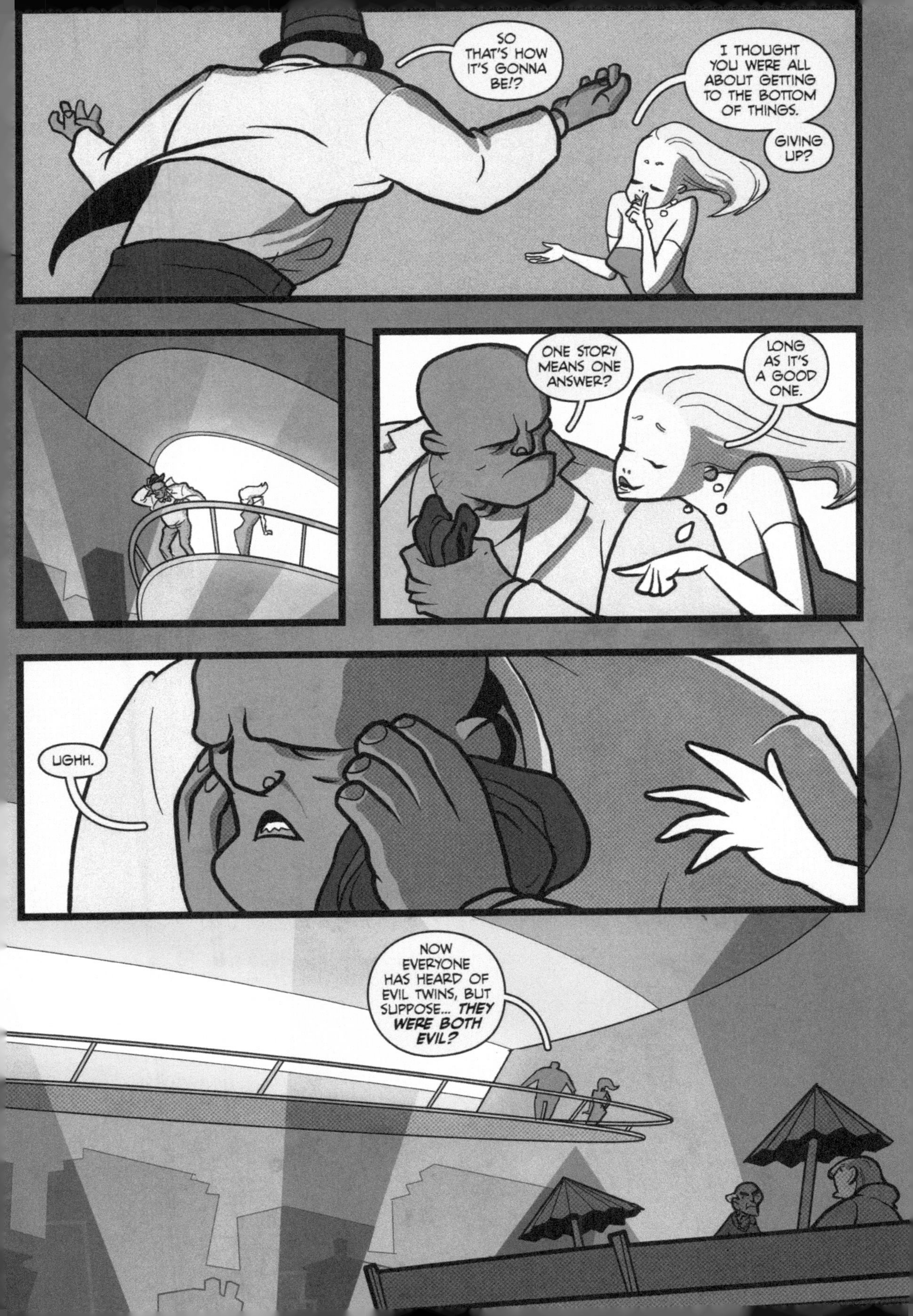
SO THAT'S HOW IT'S GONNA BE!?
I THOUGHT YOU WERE ALL ABOUT GETTING TO THE BOTTOM OF THINGS.
GIVING UP?
ONE STORY MEANS ONE ANSWER?
LONG AS IT'S A GOOD ONE.
UGHH.
NOW EVERYONE HAS HEARD OF EVIL TWINS, BUT SUPPOSE... *THEY WERE BOTH EVIL?*

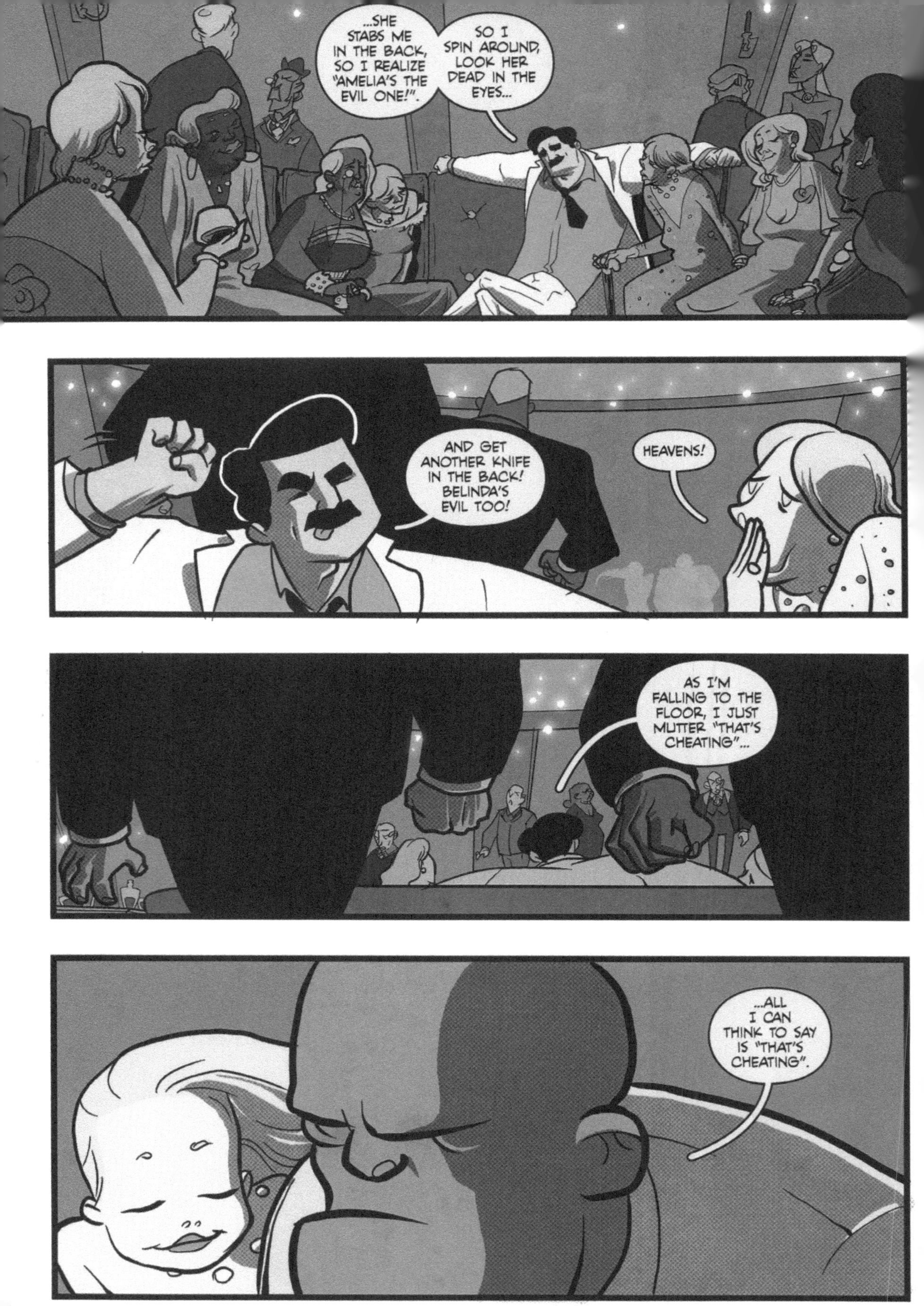
...SHE STABS ME IN THE BACK, SO I REALIZE "AMELIA'S THE EVIL ONE!".
SO I SPIN AROUND, LOOK HER DEAD IN THE EYES...
AND GET ANOTHER KNIFE IN THE BACK! BELINDA'S EVIL TOO!
HEAVENS!
AS I'M FALLING TO THE FLOOR, I JUST MUTTER "THAT'S CHEATING"...
...ALL I CAN THINK TO SAY IS "THAT'S CHEATING".

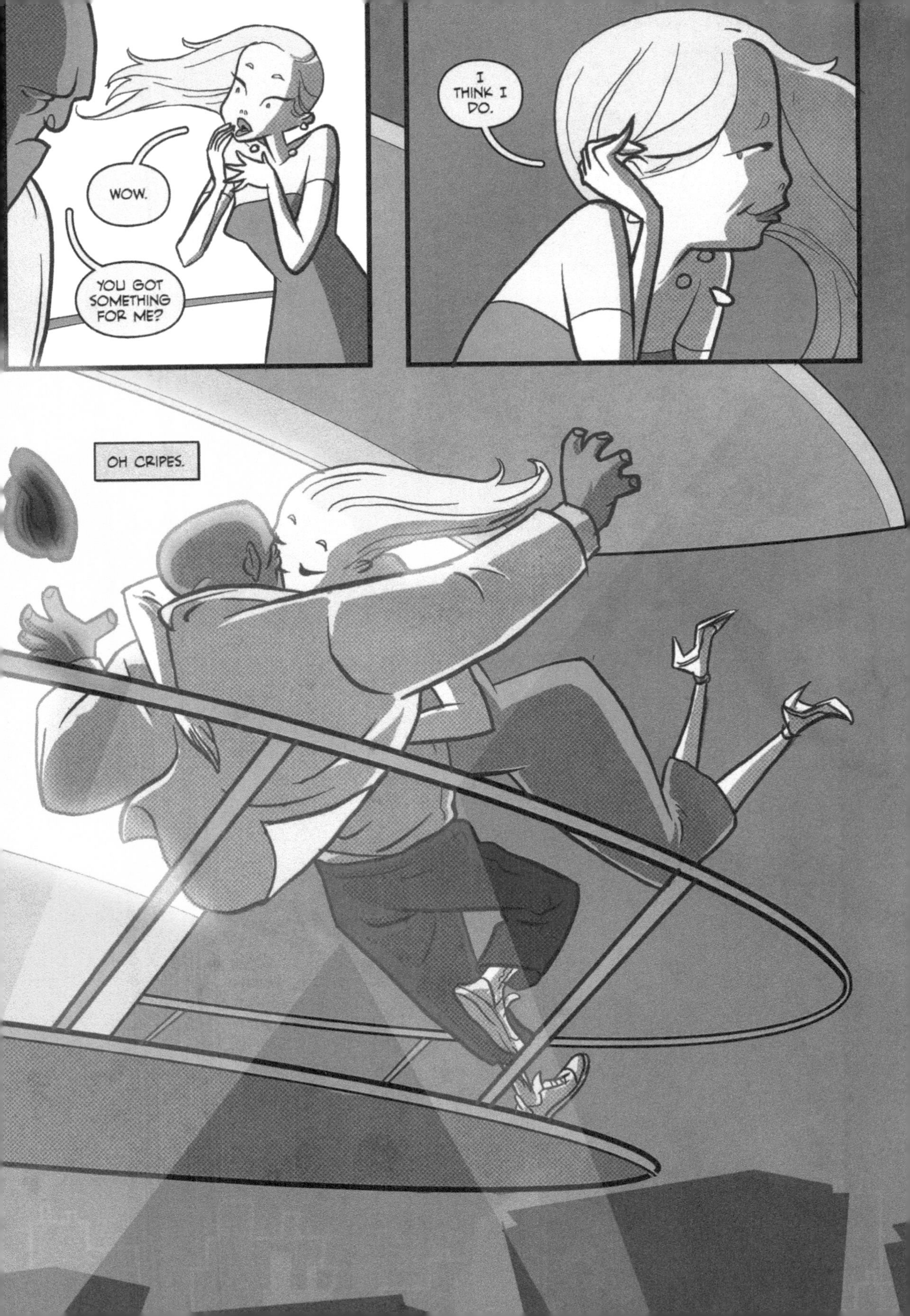
WOW.
YOU GOT SOMETHING FOR ME?
I THINK I DO.
OH CRIPES.

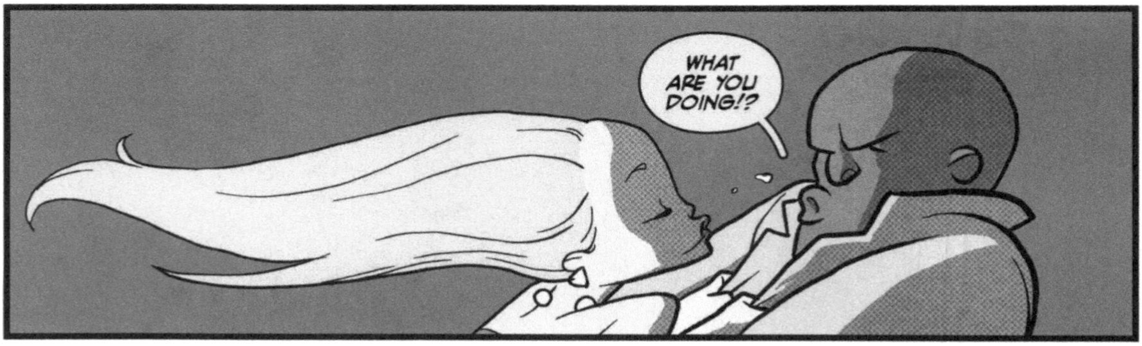
WHAT ARE YOU DOING!?
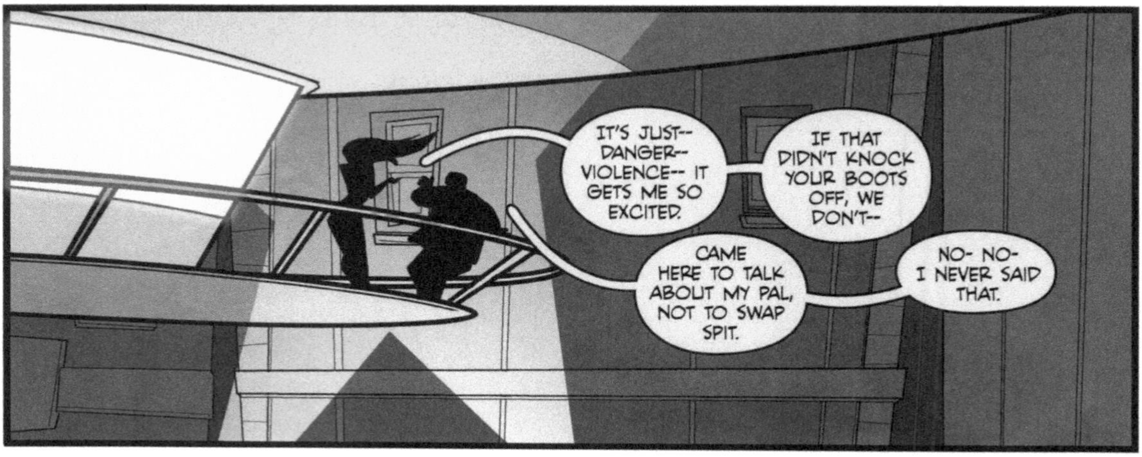
IT'S JUST-- DANGER-- VIOLENCE-- IT GETS ME SO EXCITED.
IF THAT DIDN'T KNOCK YOUR BOOTS OFF, WE DON'T--
CAME HERE TO TALK ABOUT MY PAL, NOT TO SWAP SPIT.
NO- NO- I NEVER SAID THAT.
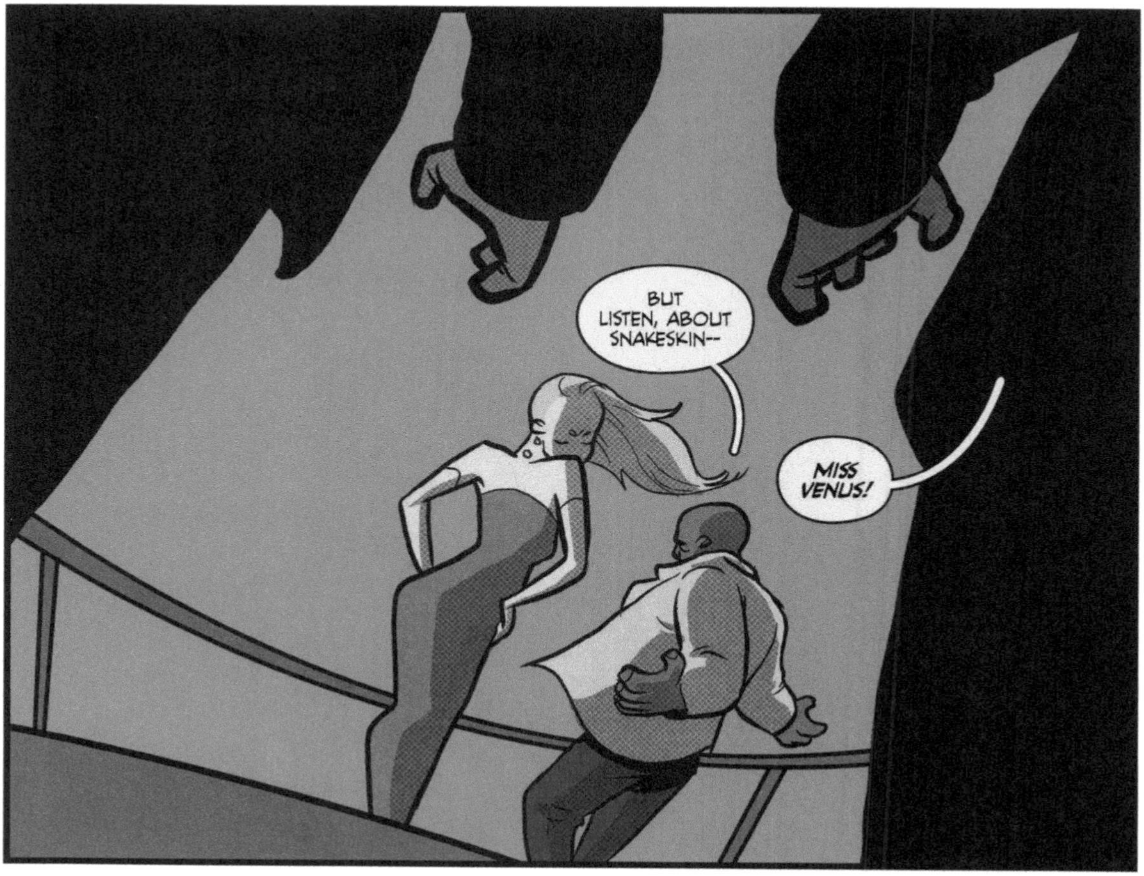
BUT LISTEN, ABOUT SNAKESKIN--
MISS VENUS!

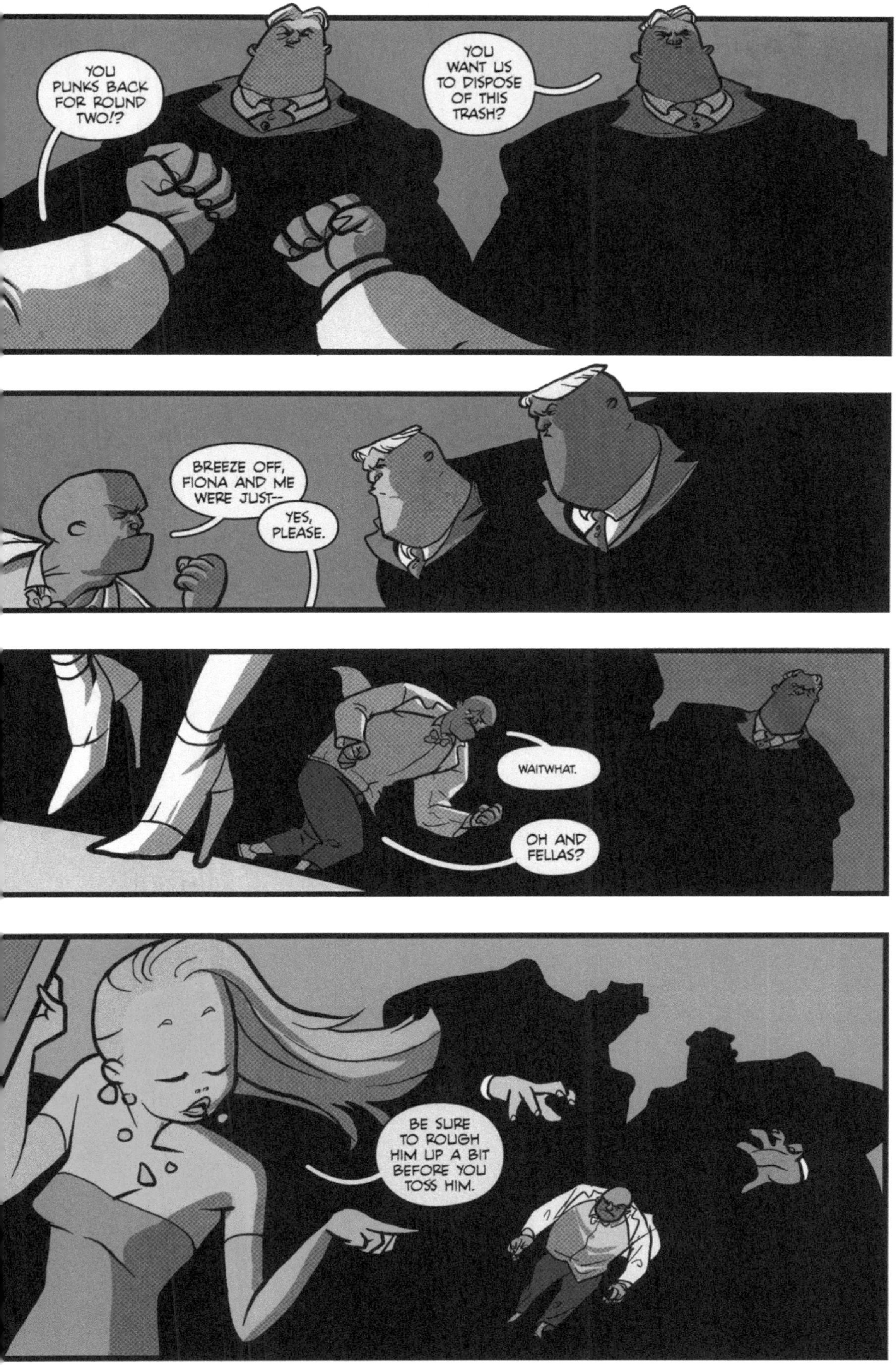
YOU PUNKS BACK FOR ROUND TWO!?
YOU WANT US TO DISPOSE OF THIS TRASH?
BREEZE OFF, FIONA AND ME WERE JUST--
YES, PLEASE.
WAITWHAT.
OH AND FELLAS?
BE SURE TO ROUGH HIM UP A BIT BEFORE YOU TOSS HIM.

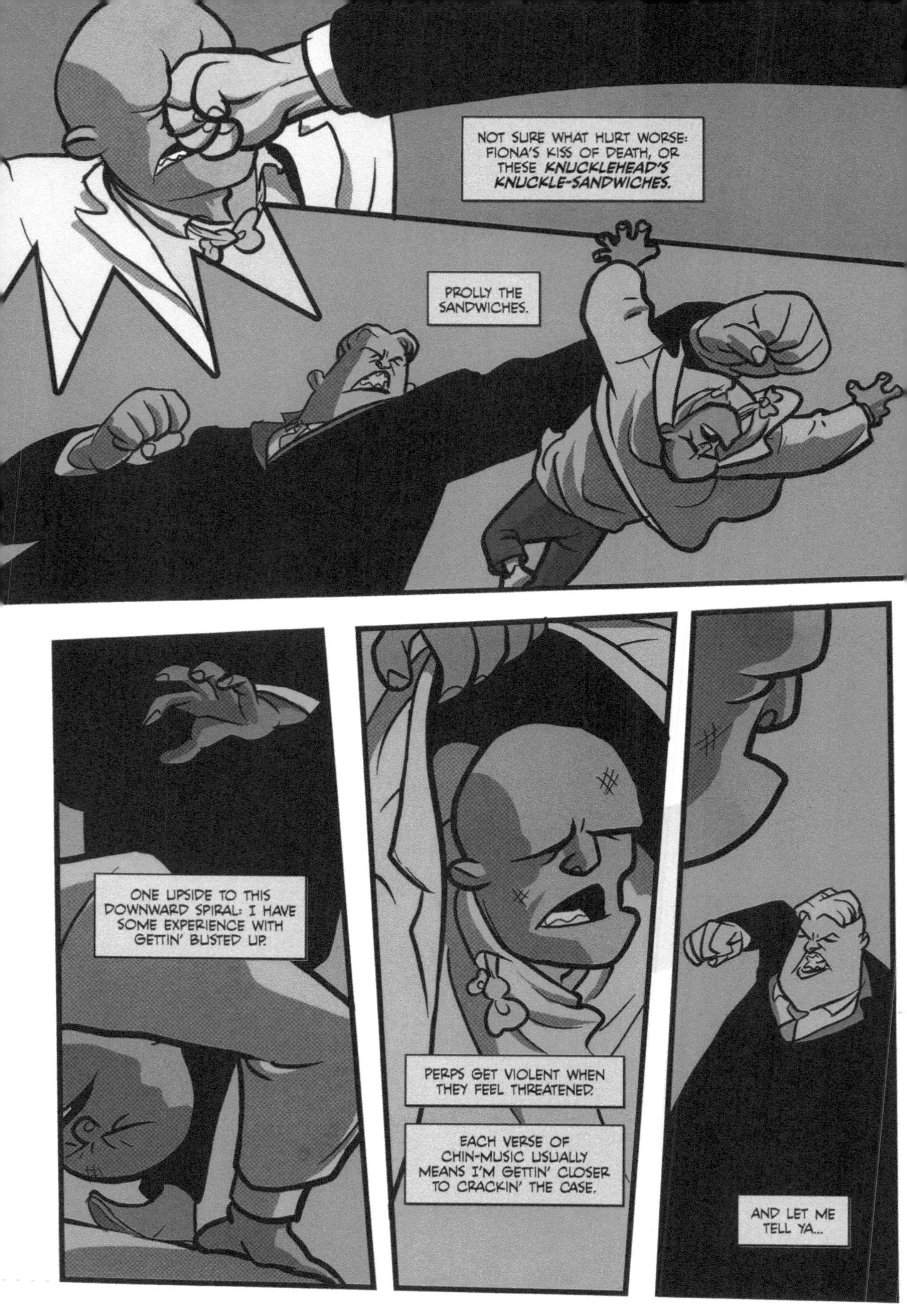
NOT SURE WHAT HURT WORSE: FIONA'S KISS OF DEATH, OR THESE ***KNUCKLEHEAD'S KNUCKLE-SANDWICHES.***
PROLLY THE SANDWICHES.
ONE UPSIDE TO THIS DOWNWARD SPIRAL: I HAVE SOME EXPERIENCE WITH GETTIN' BUSTED UP.
PERPS GET VIOLENT WHEN THEY FEEL THREATENED.
EACH VERSE OF CHIN-MUSIC USUALLY MEANS I'M GETTIN' CLOSER TO CRACKIN' THE CASE.
AND LET ME TELL YA...

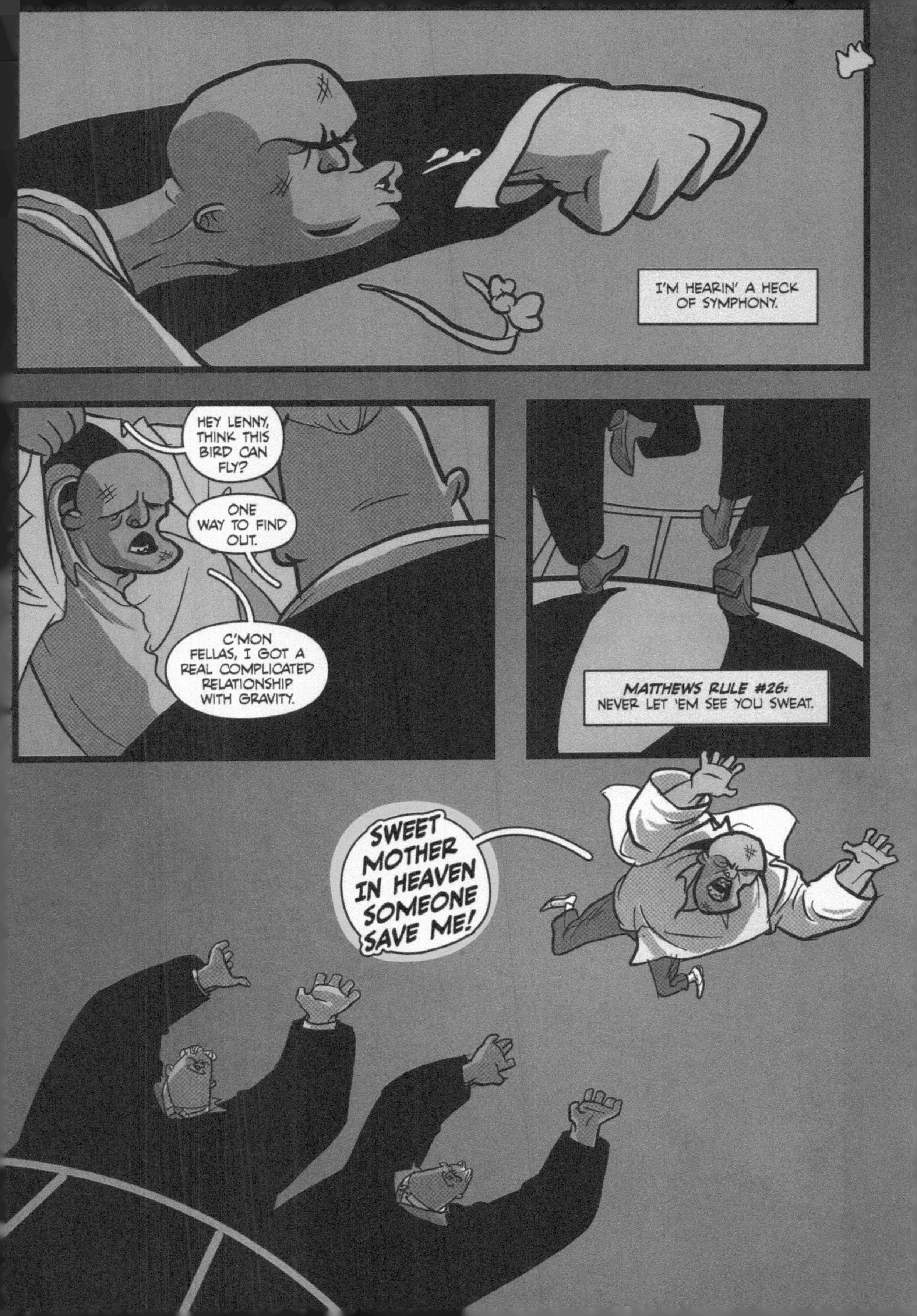
I'M HEARIN' A HECK OF SYMPHONY.
HEY LENNY, THINK THIS BIRD CAN FLY?
ONE WAY TO FIND OUT.
C'MON FELLAS, I GOT A REAL COMPLICATED RELATIONSHIP WITH GRAVITY.
MATTHEWS RULE #26: NEVER LET 'EM SEE YOU SWEAT.
SWEET MOTHER IN HEAVEN SOMEONE SAVE ME!

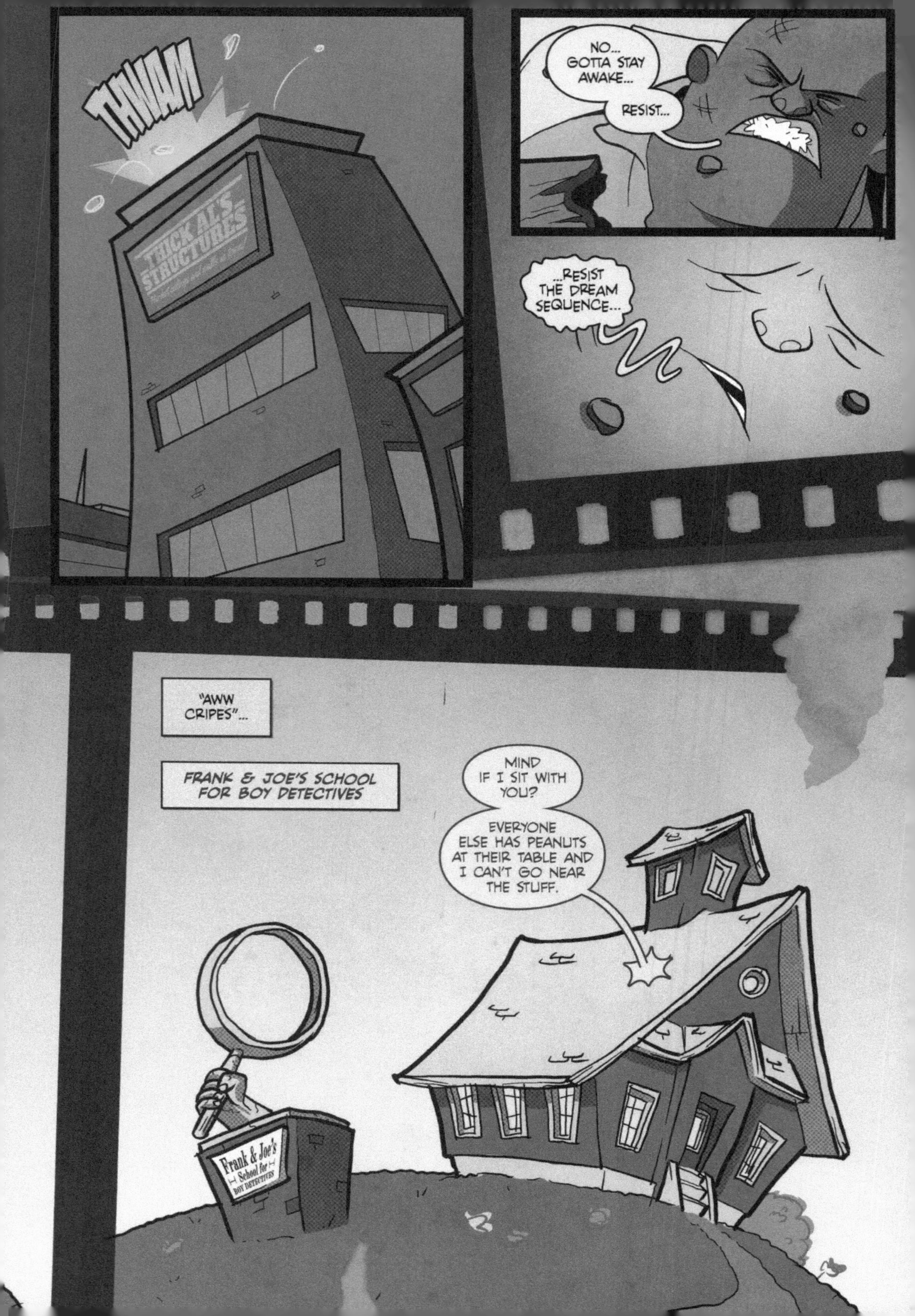
THWAM
THICK AL'S STRUCTURES
NO... GOTTA STAY AWAKE...
RESIST...
...RESIST THE DREAM SEQUENCE...
"AWW CRIPES"...
FRANK & JOE'S SCHOOL FOR BOY DETECTIVES
MIND IF I SIT WITH YOU?
EVERYONE ELSE HAS PEANUTS AT THEIR TABLE AND I CAN'T GO NEAR THE STUFF.
Frank & Joe's School for BOY DETECTIVES

CHAPTER SEVEN:

CRUEL DAZE OF SCHOOL DAYS

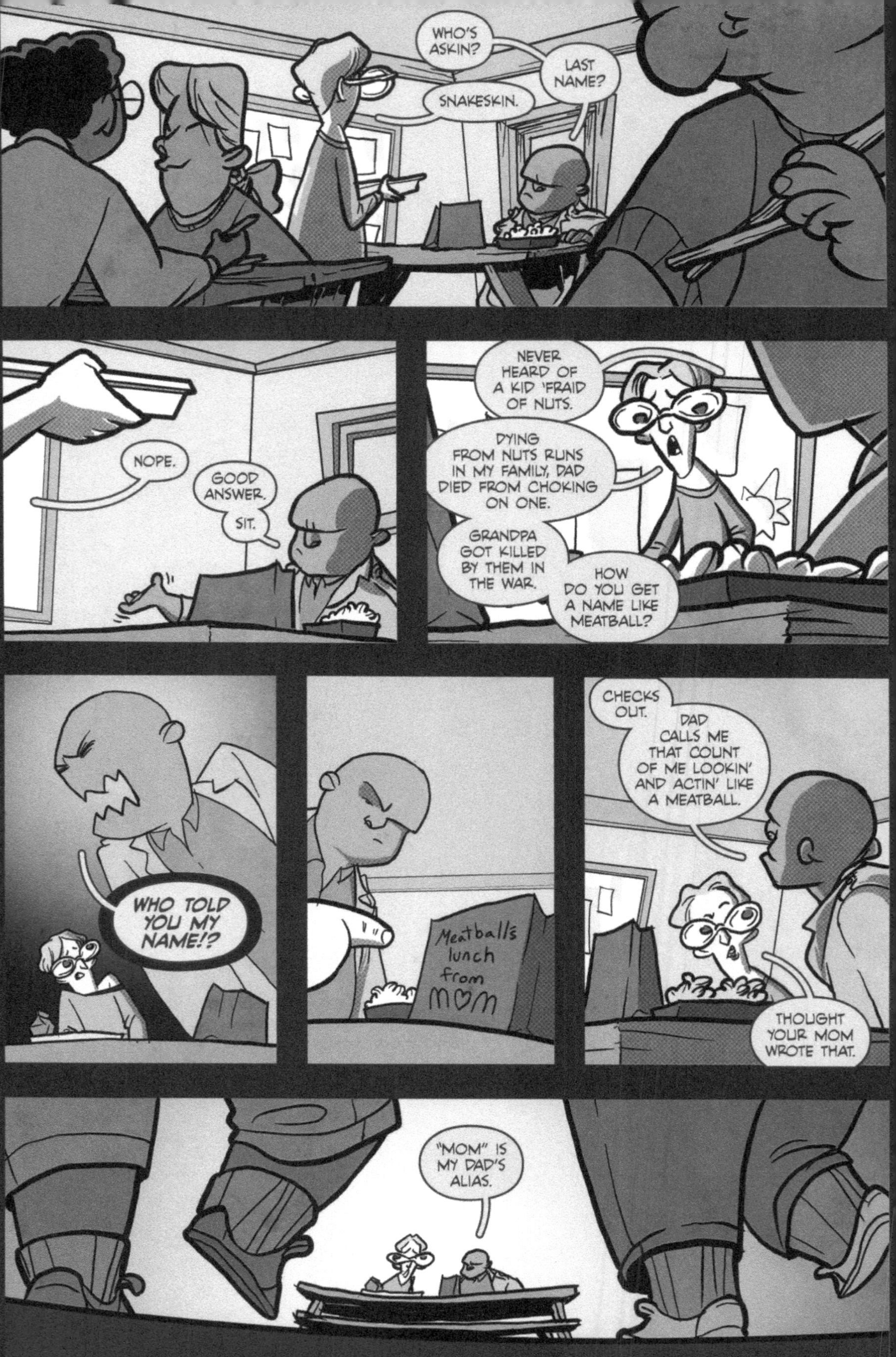
WHO'S ASKIN?
SNAKESKIN.
LAST NAME?
NOPE.
GOOD ANSWER.
SIT.
NEVER HEARD OF A KID 'FRAID OF NUTS.
DYING FROM NUTS RUNS IN MY FAMILY, DAD DIED FROM CHOKING ON ONE.
GRANDPA GOT KILLED BY THEM IN THE WAR.
HOW DO YOU GET A NAME LIKE MEATBALL?
WHO TOLD YOU MY NAME!?
Meatball's lunch from MOM
CHECKS OUT.
DAD CALLS ME THAT COUNT OF ME LOOKIN' AND ACTIN' LIKE A MEATBALL.
THOUGHT YOUR MOM WROTE THAT.
"MOM" IS MY DAD'S ALIAS.

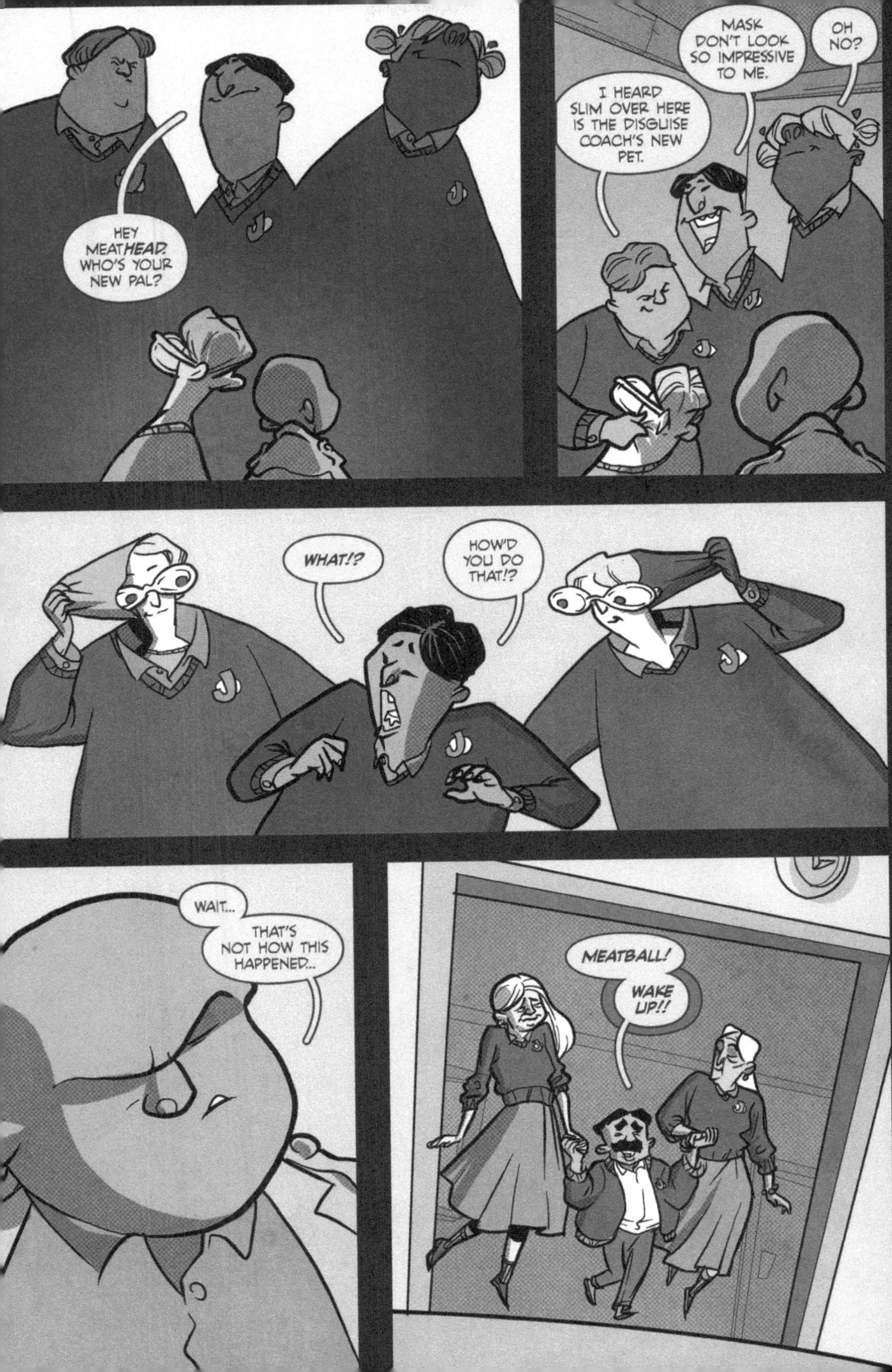
HEY MEAT*HEAD*. WHO'S YOUR NEW PAL?
I HEARD SLIM OVER HERE IS THE DISGUISE COACH'S NEW PET.
MASK DON'T LOOK SO IMPRESSIVE TO ME.
OH NO?
WHAT!?
HOW'D YOU DO THAT!?
WAIT...
THAT'S NOT HOW THIS HAPPENED...
MEATBALL!
WAKE UP!!

chapter 8:

a most UNSUSPICIOUS request.

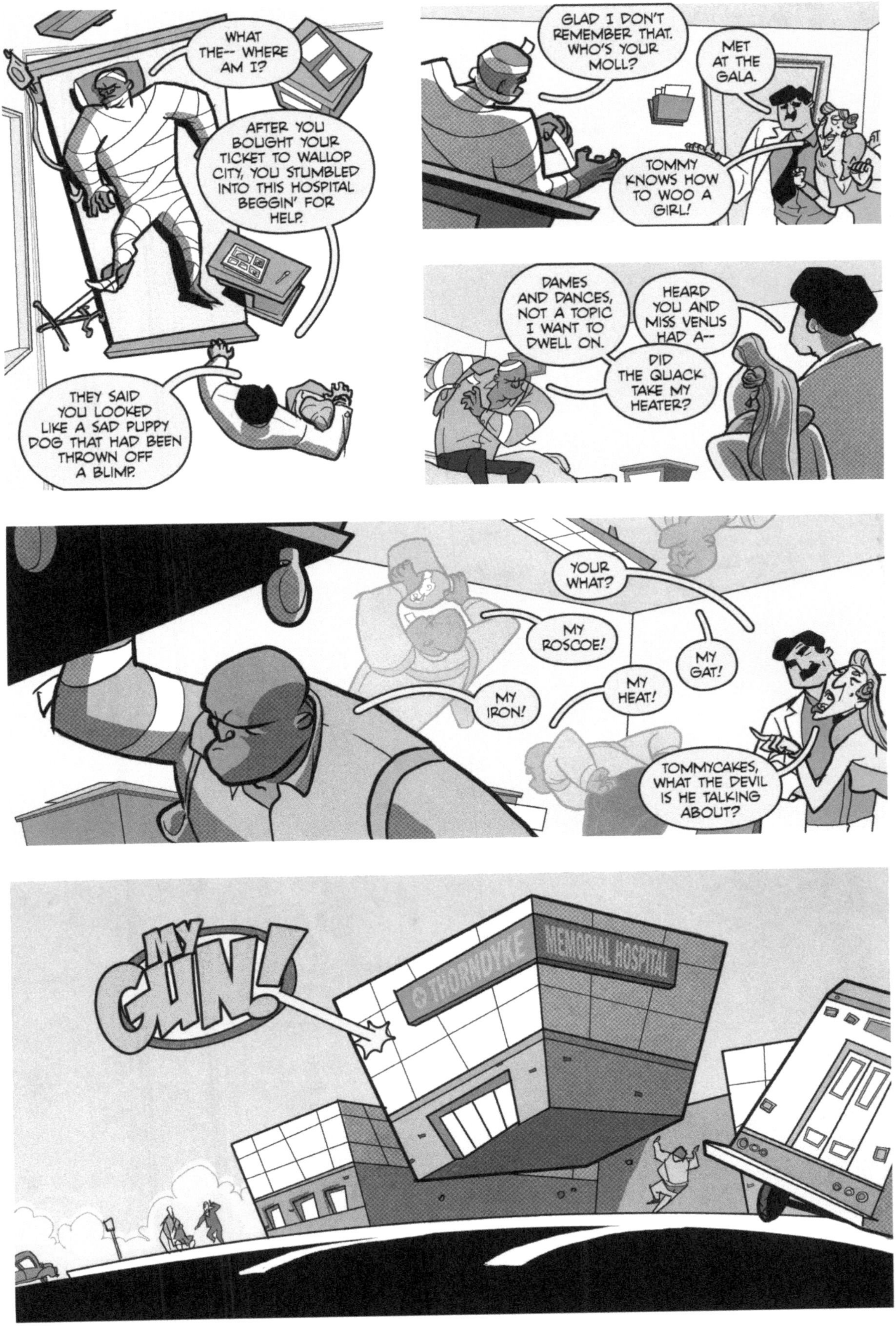

WHAT THE-- WHERE AM I?
AFTER YOU BOUGHT YOUR TICKET TO WALLOP CITY, YOU STUMBLED INTO THIS HOSPITAL BEGGIN' FOR HELP.
THEY SAID YOU LOOKED LIKE A SAD PUPPY DOG THAT HAD BEEN THROWN OFF A BLIMP.
GLAD I DON'T REMEMBER THAT. WHO'S YOUR MOLL?
MET AT THE GALA.
TOMMY KNOWS HOW TO WOO A GIRL!
HEARD YOU AND MISS VENUS HAD A--
DAMES AND DANCES, NOT A TOPIC I WANT TO DWELL ON.
DID THE QUACK TAKE MY HEATER?
YOUR WHAT?
MY ROSCOE!
MY GAT!
MY HEAT!
MY IRON!
TOMMYCAKES, WHAT THE DEVIL IS HE TALKING ABOUT?
MY GUN!
THORNDYKE
MEMORIAL HOSPITAL

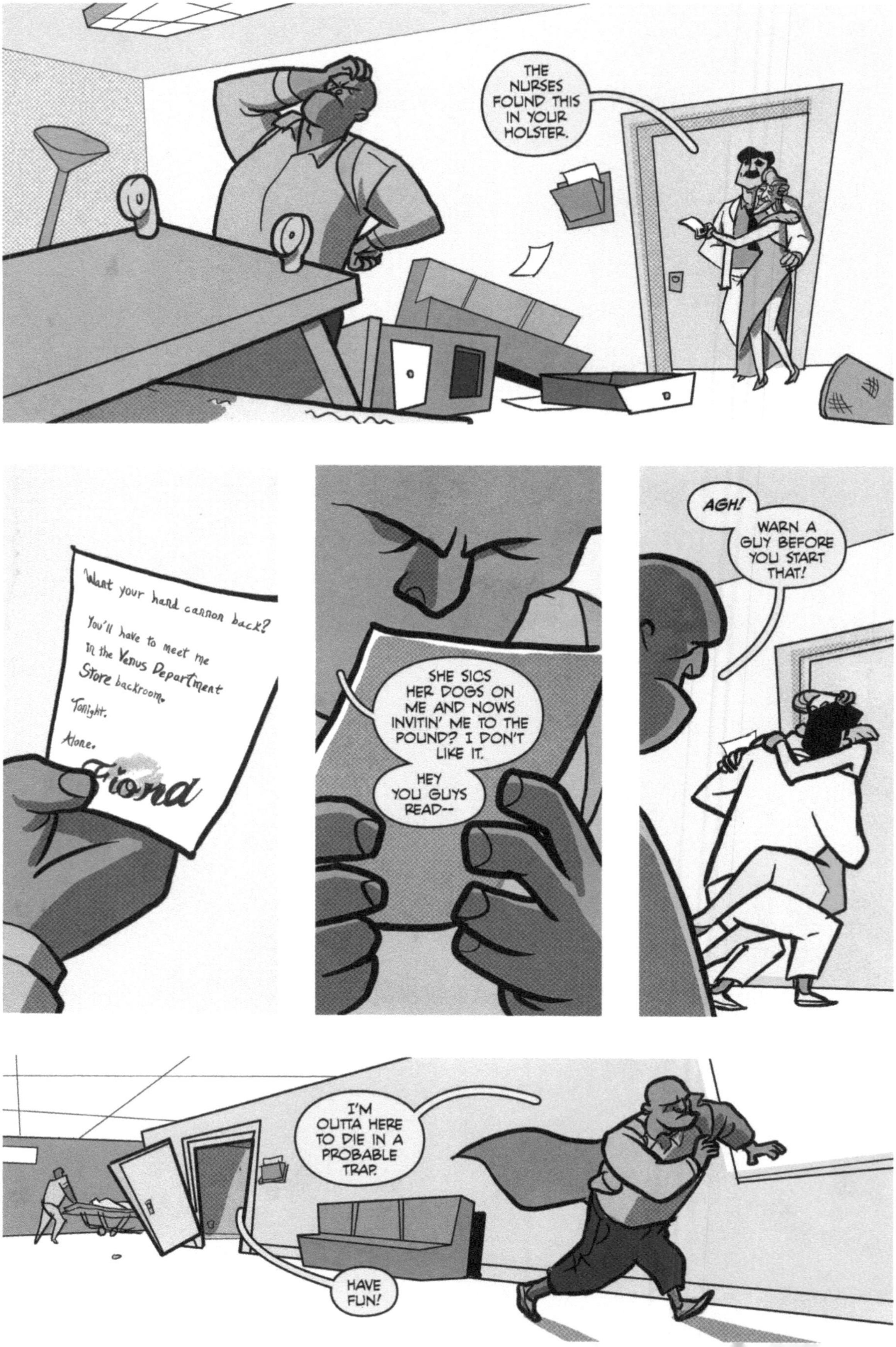
THE NURSES FOUND THIS IN YOUR HOLSTER.
Want your hand cannon back?
You'll have to meet me in the Venus Department Store backroom.
Tonight.
Alone.
Fiona
SHE SICS HER DOGS ON ME AND NOWS INVITIN' ME TO THE POUND? I DON'T LIKE IT.
HEY YOU GUYS READ--
AGH!
WARN A GUY BEFORE YOU START THAT!
I'M OUTTA HERE TO DIE IN A PROBABLE TRAP.
HAVE FUN!

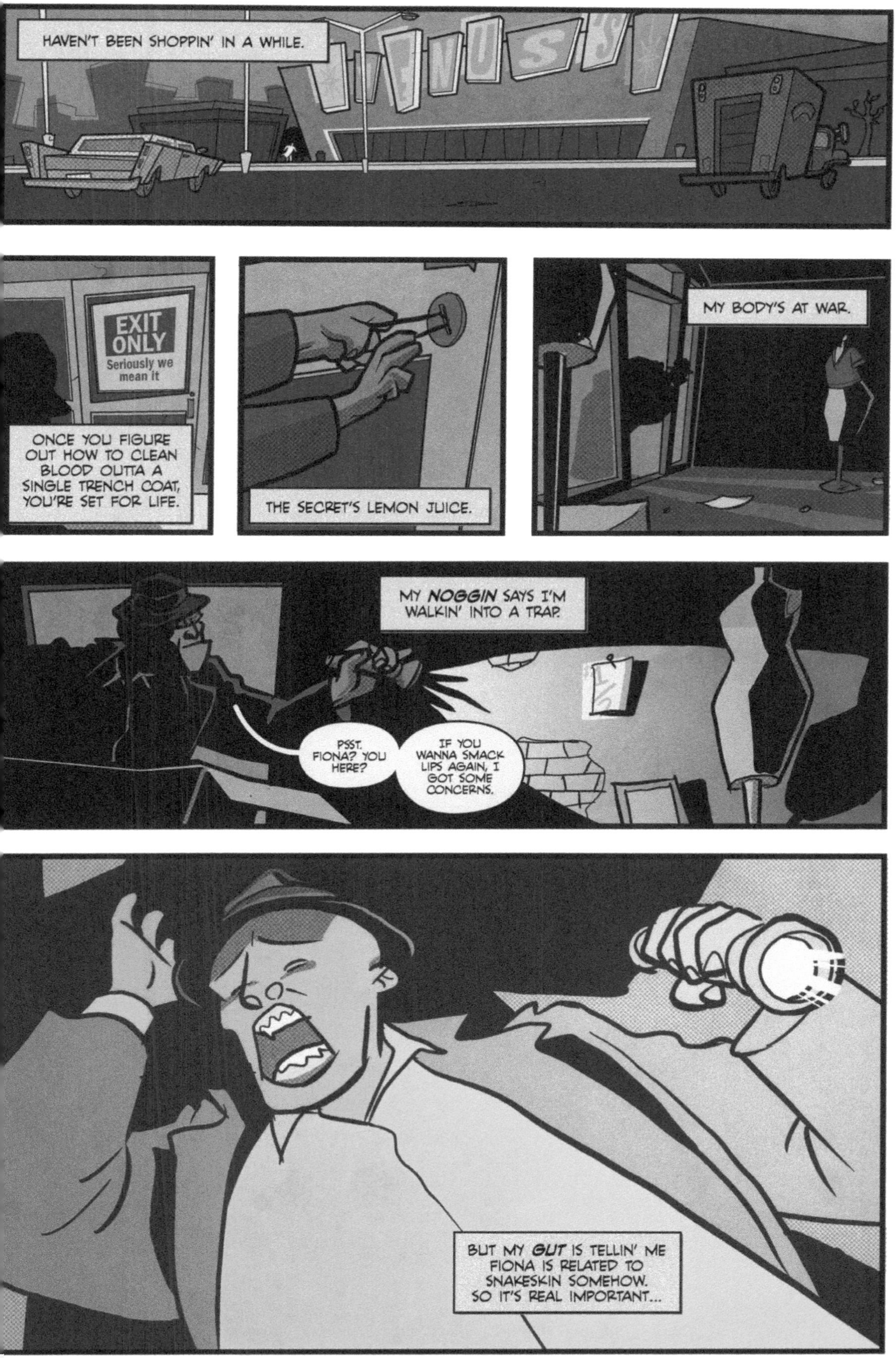
HAVEN'T BEEN SHOPPIN' IN A WHILE.
EXIT ONLY
Seriously we mean it
ONCE YOU FIGURE OUT HOW TO CLEAN BLOOD OUTTA A SINGLE TRENCH COAT, YOU'RE SET FOR LIFE.
THE SECRET'S LEMON JUICE.
MY BODY'S AT WAR.
MY NOGGIN SAYS I'M WALKIN' INTO A TRAP.
PSST. FIONA? YOU HERE?
IF YOU WANNA SMACK LIPS AGAIN, I GOT SOME CONCERNS.
BUT MY GUT IS TELLIN' ME FIONA IS RELATED TO SNAKESKIN SOMEHOW. SO IT'S REAL IMPORTANT...

A DAME WORTH
CHAPTER NINE:
BEING FRAMED FOR

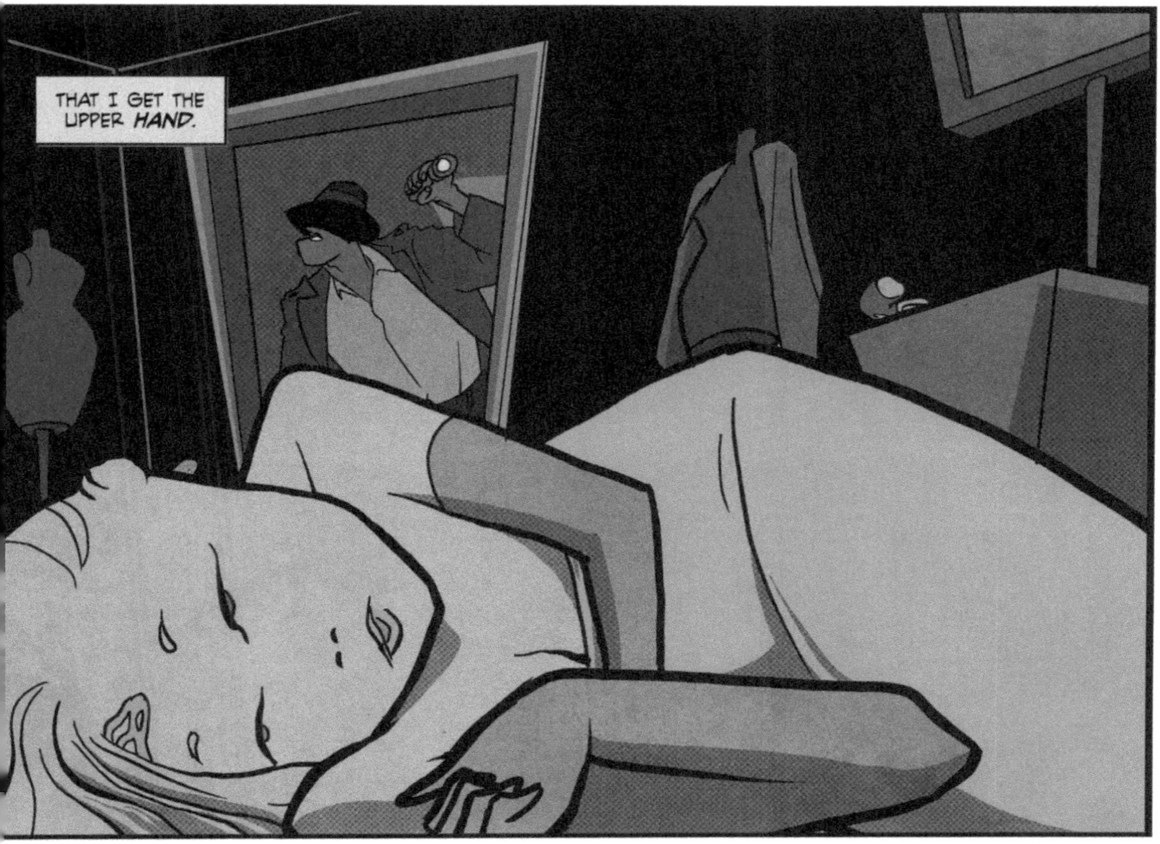
THAT I GET THE UPPER HAND.
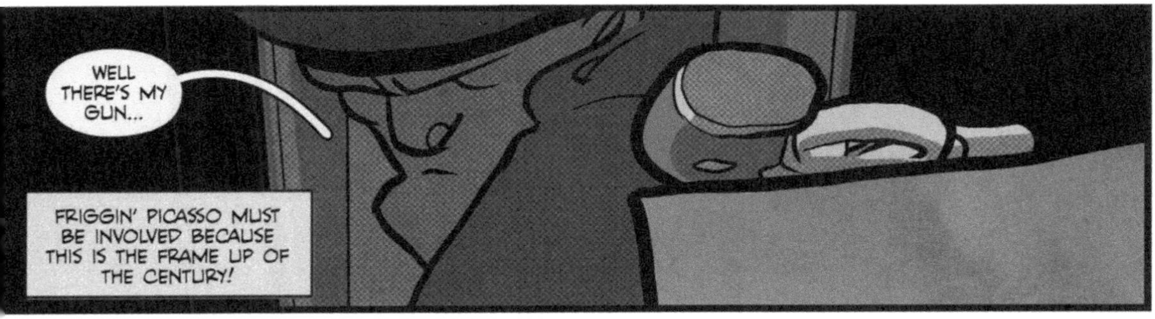
WELL THERE'S MY GUN...
FRIGGIN' PICASSO MUST BE INVOLVED BECAUSE THIS IS THE FRAME UP OF THE CENTURY!
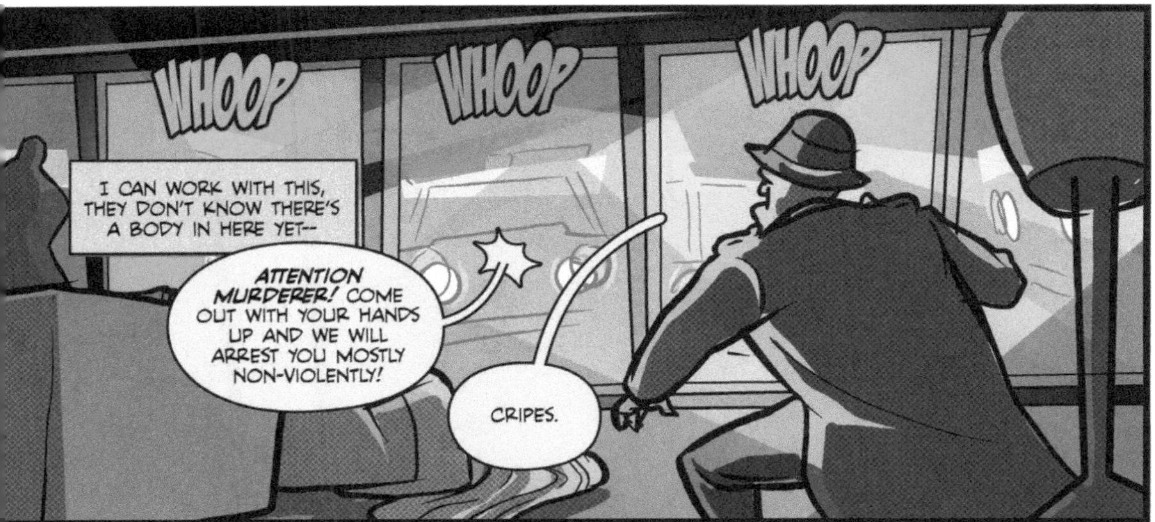
WHOOP
WHOOP
WHOOP
I CAN WORK WITH THIS, THEY DON'T KNOW THERE'S A BODY IN HERE YET--
ATTENTION MURDERER! COME OUT WITH YOUR HANDS UP AND WE WILL ARREST YOU MOSTLY NON-VIOLENTLY!
CRIPES.

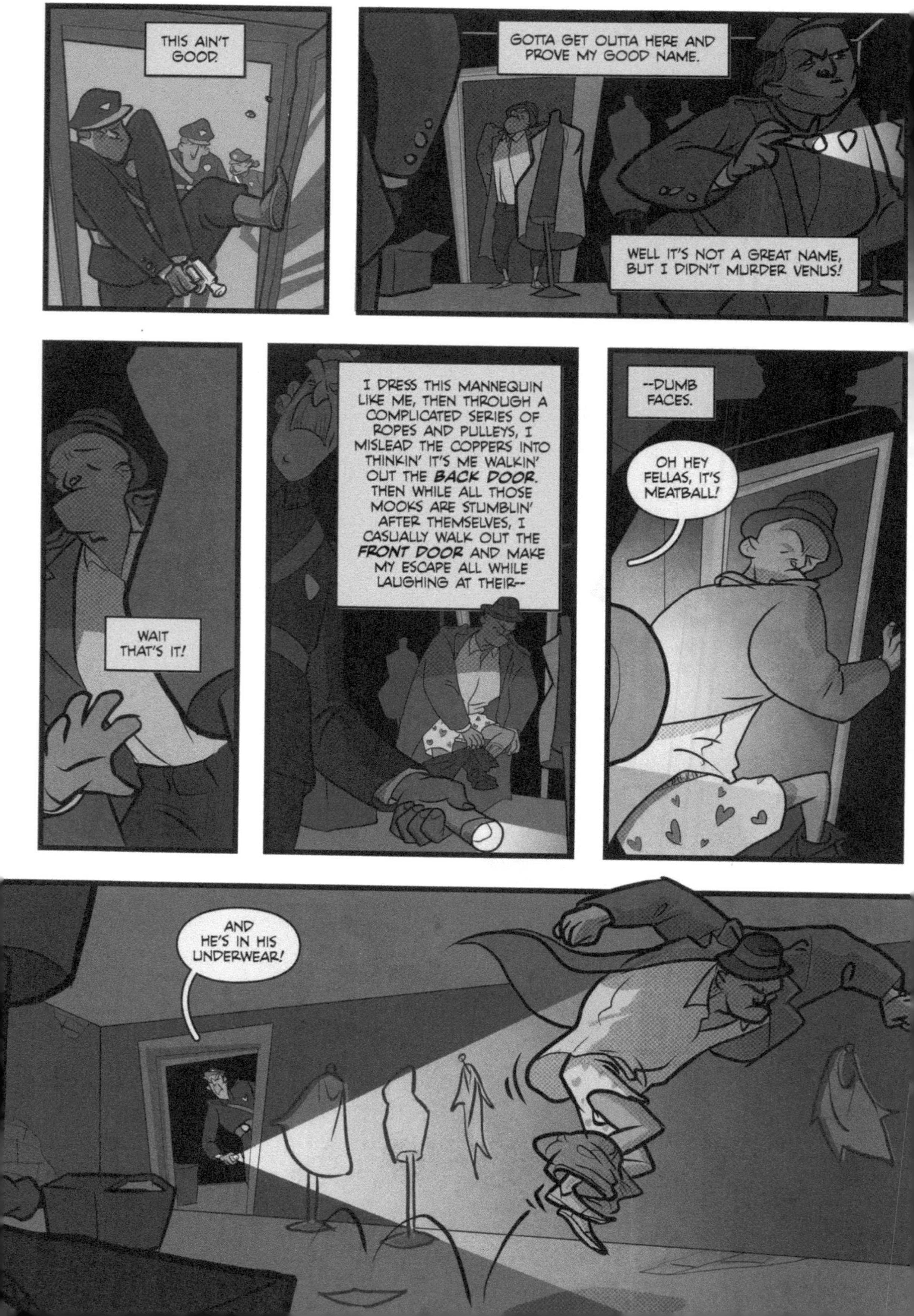
THIS AIN'T GOOD.
GOTTA GET OUTTA HERE AND PROVE MY GOOD NAME.
WELL IT'S NOT A GREAT NAME, BUT I DIDN'T MURDER VENUS!
WAIT THAT'S IT!
I DRESS THIS MANNEQUIN LIKE ME, THEN THROUGH A COMPLICATED SERIES OF ROPES AND PULLEYS, I MISLEAD THE COPPERS INTO THINKIN' IT'S ME WALKIN' OUT THE BACK DOOR. THEN WHILE ALL THOSE MOOKS ARE STUMBLIN' AFTER THEMSELVES, I CASUALLY WALK OUT THE FRONT DOOR AND MAKE MY ESCAPE ALL WHILE LAUGHING AT THEIR--
--DUMB FACES.
OH HEY FELLAS, IT'S MEATBALL!
AND HE'S IN HIS UNDERWEAR!

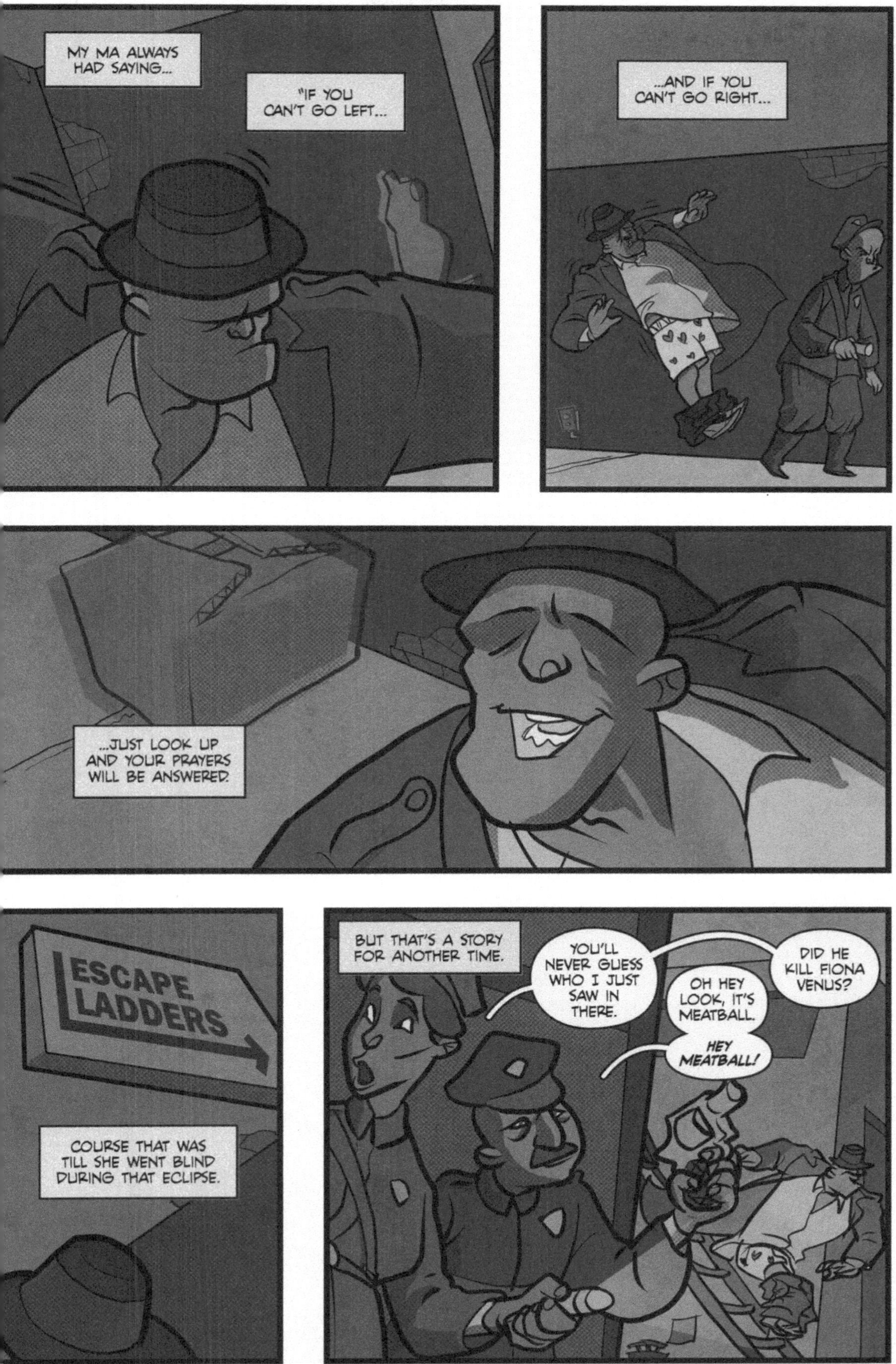
MY MA ALWAYS HAD SAYING...
"IF YOU CAN'T GO LEFT...
...AND IF YOU CAN'T GO RIGHT...
...JUST LOOK UP AND YOUR PRAYERS WILL BE ANSWERED.
ESCAPE LADDERS
COURSE THAT WAS TILL SHE WENT BLIND DURING THAT ECLIPSE.
BUT THAT'S A STORY FOR ANOTHER TIME.
YOU'LL NEVER GUESS WHO I JUST SAW IN THERE.
DID HE KILL FIONA VENUS?
OH HEY LOOK, IT'S MEATBALL.
HEY MEATBALL!

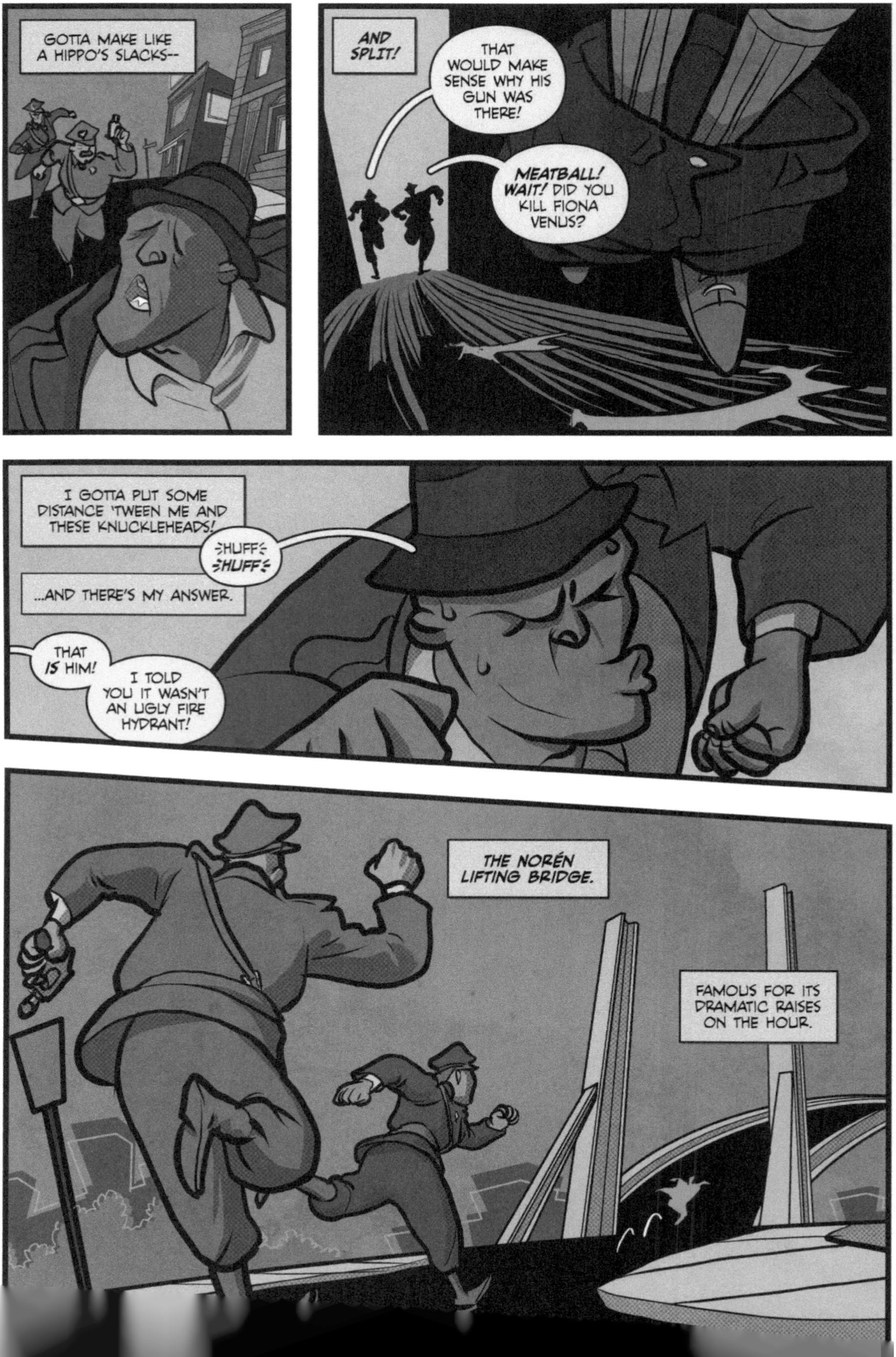
GOTTA MAKE LIKE A HIPPO'S SLACKS--
AND SPLIT!
THAT WOULD MAKE SENSE WHY HIS GUN WAS THERE!
MEATBALL! WAIT! DID YOU KILL FIONA VENUS?
I GOTTA PUT SOME DISTANCE 'TWEEN ME AND THESE KNUCKLEHEADS!
HUFF HUFF
...AND THERE'S MY ANSWER.
THAT IS HIM!
I TOLD YOU IT WASN'T AN UGLY FIRE HYDRANT!
THE NORÉN LIFTING BRIDGE.
FAMOUS FOR ITS DRAMATIC RAISES ON THE HOUR.

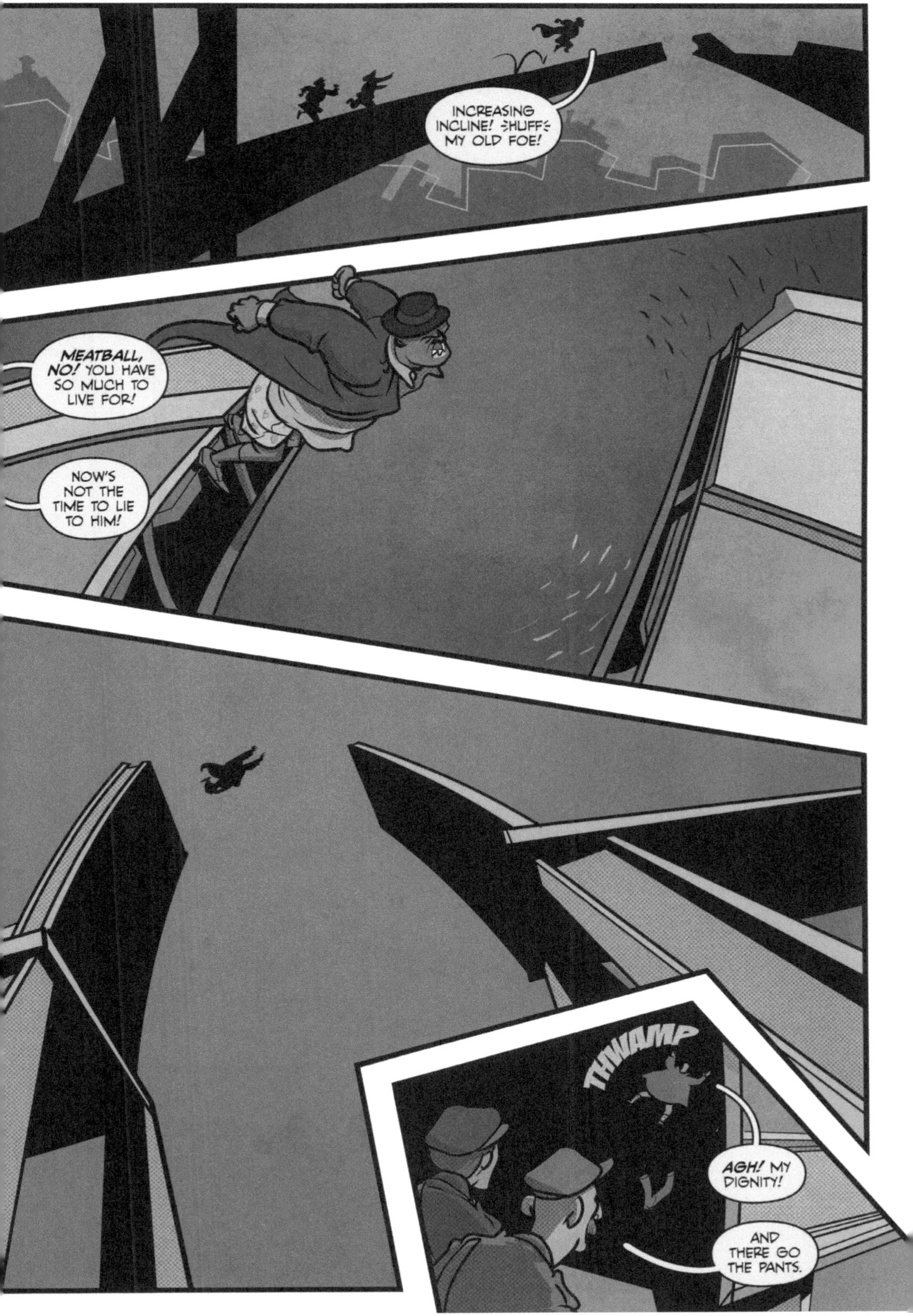
INCREASING INCLINE! ⫶HUFF⫶ MY OLD FOE!
MEATBALL, NO! YOU HAVE SO MUCH TO LIVE FOR!
NOW'S NOT THE TIME TO LIE TO HIM!
THWAMP
AGH! MY DIGNITY!
AND THERE GO THE PANTS.

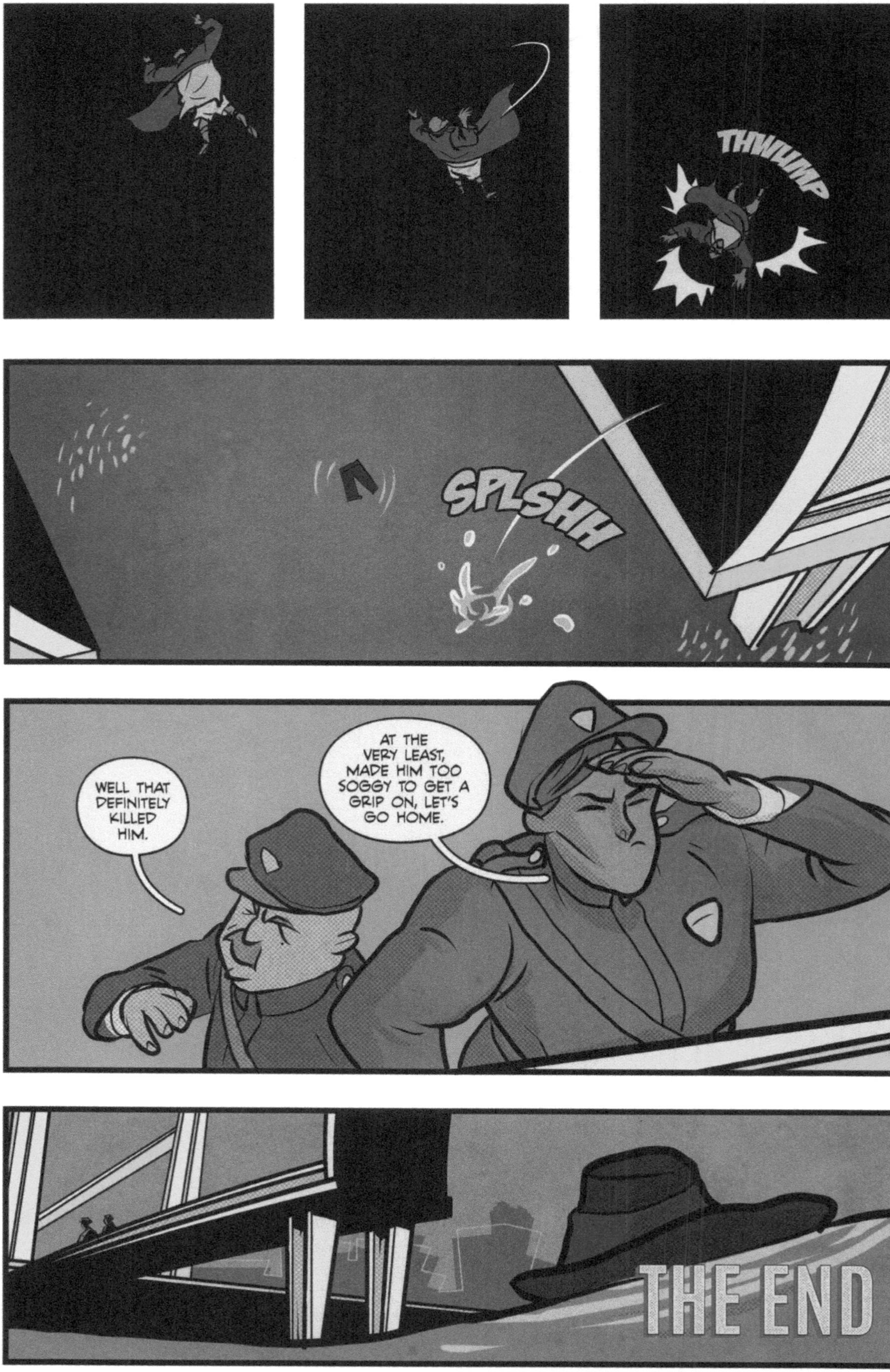
THWUMP
SPLSHH
WELL THAT DEFINITELY KILLED HIM.
AT THE VERY LEAST, MADE HIM TOO SOGGY TO GET A GRIP ON, LET'S GO HOME.
THE END

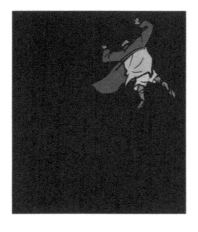

CHAPTER TEN
BIRDS-EYE'S VIEW
TO A KILL

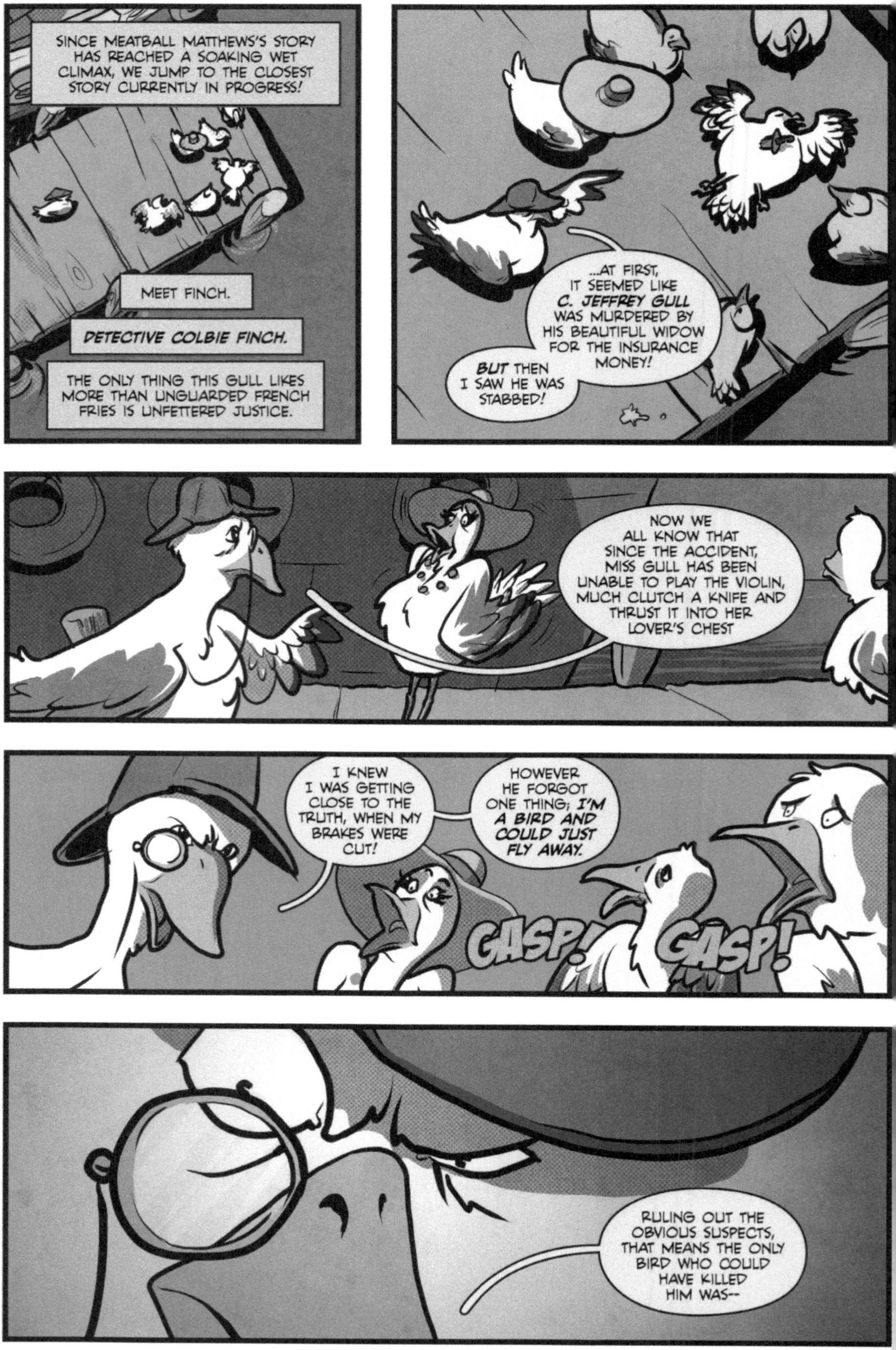
SINCE MEATBALL MATTHEWS'S STORY HAS REACHED A SOAKING WET CLIMAX, WE JUMP TO THE CLOSEST STORY CURRENTLY IN PROGRESS!
MEET FINCH.
DETECTIVE COLBIE FINCH.
THE ONLY THING THIS GULL LIKES MORE THAN UNGUARDED FRENCH FRIES IS UNFETTERED JUSTICE.
...AT FIRST, IT SEEMED LIKE C. JEFFREY GULL WAS MURDERED BY HIS BEAUTIFUL WIDOW FOR THE INSURANCE MONEY!
BUT THEN I SAW HE WAS STABBED!
NOW WE ALL KNOW THAT SINCE THE ACCIDENT, MISS GULL HAS BEEN UNABLE TO PLAY THE VIOLIN, MUCH CLUTCH A KNIFE AND THRUST IT INTO HER LOVER'S CHEST
I KNEW I WAS GETTING CLOSE TO THE TRUTH, WHEN MY BRAKES WERE CUT!
HOWEVER HE FORGOT ONE THING; I'M A BIRD AND COULD JUST FLY AWAY.
GASP!
GASP!
RULING OUT THE OBVIOUS SUSPECTS, THAT MEANS THE ONLY BIRD WHO COULD HAVE KILLED HIM WAS--

CHAPTER 11
ROCK BOTTOM
BLUES

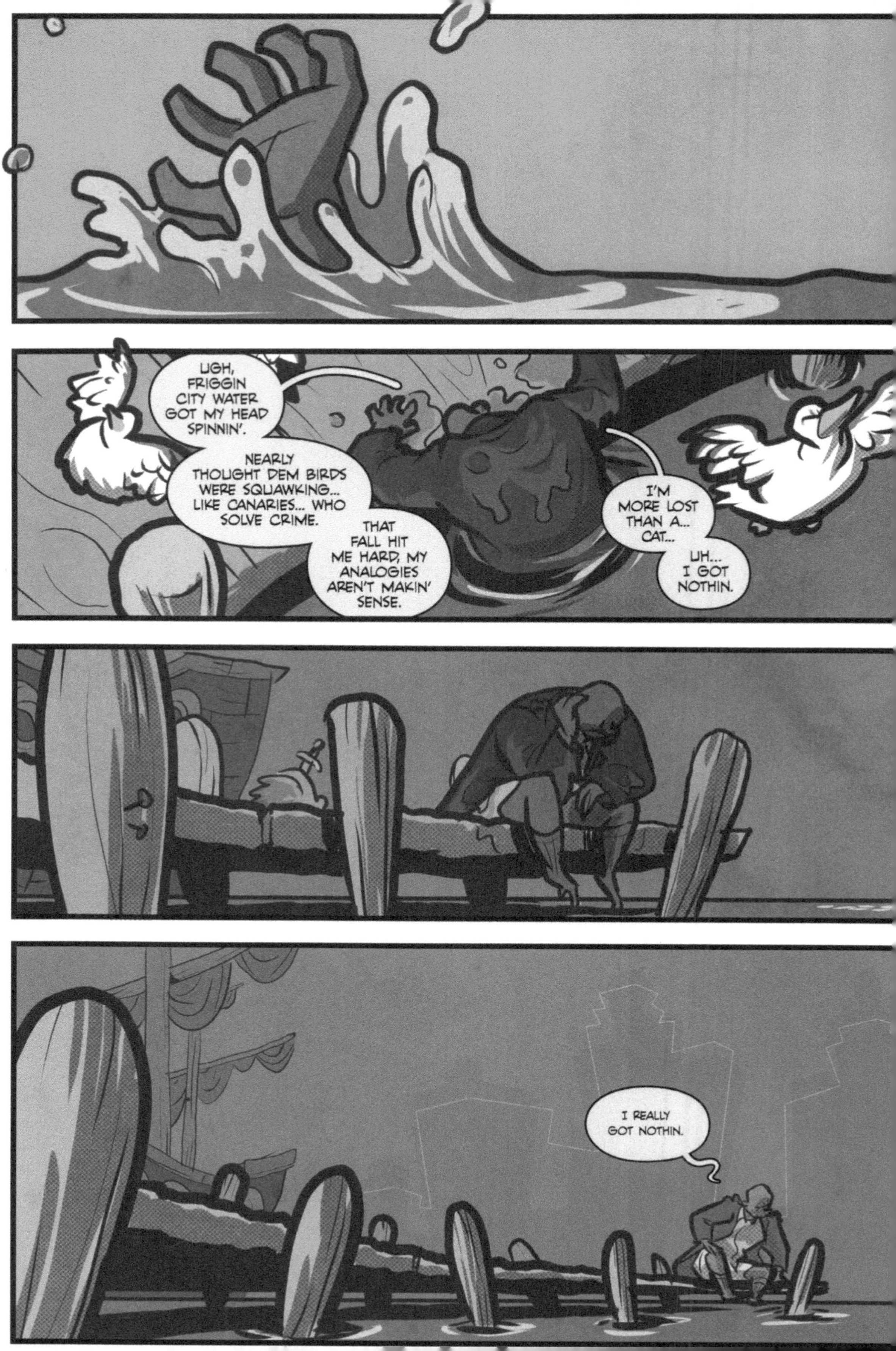
UGH, FRIGGIN CITY WATER GOT MY HEAD SPINNIN'.
NEARLY THOUGHT DEM BIRDS WERE SQUAWKING... LIKE CANARIES... WHO SOLVE CRIME.
THAT FALL HIT ME HARD, MY ANALOGIES AREN'T MAKIN' SENSE.
I'M MORE LOST THAN A... CAT...
UH... I GOT NOTHIN.
I REALLY GOT NOTHIN.

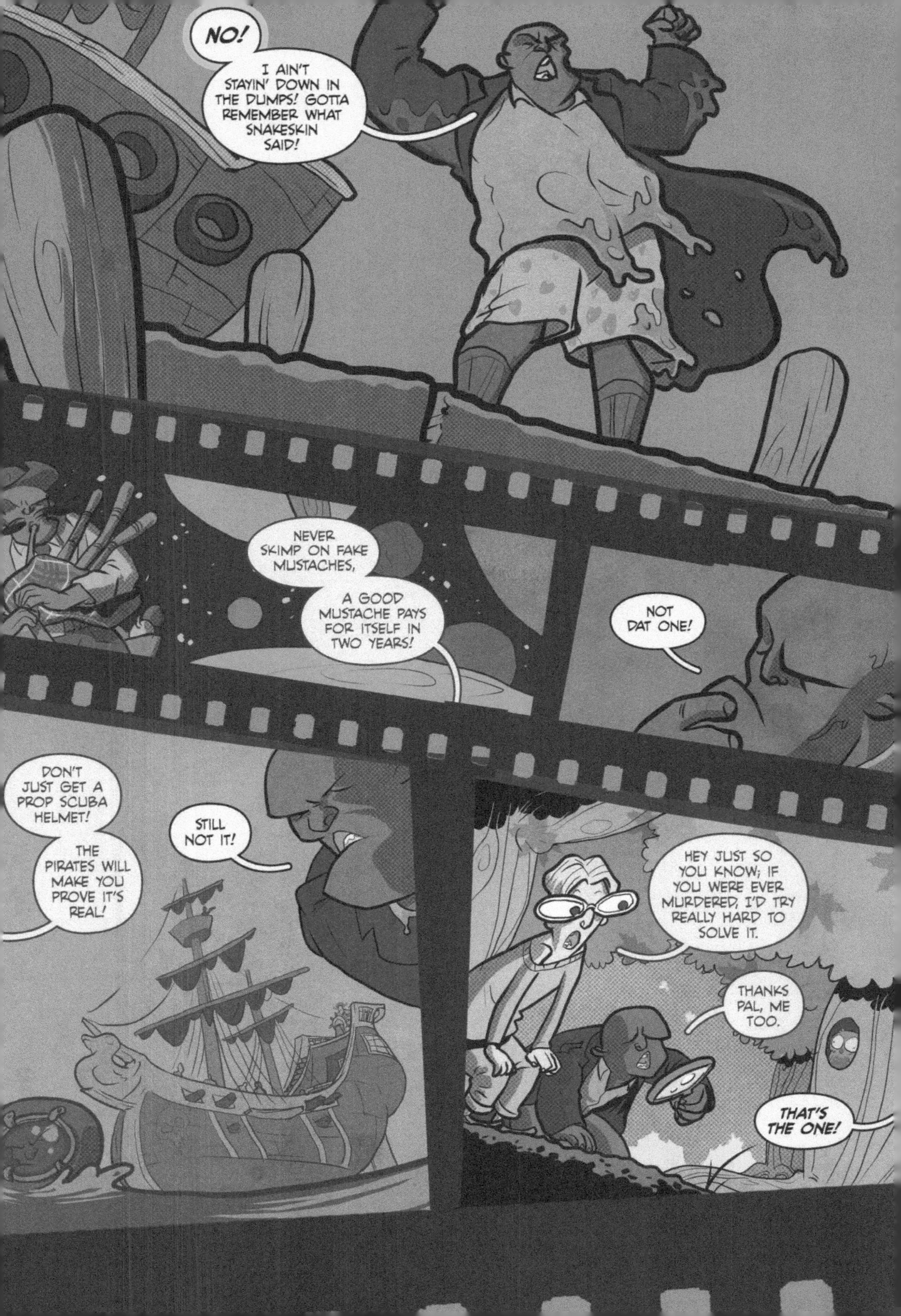
NO!
I AIN'T STAYIN' DOWN IN THE DUMPS! GOTTA REMEMBER WHAT SNAKESKIN SAID!
NEVER SKIMP ON FAKE MUSTACHES,
A GOOD MUSTACHE PAYS FOR ITSELF IN TWO YEARS!
NOT DAT ONE!
DON'T JUST GET A PROP SCUBA HELMET!
THE PIRATES WILL MAKE YOU PROVE IT'S REAL!
STILL NOT IT!
HEY JUST SO YOU KNOW; IF YOU WERE EVER MURDERED, I'D TRY REALLY HARD TO SOLVE IT.
THANKS PAL, ME TOO.
THAT'S THE ONE!

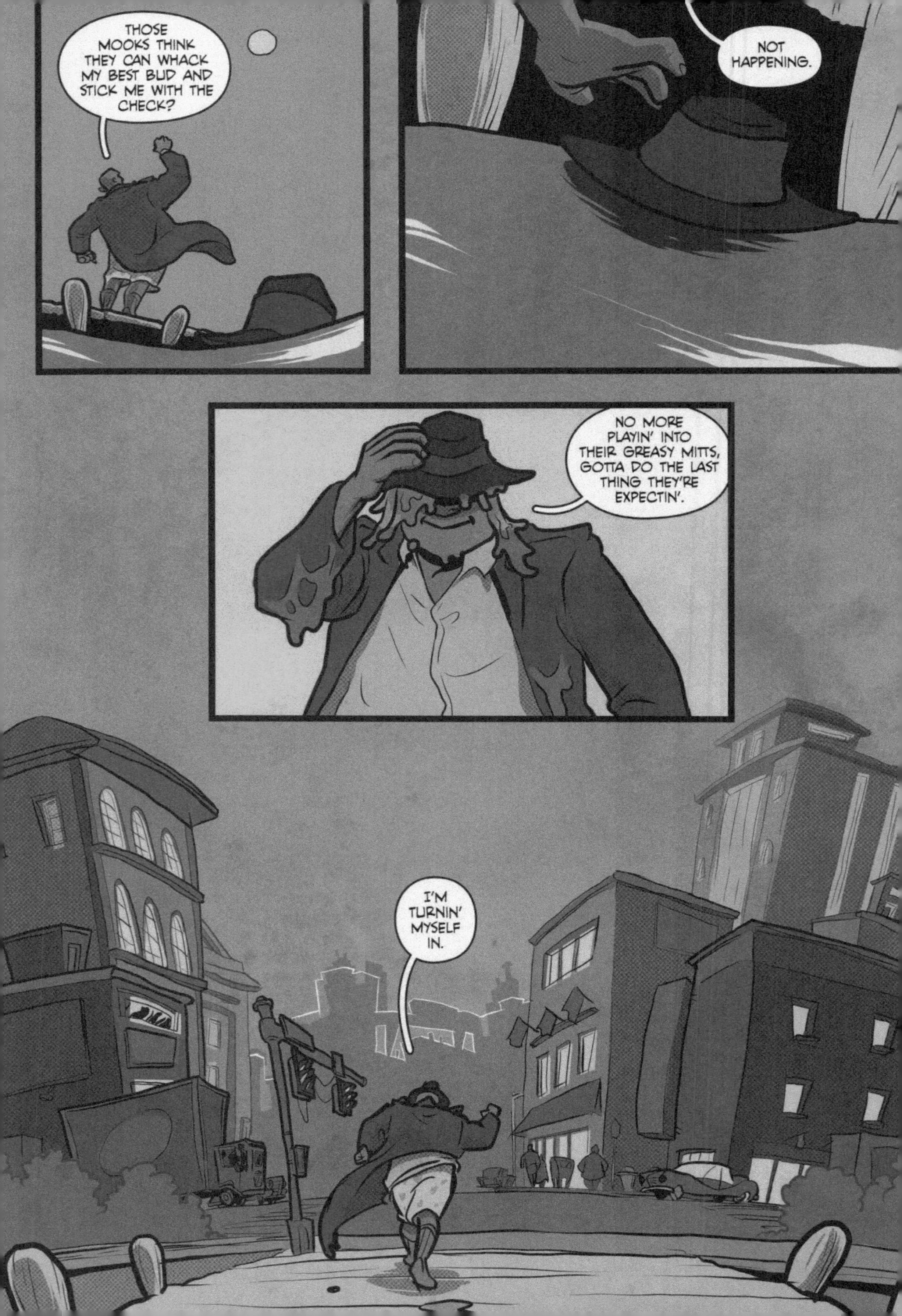
THOSE MOOKS THINK THEY CAN WHACK MY BEST BUD AND STICK ME WITH THE CHECK?
NOT HAPPENING.
NO MORE PLAYIN' INTO THEIR GREASY MITTS, GOTTA DO THE LAST THING THEY'RE EXPECTIN'.
I'M TURNIN' MYSELF IN.

CHAPTER TWELVE

SURRENDERING TO REVELATIONS

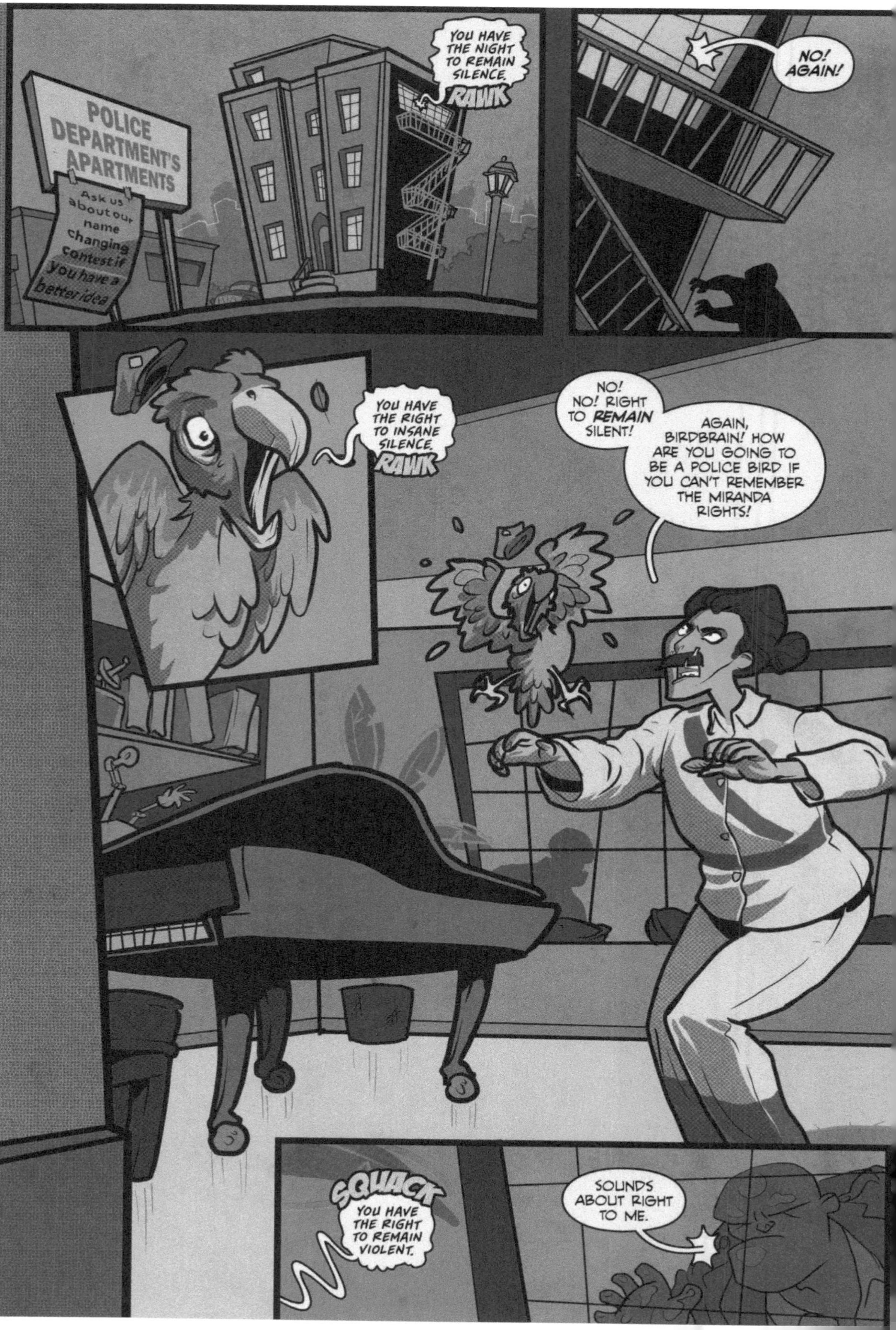
POLICE DEPARTMENT'S APARTMENTS
Ask us about our name changing contest if you have a better idea
YOU HAVE THE NIGHT TO REMAIN SILENCE.
RAWK
NO! AGAIN!
YOU HAVE THE RIGHT TO INSANE SILENCE.
RAWK
NO! NO! RIGHT TO REMAIN SILENT!
AGAIN, BIRDBRAIN! HOW ARE YOU GOING TO BE A POLICE BIRD IF YOU CAN'T REMEMBER THE MIRANDA RIGHTS!
SQUACK
YOU HAVE THE RIGHT TO REMAIN VIOLENT.
SOUNDS ABOUT RIGHT TO ME.

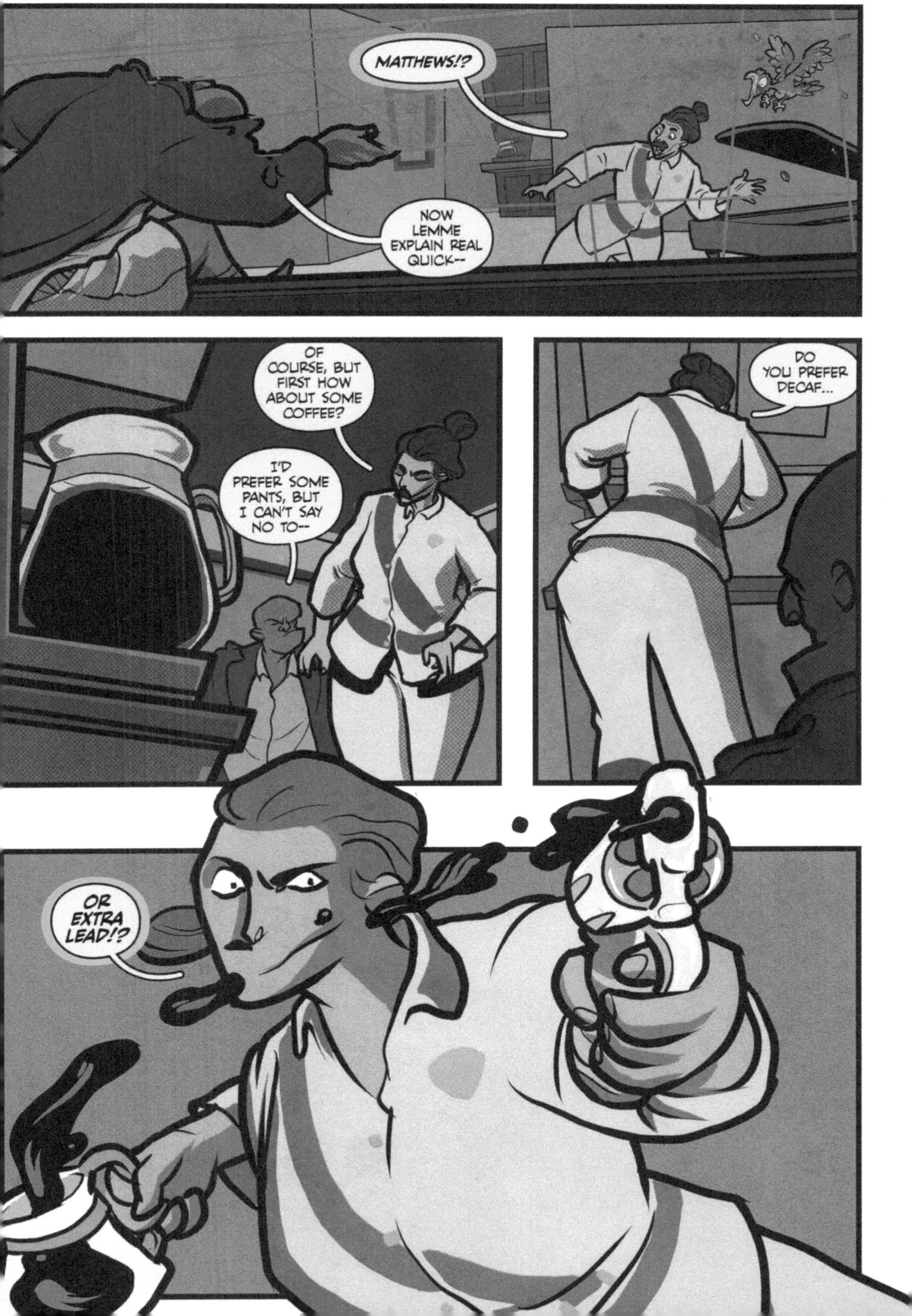
MATTHEWS!?
NOW LEMME EXPLAIN REAL QUICK--
OF COURSE, BUT FIRST HOW ABOUT SOME COFFEE?
I'D PREFER SOME PANTS, BUT I CAN'T SAY NO TO--
DO YOU PREFER DECAF...
OR EXTRA LEAD!?

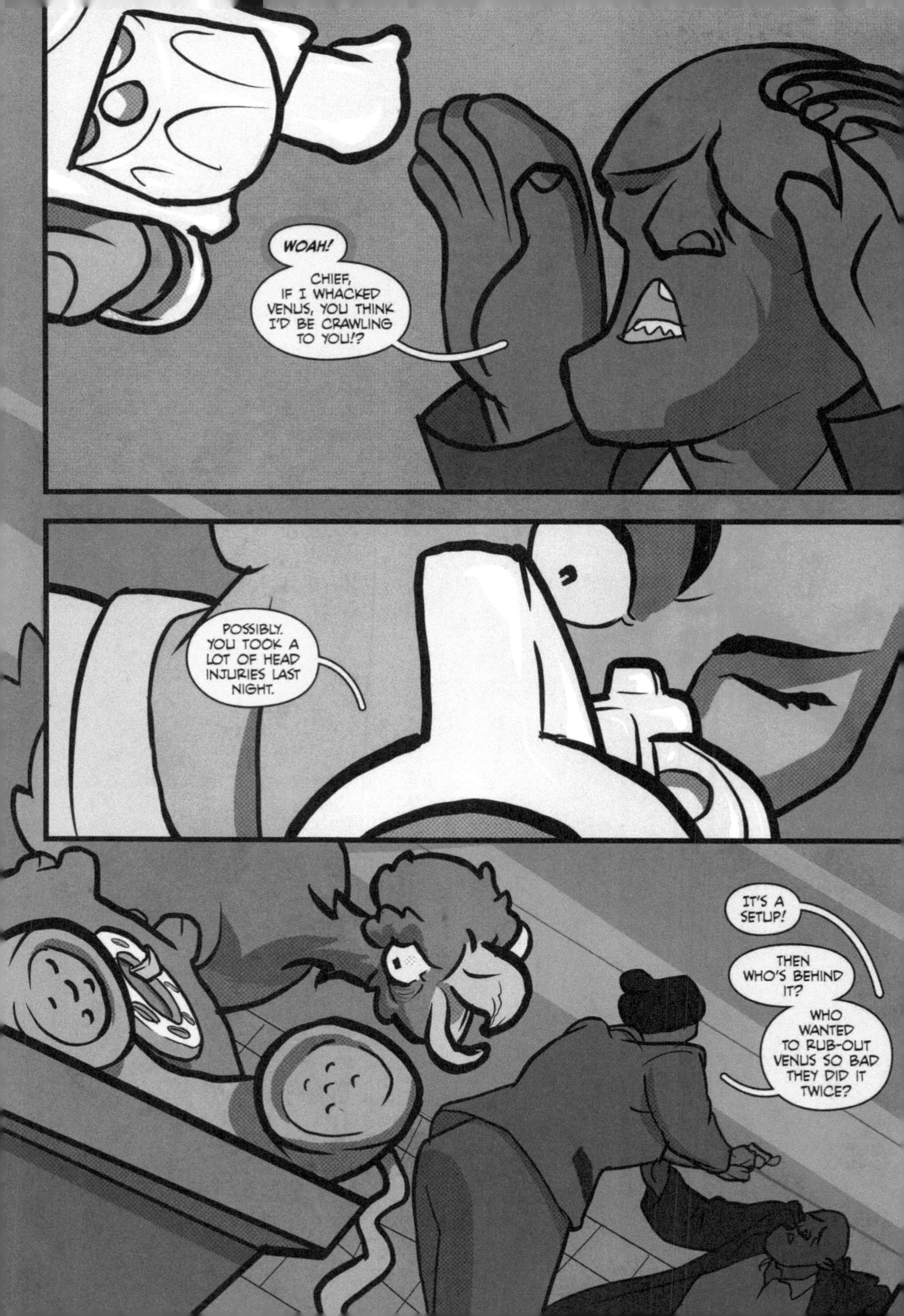
WOAH!
CHIEF, IF I WHACKED VENUS, YOU THINK I'D BE CRAWLING TO YOU!?
POSSIBLY. YOU TOOK A LOT OF HEAD INJURIES LAST NIGHT.
IT'S A SETUP!
THEN WHO'S BEHIND IT?
WHO WANTED TO RUB-OUT VENUS SO BAD THEY DID IT TWICE?

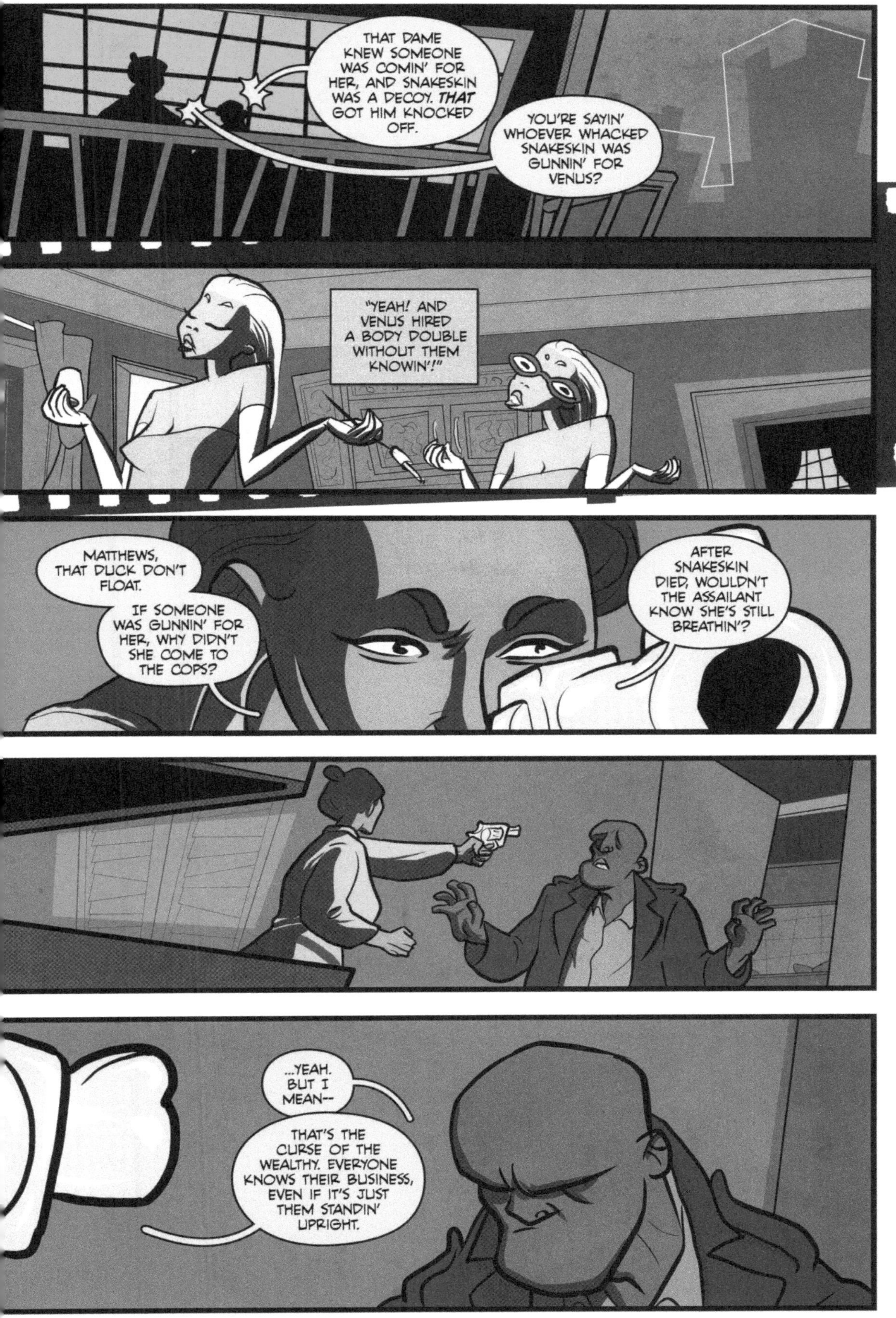
THAT DAME KNEW SOMEONE WAS COMIN' FOR HER, AND SNAKESKIN WAS A DECOY. *THAT* GOT HIM KNOCKED OFF.
YOU'RE SAYIN' WHOEVER WHACKED SNAKESKIN WAS GUNNIN' FOR VENUS?
"YEAH! AND VENUS HIRED A BODY DOUBLE WITHOUT THEM KNOWIN'!"
MATTHEWS, THAT DUCK DON'T FLOAT.
IF SOMEONE WAS GUNNIN' FOR HER, WHY DIDN'T SHE COME TO THE COPS?
AFTER SNAKESKIN DIED, WOULDN'T THE ASSAILANT KNOW SHE'S STILL BREATHIN'?
...YEAH. BUT I MEAN--
THAT'S THE CURSE OF THE WEALTHY. EVERYONE KNOWS THEIR BUSINESS, EVEN IF IT'S JUST THEM STANDIN' UPRIGHT.

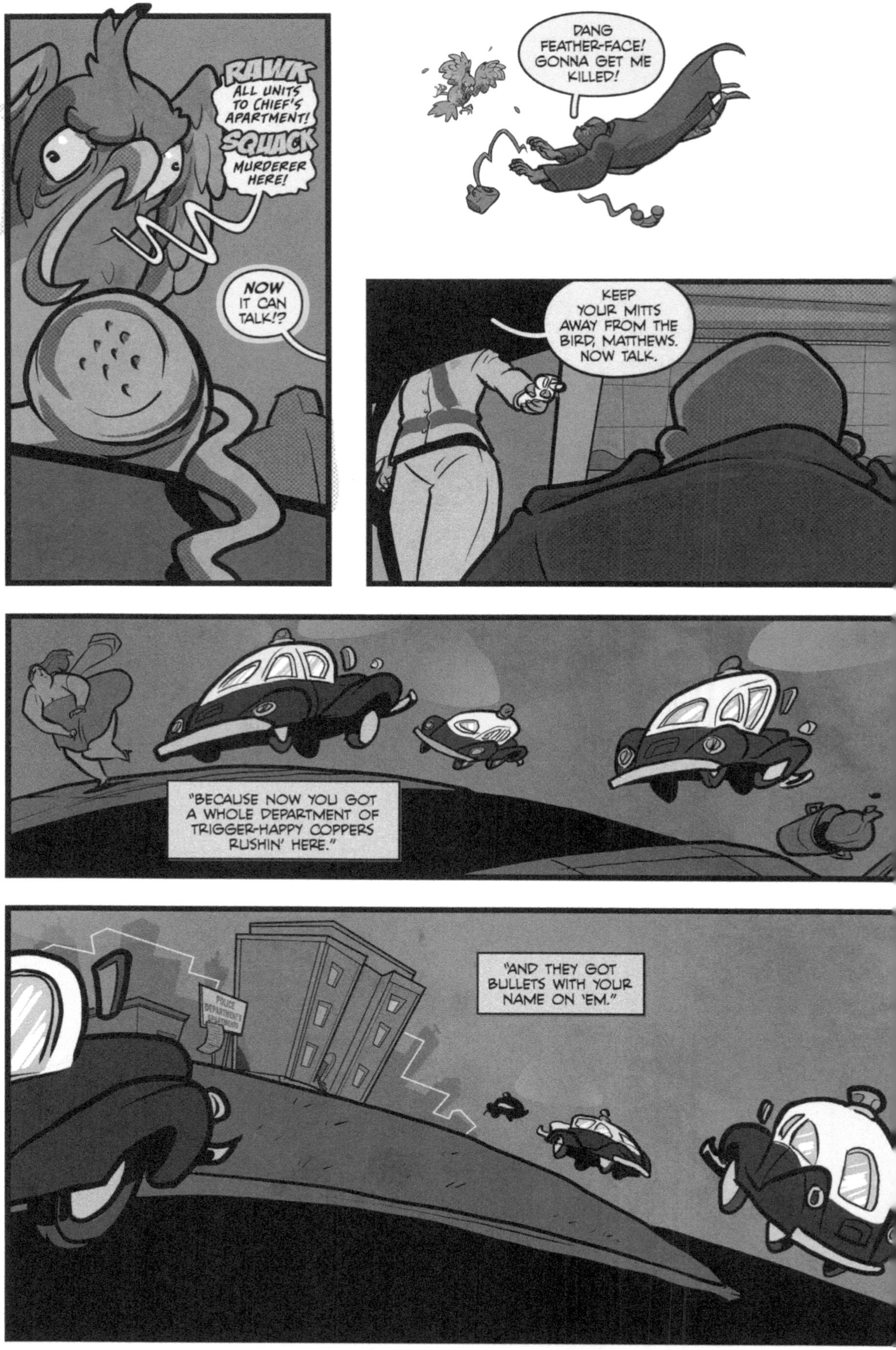
RAWK ALL UNITS TO CHIEF'S APARTMENT! SQUACK MURDERER HERE!
NOW IT CAN TALK!?
DANG FEATHER-FACE! GONNA GET ME KILLED!
KEEP YOUR MITTS AWAY FROM THE BIRD, MATTHEWS. NOW TALK.
"BECAUSE NOW YOU GOT A WHOLE DEPARTMENT OF TRIGGER-HAPPY COPPERS RUSHIN' HERE."
"AND THEY GOT BULLETS WITH YOUR NAME ON 'EM."

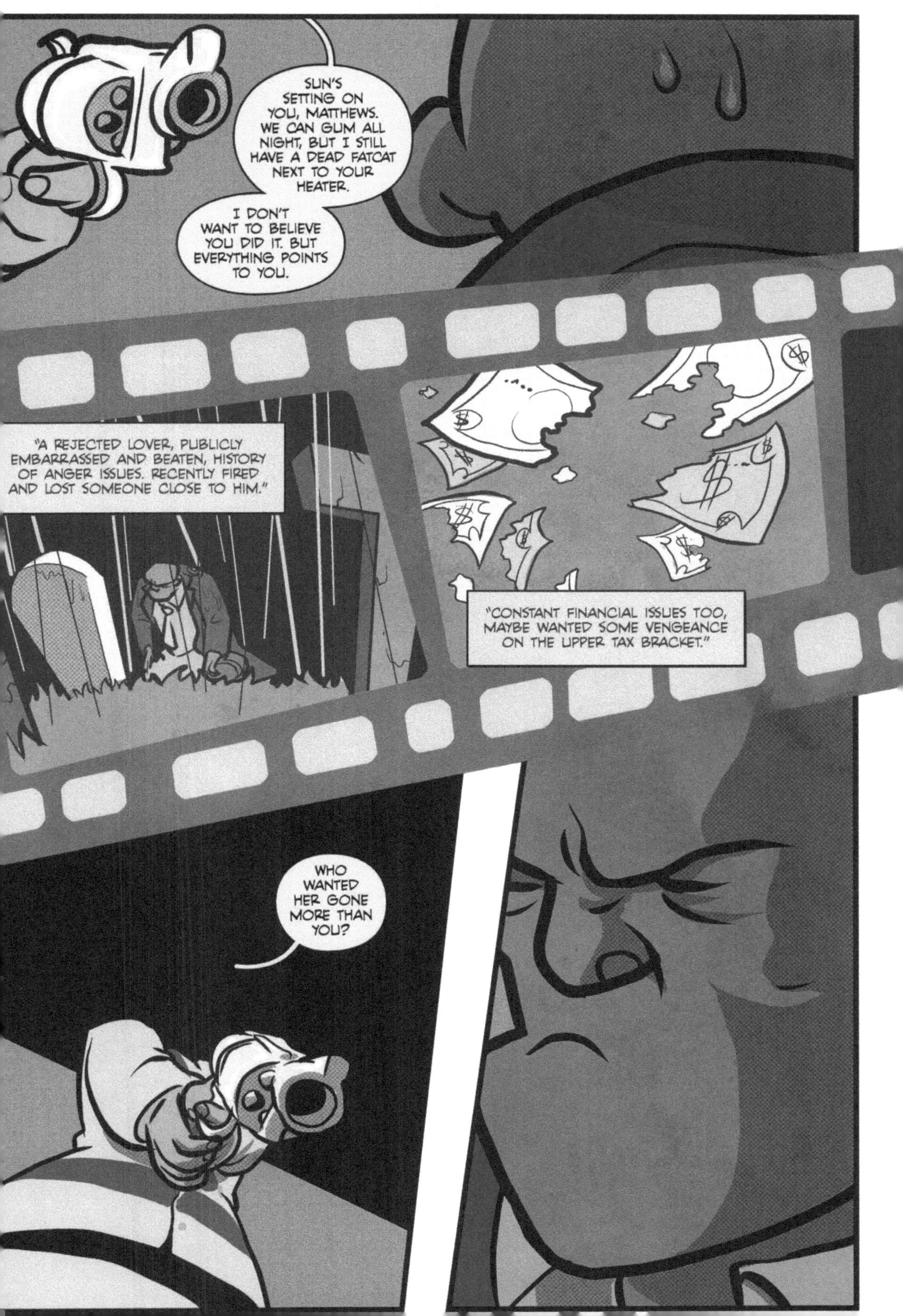
SUN'S SETTING ON YOU, MATTHEWS. WE CAN GUM ALL NIGHT, BUT I STILL HAVE A DEAD FATCAT NEXT TO YOUR HEATER.
I DON'T WANT TO BELIEVE YOU DID IT. BUT EVERYTHING POINTS TO YOU.
"A REJECTED LOVER, PUBLICLY EMBARRASSED AND BEATEN, HISTORY OF ANGER ISSUES. RECENTLY FIRED AND LOST SOMEONE CLOSE TO HIM."
"CONSTANT FINANCIAL ISSUES TOO, MAYBE WANTED SOME VENGEANCE ON THE UPPER TAX BRACKET."
WHO WANTED HER GONE MORE THAN YOU?

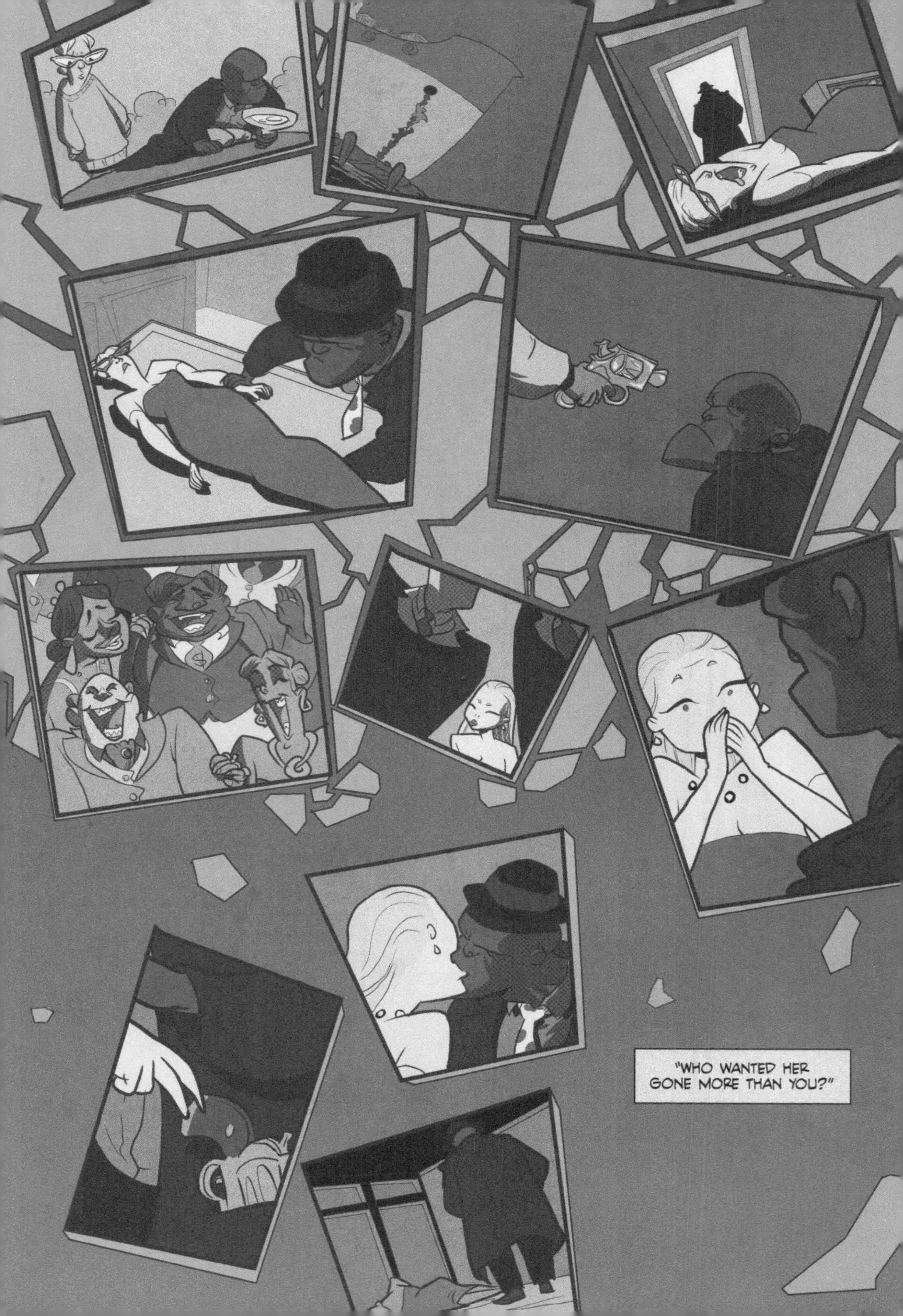
"WHO WANTED HER
GONE MORE THAN YOU?"

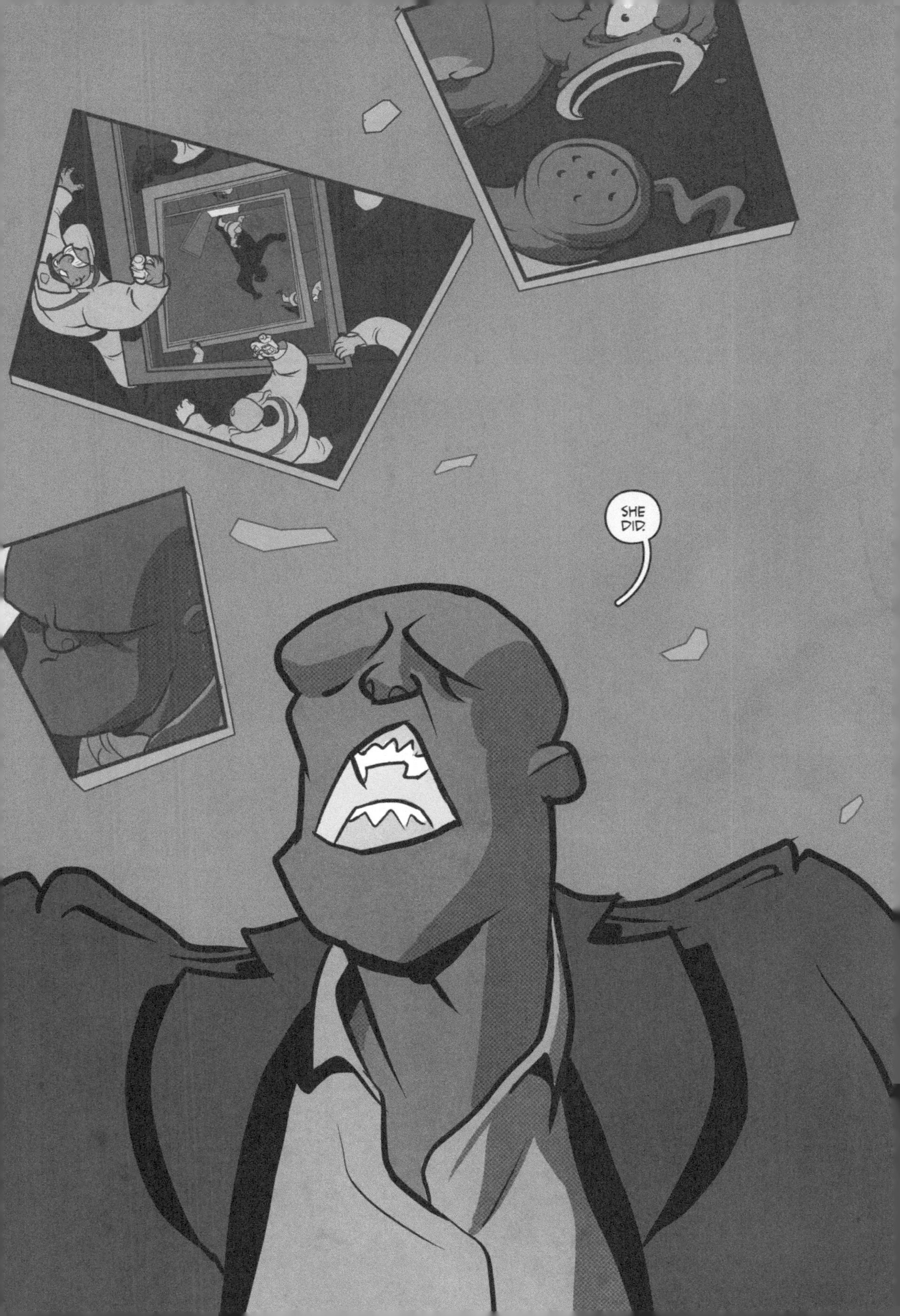
SHE DID.

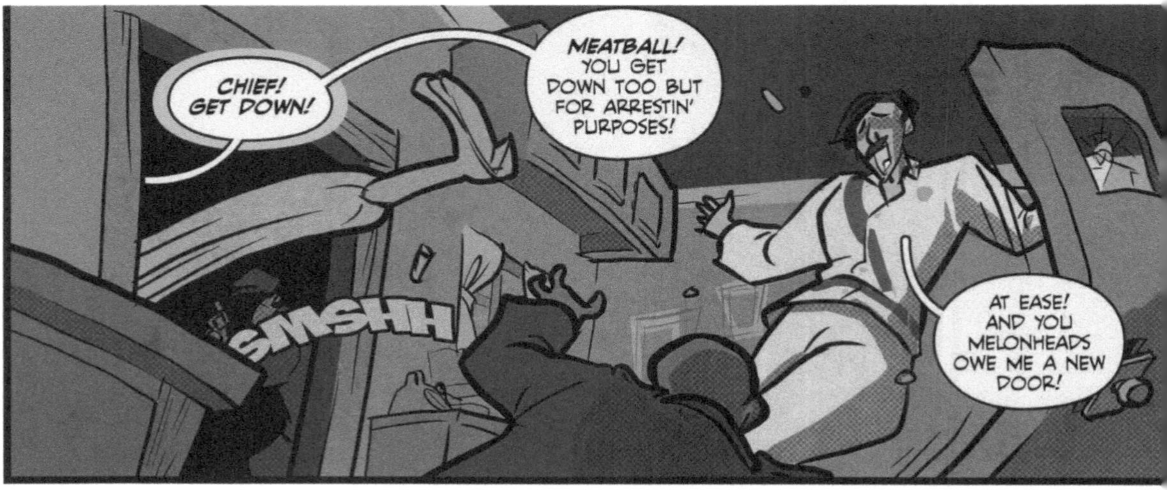
CHIEF! GET DOWN!
MEATBALL! YOU GET DOWN TOO BUT FOR ARRESTIN' PURPOSES!
SMSHH
AT EASE! AND YOU MELONHEADS OWE ME A NEW DOOR!

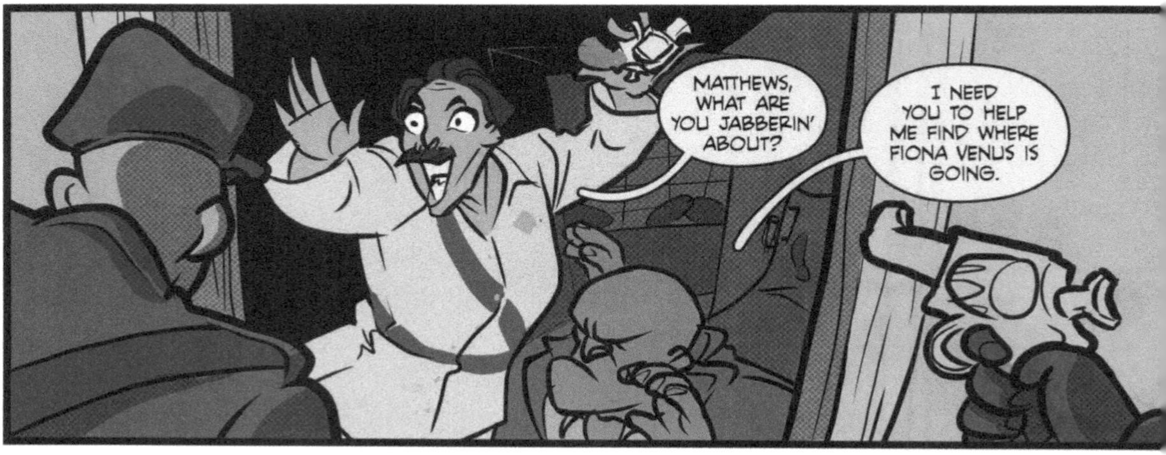
MATTHEWS, WHAT ARE YOU JABBERIN' ABOUT?
I NEED YOU TO HELP ME FIND WHERE FIONA VENUS IS GOING.

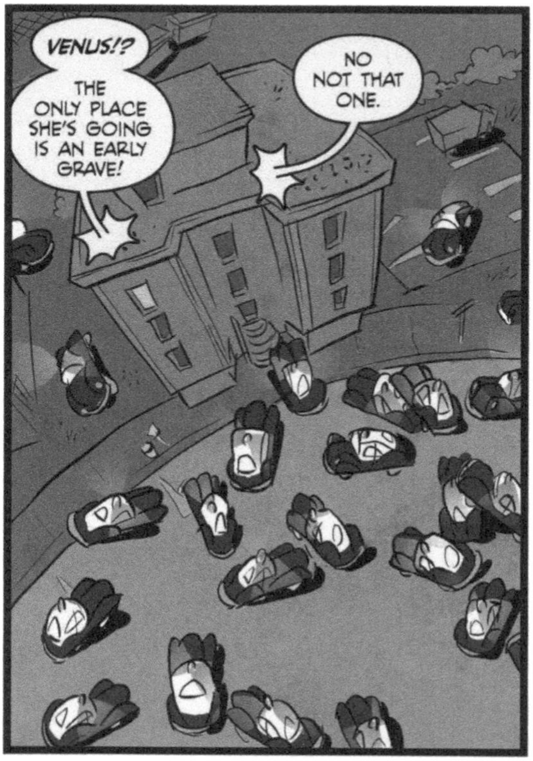
VENUS!? THE ONLY PLACE SHE'S GOING IS AN EARLY GRAVE!
NO NOT THAT ONE.

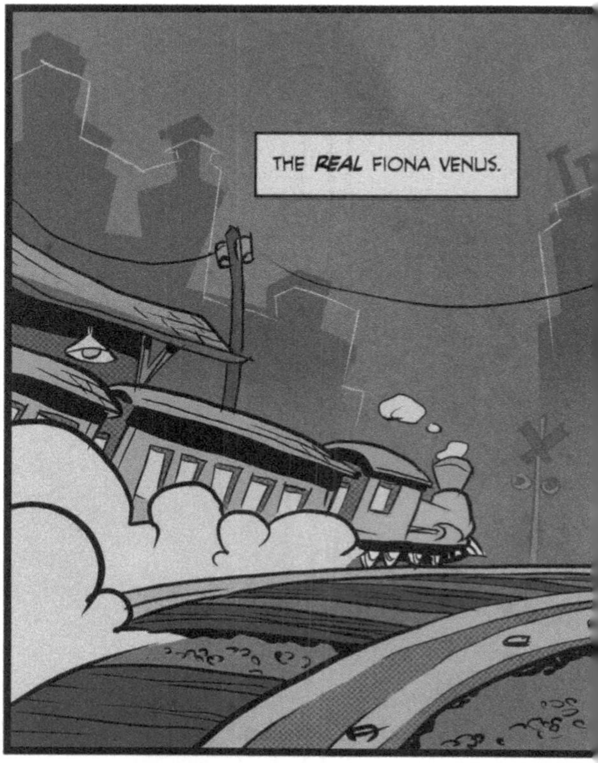
THE REAL FIONA VENUS.

CHAPTER 13

NOW ARRIVING... TO CONCLUSIONS

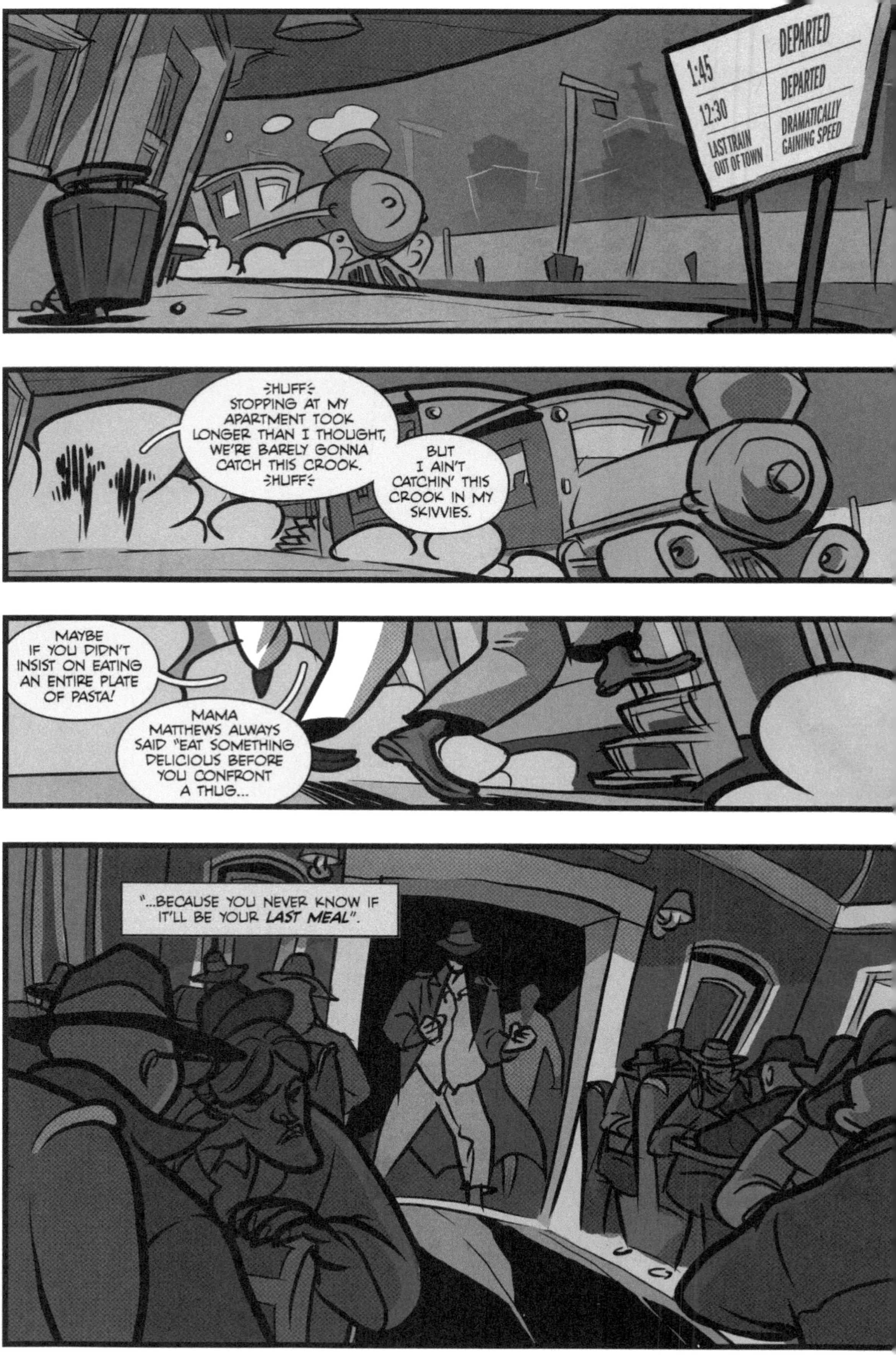
1:45 DEPARTED
12:30 DEPARTED
LAST TRAIN OUT OF TOWN DRAMATICALLY GAINING SPEED
-HUFF- STOPPING AT MY APARTMENT TOOK LONGER THAN I THOUGHT, WE'RE BARELY GONNA CATCH THIS CROOK. -HUFF-
BUT I AIN'T CATCHIN' THIS CROOK IN MY SKIVVIES.
MAYBE IF YOU DIDN'T INSIST ON EATING AN ENTIRE PLATE OF PASTA!
MAMA MATTHEWS ALWAYS SAID "EAT SOMETHING DELICIOUS BEFORE YOU CONFRONT A THUG...
"...BECAUSE YOU NEVER KNOW IF IT'LL BE YOUR *LAST MEAL*".

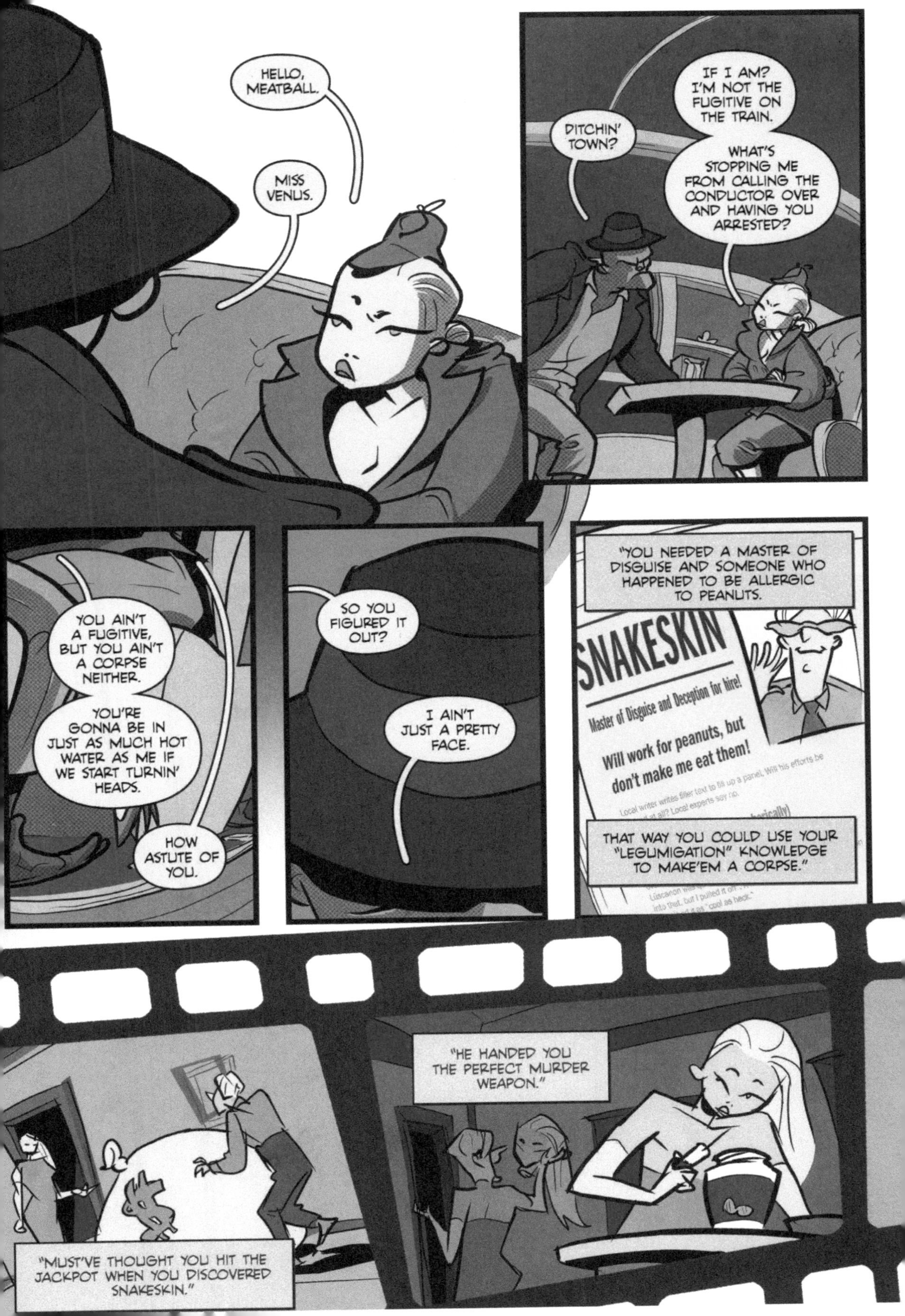
HELLO, MEATBALL.
MISS VENUS.
DITCHIN' TOWN?
IF I AM? I'M NOT THE FUGITIVE ON THE TRAIN.
WHAT'S STOPPING ME FROM CALLING THE CONDUCTOR OVER AND HAVING YOU ARRESTED?
YOU AIN'T A FUGITIVE, BUT YOU AIN'T A CORPSE NEITHER.
YOU'RE GONNA BE IN JUST AS MUCH HOT WATER AS ME IF WE START TURNIN' HEADS.
HOW ASTUTE OF YOU.
SO YOU FIGURED IT OUT?
I AIN'T JUST A PRETTY FACE.
"YOU NEEDED A MASTER OF DISGUISE AND SOMEONE WHO HAPPENED TO BE ALLERGIC TO PEANUTS.
SNAKESKIN
Master of Disguise and Deception for hire!
Will work for peanuts, but don't make me eat them!
THAT WAY YOU COULD USE YOUR "LEGUMIGATION" KNOWLEDGE TO MAKE'EM A CORPSE."
"MUST'VE THOUGHT YOU HIT THE JACKPOT WHEN YOU DISCOVERED SNAKESKIN."
"HE HANDED YOU THE PERFECT MURDER WEAPON."

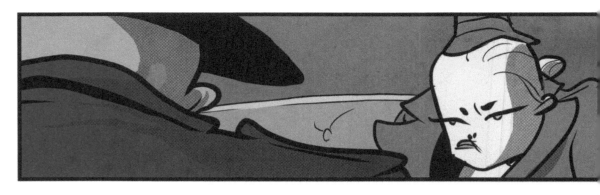

YOU MOOKS READY FOR GRUB?

FOIE GRAS. RARE.

PASS.

YOU KNOW, THOSE THINGS I SAID ON THE BLIMP. THEY WERE TRUE.

ABOUT ME BEING PUNCHED? YEAH, I KNOW.

ABOUT YOU LIVING A *REAL LIFE.*

YOU SHOULD TAKE A LOOK AT MY APARTMENT BEFORE YOU START GETTIN' GREEN EYES.

MY ENTIRE EXISTENCE IS IN FRONT OF THE WORLD; I CAN'T GET A COFFEE WITHOUT HALF THE CITY'S EYEBALLS ON ME.

I NEVER GOT A SAY IN ANYTHING IN LIFE.

SO YOU THOUGHT YOU'D GET A CHANCE IN DEATH.

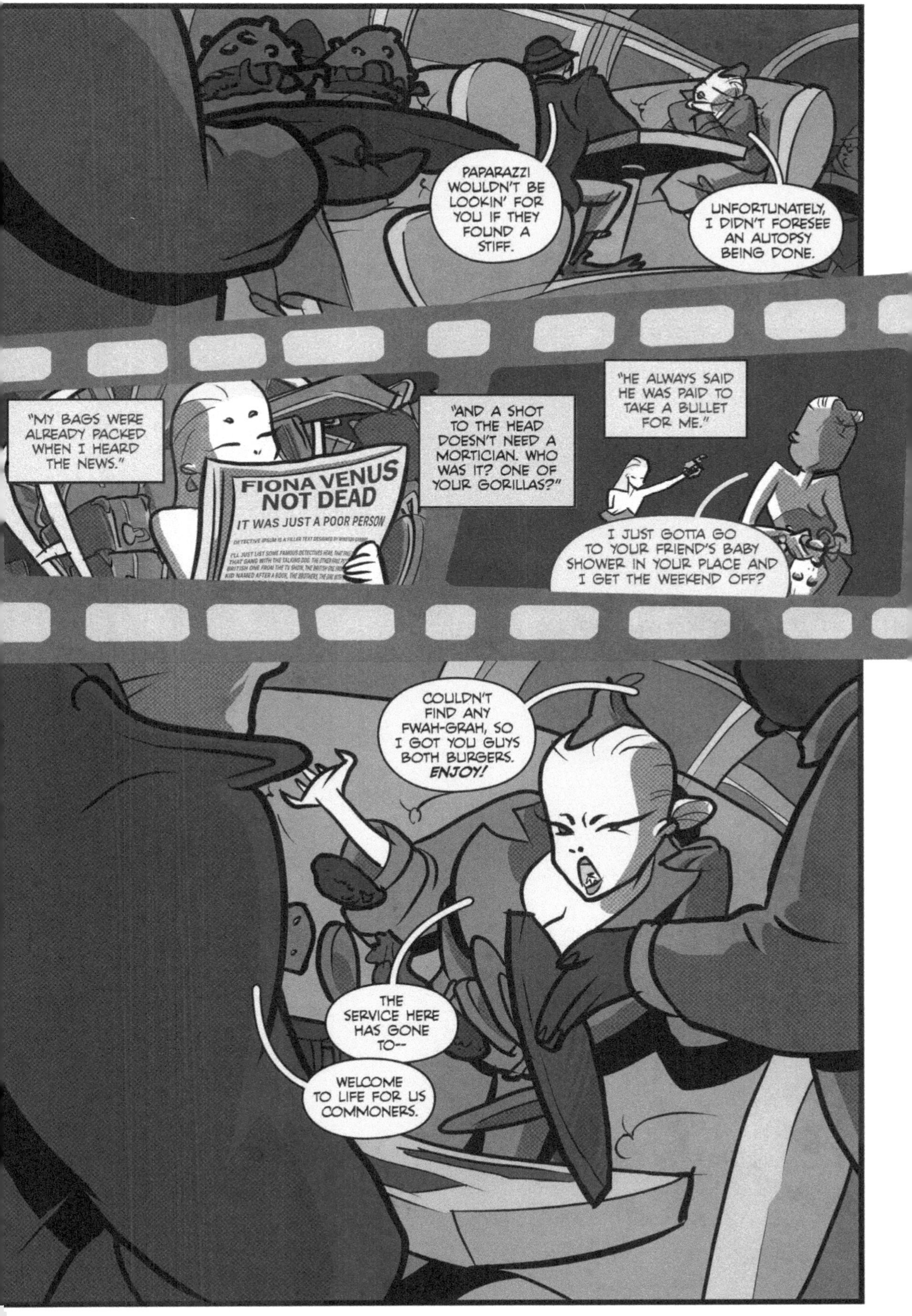
PAPARAZZI WOULDN'T BE LOOKIN' FOR YOU IF THEY FOUND A STIFF.
UNFORTUNATELY, I DIDN'T FORESEE AN AUTOPSY BEING DONE.
"MY BAGS WERE ALREADY PACKED WHEN I HEARD THE NEWS."
FIONA VENUS NOT DEAD
IT WAS JUST A POOR PERSON
"AND A SHOT TO THE HEAD DOESN'T NEED A MORTICIAN. WHO WAS IT? ONE OF YOUR GORILLAS?"
"HE ALWAYS SAID HE WAS PAID TO TAKE A BULLET FOR ME."
I JUST GOTTA GO TO YOUR FRIEND'S BABY SHOWER IN YOUR PLACE AND I GET THE WEEKEND OFF?
COULDN'T FIND ANY FWAH-GRAH, SO I GOT YOU GUYS BOTH BURGERS. *ENJOY!*
THE SERVICE HERE HAS GONE TO--
WELCOME TO LIFE FOR US COMMONERS.

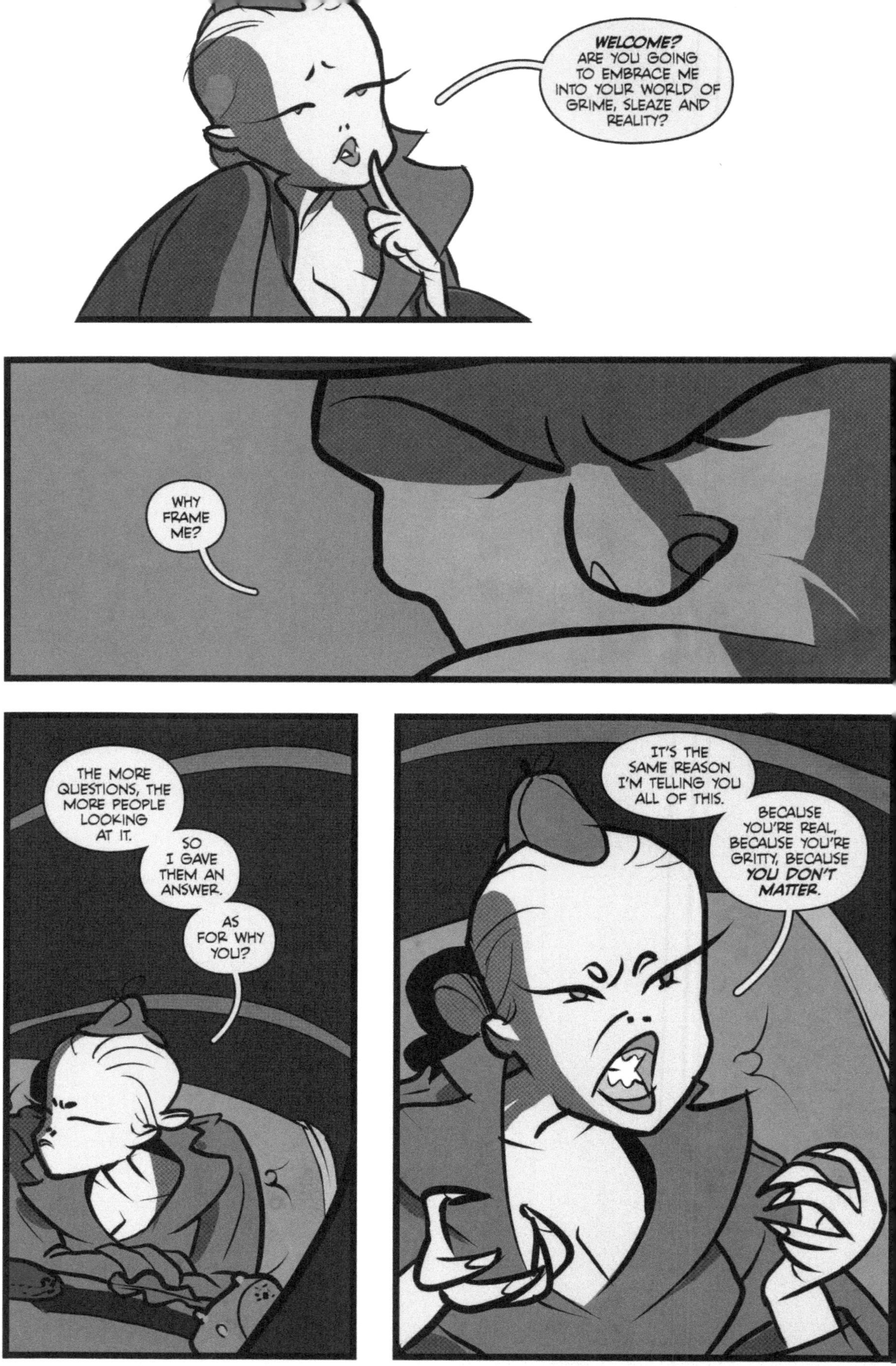
WELCOME? ARE YOU GOING TO EMBRACE ME INTO YOUR WORLD OF GRIME, SLEAZE AND REALITY?
WHY FRAME ME?
THE MORE QUESTIONS, THE MORE PEOPLE LOOKING AT IT.
SO I GAVE THEM AN ANSWER.
AS FOR WHY YOU?
IT'S THE SAME REASON I'M TELLING YOU ALL OF THIS.
BECAUSE YOU'RE REAL, BECAUSE YOU'RE GRITTY, BECAUSE YOU DON'T MATTER.

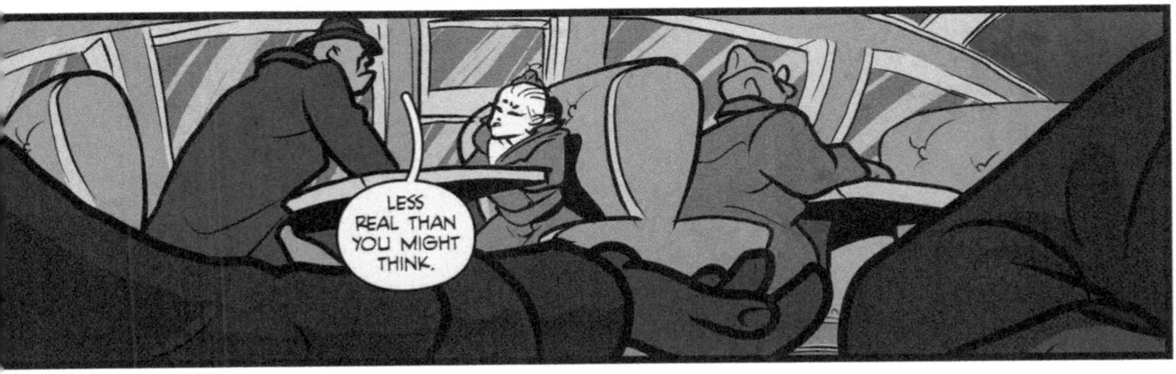
LESS REAL THAN YOU MIGHT THINK.

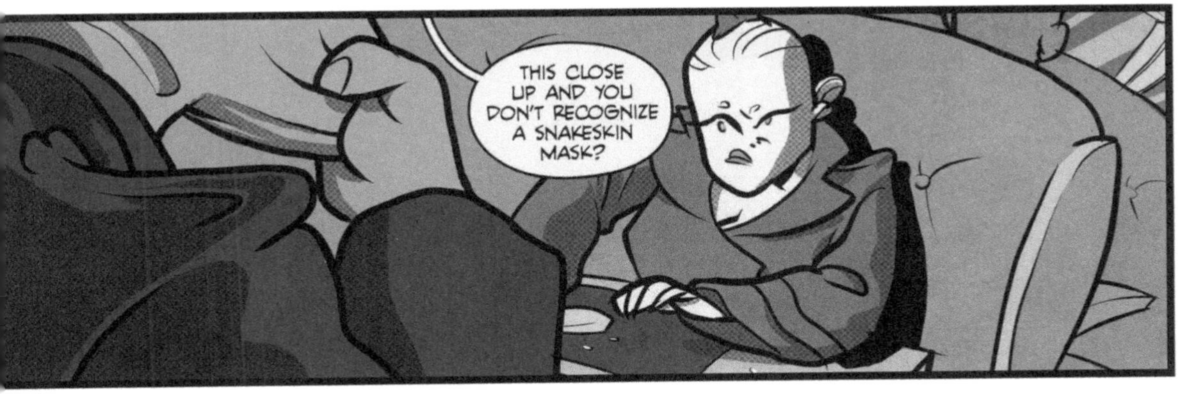
THIS CLOSE UP AND YOU DON'T RECOGNIZE A SNAKESKIN MASK?

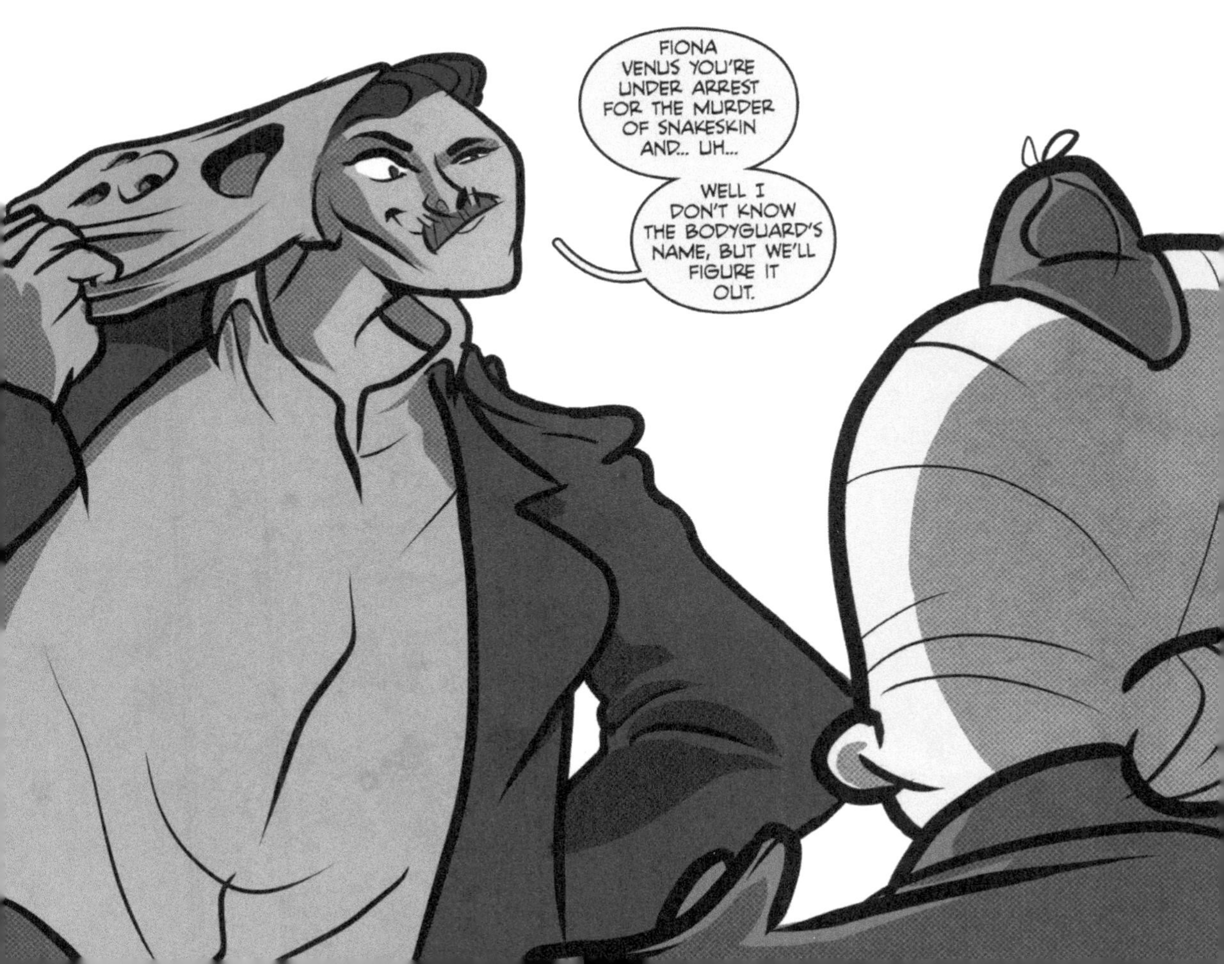
FIONA VENUS YOU'RE UNDER ARREST FOR THE MURDER OF SNAKESKIN AND... UH...
WELL I DON'T KNOW THE BODYGUARD'S NAME, BUT WE'LL FIGURE IT OUT.

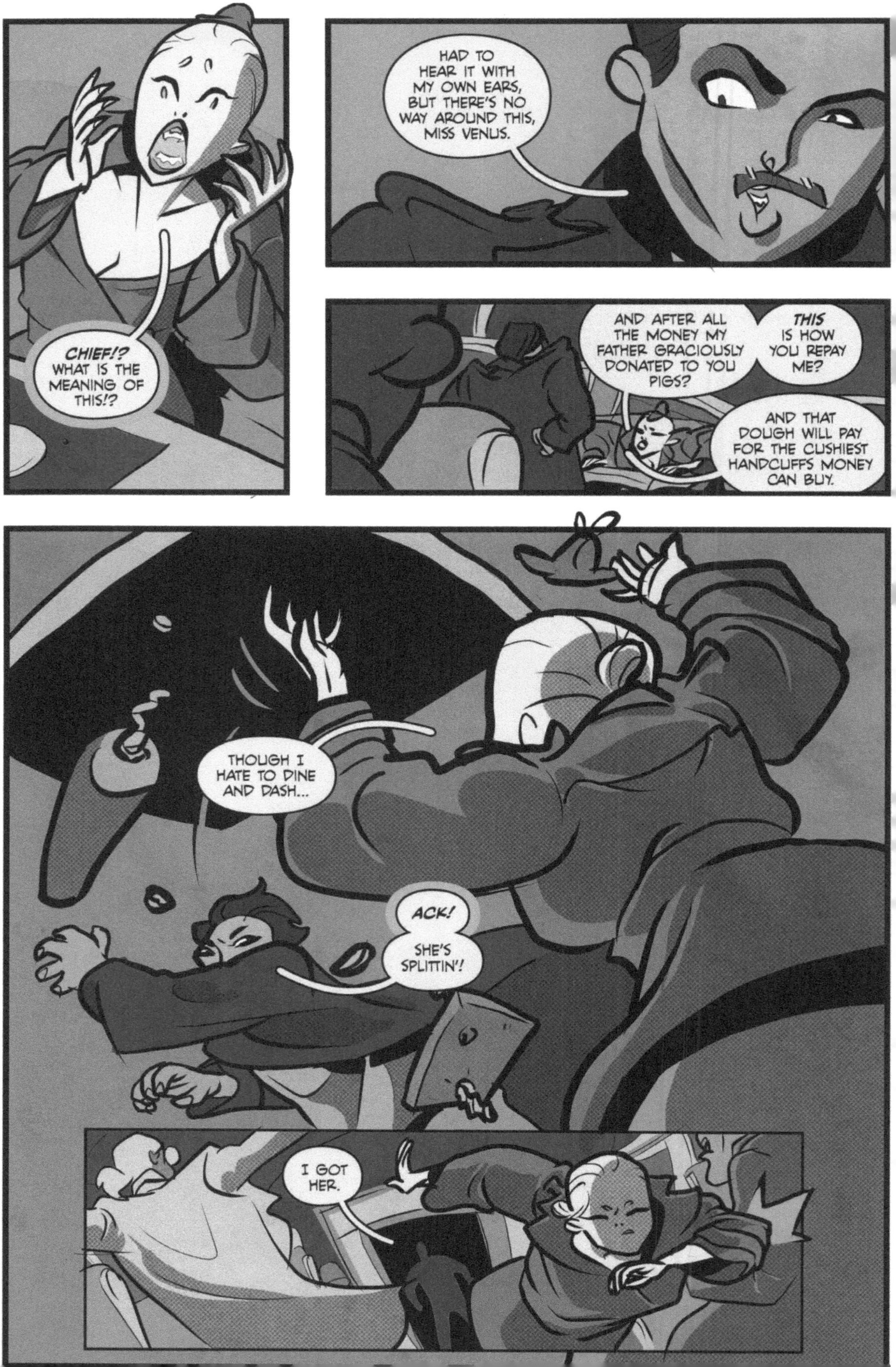
CHIEF!? WHAT IS THE MEANING OF THIS!?
HAD TO HEAR IT WITH MY OWN EARS, BUT THERE'S NO WAY AROUND THIS, MISS VENUS.
AND AFTER ALL THE MONEY MY FATHER GRACIOUSLY DONATED TO YOU PIGS?
THIS IS HOW YOU REPAY ME?
AND THAT DOUGH WILL PAY FOR THE CUSHIEST HANDCUFFS MONEY CAN BUY.
THOUGH I HATE TO DINE AND DASH...
ACK!
SHE'S SPLITTIN'!
I GOT HER.

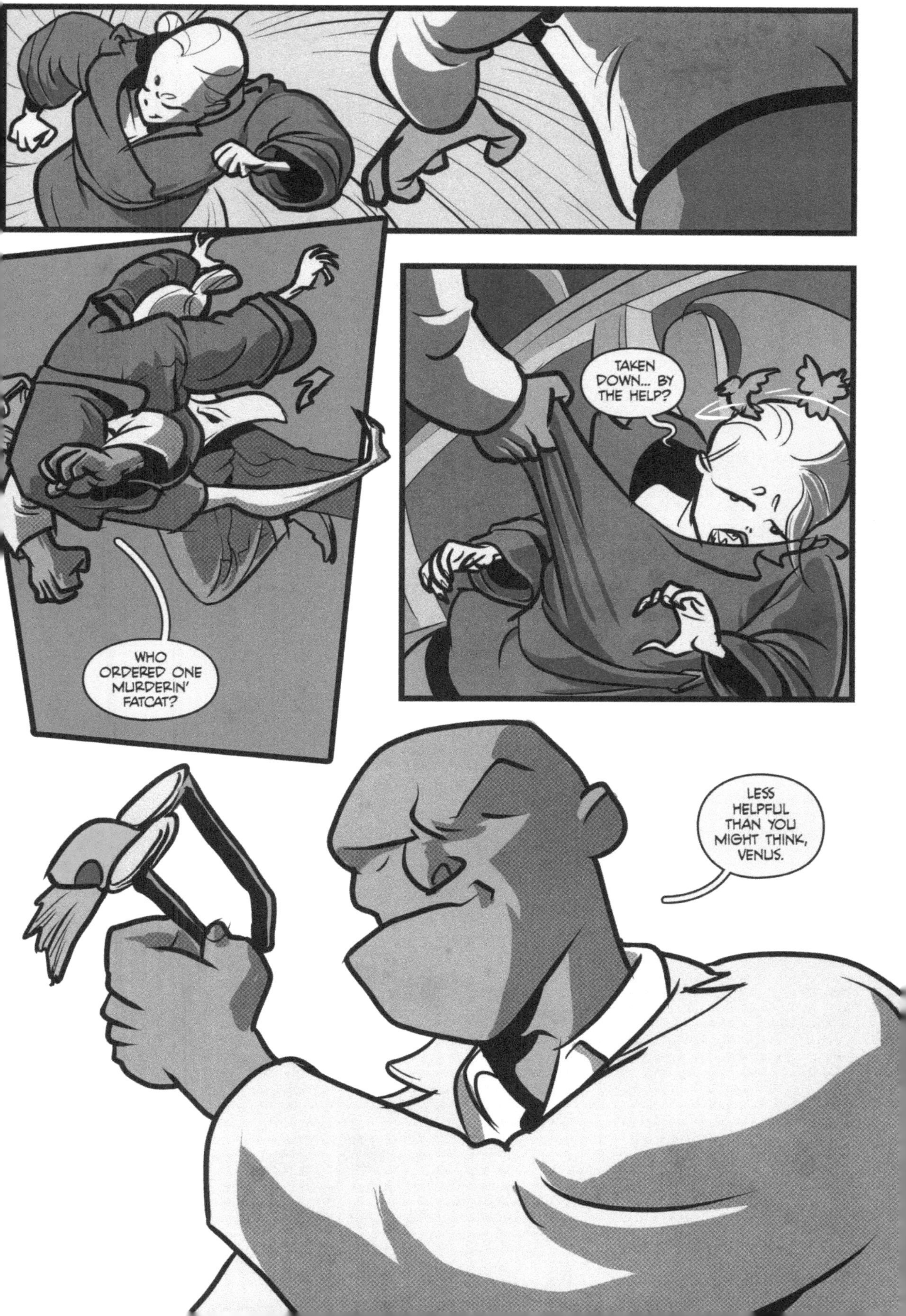
WHO ORDERED ONE MURDERIN' FATCAT?
TAKEN DOWN... BY THE HELP?
LESS HELPFUL THAN YOU MIGHT THINK, VENUS.

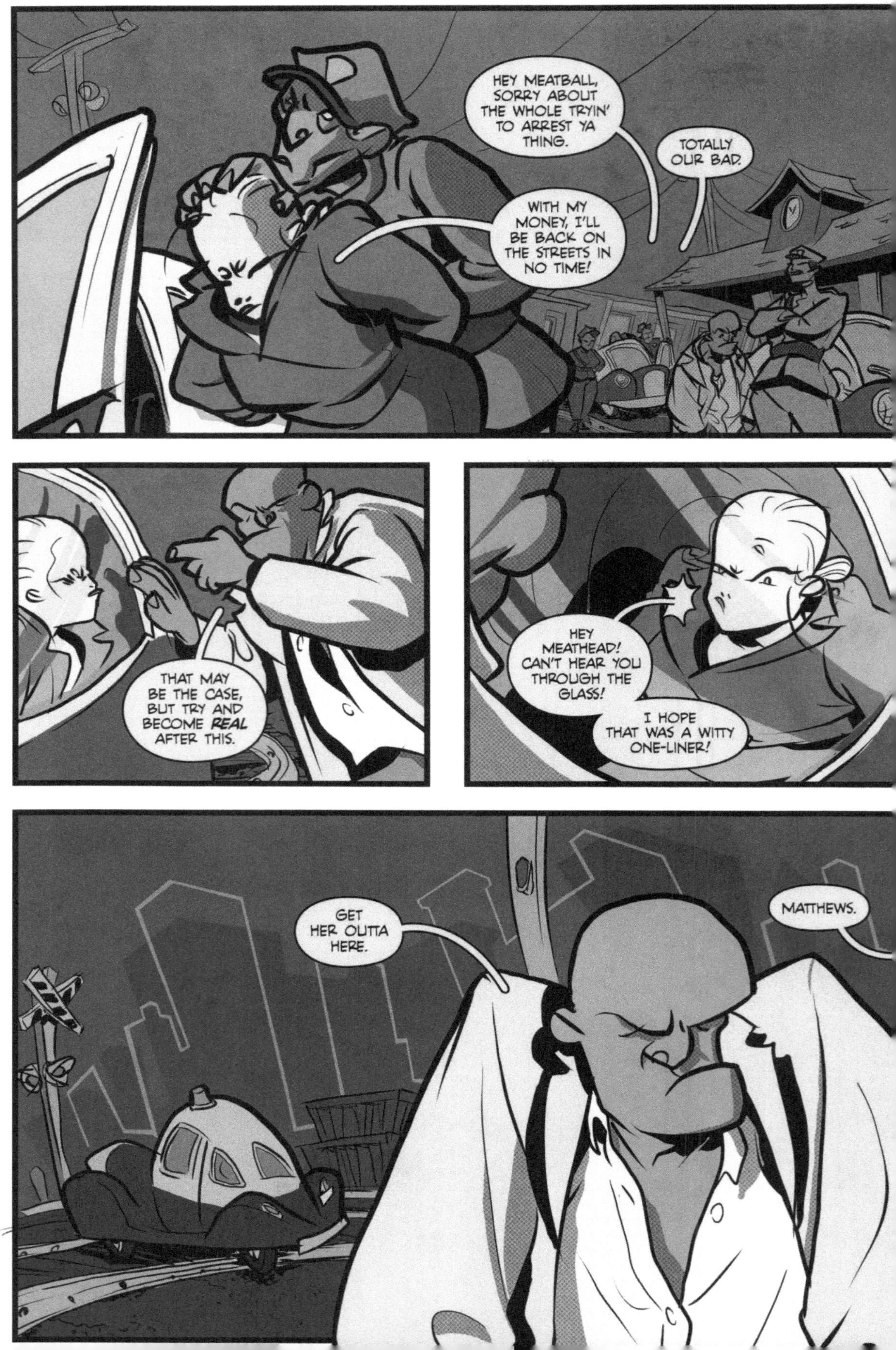
HEY MEATBALL, SORRY ABOUT THE WHOLE TRYIN' TO ARREST YA THING.
TOTALLY OUR BAD.
WITH MY MONEY, I'LL BE BACK ON THE STREETS IN NO TIME!
THAT MAY BE THE CASE, BUT TRY AND BECOME REAL AFTER THIS.
HEY MEATHEAD! CAN'T HEAR YOU THROUGH THE GLASS!
I HOPE THAT WAS A WITTY ONE-LINER!
GET HER OUTTA HERE.
MATTHEWS.

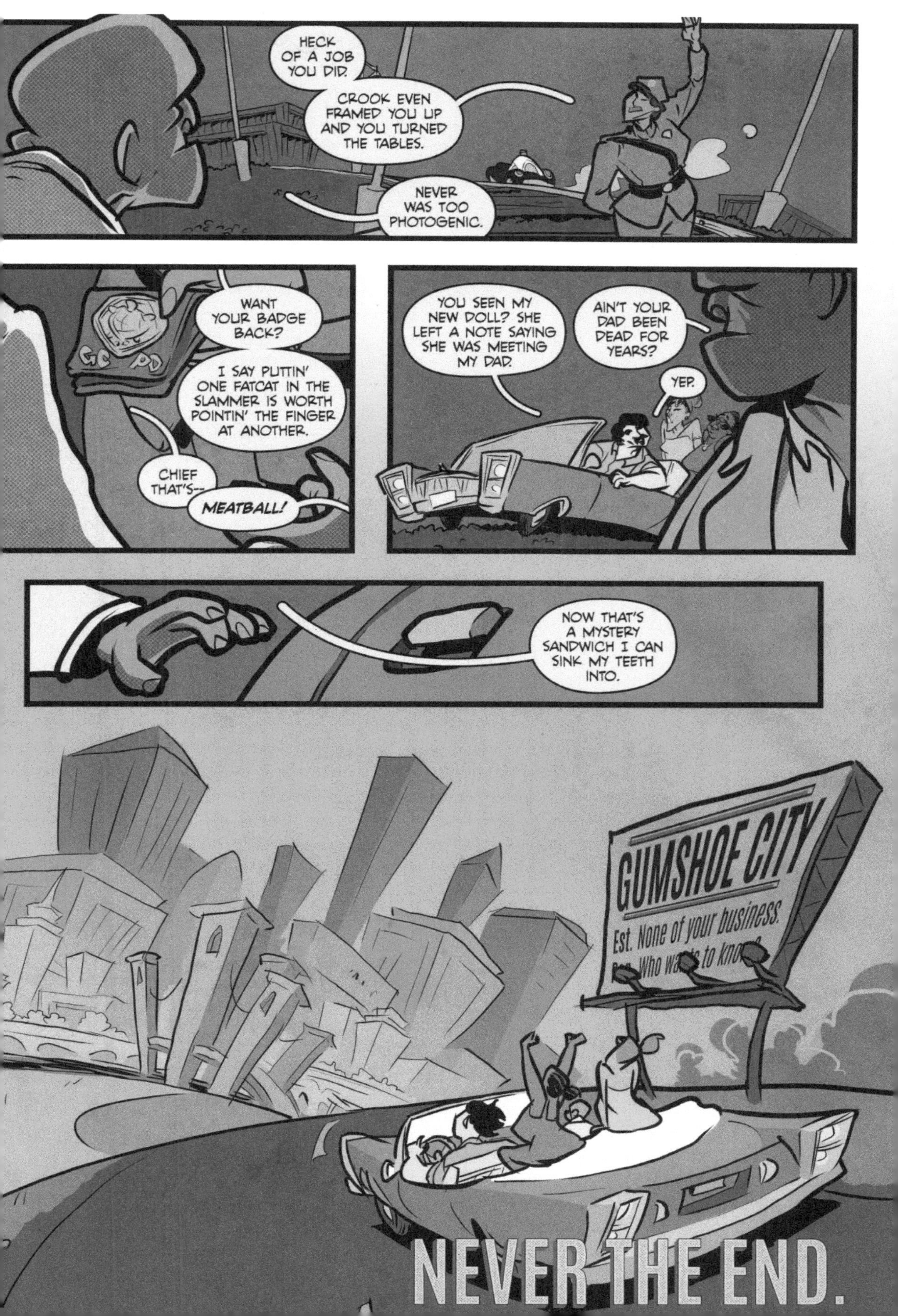
HECK OF A JOB YOU DID.
CROOK EVEN FRAMED YOU UP AND YOU TURNED THE TABLES.
NEVER WAS TOO PHOTOGENIC.
WANT YOUR BADGE BACK?
I SAY PUTTIN' ONE FATCAT IN THE SLAMMER IS WORTH POINTIN' THE FINGER AT ANOTHER.
CHIEF THAT'S--
MEATBALL!
GC PD
YOU SEEN MY NEW DOLL? SHE LEFT A NOTE SAYING SHE WAS MEETING MY DAD.
AIN'T YOUR DAD BEEN DEAD FOR YEARS?
YEP.
NOW THAT'S A MYSTERY SANDWICH I CAN SINK MY TEETH INTO.
GUMSHOE CITY
Est. None of your business.
NEVER THE END.

THE CASE OF
THE OVERDUE JUSTICE

PROLOGUE
FATAL HARDWARE

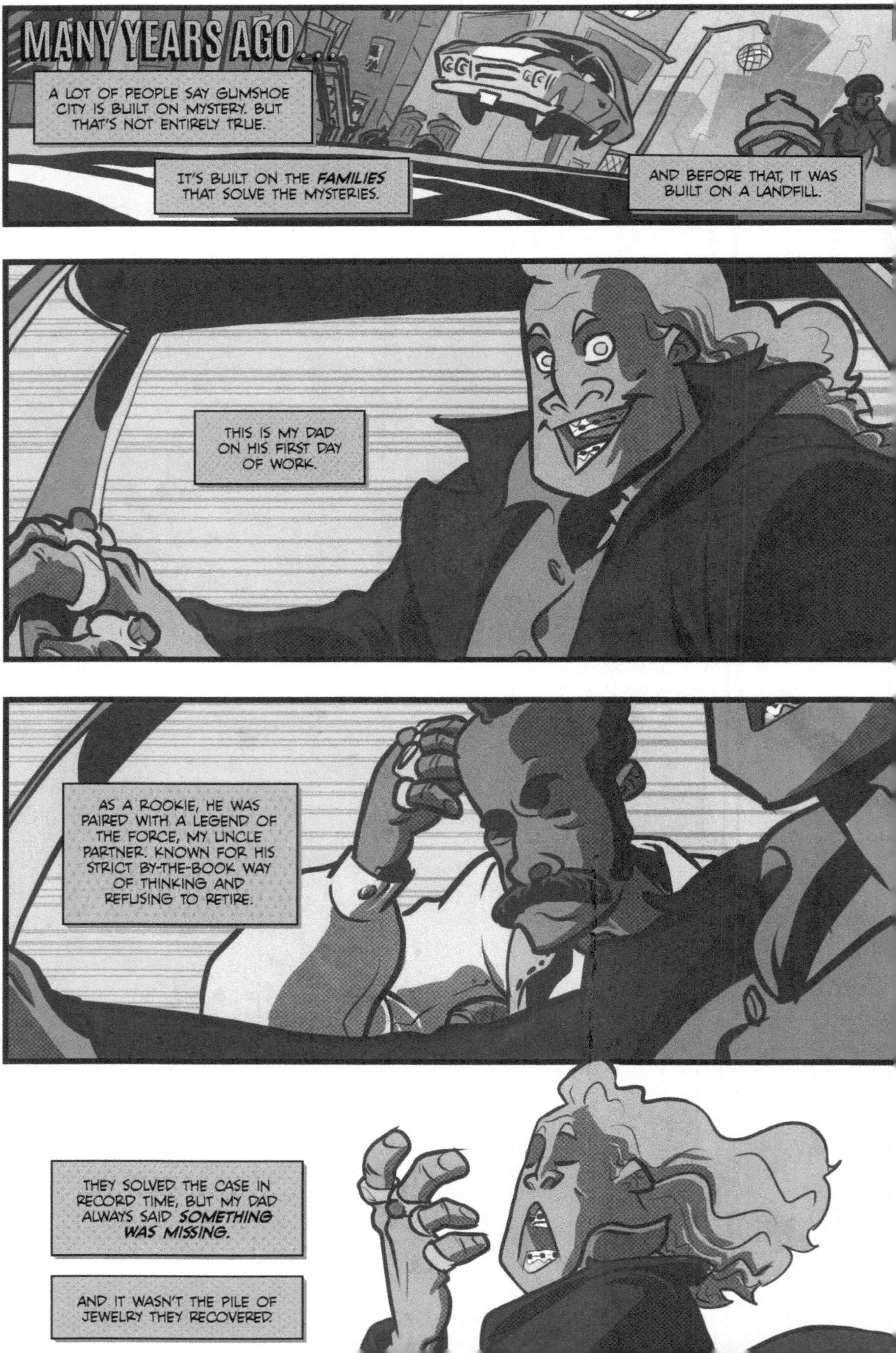
MANY YEARS AGO...
A LOT OF PEOPLE SAY GUMSHOE CITY IS BUILT ON MYSTERY. BUT THAT'S NOT ENTIRELY TRUE.
IT'S BUILT ON THE *FAMILIES* THAT SOLVE THE MYSTERIES.
AND BEFORE THAT, IT WAS BUILT ON A LANDFILL.
THIS IS MY DAD ON HIS FIRST DAY OF WORK.
AS A ROOKIE, HE WAS PAIRED WITH A LEGEND OF THE FORCE, MY UNCLE PARTNER. KNOWN FOR HIS STRICT BY-THE-BOOK WAY OF THINKING AND REFUSING TO RETIRE.
THEY SOLVED THE CASE IN RECORD TIME, BUT MY DAD ALWAYS SAID ***SOMETHING WAS MISSING.***
AND IT WASN'T THE PILE OF JEWELRY THEY RECOVERED.

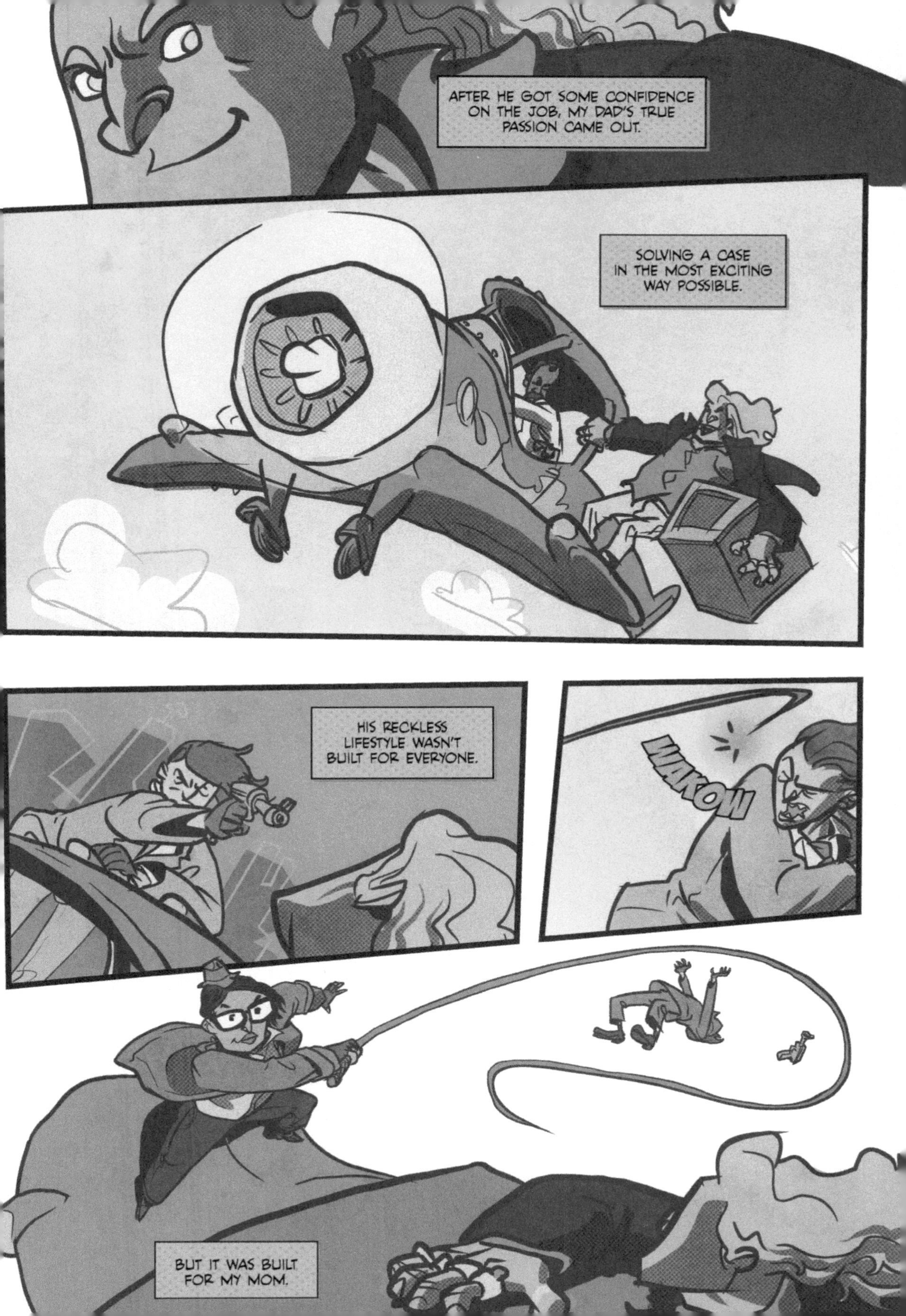
AFTER HE GOT SOME CONFIDENCE ON THE JOB, MY DAD'S TRUE PASSION CAME OUT.
SOLVING A CASE IN THE MOST EXCITING WAY POSSIBLE.
HIS RECKLESS LIFESTYLE WASN'T BUILT FOR EVERYONE.
WAKOW
BUT IT WAS BUILT FOR MY MOM.

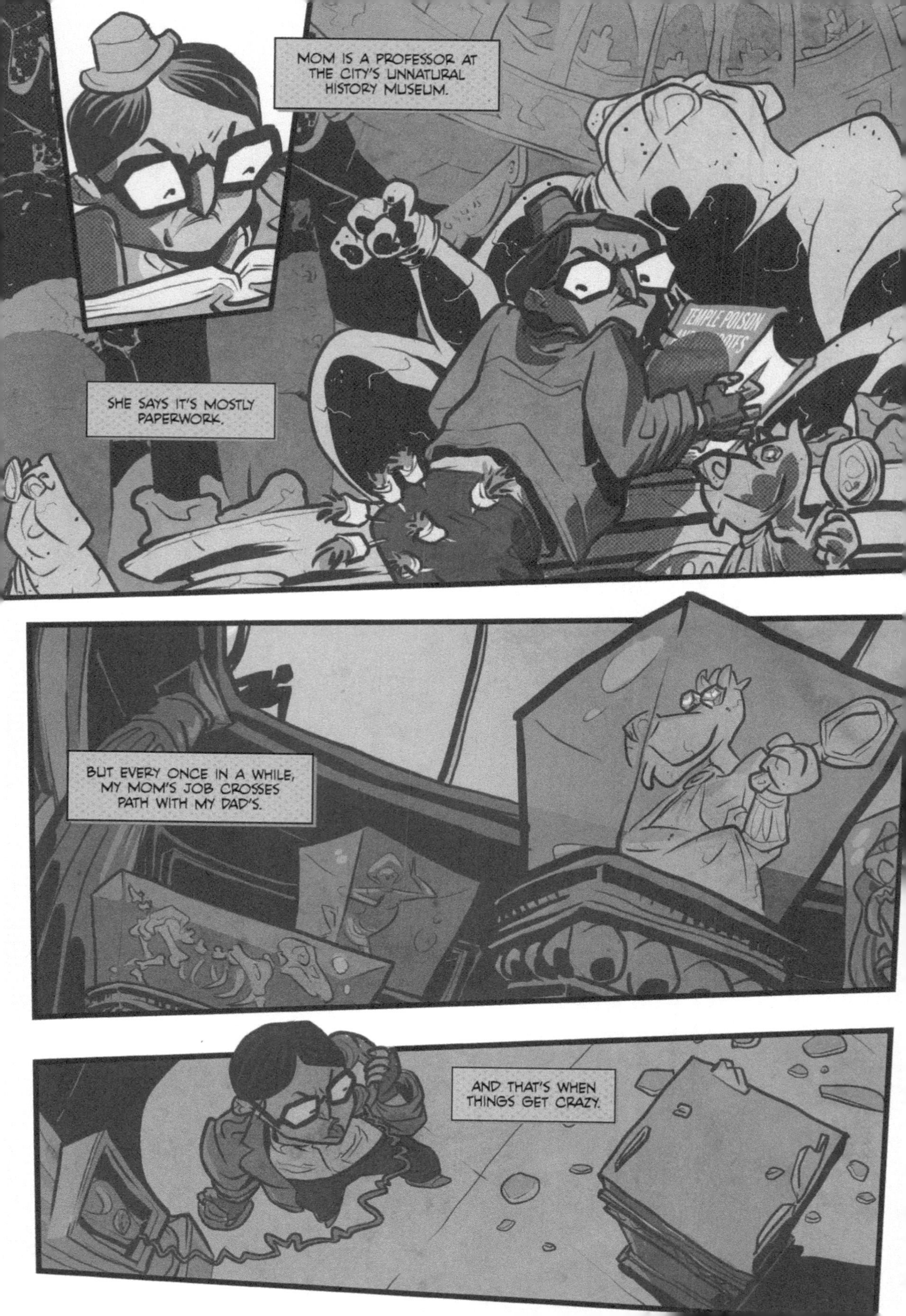
MOM IS A PROFESSOR AT THE CITY'S UNNATURAL HISTORY MUSEUM.
TEMPLE POISON
SHE SAYS IT'S MOSTLY PAPERWORK.
BUT EVERY ONCE IN A WHILE, MY MOM'S JOB CROSSES PATH WITH MY DAD'S.
AND THAT'S WHEN THINGS GET CRAZY.

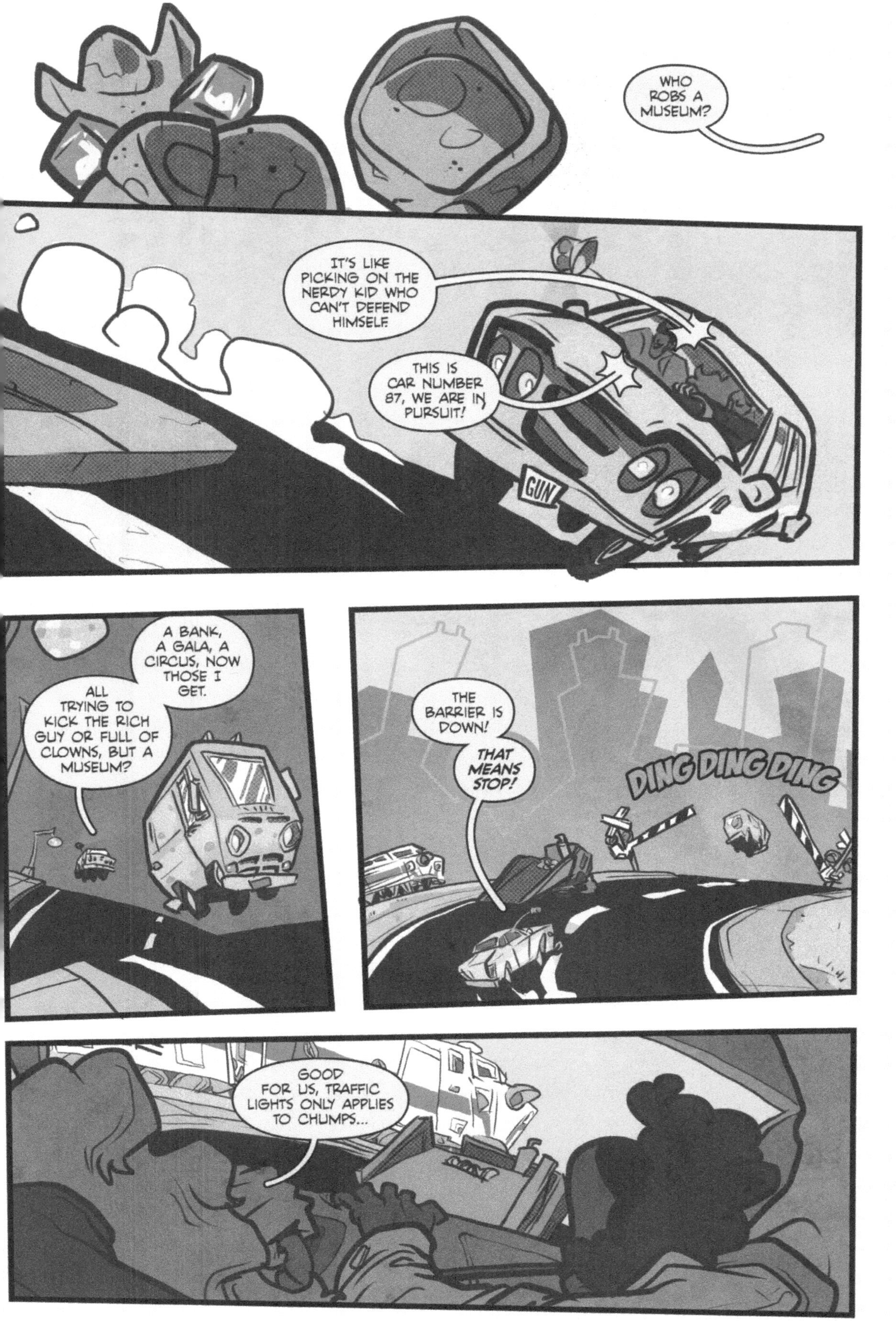
WHO ROBS A MUSEUM?
IT'S LIKE PICKING ON THE NERDY KID WHO CAN'T DEFEND HIMSELF.
THIS IS CAR NUMBER 87, WE ARE IN PURSUIT!
GUN
A BANK, A GALA, A CIRCUS, NOW THOSE I GET.
ALL TRYING TO KICK THE RICH GUY OR FULL OF CLOWNS, BUT A MUSEUM?
THE BARRIER IS DOWN!
THAT MEANS STOP!
DING DING DING
GOOD FOR US, TRAFFIC LIGHTS ONLY APPLIES TO CHUMPS...

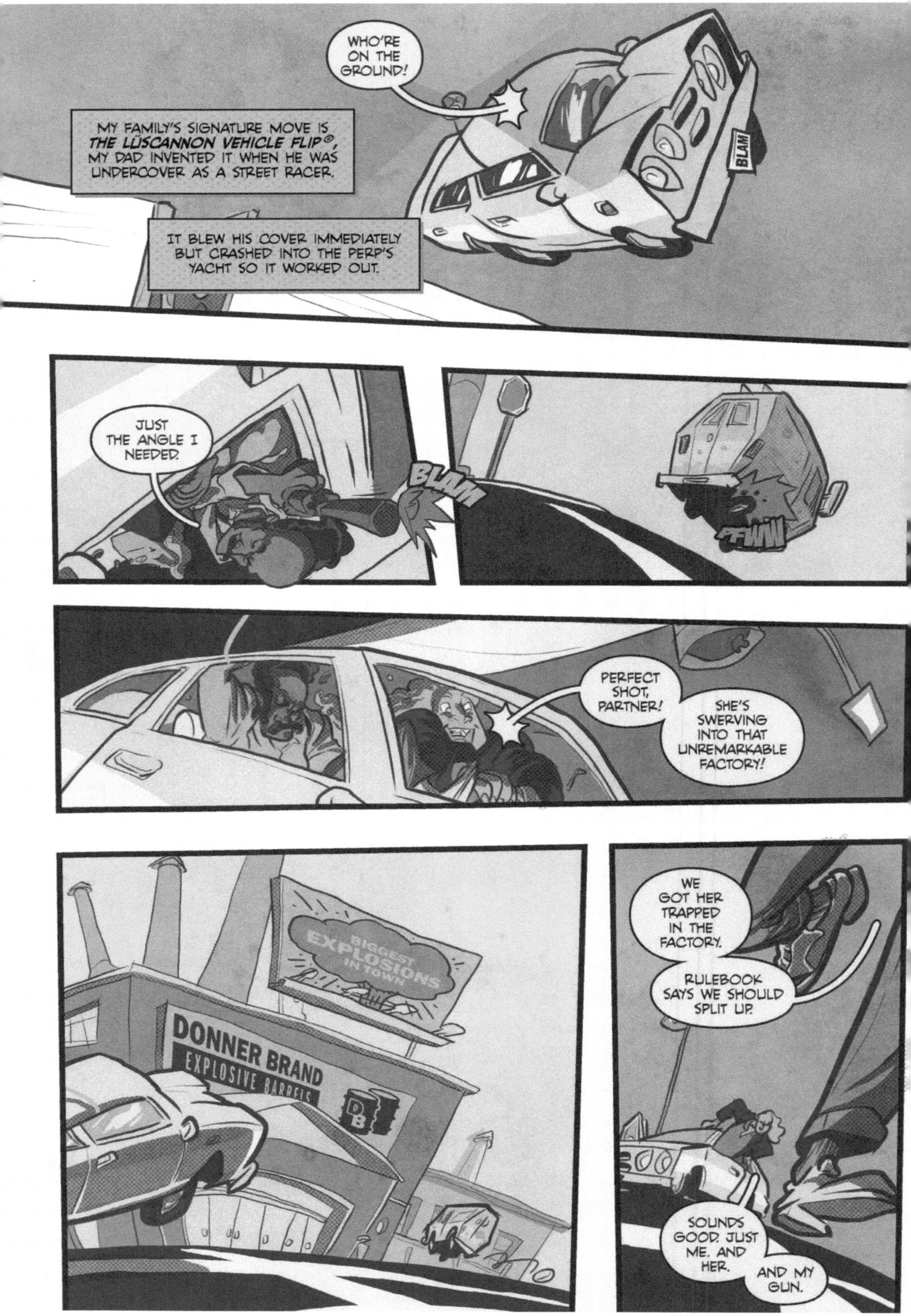
WHO'RE ON THE GROUND!
MY FAMILY'S SIGNATURE MOVE IS ***THE LÜSCANNON VEHICLE FLIP®***, MY DAD INVENTED IT WHEN HE WAS UNDERCOVER AS A STREET RACER.
BLAM
IT BLEW HIS COVER IMMEDIATELY BUT CRASHED INTO THE PERP'S YACHT SO IT WORKED OUT.
JUST THE ANGLE I NEEDED.
BLAM
PFWM
PERFECT SHOT, PARTNER!
SHE'S SWERVING INTO THAT UNREMARKABLE FACTORY!
BIGGEST EXPLOSIONS IN TOWN
DONNER BRAND
EXPLOSIVE BARRELS
DB
WE GOT HER TRAPPED IN THE FACTORY.
RULEBOOK SAYS WE SHOULD SPLIT UP.
SOUNDS GOOD. JUST ME. AND HER.
AND MY GUN.

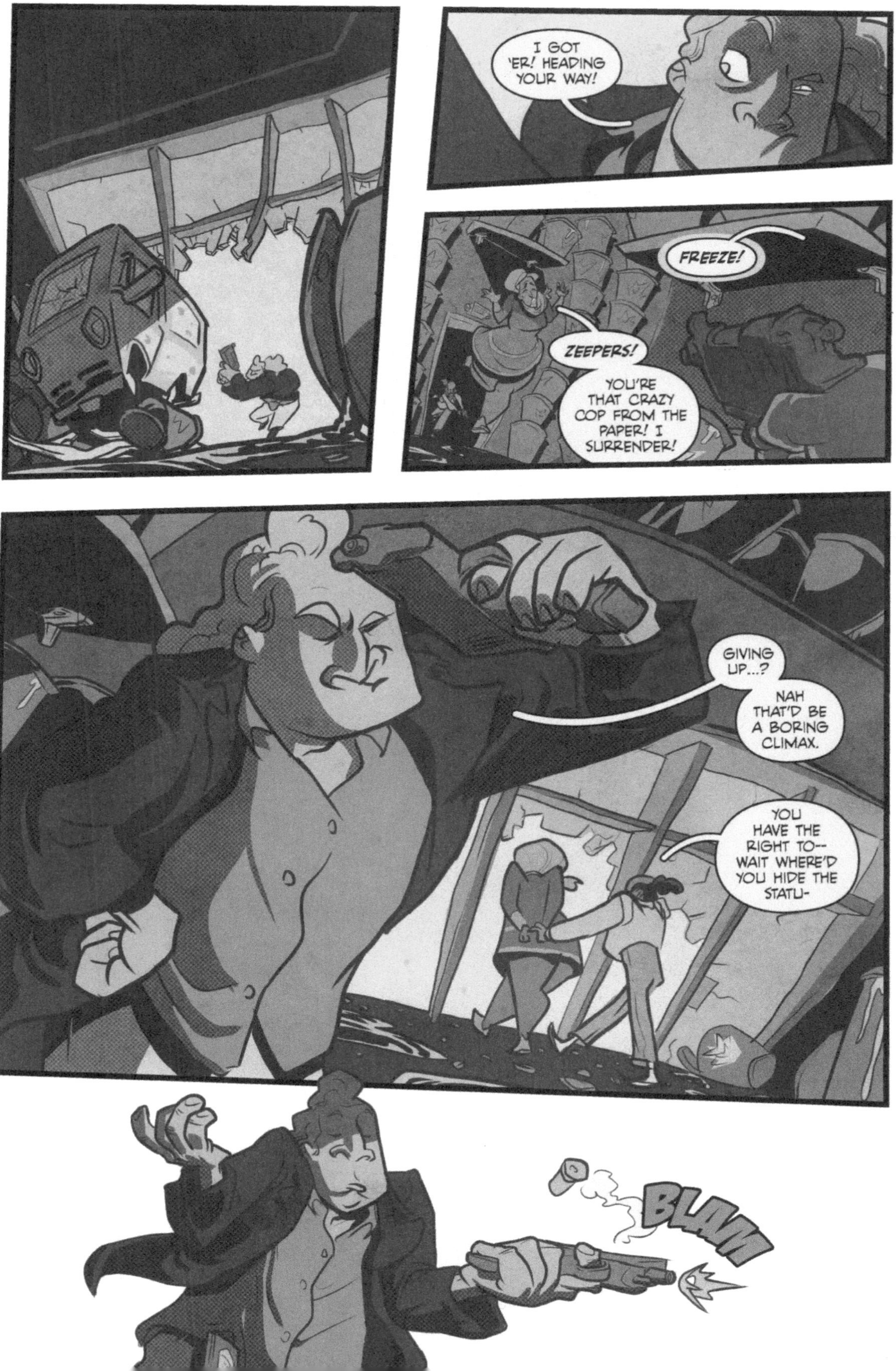
I GOT 'ER! HEADING YOUR WAY!
FREEZE!
ZEEPERS!
YOU'RE THAT CRAZY COP FROM THE PAPER! I SURRENDER!
GIVING UP...?
NAH THAT'D BE A BORING CLIMAX.
YOU HAVE THE RIGHT TO--
WAIT WHERE'D YOU HIDE THE STATU-
BLAM

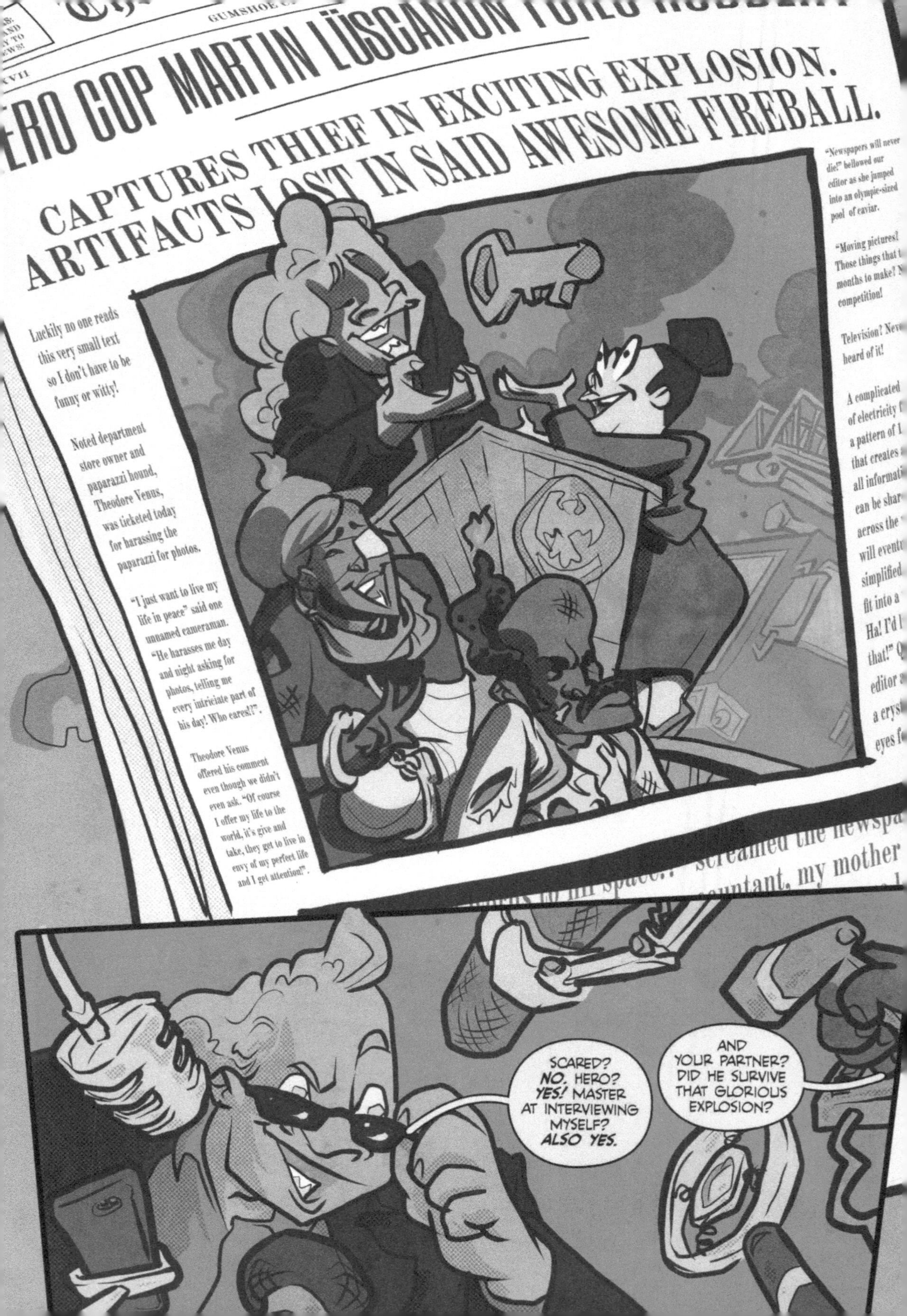

GUMSHOE
ERO COP MARTIN LÜSCANON
CAPTURES THIEF IN EXCITING EXPLOSION.
ARTIFACTS LOST IN SAID AWESOME FIREBALL.
Luckily no one reads this very small text so I don't have to be funny or witty!
Noted department store owner and paparazzi hound, Theodore Venus, was ticketed today for harassing the paparazzi for photos.
"I just want to live my life in peace" said one unnamed cameraman. "He harasses me day and night asking for photos, telling me every intricate part of his day! Who cares!?".
Theodore Venus offered his comment even though we didn't even ask. "Of course I offer my life to the world, it's give and take, they get to live in envy of my perfect life and I get attention!".
"Newspapers will never die!" bellowed our editor as she jumped into an olympic-sized pool of caviar.
"Moving pictures? Those things that
months to make?
competition!
Television?
heard of it!
A complicated
of electricity
a pattern of
that creates
all
can be
across the
will
simplified
fit into a
Ha!
that!"
editor
a
eyes
screamed the
my mother
SCARED? NO. HERO? YES! MASTER AT INTERVIEWING MYSELF? ALSO YES.
AND YOUR PARTNER? DID HE SURVIVE THAT GLORIOUS EXPLOSION?

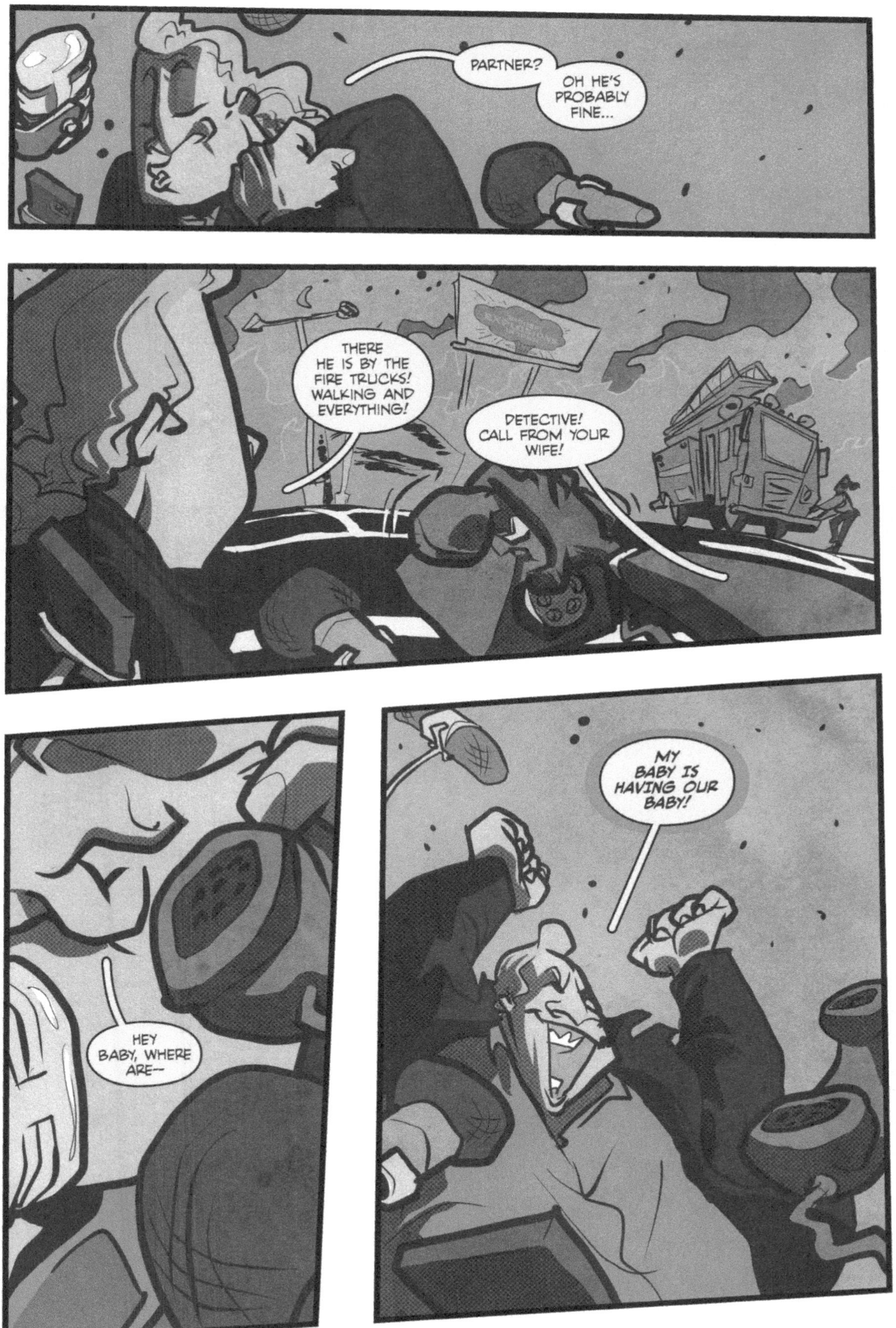
PARTNER?
OH HE'S PROBABLY FINE...
THERE HE IS BY THE FIRE TRUCKS! WALKING AND EVERYTHING!
DETECTIVE! CALL FROM YOUR WIFE!
HEY BABY, WHERE ARE--
MY BABY IS HAVING OUR BABY!

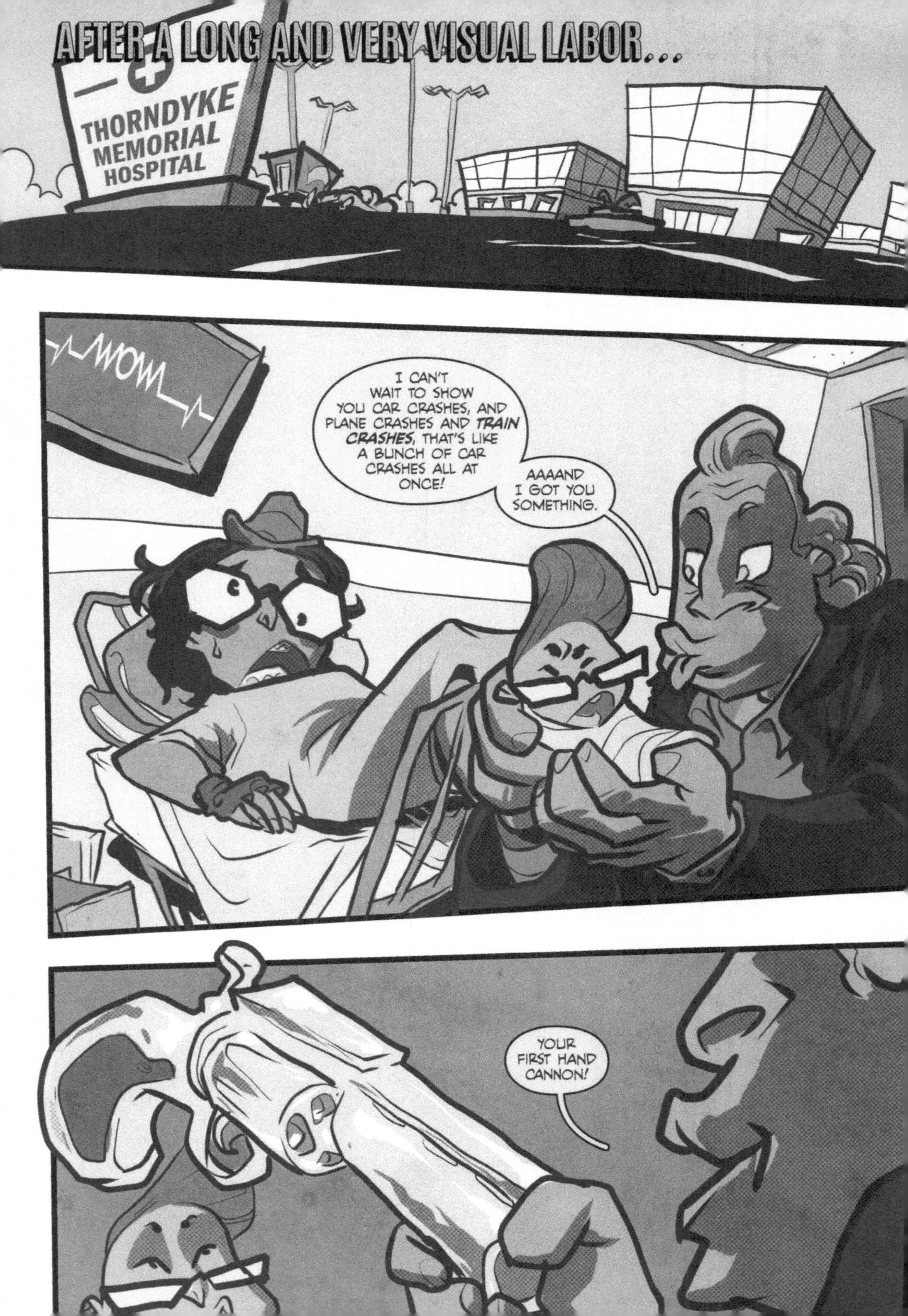
AFTER A LONG AND VERY VISUAL LABOR...
THORNDYKE MEMORIAL HOSPITAL
WOW
I CAN'T WAIT TO SHOW YOU CAR CRASHES, AND PLANE CRASHES AND TRAIN CRASHES, THAT'S LIKE A BUNCH OF CAR CRASHES ALL AT ONCE!
AAAAND I GOT YOU SOMETHING.
YOUR FIRST HAND CANNON!

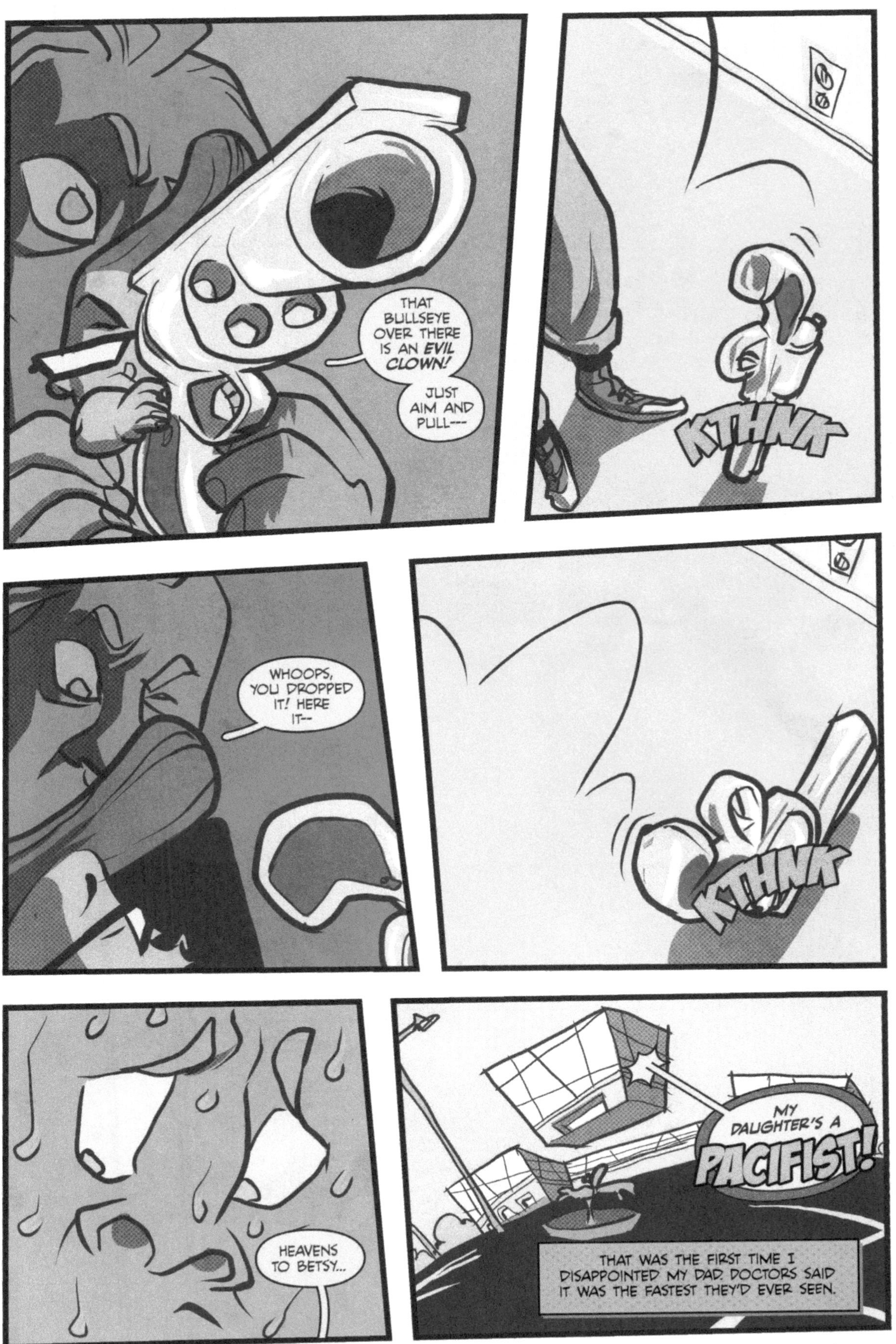
THAT BULLSEYE OVER THERE IS AN *EVIL CLOWN!*
JUST AIM AND PULL---
KTHNK
WHOOPS, YOU DROPPED IT! HERE IT--
KTHNK
HEAVENS TO BETSY...
MY DAUGHTER'S A PACIFIST!
THAT WAS THE FIRST TIME I DISAPPOINTED MY DAD. DOCTORS SAID IT WAS THE FASTEST THEY'D EVER SEEN.

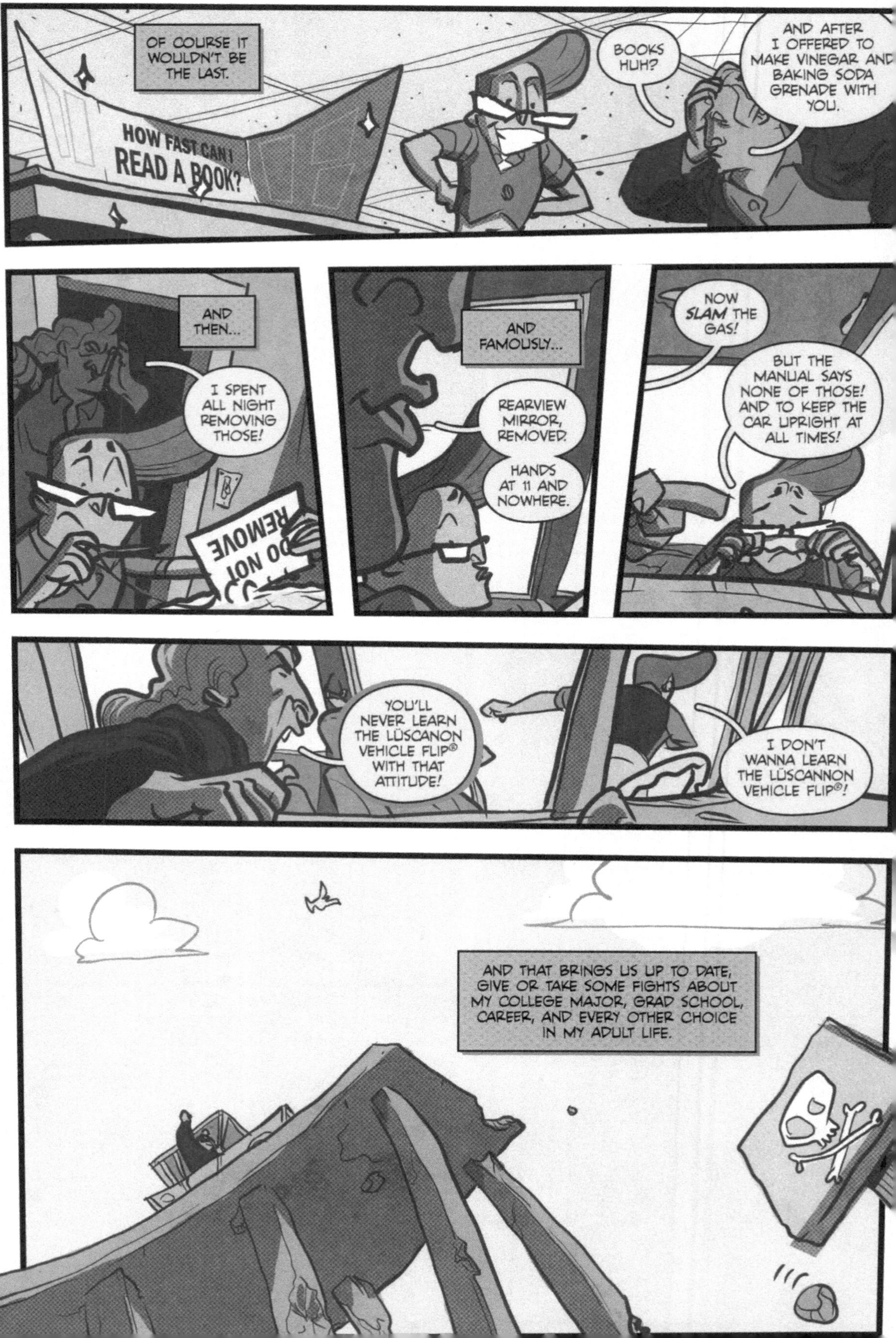
OF COURSE IT WOULDN'T BE THE LAST.
HOW FAST CAN I READ A BOOK?
BOOKS HUH?
AND AFTER I OFFERED TO MAKE VINEGAR AND BAKING SODA GRENADE WITH YOU.
AND THEN...
I SPENT ALL NIGHT REMOVING THOSE!
DO NOT REMOVE
AND FAMOUSLY...
REARVIEW MIRROR, REMOVED.
HANDS AT 11 AND NOWHERE.
NOW *SLAM* THE GAS!
BUT THE MANUAL SAYS NONE OF THOSE! AND TO KEEP THE CAR UPRIGHT AT ALL TIMES!
YOU'LL NEVER LEARN THE LÜSCANON VEHICLE FLIP® WITH THAT ATTITUDE!
I DON'T WANNA LEARN THE LÜSCANNON VEHICLE FLIP®!
AND THAT BRINGS US UP TO DATE, GIVE OR TAKE SOME FIGHTS ABOUT MY COLLEGE MAJOR, GRAD SCHOOL, CAREER, AND EVERY OTHER CHOICE IN MY ADULT LIFE.

Chapter One: Checking In & Checking Out

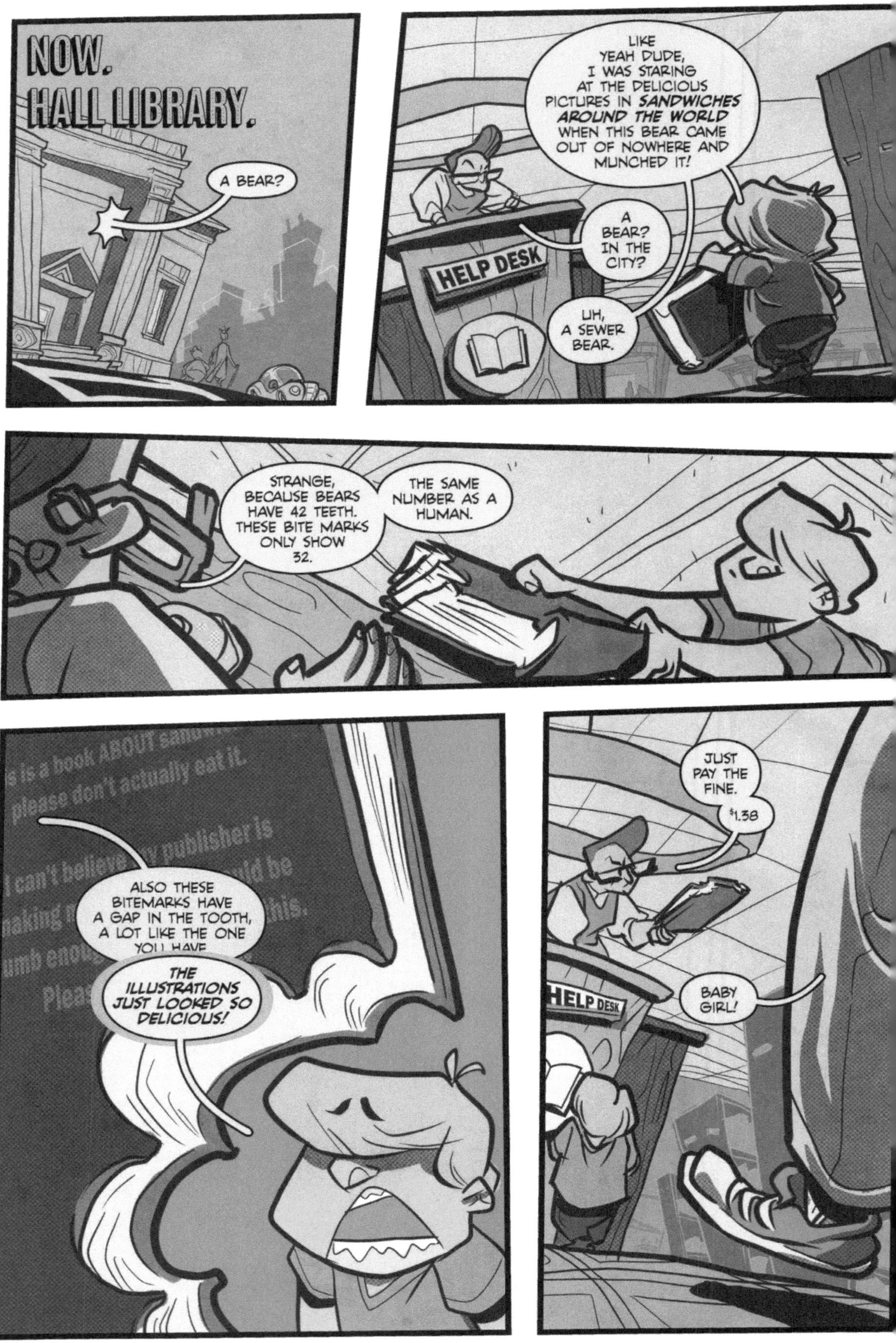
NOW.
HALL LIBRARY.
A BEAR?
LIKE YEAH DUDE, I WAS STARING AT THE DELICIOUS PICTURES IN SANDWICHES AROUND THE WORLD WHEN THIS BEAR CAME OUT OF NOWHERE AND MUNCHED IT!
A BEAR? IN THE CITY?
UH, A SEWER BEAR.
HELP DESK
STRANGE, BECAUSE BEARS HAVE 42 TEETH. THESE BITE MARKS ONLY SHOW 32.
THE SAME NUMBER AS A HUMAN.
ALSO THESE BITEMARKS HAVE A GAP IN THE TOOTH, A LOT LIKE THE ONE YOU HAVE
THE ILLUSTRATIONS JUST LOOKED SO DELICIOUS!
JUST PAY THE FINE.
$1.38
HELP DESK
BABY GIRL!

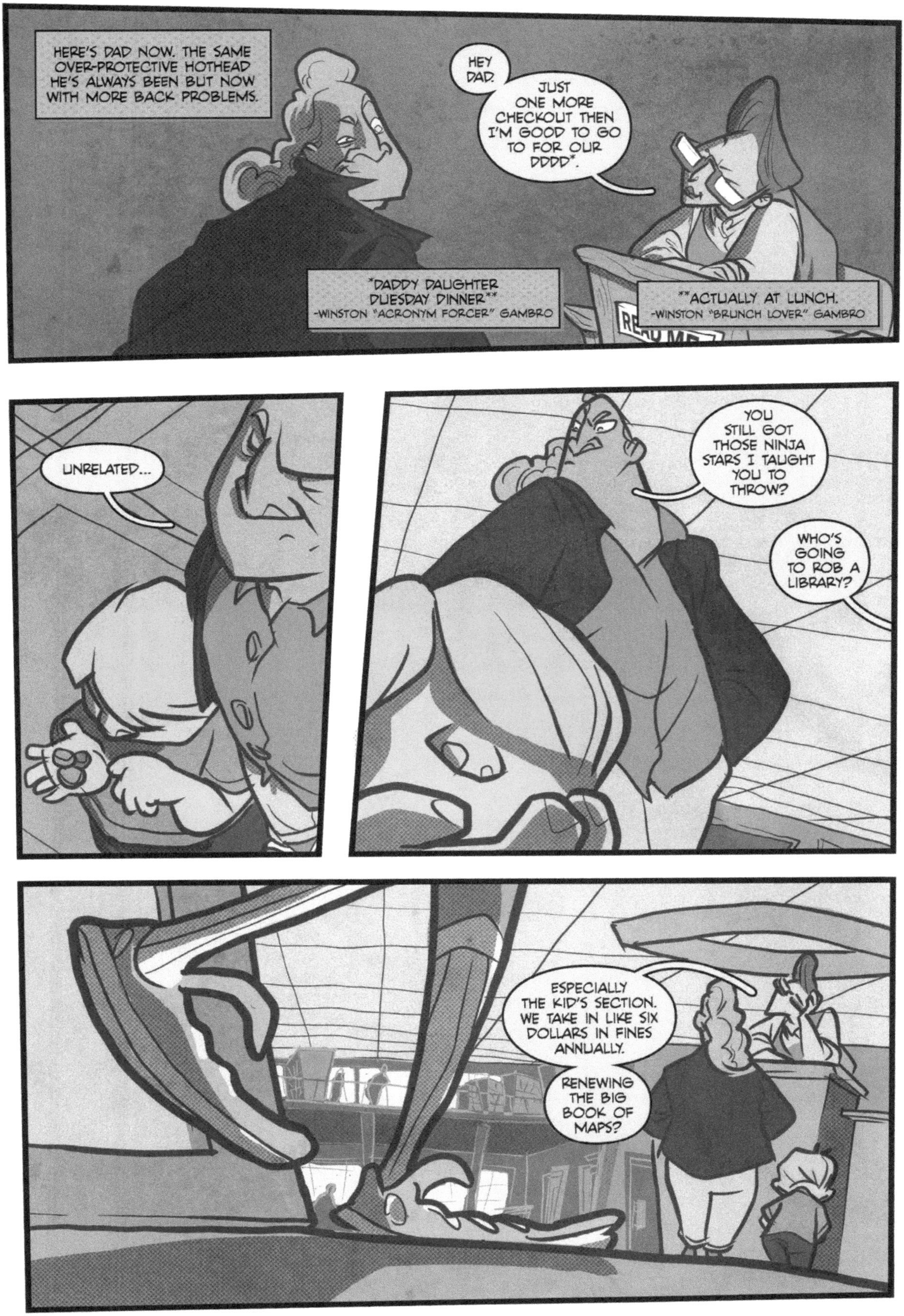
HERE'S DAD NOW. THE SAME OVER-PROTECTIVE HOTHEAD HE'S ALWAYS BEEN BUT NOW WITH MORE BACK PROBLEMS.
HEY DAD.
JUST ONE MORE CHECKOUT THEN I'M GOOD TO GO TO FOR OUR DDDD*.
*DADDY DAUGHTER DUESDAY DINNER** -WINSTON "ACRONYM FORCER" GAMBRO
**ACTUALLY AT LUNCH. -WINSTON "BRUNCH LOVER" GAMBRO
UNRELATED...
YOU STILL GOT THOSE NINJA STARS I TAUGHT YOU TO THROW?
WHO'S GOING TO ROB A LIBRARY?
ESPECIALLY THE KID'S SECTION. WE TAKE IN LIKE SIX DOLLARS IN FINES ANNUALLY.
RENEWING THE BIG BOOK OF MAPS?

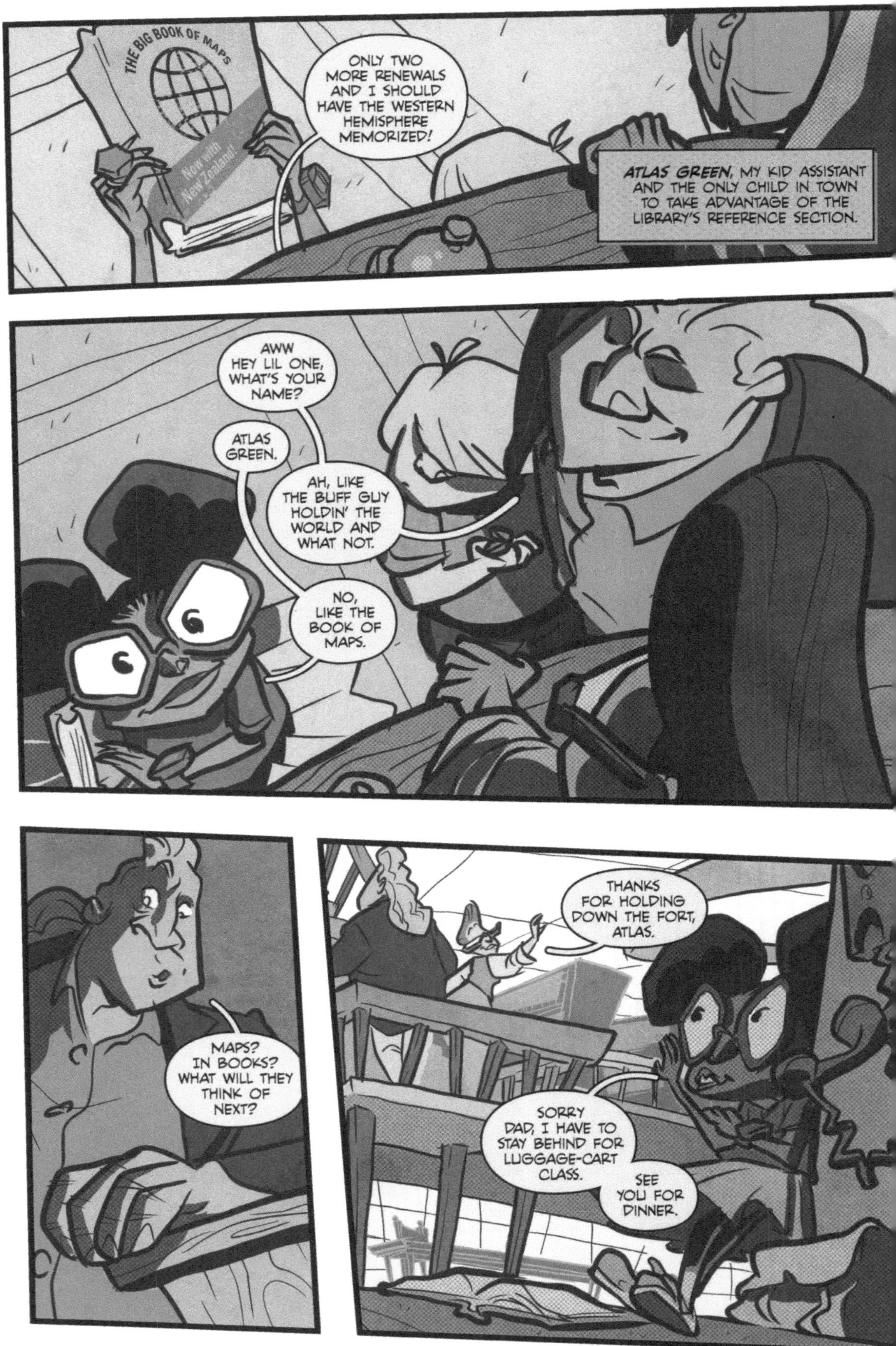
THE BIG BOOK OF MAPS
Now with New Zealand!
ONLY TWO MORE RENEWALS AND I SHOULD HAVE THE WESTERN HEMISPHERE MEMORIZED!
ATLAS GREEN, MY KID ASSISTANT AND THE ONLY CHILD IN TOWN TO TAKE ADVANTAGE OF THE LIBRARY'S REFERENCE SECTION.
AWW HEY LIL ONE, WHAT'S YOUR NAME?
ATLAS GREEN.
AH, LIKE THE BUFF GUY HOLDIN' THE WORLD AND WHAT NOT.
NO, LIKE THE BOOK OF MAPS.
MAPS? IN BOOKS? WHAT WILL THEY THINK OF NEXT?
THANKS FOR HOLDING DOWN THE FORT, ATLAS.
SORRY DAD, I HAVE TO STAY BEHIND FOR LUGGAGE-CART CLASS.
SEE YOU FOR DINNER.

CHAPTER 2

SECOND TO LAND TO

Last Supper

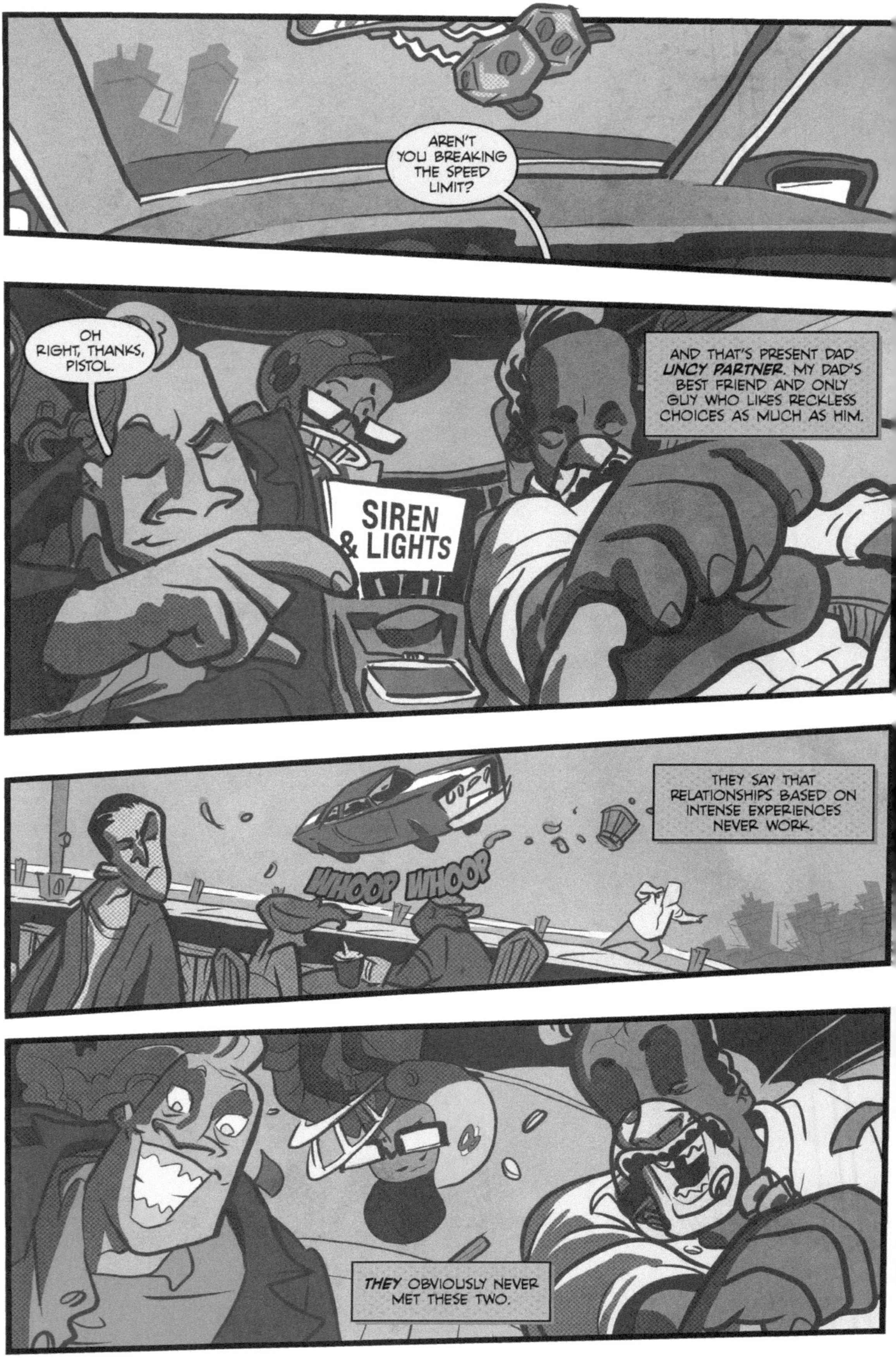
AREN'T YOU BREAKING THE SPEED LIMIT?
OH RIGHT, THANKS, PISTOL.
AND THAT'S PRESENT DAD *UNCY PARTNER*. MY DAD'S BEST FRIEND AND ONLY GUY WHO LIKES RECKLESS CHOICES AS MUCH AS HIM.
SIREN & LIGHTS
THEY SAY THAT RELATIONSHIPS BASED ON INTENSE EXPERIENCES NEVER WORK.
WHOOP WHOOP
THEY OBVIOUSLY NEVER MET THESE TWO.

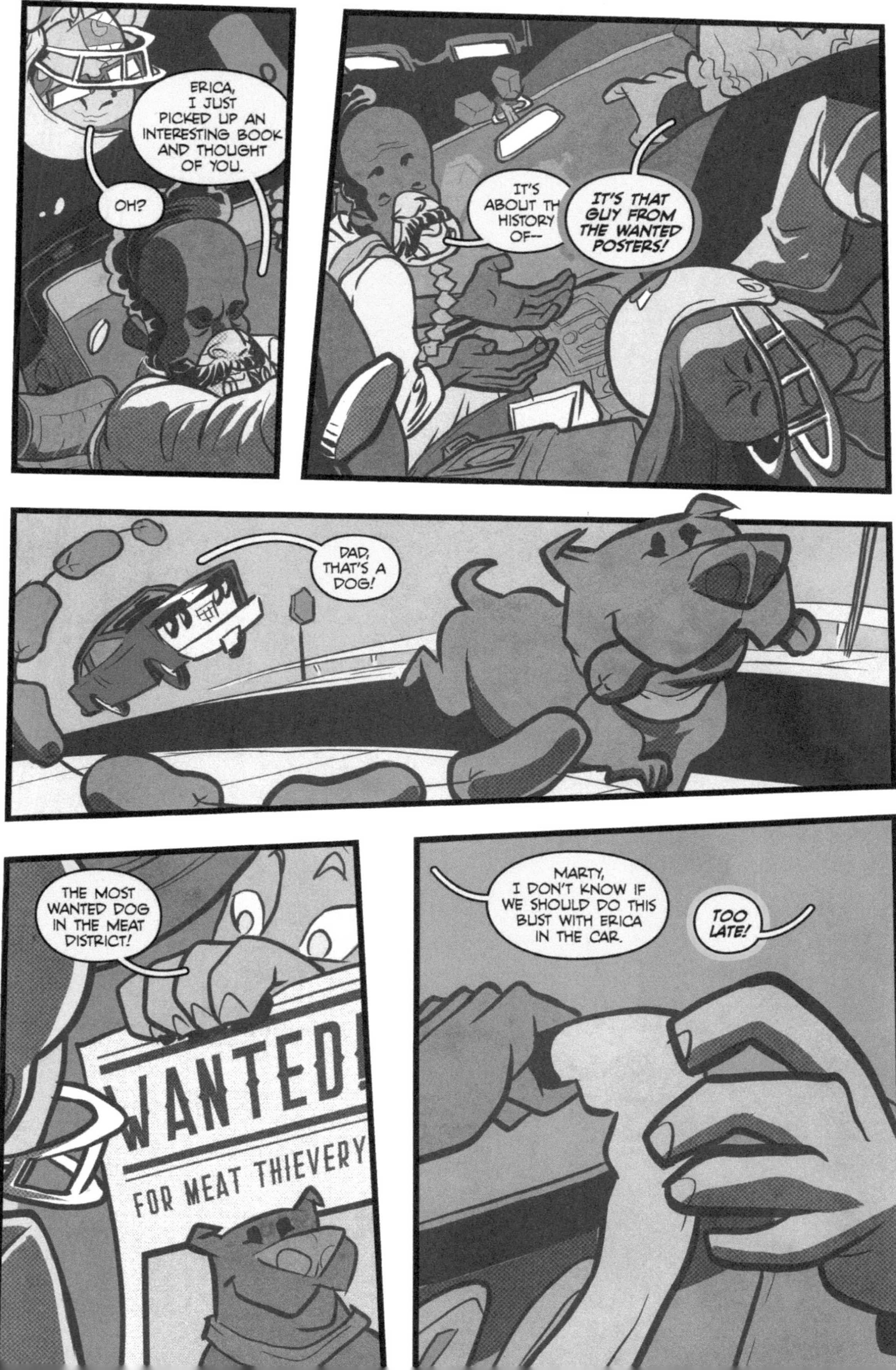
ERICA, I JUST PICKED UP AN INTERESTING BOOK AND THOUGHT OF YOU.
OH?
IT'S ABOUT TH HISTORY OF--
IT'S THAT GUY FROM THE WANTED POSTERS!
DAD, THAT'S A DOG!
THE MOST WANTED DOG IN THE MEAT DISTRICT!
WANTED!
FOR MEAT THIEVERY
MARTY, I DON'T KNOW IF WE SHOULD DO THIS BUST WITH ERICA IN THE CAR.
TOO LATE!

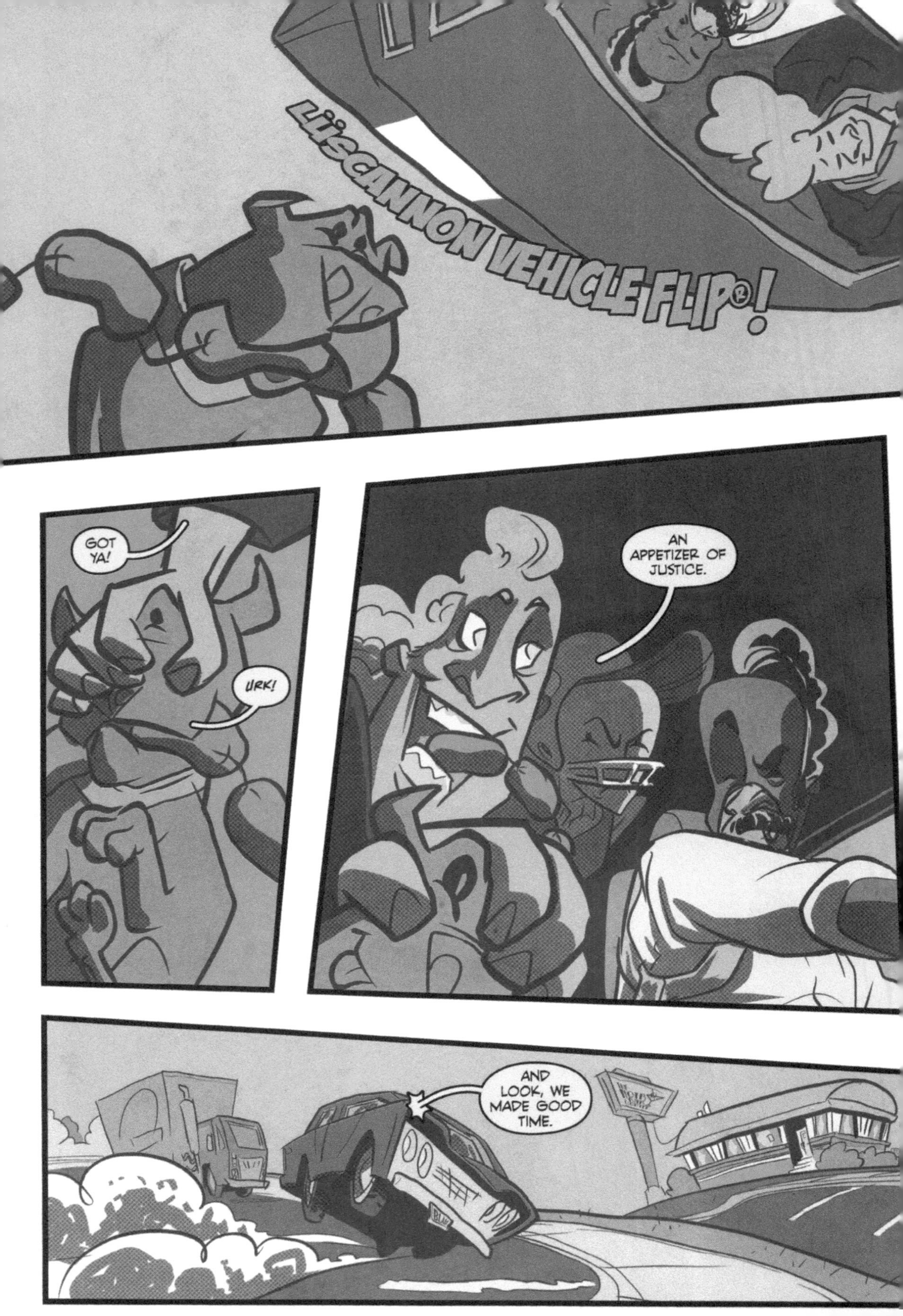
LÏSCANNON VEHICLE FLIP®!
GOT YA!
URK!
AN APPETIZER OF JUSTICE.
AND LOOK, WE MADE GOOD TIME.

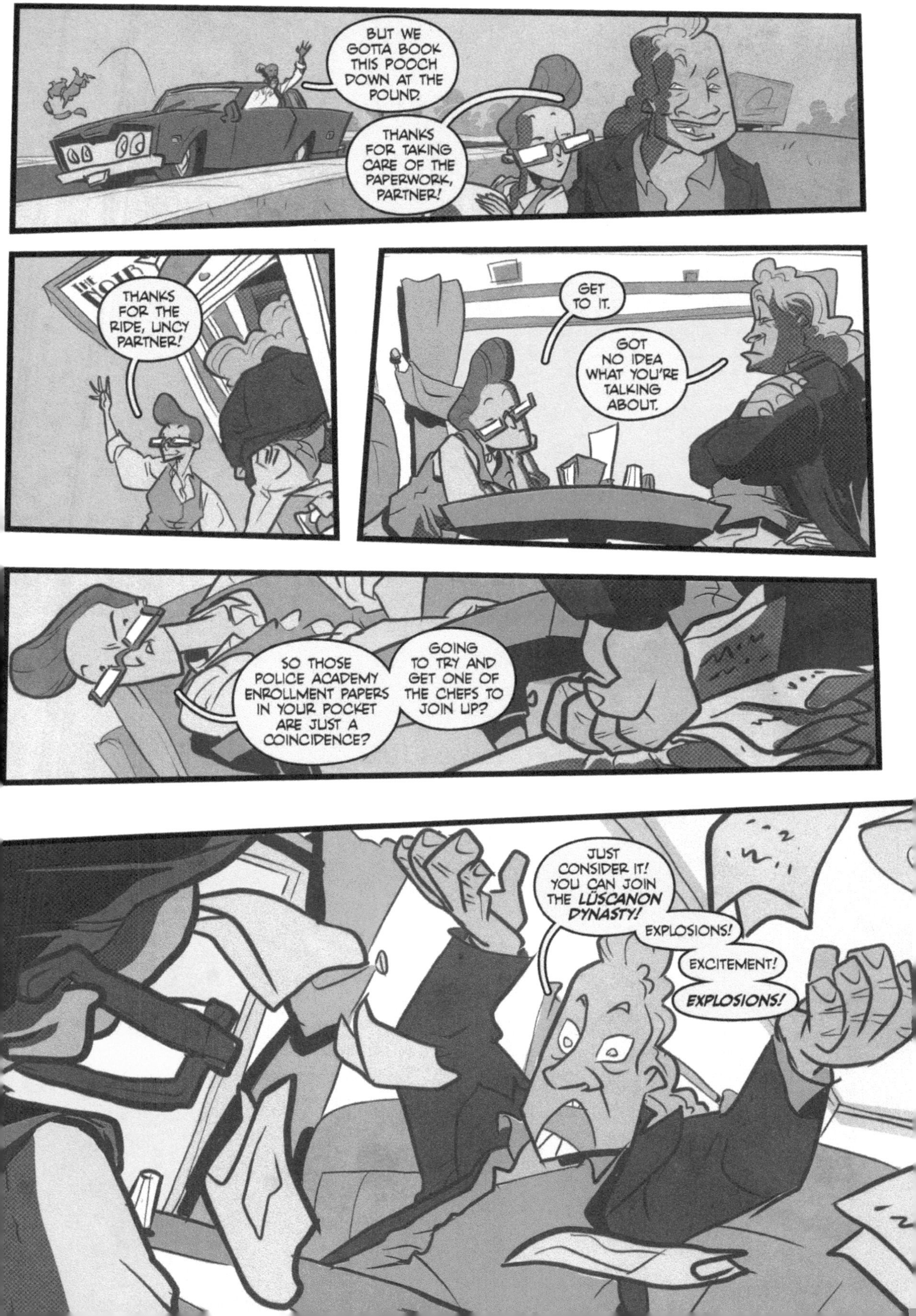
BUT WE GOTTA BOOK THIS POOCH DOWN AT THE POUND.
THANKS FOR TAKING CARE OF THE PAPERWORK, PARTNER!
THANKS FOR THE RIDE, UNCY PARTNER!
GET TO IT.
GOT NO IDEA WHAT YOU'RE TALKING ABOUT.
SO THOSE POLICE ACADEMY ENROLLMENT PAPERS IN YOUR POCKET ARE JUST A COINCIDENCE?
GOING TO TRY AND GET ONE OF THE CHEFS TO JOIN UP?
JUST CONSIDER IT! YOU CAN JOIN THE LÜSCANON DYNASTY!
EXPLOSIONS!
EXCITEMENT!
EXPLOSIONS!

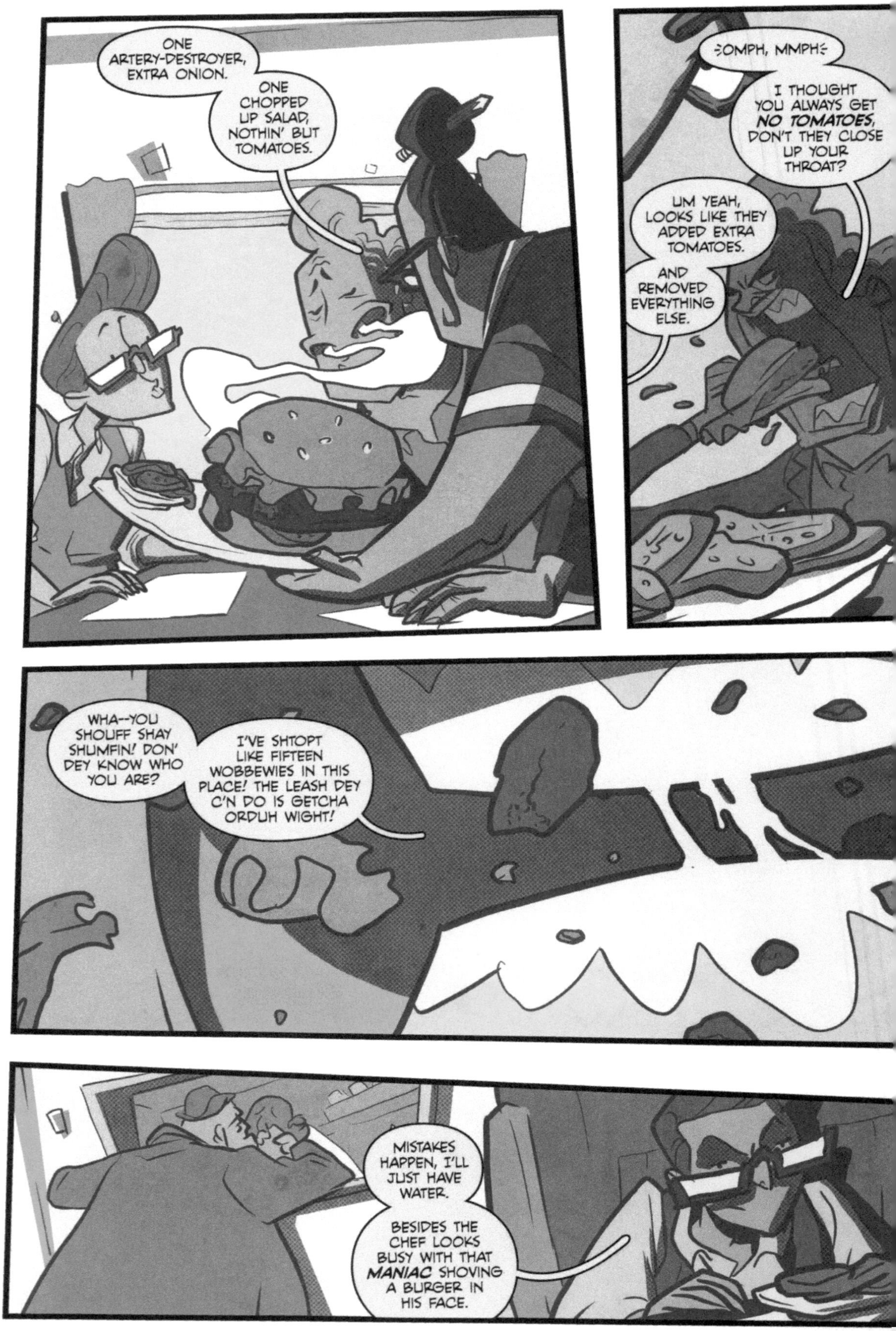
ONE ARTERY-DESTROYER, EXTRA ONION.
ONE CHOPPED UP SALAD, NOTHIN' BUT TOMATOES.
OMPH, MMPH
I THOUGHT YOU ALWAYS GET NO TOMATOES, DON'T THEY CLOSE UP YOUR THROAT?
UM YEAH, LOOKS LIKE THEY ADDED EXTRA TOMATOES.
AND REMOVED EVERYTHING ELSE.
WHA--YOU SHOUFF SHAY SHUMFIN! DON' DEY KNOW WHO YOU ARE?
I'VE SHTOPT LIKE FIFTEEN WOBBEWIES IN THIS PLACE! THE LEASH DEY C'N DO IS GETCHA ORDUH WIGHT!
MISTAKES HAPPEN, I'LL JUST HAVE WATER.
BESIDES THE CHEF LOOKS BUSY WITH THAT MANIAC SHOVING A BURGER IN HIS FACE.

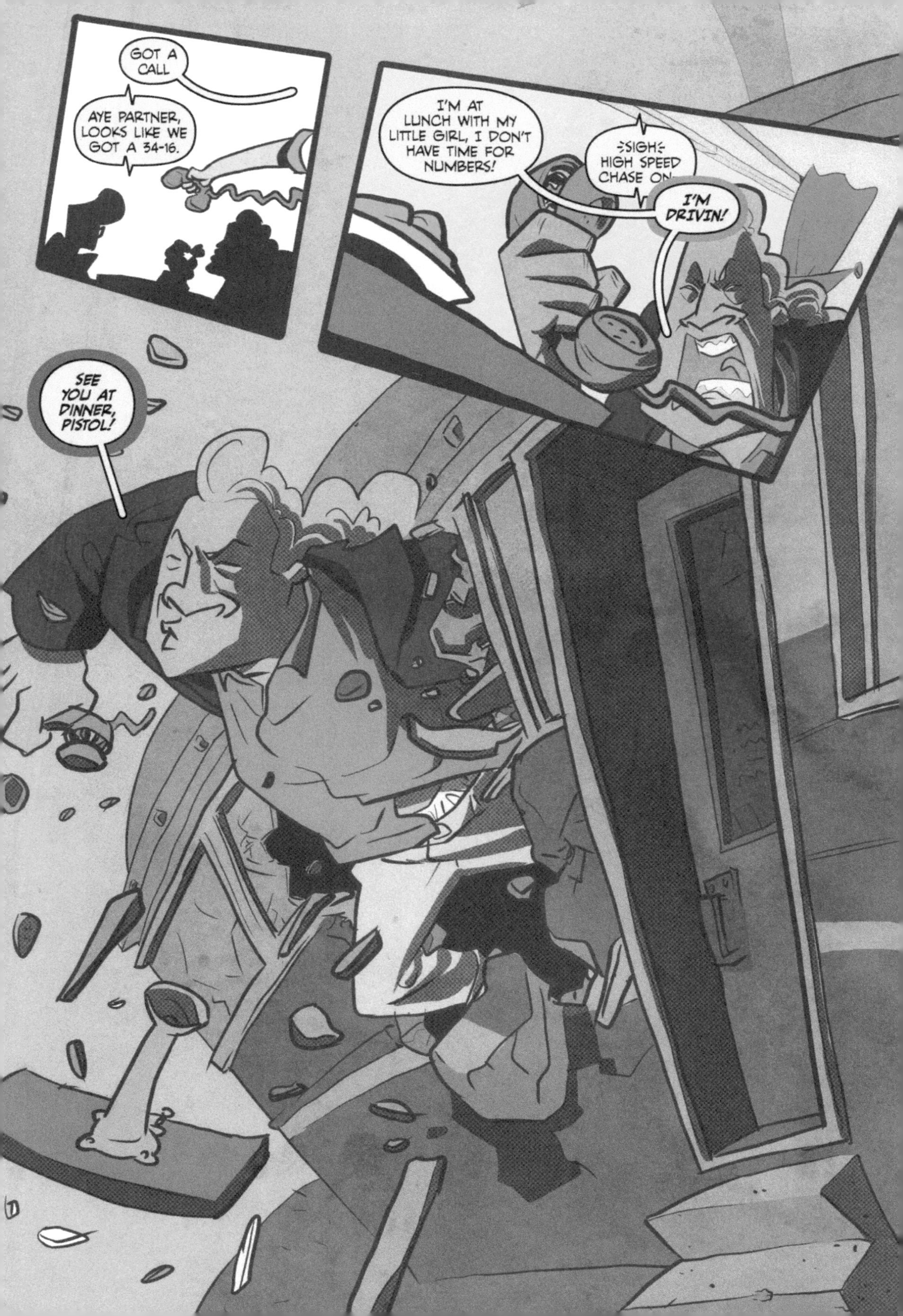
GOT A CALL
AYE PARTNER, LOOKS LIKE WE GOT A 34-16.
I'M AT LUNCH WITH MY LITTLE GIRL, I DON'T HAVE TIME FOR NUMBERS!
SIGH HIGH SPEED CHASE ON
I'M DRIVIN!
SEE YOU AT DINNER, PISTOL!

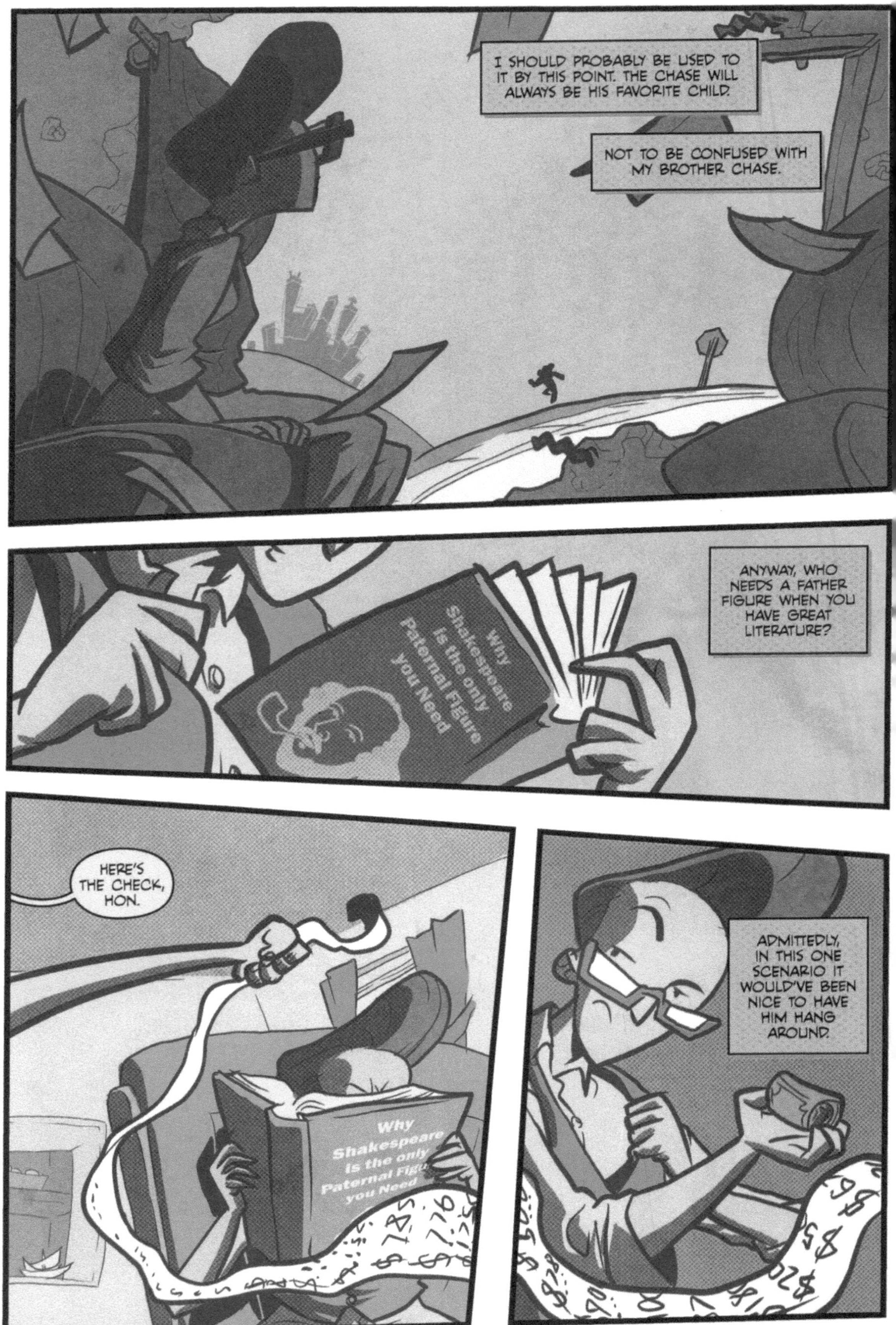
I SHOULD PROBABLY BE USED TO IT BY THIS POINT. THE CHASE WILL ALWAYS BE HIS FAVORITE CHILD.
NOT TO BE CONFUSED WITH MY BROTHER CHASE.
ANYWAY, WHO NEEDS A FATHER FIGURE WHEN YOU HAVE GREAT LITERATURE?
Why Shakespeare is the only Paternal Figure you Need
HERE'S THE CHECK, HON.
Why Shakespeare is the only Paternal Figu you Need
ADMITTEDLY, IN THIS ONE SCENARIO IT WOULD'VE BEEN NICE TO HAVE HIM HANG AROUND.

CHAPTER THREE

BATTLE

ON THE HOMEFRONT

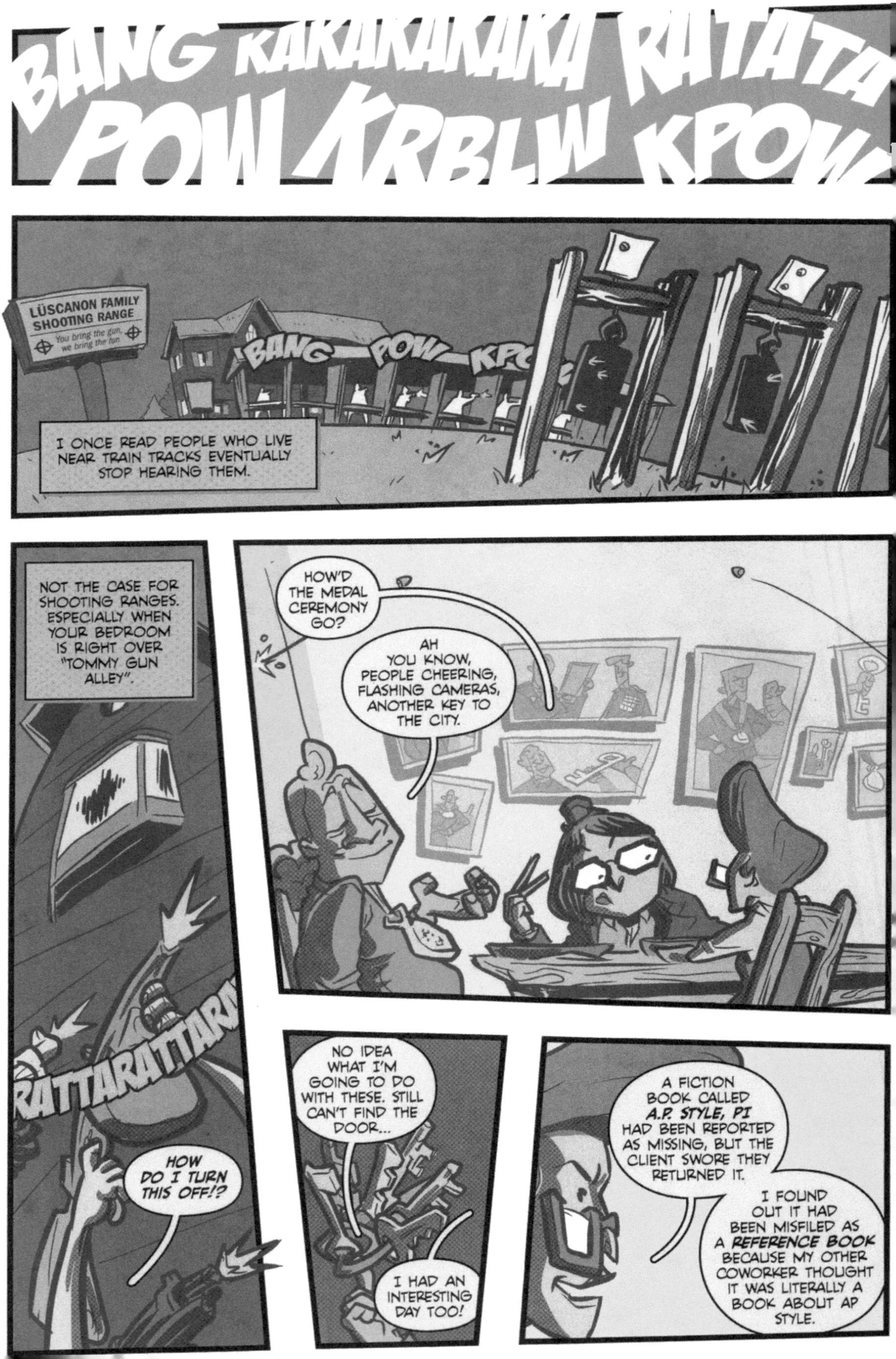
BANG KAKAKAKAKAKA RATATA
POW KRBLW KPOW
LÜSCANON FAMILY SHOOTING RANGE
You bring the gun, we bring the fun
BANG POW KPOW
I ONCE READ PEOPLE WHO LIVE NEAR TRAIN TRACKS EVENTUALLY STOP HEARING THEM.
NOT THE CASE FOR SHOOTING RANGES. ESPECIALLY WHEN YOUR BEDROOM IS RIGHT OVER "TOMMY GUN ALLEY".
RATTARATTARA
HOW DO I TURN THIS OFF!?
HOW'D THE MEDAL CEREMONY GO?
AH YOU KNOW, PEOPLE CHEERING, FLASHING CAMERAS, ANOTHER KEY TO THE CITY.
NO IDEA WHAT I'M GOING TO DO WITH THESE. STILL CAN'T FIND THE DOOR...
I HAD AN INTERESTING DAY TOO!
A FICTION BOOK CALLED *A.P. STYLE, PI* HAD BEEN REPORTED AS MISSING, BUT THE CLIENT SWORE THEY RETURNED IT.
I FOUND OUT IT HAD BEEN MISFILED AS A *REFERENCE BOOK* BECAUSE MY OTHER COWORKER THOUGHT IT WAS LITERALLY A BOOK ABOUT AP STYLE.

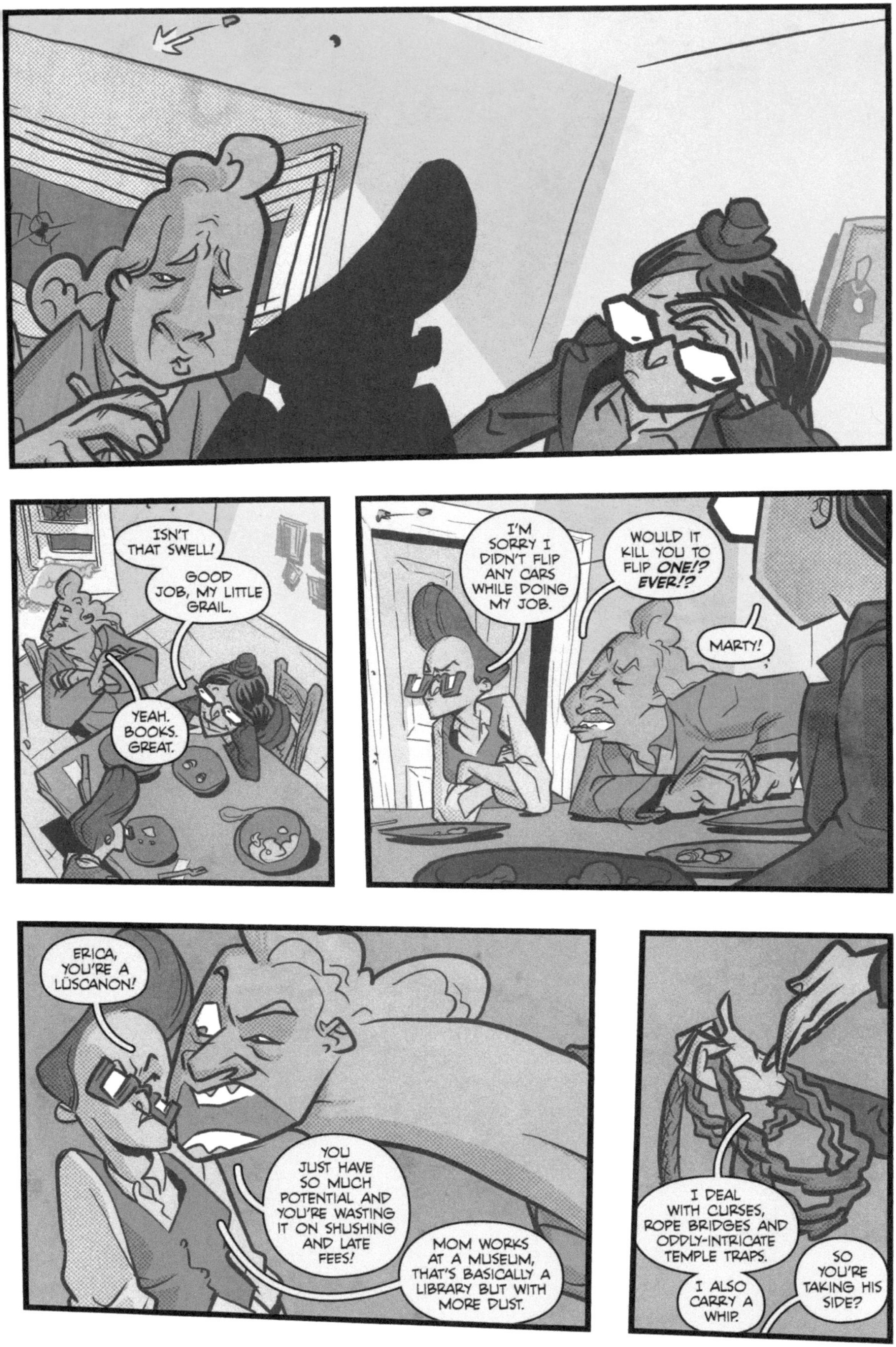
ISN'T THAT SWELL!
GOOD JOB, MY LITTLE GRAIL.
YEAH. BOOKS. GREAT.
I'M SORRY I DIDN'T FLIP ANY CARS WHILE DOING MY JOB.
WOULD IT KILL YOU TO FLIP ONE!? EVER!?
MARTY!
ERICA, YOU'RE A LÜSCANON!
YOU JUST HAVE SO MUCH POTENTIAL AND YOU'RE WASTING IT ON SHUSHING AND LATE FEES!
MOM WORKS AT A MUSEUM, THAT'S BASICALLY A LIBRARY BUT WITH MORE DUST.
I DEAL WITH CURSES, ROPE BRIDGES AND ODDLY-INTRICATE TEMPLE TRAPS.
I ALSO CARRY A WHIP.
SO YOU'RE TAKING HIS SIDE?

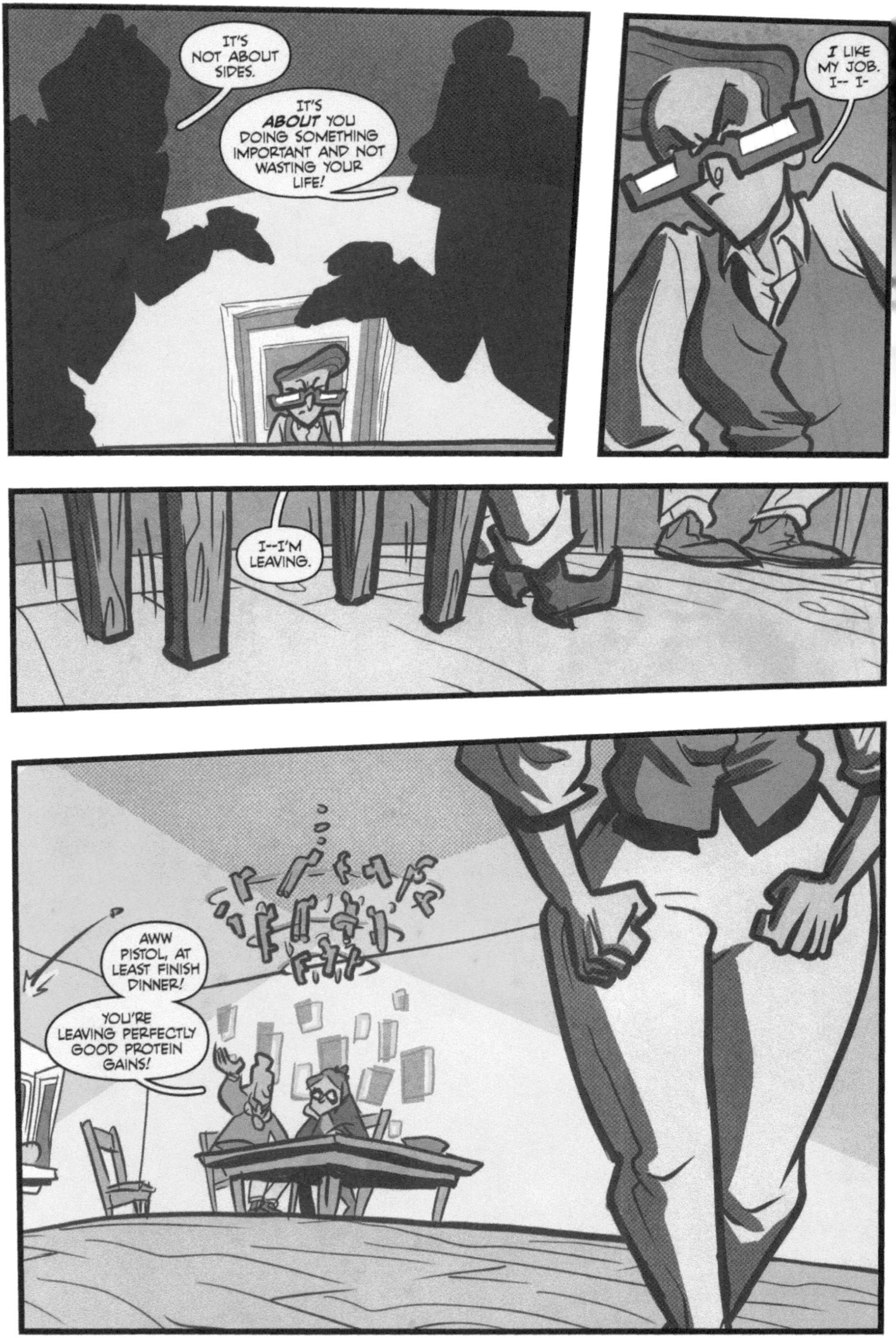
IT'S NOT ABOUT SIDES.
IT'S ABOUT YOU DOING SOMETHING IMPORTANT AND NOT WASTING YOUR LIFE!
I LIKE MY JOB. I-- I-
I--I'M LEAVING.
AWW PISTOL, AT LEAST FINISH DINNER!
YOU'RE LEAVING PERFECTLY GOOD PROTEIN GAINS!

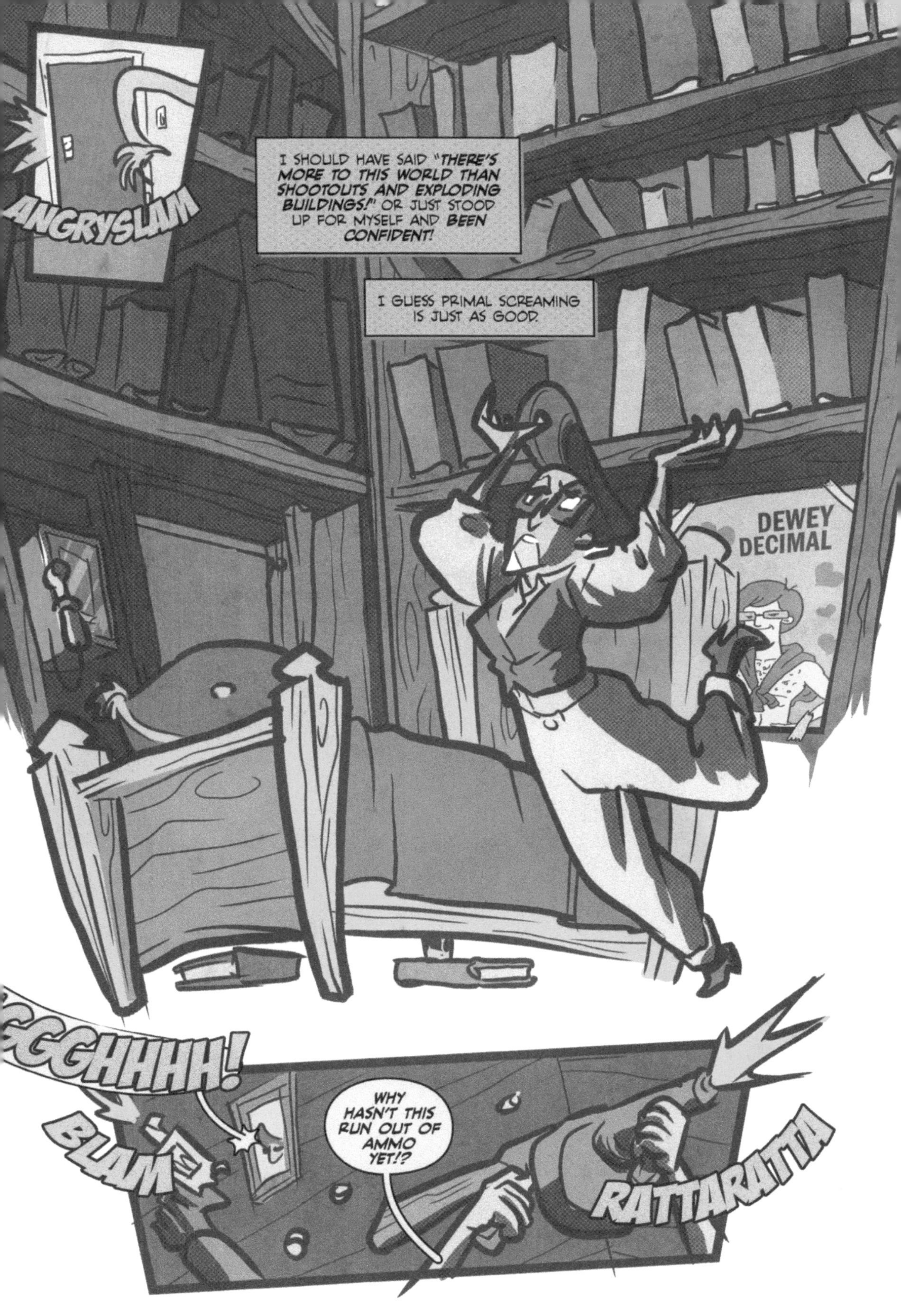
ANGRYSLAM
I SHOULD HAVE SAID "THERE'S MORE TO THIS WORLD THAN SHOOTOUTS AND EXPLODING BUILDINGS!" OR JUST STOOD UP FOR MYSELF AND BEEN CONFIDENT!
I GUESS PRIMAL SCREAMING IS JUST AS GOOD.
DEWEY DECIMAL
GGGHHHH!
BLAM
WHY HASN'T THIS RUN OUT OF AMMO YET!?
RATTARATTA

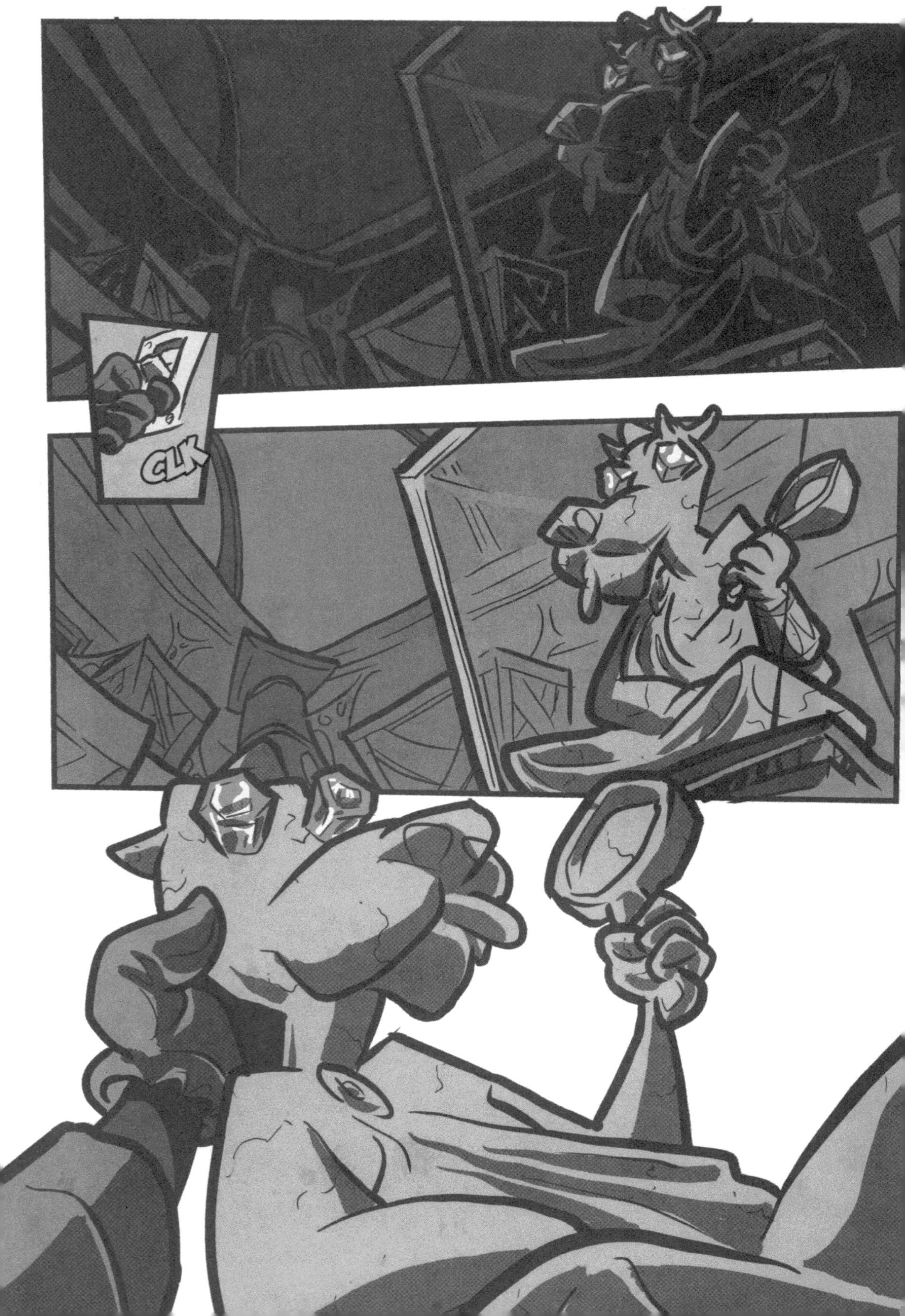
CLK

CHAPTER FOUR: A CALL TO MYSTERY

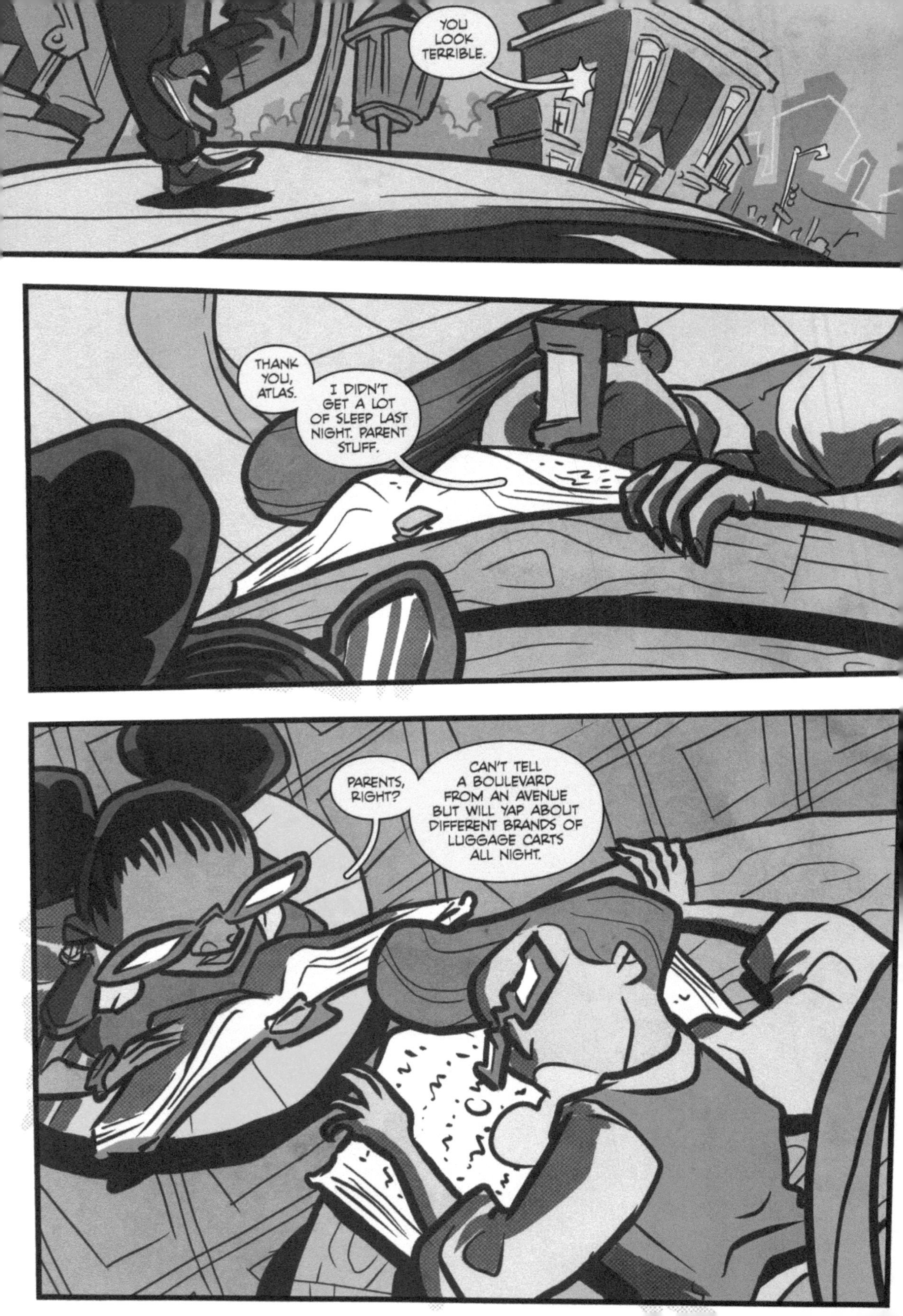
YOU LOOK TERRIBLE.
THANK YOU, ATLAS.
I DIDN'T GET A LOT OF SLEEP LAST NIGHT. PARENT STUFF.
PARENTS, RIGHT?
CAN'T TELL A BOULEVARD FROM AN AVENUE BUT WILL YAP ABOUT DIFFERENT BRANDS OF LUGGAGE CARTS ALL NIGHT.

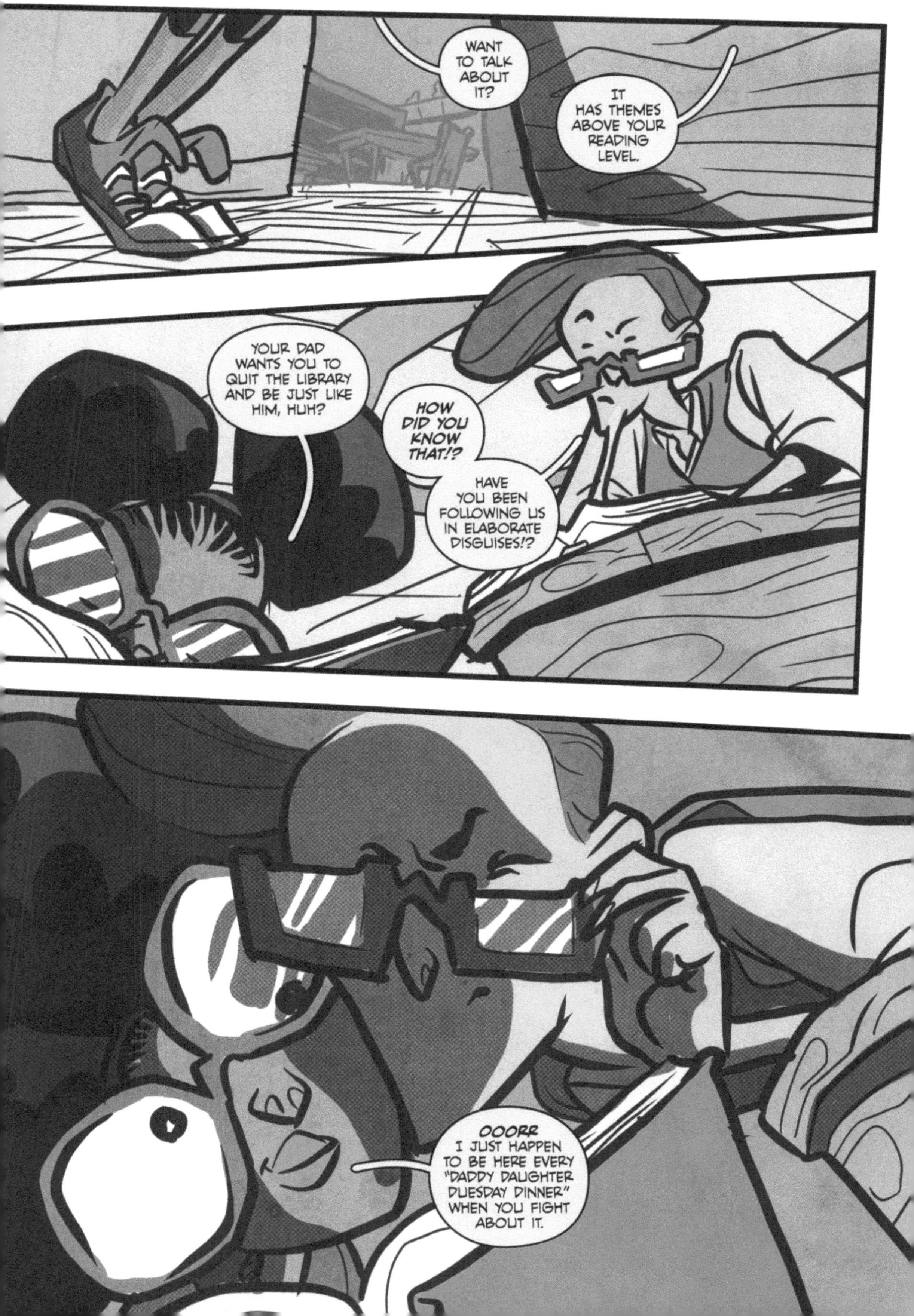
WANT TO TALK ABOUT IT?
IT HAS THEMES ABOVE YOUR READING LEVEL.
YOUR DAD WANTS YOU TO QUIT THE LIBRARY AND BE JUST LIKE HIM, HUH?
HOW DID YOU KNOW THAT!?
HAVE YOU BEEN FOLLOWING US IN ELABORATE DISGUISES!?
OOORR I JUST HAPPEN TO BE HERE EVERY "DADDY DAUGHTER DUESDAY DINNER" WHEN YOU FIGHT ABOUT IT.

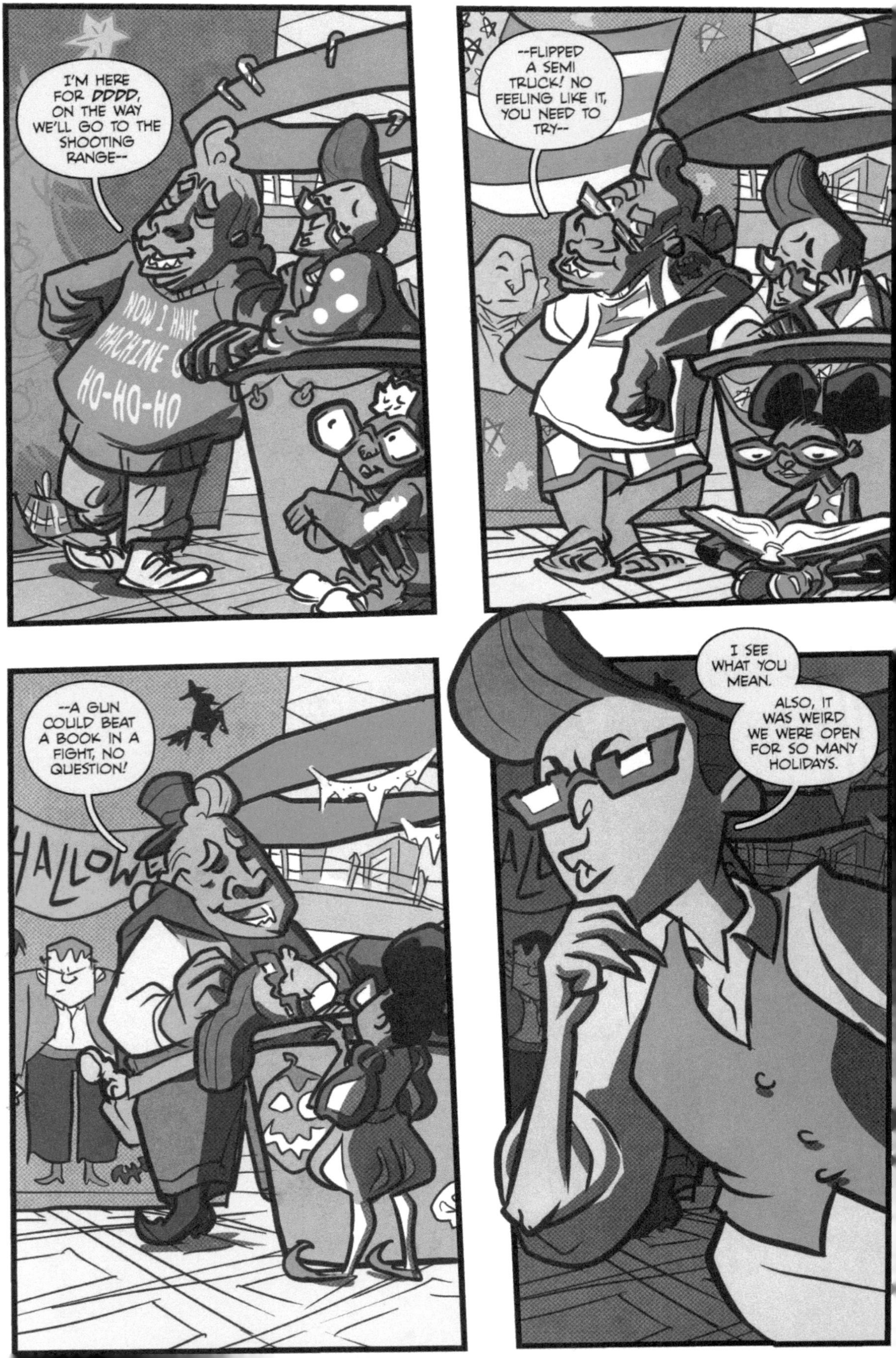
I'M HERE FOR DDDD, ON THE WAY WE'LL GO TO THE SHOOTING RANGE--
NOW I HAVE MACHINE G
HO-HO-HO
--FLIPPED A SEMI TRUCK! NO FEELING LIKE IT, YOU NEED TO TRY--
--A GUN COULD BEAT A BOOK IN A FIGHT, NO QUESTION!
HALLOW
I SEE WHAT YOU MEAN.
ALSO, IT WAS WEIRD WE WERE OPEN FOR SO MANY HOLIDAYS.

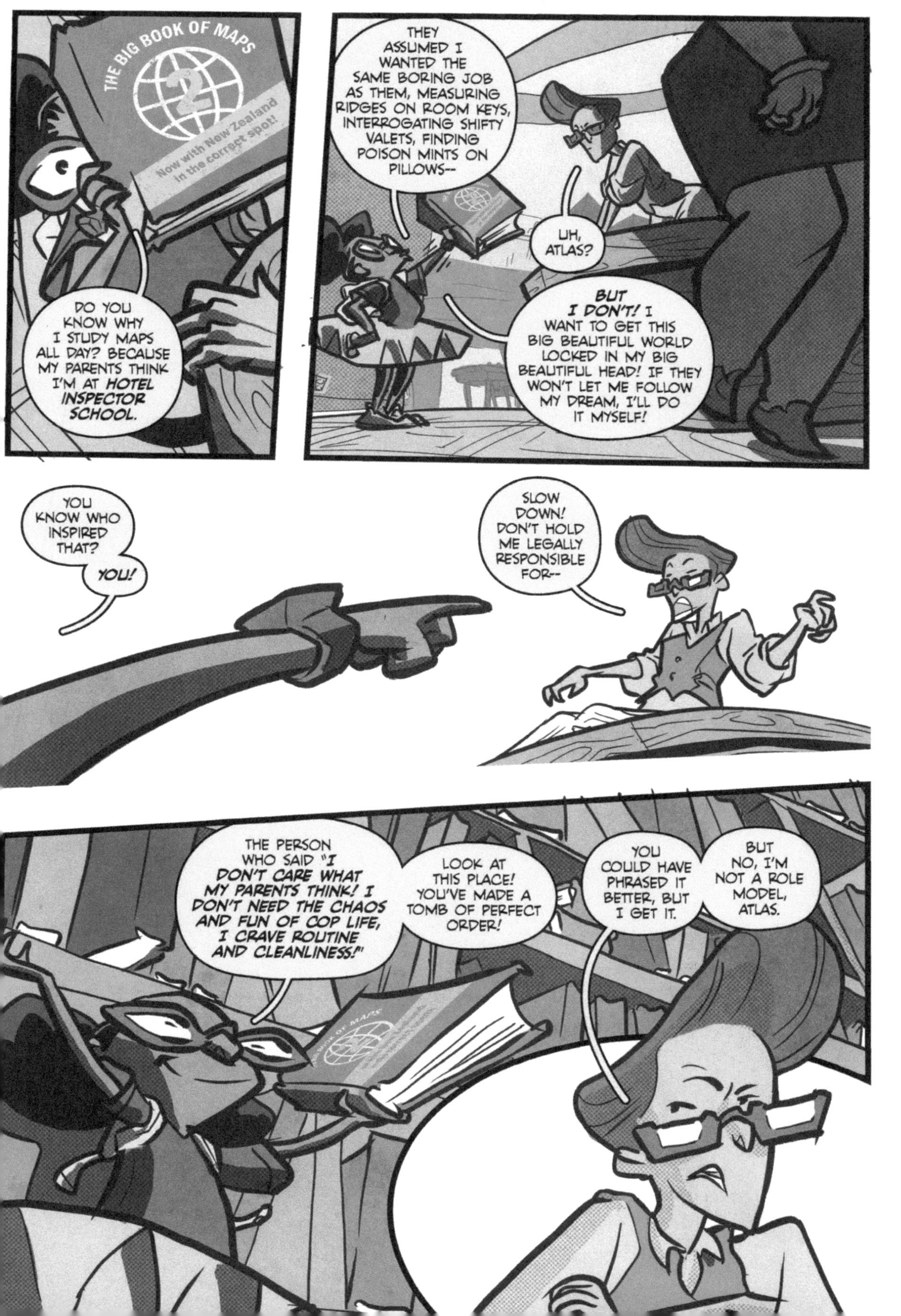
THE BIG BOOK OF MAPS
2
Now with New Zealand in the correct spot!
DO YOU KNOW WHY I STUDY MAPS ALL DAY? BECAUSE MY PARENTS THINK I'M AT HOTEL INSPECTOR SCHOOL.
THEY ASSUMED I WANTED THE SAME BORING JOB AS THEM, MEASURING RIDGES ON ROOM KEYS, INTERROGATING SHIFTY VALETS, FINDING POISON MINTS ON PILLOWS--
UH, ATLAS?
BUT I DON'T! I WANT TO GET THIS BIG BEAUTIFUL WORLD LOCKED IN MY BIG BEAUTIFUL HEAD! IF THEY WON'T LET ME FOLLOW MY DREAM, I'LL DO IT MYSELF!
YOU KNOW WHO INSPIRED THAT?
YOU!
SLOW DOWN! DON'T HOLD ME LEGALLY RESPONSIBLE FOR--
THE PERSON WHO SAID "I DON'T CARE WHAT MY PARENTS THINK! I DON'T NEED THE CHAOS AND FUN OF COP LIFE, I CRAVE ROUTINE AND CLEANLINESS!"
LOOK AT THIS PLACE! YOU'VE MADE A TOMB OF PERFECT ORDER!
YOU COULD HAVE PHRASED IT BETTER, BUT I GET IT.
BUT NO, I'M NOT A ROLE MODEL, ATLAS.

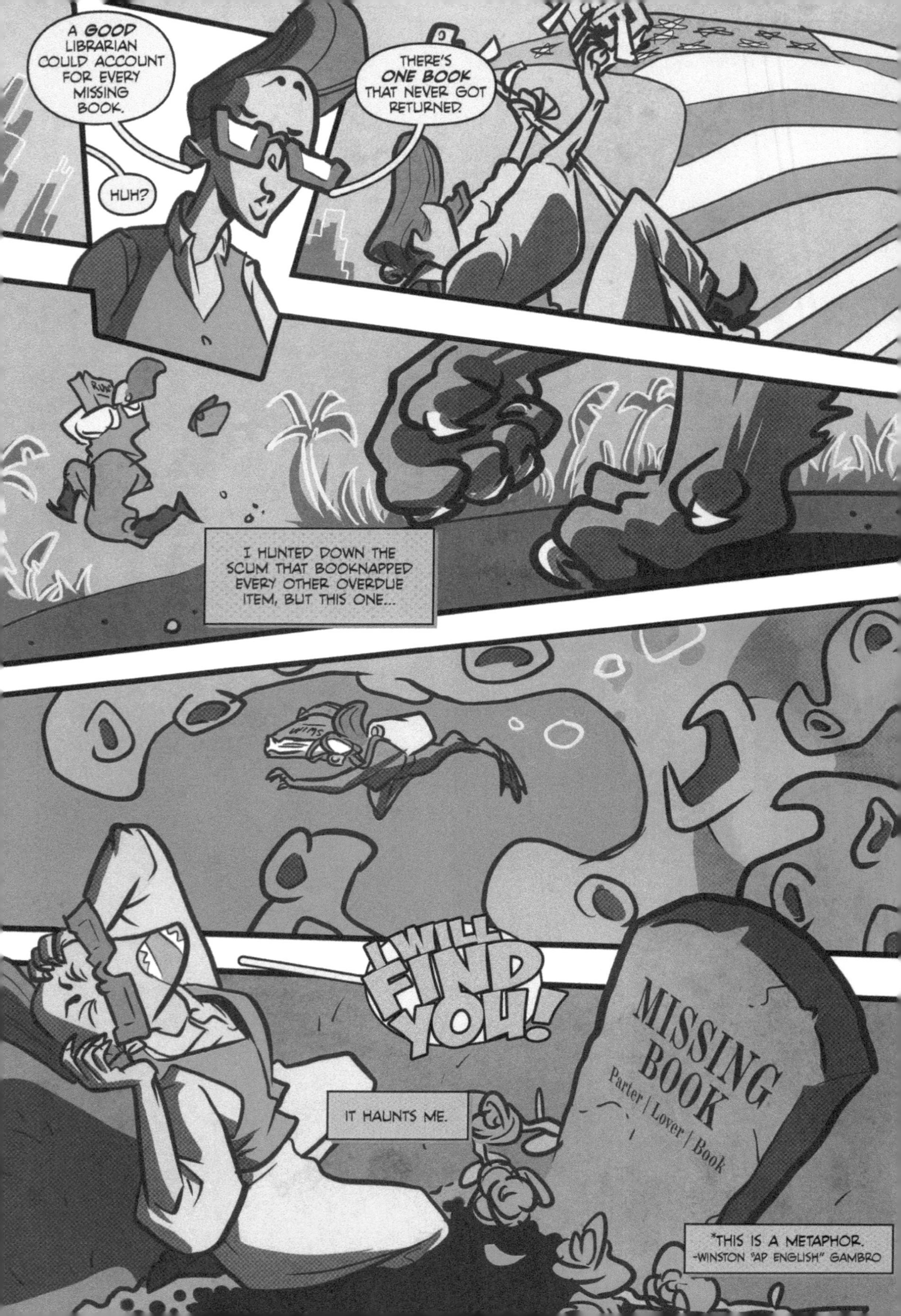
A GOOD LIBRARIAN COULD ACCOUNT FOR EVERY MISSING BOOK.
HUH?
THERE'S ONE BOOK THAT NEVER GOT RETURNED.
I HUNTED DOWN THE SCUM THAT BOOKNAPPED EVERY OTHER OVERDUE ITEM, BUT THIS ONE...
I WILL FIND YOU!
IT HAUNTS ME.
MISSING BOOK
Parter / Lover / Book
*THIS IS A METAPHOR.
-WINSTON "AP ENGLISH" GAMBRO

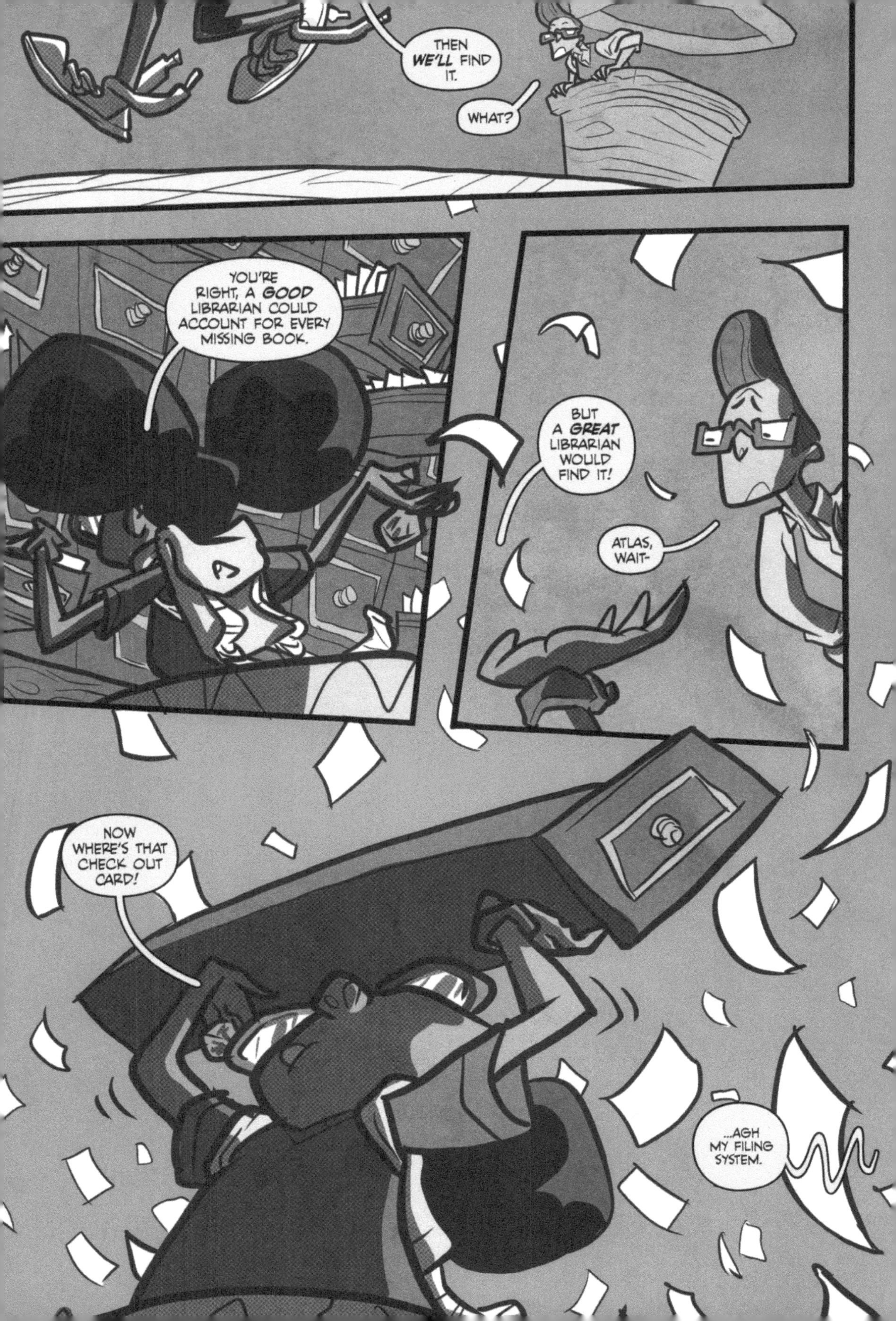
THEN WE'LL FIND IT.
WHAT?
YOU'RE RIGHT, A GOOD LIBRARIAN COULD ACCOUNT FOR EVERY MISSING BOOK.
BUT A GREAT LIBRARIAN WOULD FIND IT!
ATLAS, WAIT-
NOW WHERE'S THAT CHECK OUT CARD!
...AGH MY FILING SYSTEM.

CHAPTER FIVE: BOOKING FOR TROUBLE

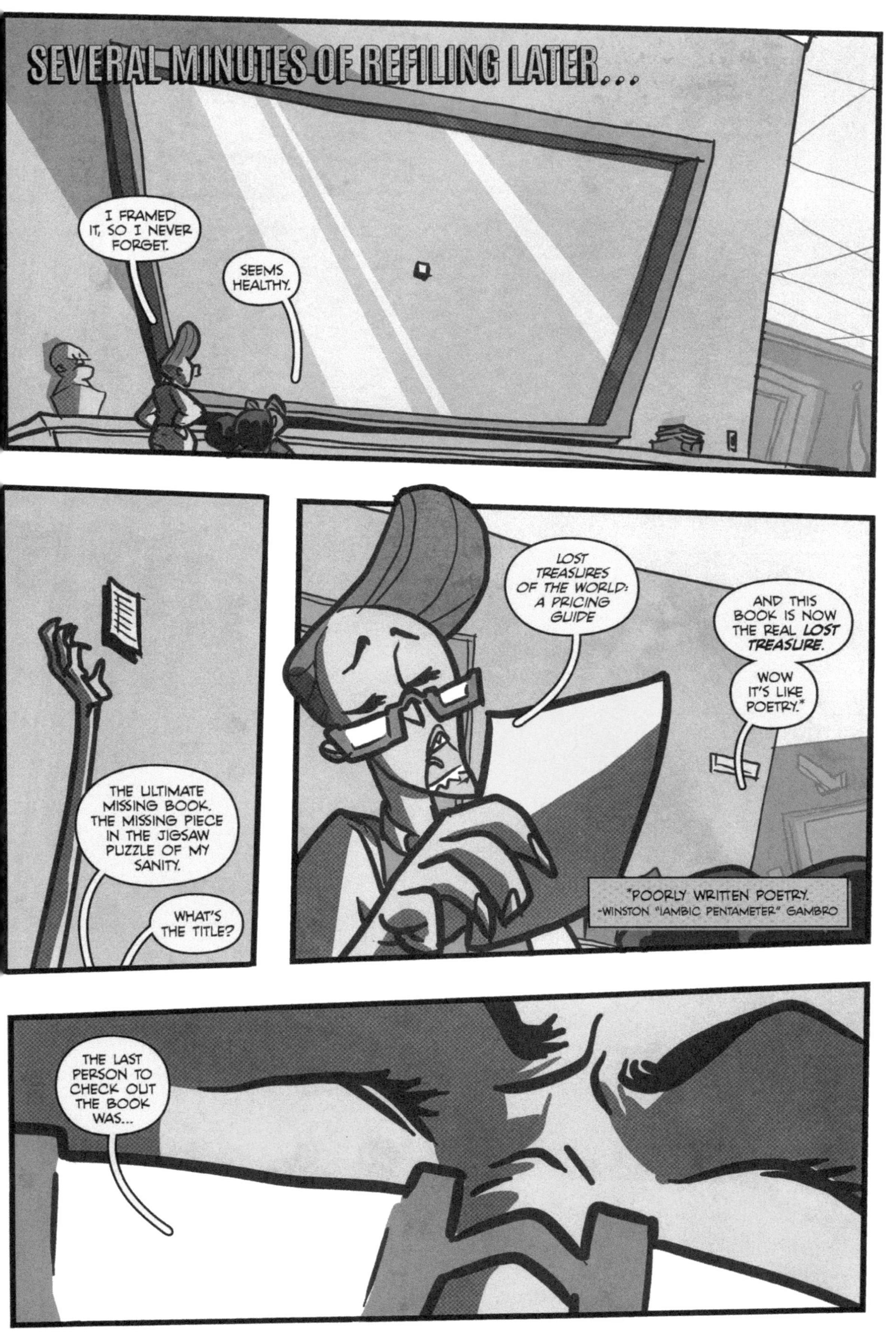
SEVERAL MINUTES OF REFILING LATER...
I FRAMED IT, SO I NEVER FORGET.
SEEMS HEALTHY.
THE ULTIMATE MISSING BOOK. THE MISSING PIECE IN THE JIGSAW PUZZLE OF MY SANITY.
WHAT'S THE TITLE?
LOST TREASURES OF THE WORLD: A PRICING GUIDE
AND THIS BOOK IS NOW THE REAL LOST TREASURE.
WOW IT'S LIKE POETRY.*
*POORLY WRITTEN POETRY. -WINSTON "IAMBIC PENTAMETER" GAMBRO
THE LAST PERSON TO CHECK OUT THE BOOK WAS...

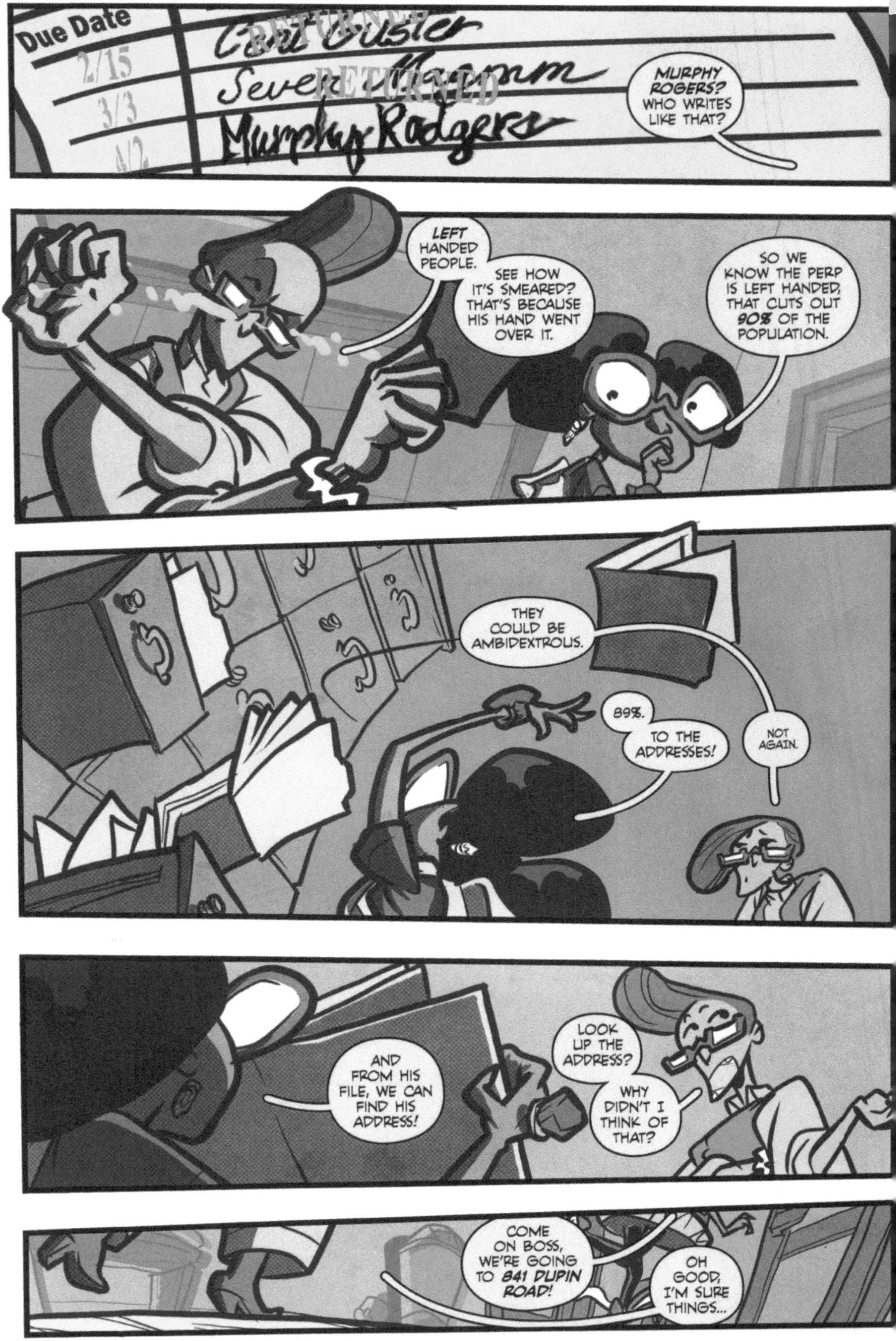
Due Date
2/15
3/3
4/2
RETURNED
RETURNED
Murphy Rodgers
MURPHY ROGERS? WHO WRITES LIKE THAT?
LEFT HANDED PEOPLE.
SEE HOW IT'S SMEARED? THAT'S BECAUSE HIS HAND WENT OVER IT.
SO WE KNOW THE PERP IS LEFT HANDED, THAT CUTS OUT 90% OF THE POPULATION.
THEY COULD BE AMBIDEXTROUS.
89%.
TO THE ADDRESSES!
NOT AGAIN.
AND FROM HIS FILE, WE CAN FIND HIS ADDRESS!
LOOK UP THE ADDRESS?
WHY DIDN'T I THINK OF THAT?
COME ON BOSS, WE'RE GOING TO 841 DUPIN ROAD!
OH GOOD, I'M SURE THINGS...

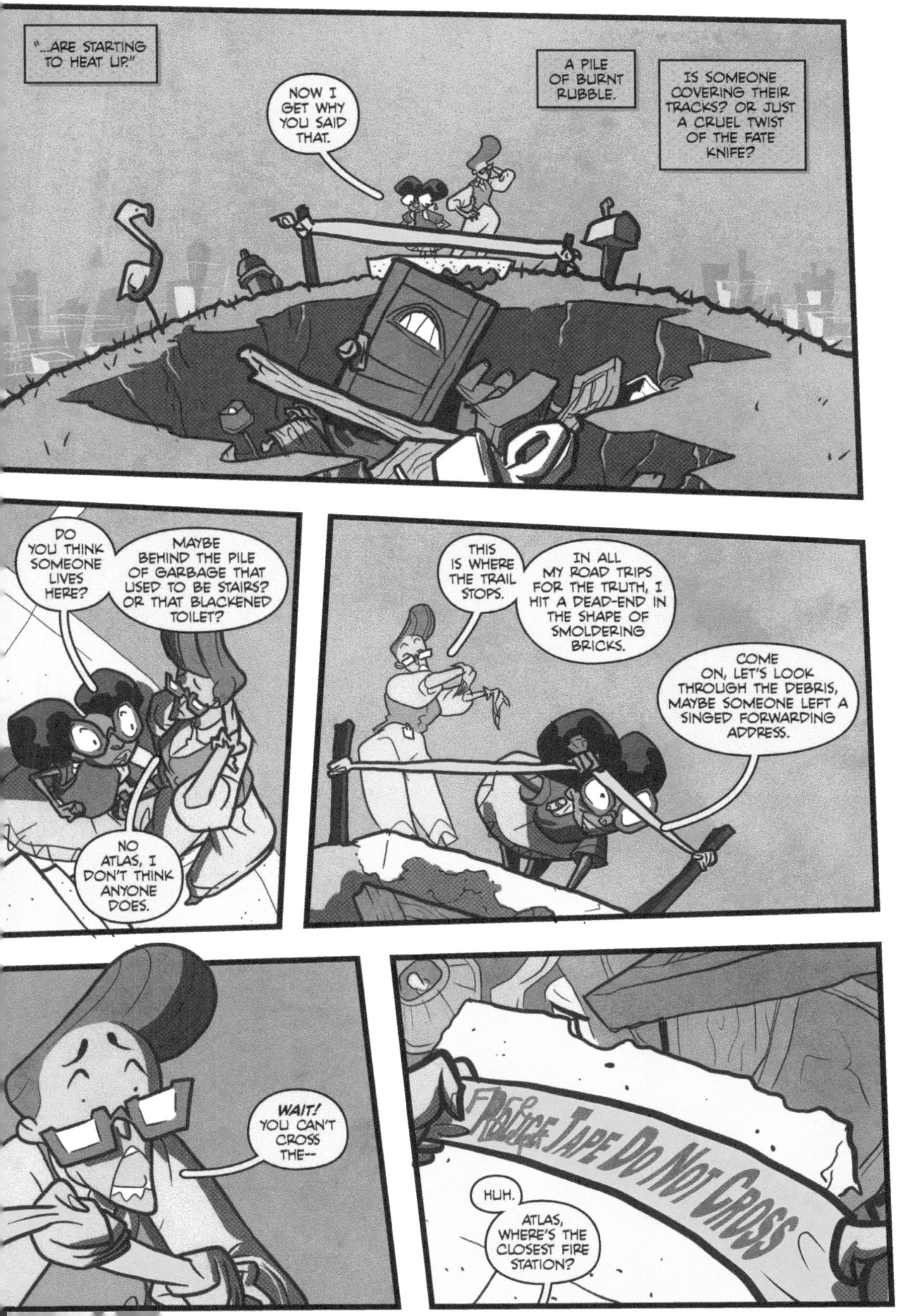
"...ARE STARTING TO HEAT UP."
NOW I GET WHY YOU SAID THAT.
A PILE OF BURNT RUBBLE.
IS SOMEONE COVERING THEIR TRACKS? OR JUST A CRUEL TWIST OF THE FATE KNIFE?
DO YOU THINK SOMEONE LIVES HERE?
MAYBE BEHIND THE PILE OF GARBAGE THAT USED TO BE STAIRS? OR THAT BLACKENED TOILET?
NO ATLAS, I DON'T THINK ANYONE DOES.
THIS IS WHERE THE TRAIL STOPS.
IN ALL MY ROAD TRIPS FOR THE TRUTH, I HIT A DEAD-END IN THE SHAPE OF SMOLDERING BRICKS.
COME ON, LET'S LOOK THROUGH THE DEBRIS, MAYBE SOMEONE LEFT A SINGED FORWARDING ADDRESS.
WAIT! YOU CAN'T CROSS THE--
FIRE
POLICE TAPE DO NOT CROSS
HUH.
ATLAS, WHERE'S THE CLOSEST FIRE STATION?

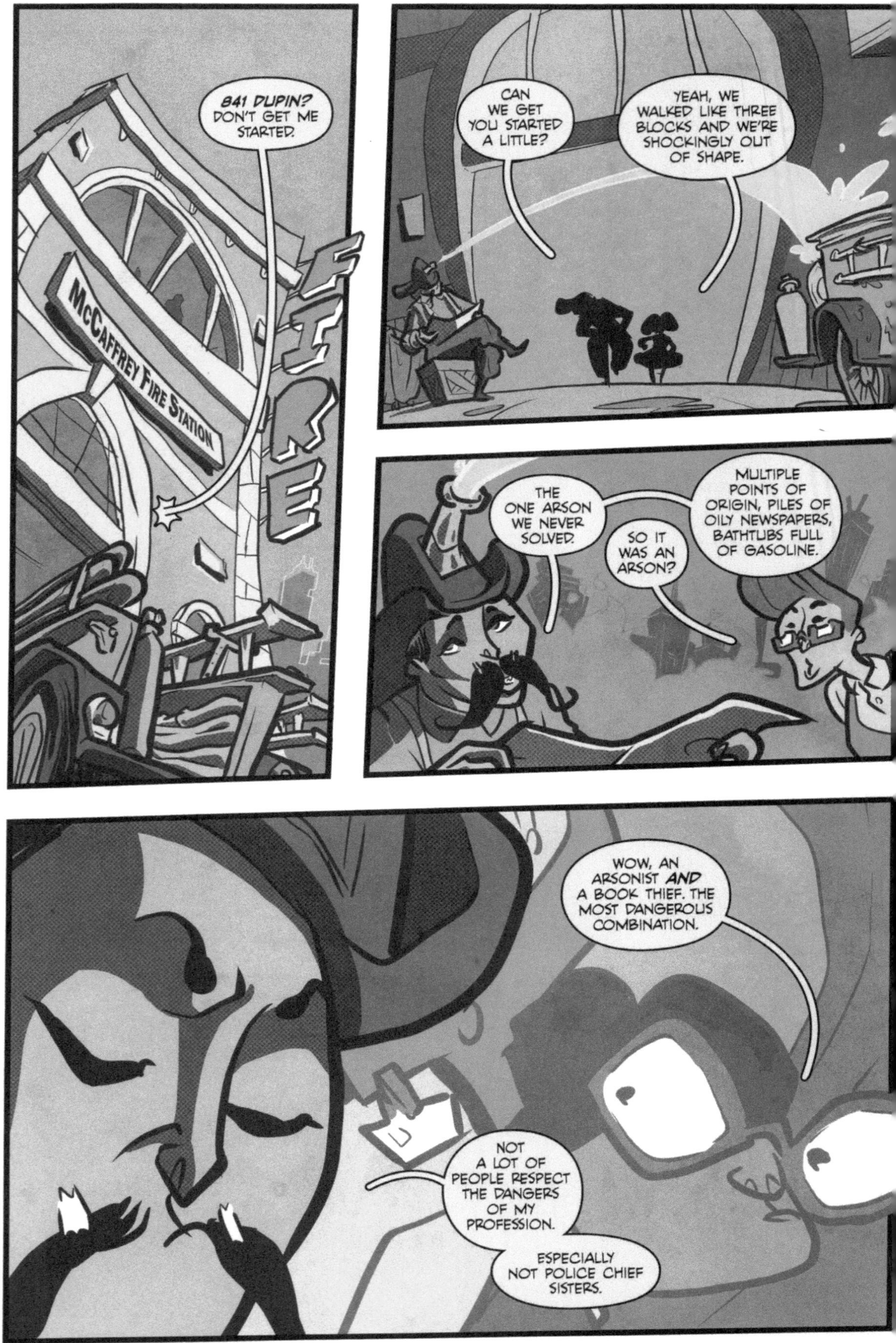

841 DUPIN? DON'T GET ME STARTED.
McCAFFREY FIRE STATION
FIRE
CAN WE GET YOU STARTED A LITTLE?
YEAH, WE WALKED LIKE THREE BLOCKS AND WE'RE SHOCKINGLY OUT OF SHAPE.
THE ONE ARSON WE NEVER SOLVED.
MULTIPLE POINTS OF ORIGIN, PILES OF OILY NEWSPAPERS, BATHTUBS FULL OF GASOLINE.
SO IT WAS AN ARSON?
WOW, AN ARSONIST AND A BOOK THIEF. THE MOST DANGEROUS COMBINATION.
NOT A LOT OF PEOPLE RESPECT THE DANGERS OF MY PROFESSION.
ESPECIALLY NOT POLICE CHIEF SISTERS.

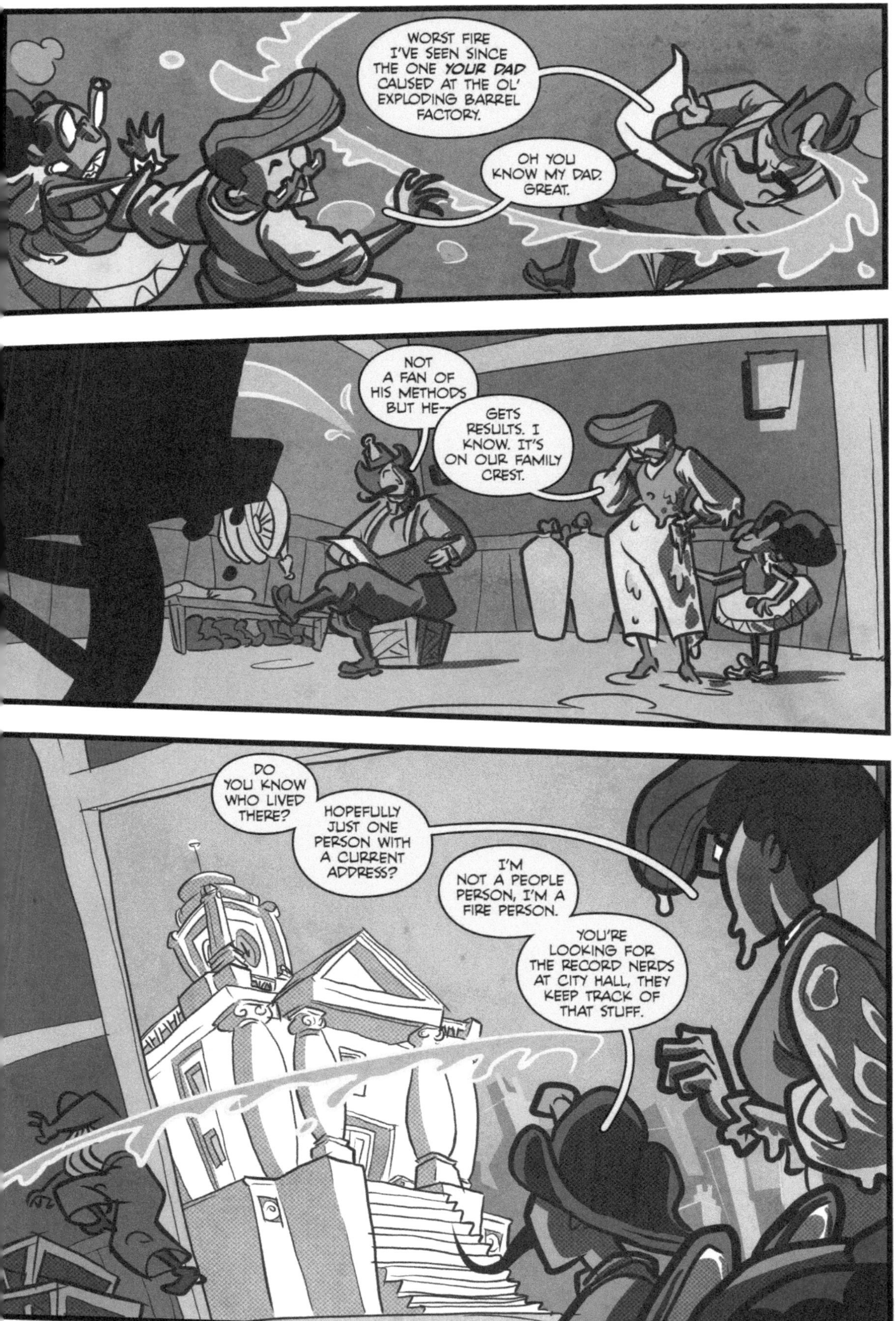
WORST FIRE I'VE SEEN SINCE THE ONE YOUR DAD CAUSED AT THE OL' EXPLODING BARREL FACTORY.
OH YOU KNOW MY DAD. GREAT.
NOT A FAN OF HIS METHODS BUT HE--
GETS RESULTS. I KNOW. IT'S ON OUR FAMILY CREST.
DO YOU KNOW WHO LIVED THERE?
HOPEFULLY JUST ONE PERSON WITH A CURRENT ADDRESS?
I'M NOT A PEOPLE PERSON, I'M A FIRE PERSON.
YOU'RE LOOKING FOR THE RECORD NERDS AT CITY HALL, THEY KEEP TRACK OF THAT STUFF.

Chapter Six:
Planning for
TROUBLE

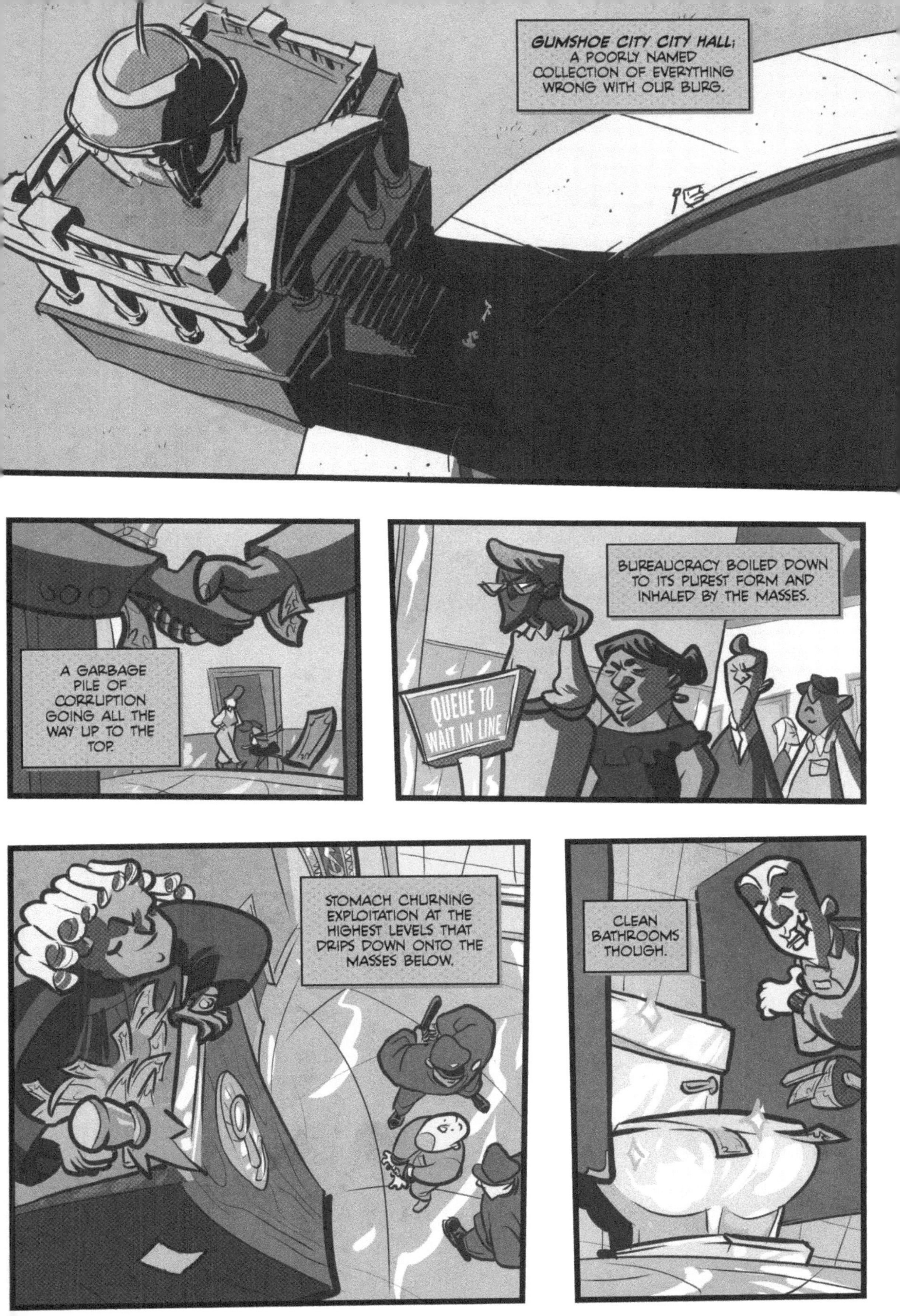
GUMSHOE CITY CITY HALL; A POORLY NAMED COLLECTION OF EVERYTHING WRONG WITH OUR BURG.
A GARBAGE PILE OF CORRUPTION GOING ALL THE WAY UP TO THE TOP.
BUREAUCRACY BOILED DOWN TO ITS PUREST FORM AND INHALED BY THE MASSES.
QUEUE TO WAIT IN LINE
STOMACH CHURNING EXPLOITATION AT THE HIGHEST LEVELS THAT DRIPS DOWN ONTO THE MASSES BELOW.
CLEAN BATHROOMS THOUGH.

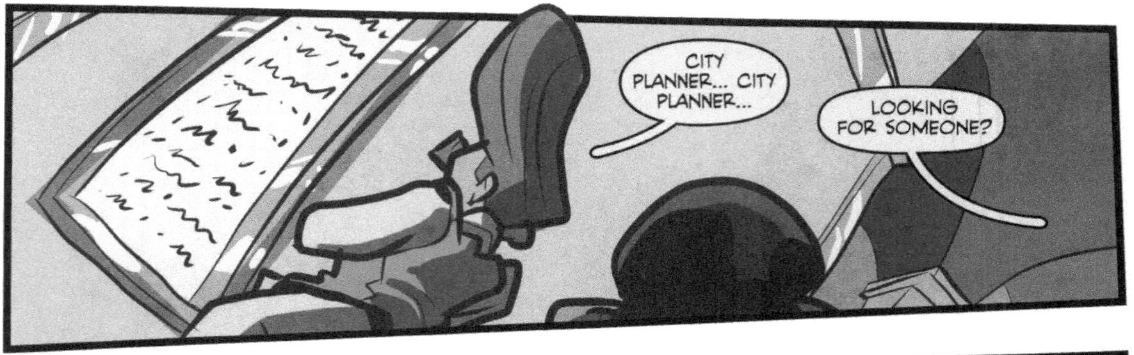
CITY PLANNER... CITY PLANNER...
LOOKING FOR SOMEONE?

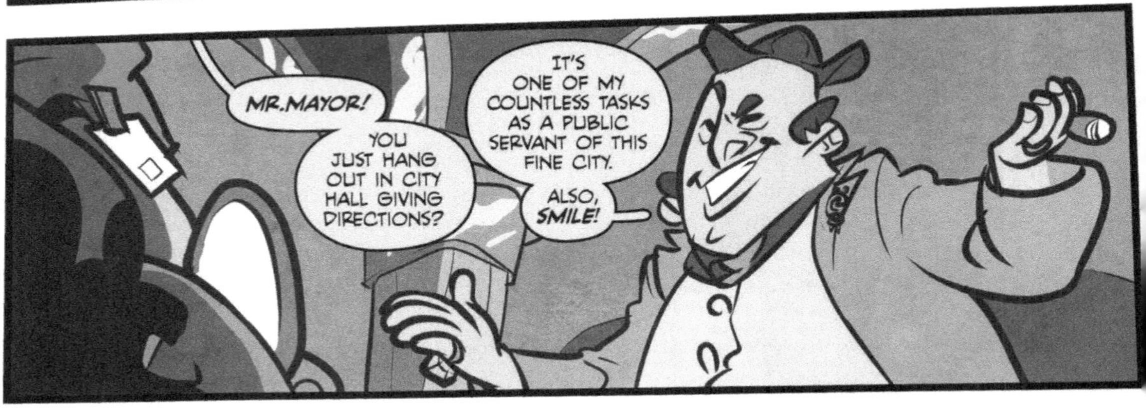
MR.MAYOR!
YOU JUST HANG OUT IN CITY HALL GIVING DIRECTIONS?
IT'S ONE OF MY COUNTLESS TASKS AS A PUBLIC SERVANT OF THIS FINE CITY.
ALSO, SMILE!

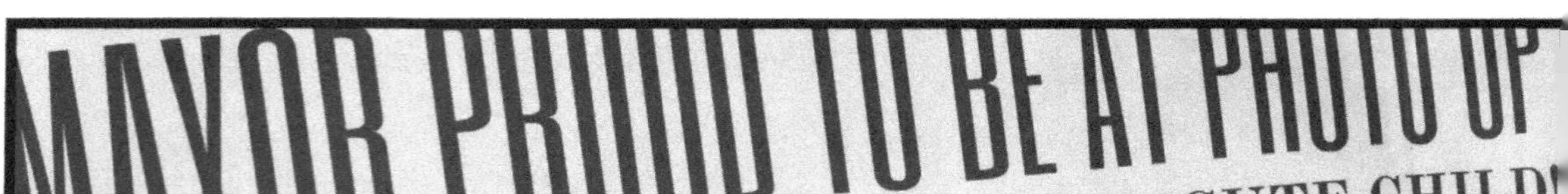
MAYOR PROUD TO BE AT PHOTO OP
WITH FEMALE VOTER AND CUTE CHILD!

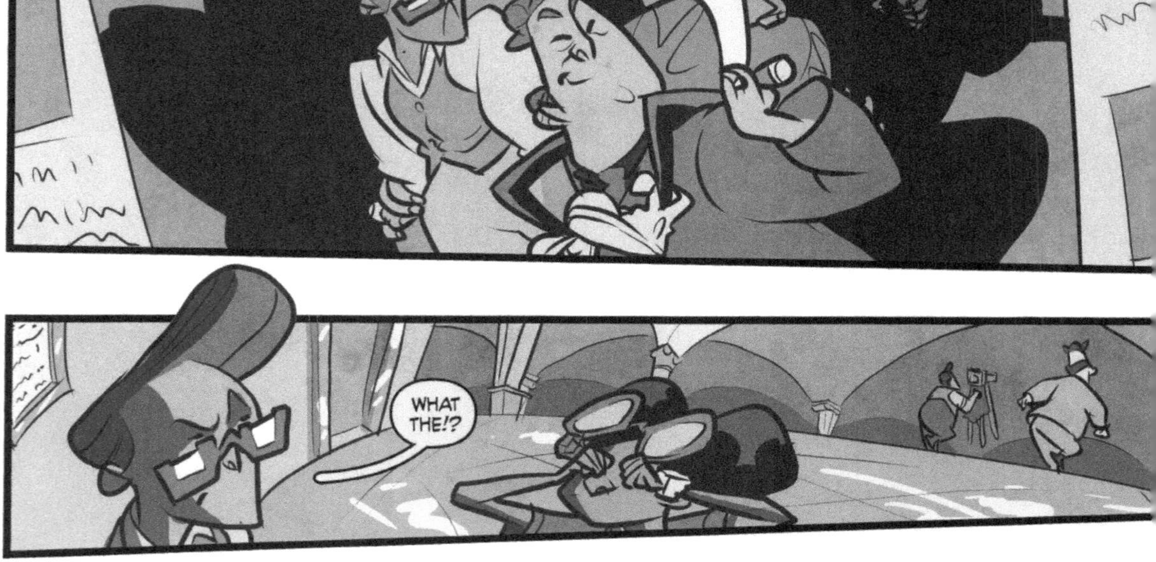
WHAT THE!?

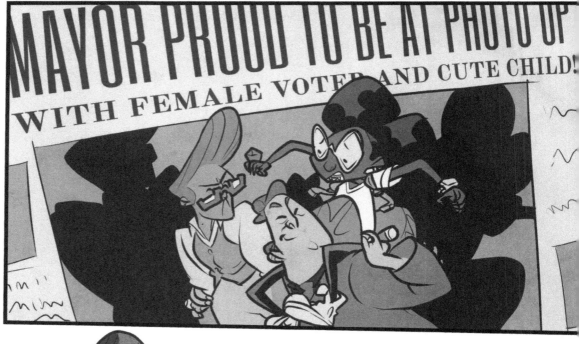

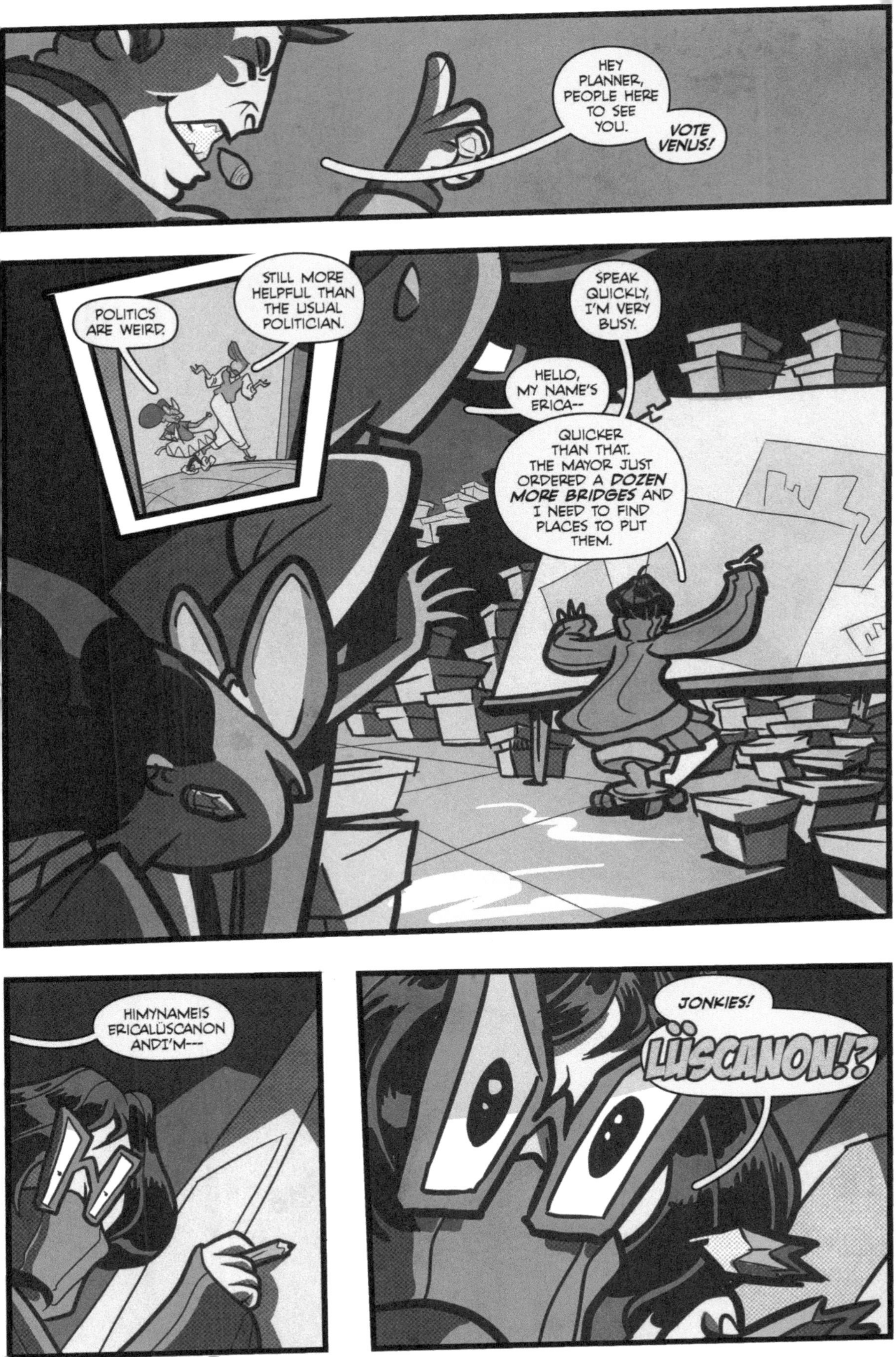
HEY PLANNER, PEOPLE HERE TO SEE YOU.
VOTE VENUS!
POLITICS ARE WEIRD.
STILL MORE HELPFUL THAN THE USUAL POLITICIAN.
SPEAK QUICKLY, I'M VERY BUSY.
HELLO, MY NAME'S ERICA--
QUICKER THAN THAT. THE MAYOR JUST ORDERED A DOZEN MORE BRIDGES AND I NEED TO FIND PLACES TO PUT THEM.
HIMYNAMEIS ERICALÜSCANON ANDI'M---
JONKIES!
LÜSCANON!?

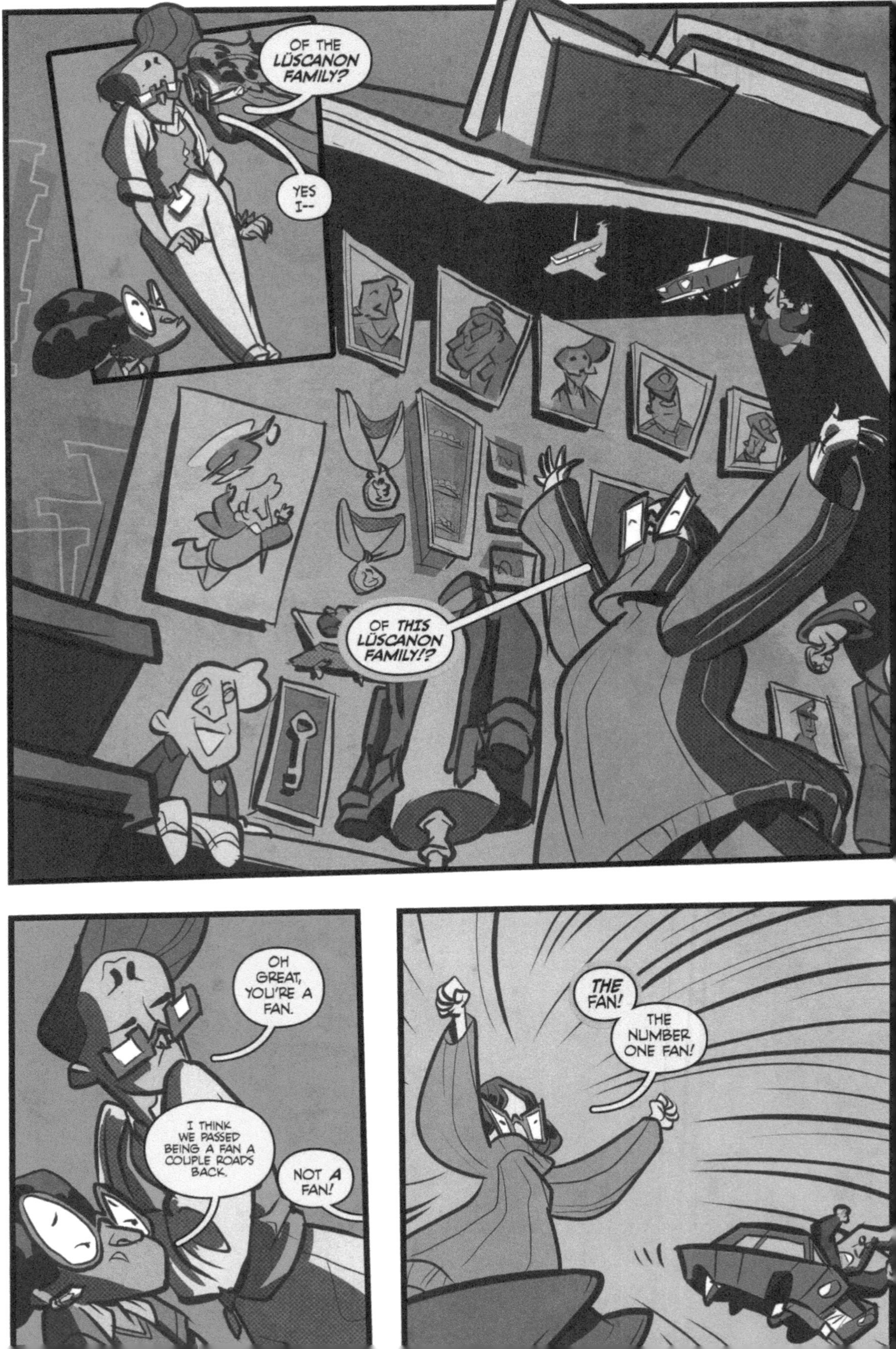

OF THE LÜSCANON FAMILY?
YES I--
OF THIS LÜSCANON FAMILY!?
OH GREAT, YOU'RE A FAN.
I THINK WE PASSED BEING A FAN A COUPLE ROADS BACK.
NOT A FAN!
THE FAN!
THE NUMBER ONE FAN!

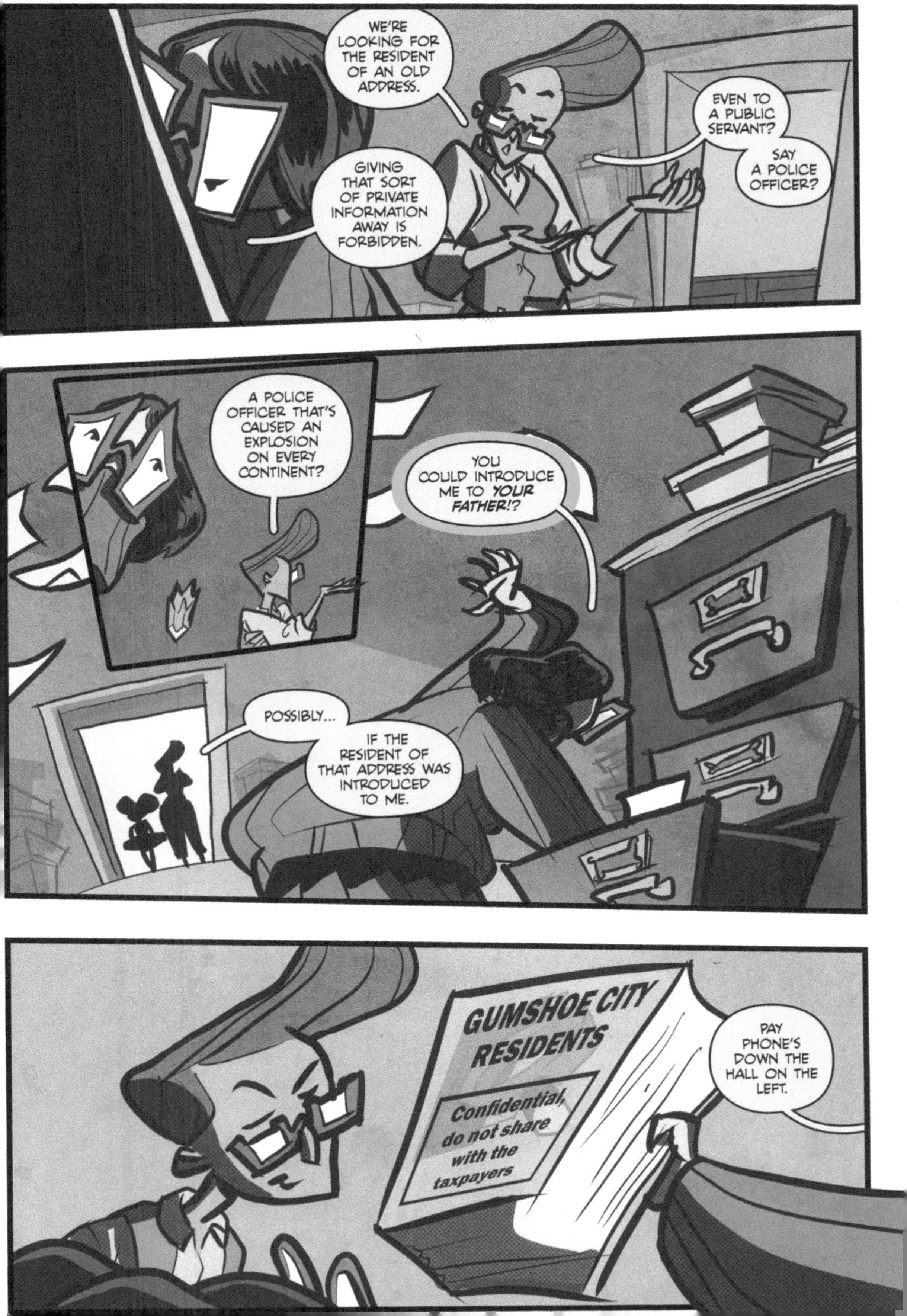
WE'RE LOOKING FOR THE RESIDENT OF AN OLD ADDRESS.
GIVING THAT SORT OF PRIVATE INFORMATION AWAY IS FORBIDDEN.
EVEN TO A PUBLIC SERVANT?
SAY A POLICE OFFICER?
A POLICE OFFICER THAT'S CAUSED AN EXPLOSION ON EVERY CONTINENT?
YOU COULD INTRODUCE ME TO YOUR FATHER!?
POSSIBLY...
IF THE RESIDENT OF THAT ADDRESS WAS INTRODUCED TO ME.
GUMSHOE CITY RESIDENTS
Confidential, do not share with the taxpayers
PAY PHONE'S DOWN THE HALL ON THE LEFT.

CHAPTER SEVEN:
Reunions: Family & Otherwise

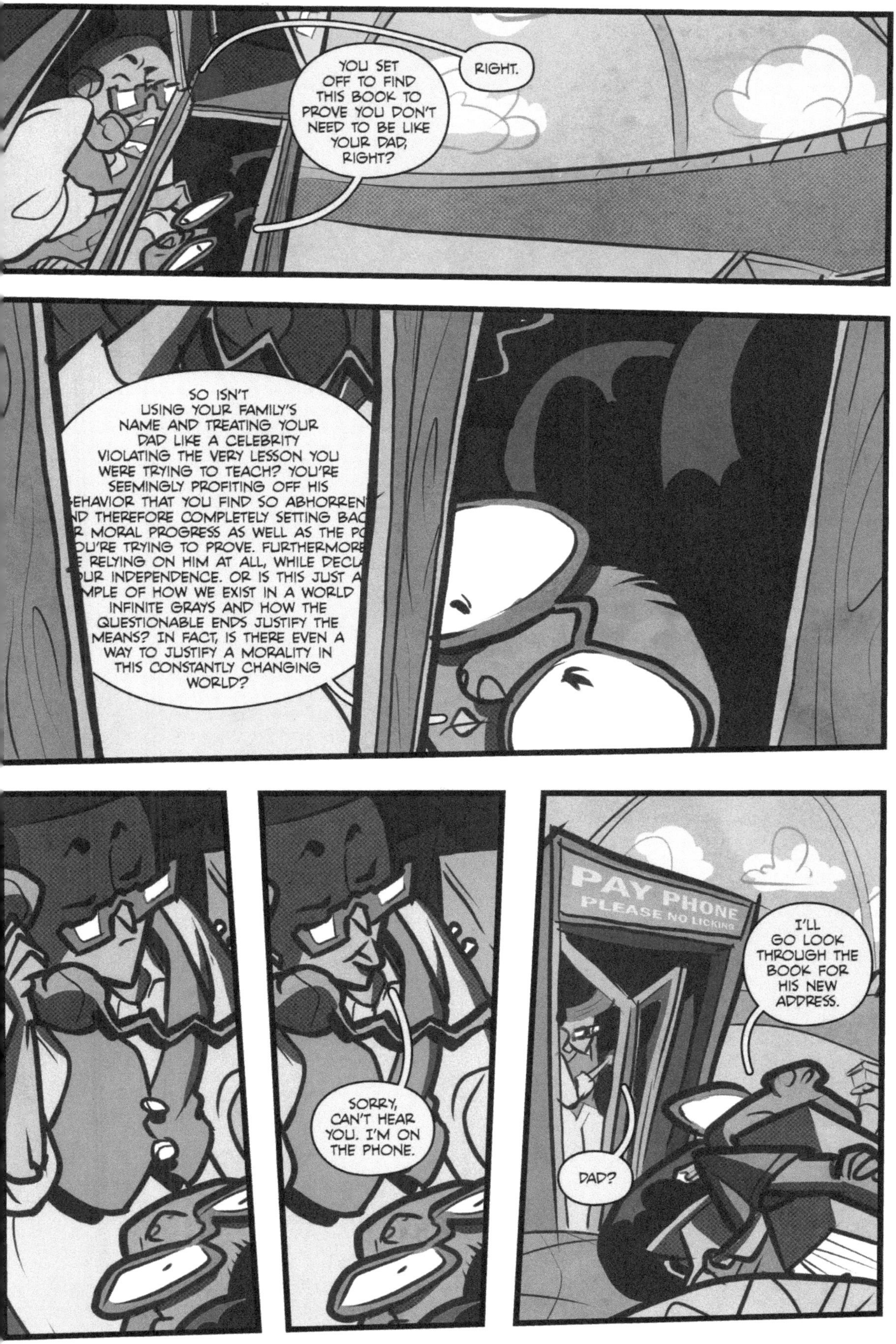
YOU SET OFF TO FIND THIS BOOK TO PROVE YOU DON'T NEED TO BE LIKE YOUR DAD, RIGHT?
RIGHT.
SO ISN'T USING YOUR FAMILY'S NAME AND TREATING YOUR DAD LIKE A CELEBRITY VIOLATING THE VERY LESSON YOU WERE TRYING TO TEACH? YOU'RE SEEMINGLY PROFITING OFF HIS EHAVIOR THAT YOU FIND SO ABHORREN ND THEREFORE COMPLETELY SETTING BAC R MORAL PROGRESS AS WELL AS THE PO OU'RE TRYING TO PROVE. FURTHERMORE E RELYING ON HIM AT ALL, WHILE DECLA OUR INDEPENDENCE. OR IS THIS JUST A MPLE OF HOW WE EXIST IN A WORLD INFINITE GRAYS AND HOW THE QUESTIONABLE ENDS JUSTIFY THE MEANS? IN FACT, IS THERE EVEN A WAY TO JUSTIFY A MORALITY IN THIS CONSTANTLY CHANGING WORLD?
SORRY, CAN'T HEAR YOU. I'M ON THE PHONE.
PAY PHONE
PLEASE NO LICKING
I'LL GO LOOK THROUGH THE BOOK FOR HIS NEW ADDRESS.
DAD?

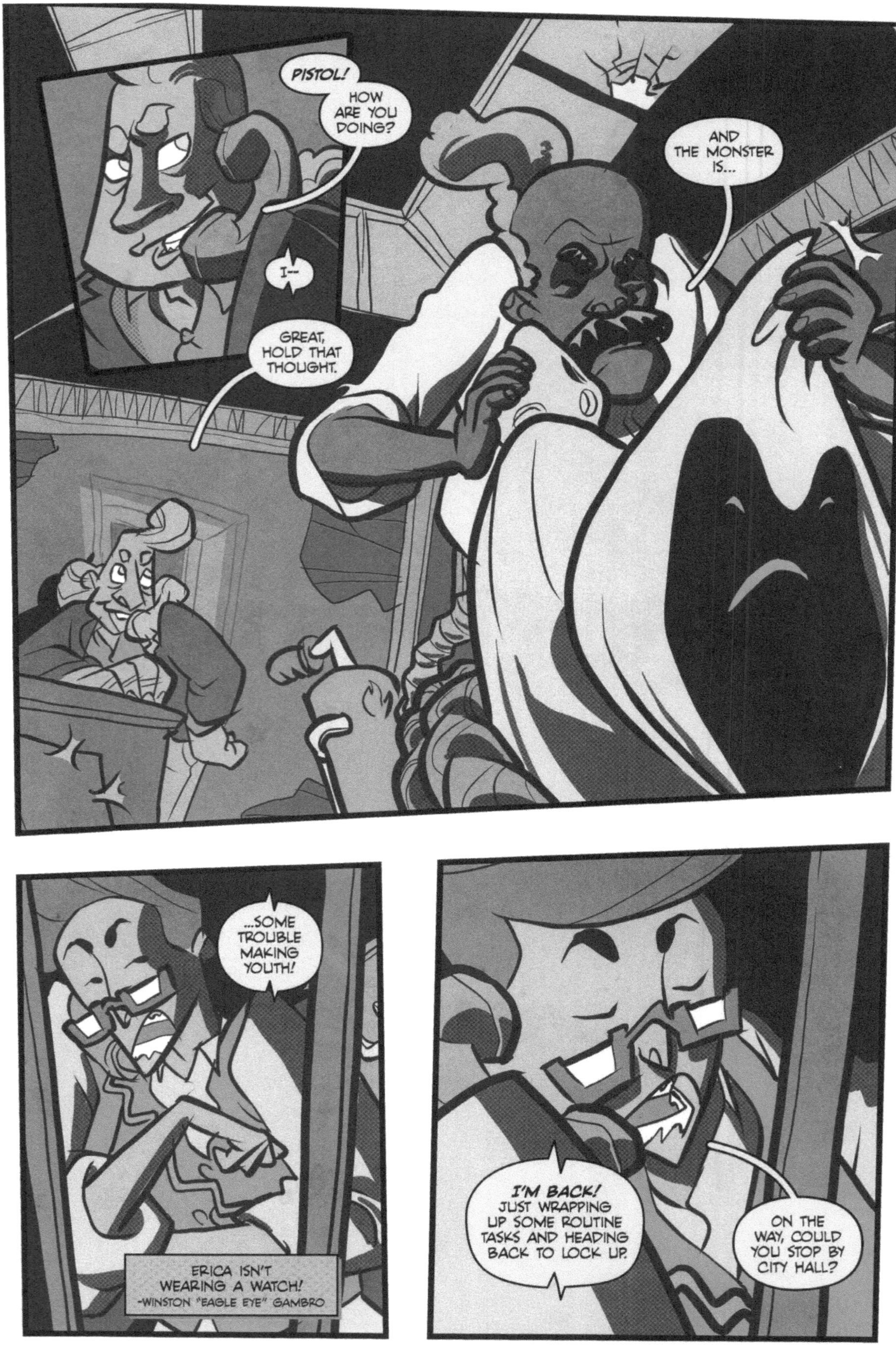
PISTOL! HOW ARE YOU DOING?
I--
GREAT, HOLD THAT THOUGHT.
AND THE MONSTER IS...
...SOME TROUBLE MAKING YOUTH!
ERICA ISN'T WEARING A WATCH! -WINSTON "EAGLE EYE" GAMBRO
I'M BACK! JUST WRAPPING UP SOME ROUTINE TASKS AND HEADING BACK TO LOCK UP.
ON THE WAY, COULD YOU STOP BY CITY HALL?

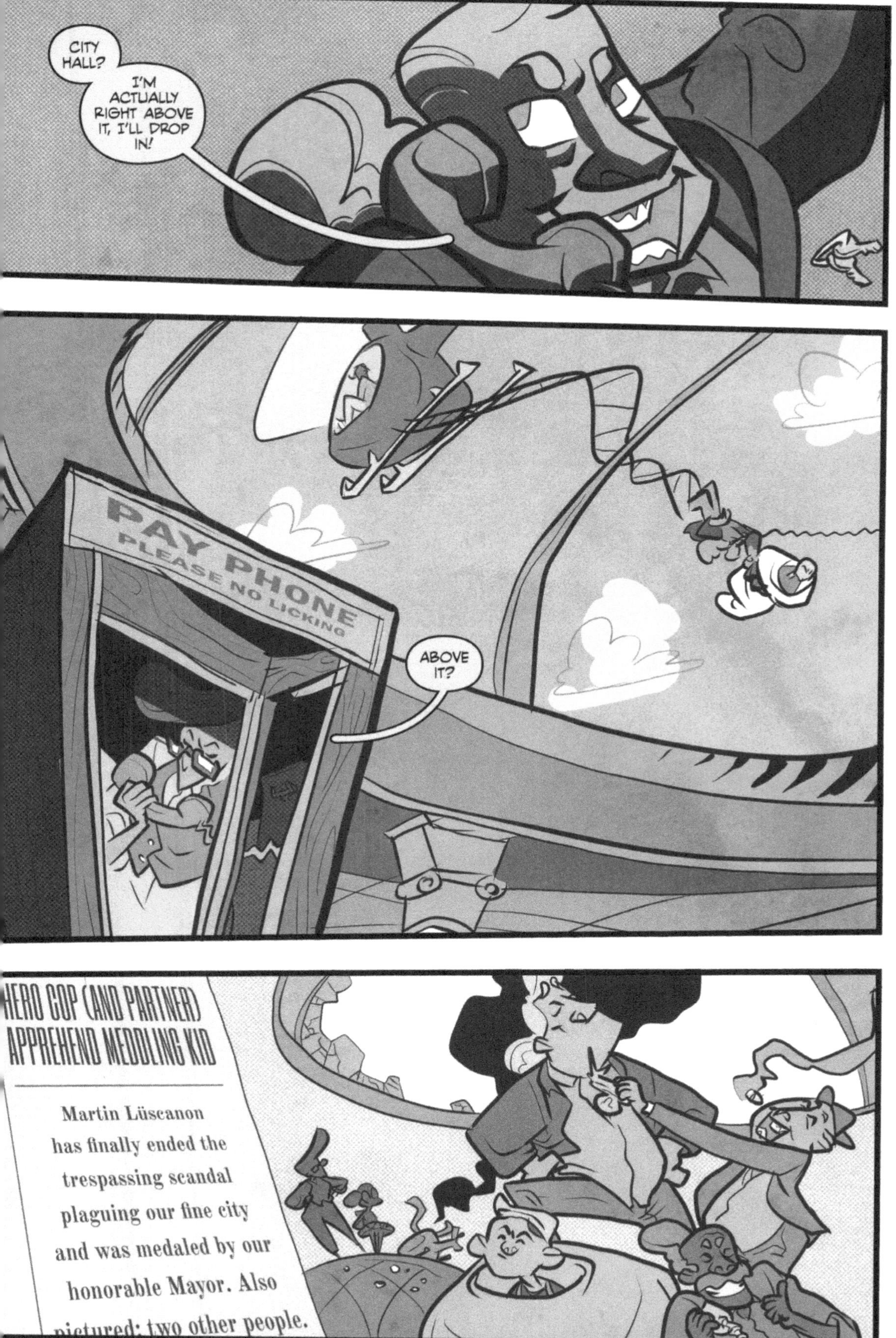
CITY HALL?
I'M ACTUALLY RIGHT ABOVE IT, I'LL DROP IN!
PAY PHONE
PLEASE NO LICKING
ABOVE IT?
HERO COP (AND PARTNER) APPREHEND MEDDLING KID
Martin Lüscanon has finally ended the trespassing scandal plaguing our fine city and was medaled by our honorable Mayor. Also pictured: two other people.

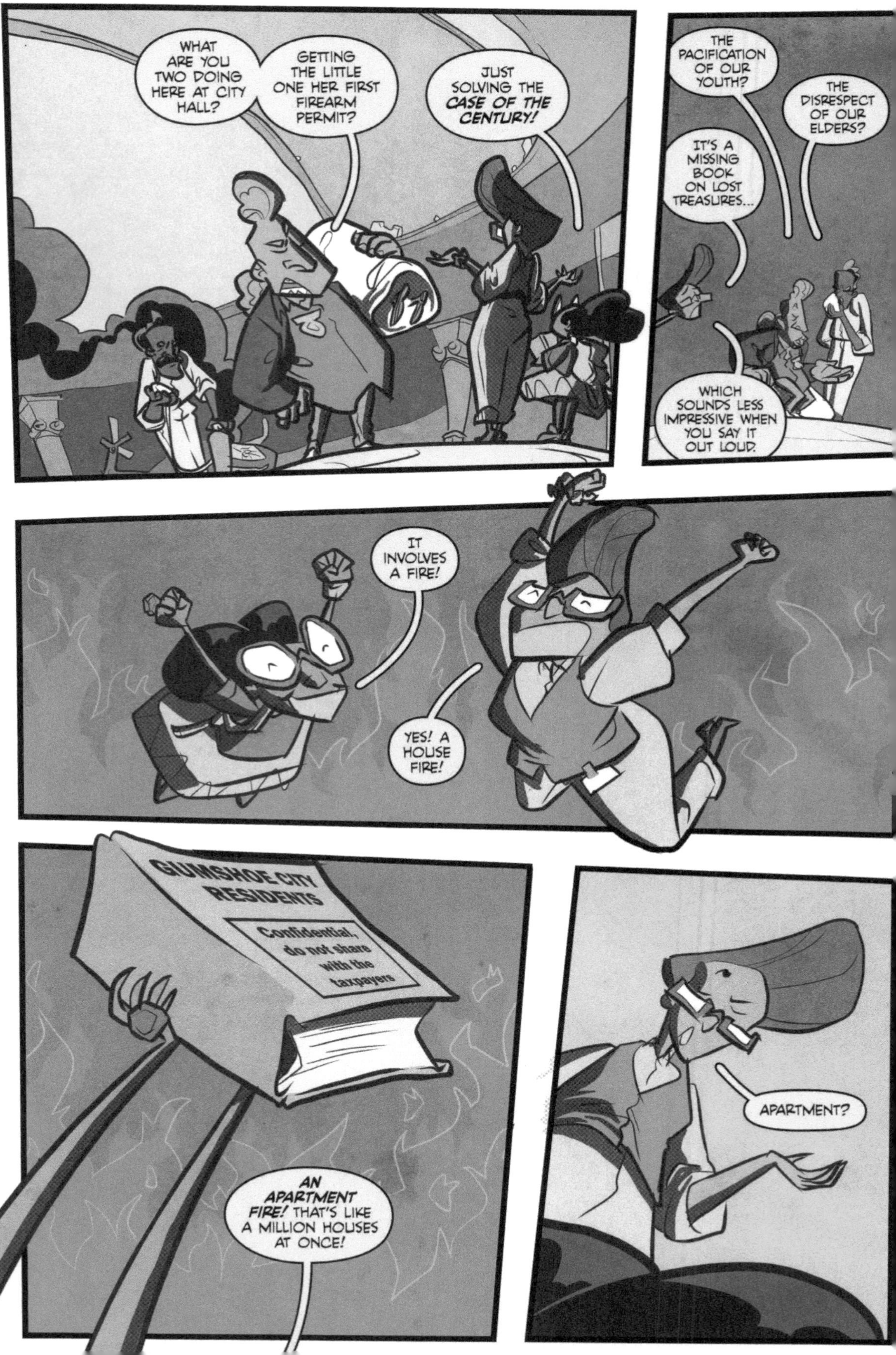
WHAT ARE YOU TWO DOING HERE AT CITY HALL?
GETTING THE LITTLE ONE HER FIRST FIREARM PERMIT?
JUST SOLVING THE ***CASE OF THE CENTURY!***
THE PACIFICATION OF OUR YOUTH?
THE DISRESPECT OF OUR ELDERS?
IT'S A MISSING BOOK ON LOST TREASURES...
WHICH SOUNDS LESS IMPRESSIVE WHEN YOU SAY IT OUT LOUD.
IT INVOLVES A FIRE!
YES! A HOUSE FIRE!
GUMSHOE CITY RESIDENTS
Confidential, do not share with the taxpayers
AN APARTMENT FIRE! THAT'S LIKE A MILLION HOUSES AT ONCE!
APARTMENT?

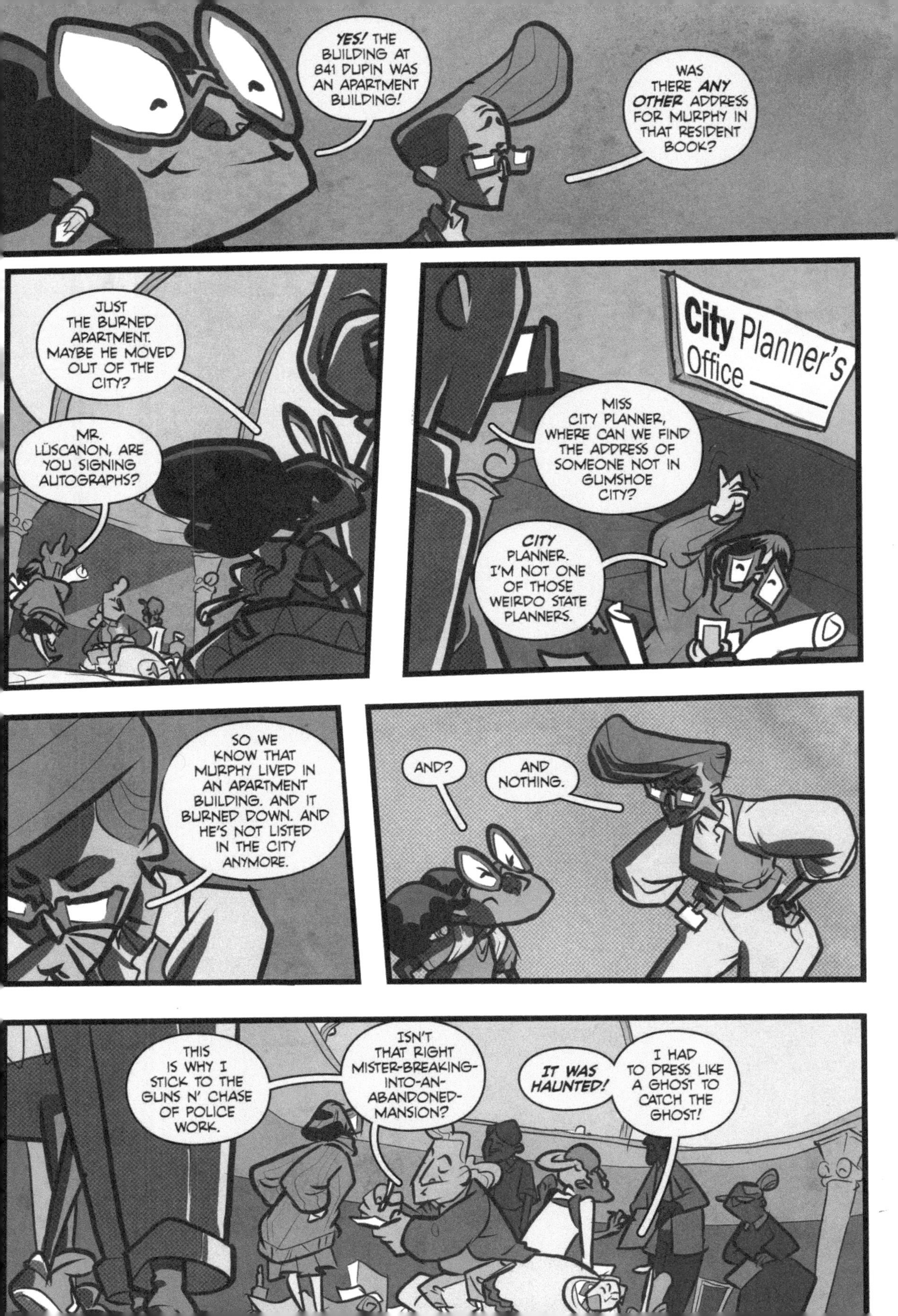
YES! THE BUILDING AT 841 DUPIN WAS AN APARTMENT BUILDING!
WAS THERE ANY OTHER ADDRESS FOR MURPHY IN THAT RESIDENT BOOK?
JUST THE BURNED APARTMENT. MAYBE HE MOVED OUT OF THE CITY?
MR. LÜSCANON, ARE YOU SIGNING AUTOGRAPHS?
City Planner's Office
MISS CITY PLANNER, WHERE CAN WE FIND THE ADDRESS OF SOMEONE NOT IN GUMSHOE CITY?
CITY PLANNER. I'M NOT ONE OF THOSE WEIRDO STATE PLANNERS.
SO WE KNOW THAT MURPHY LIVED IN AN APARTMENT BUILDING. AND IT BURNED DOWN. AND HE'S NOT LISTED IN THE CITY ANYMORE.
AND?
AND NOTHING.
THIS IS WHY I STICK TO THE GUNS N' CHASE OF POLICE WORK.
ISN'T THAT RIGHT MISTER-BREAKING-INTO-AN-ABANDONED-MANSION?
IT WAS HAUNTED!
I HAD TO DRESS LIKE A GHOST TO CATCH THE GHOST!

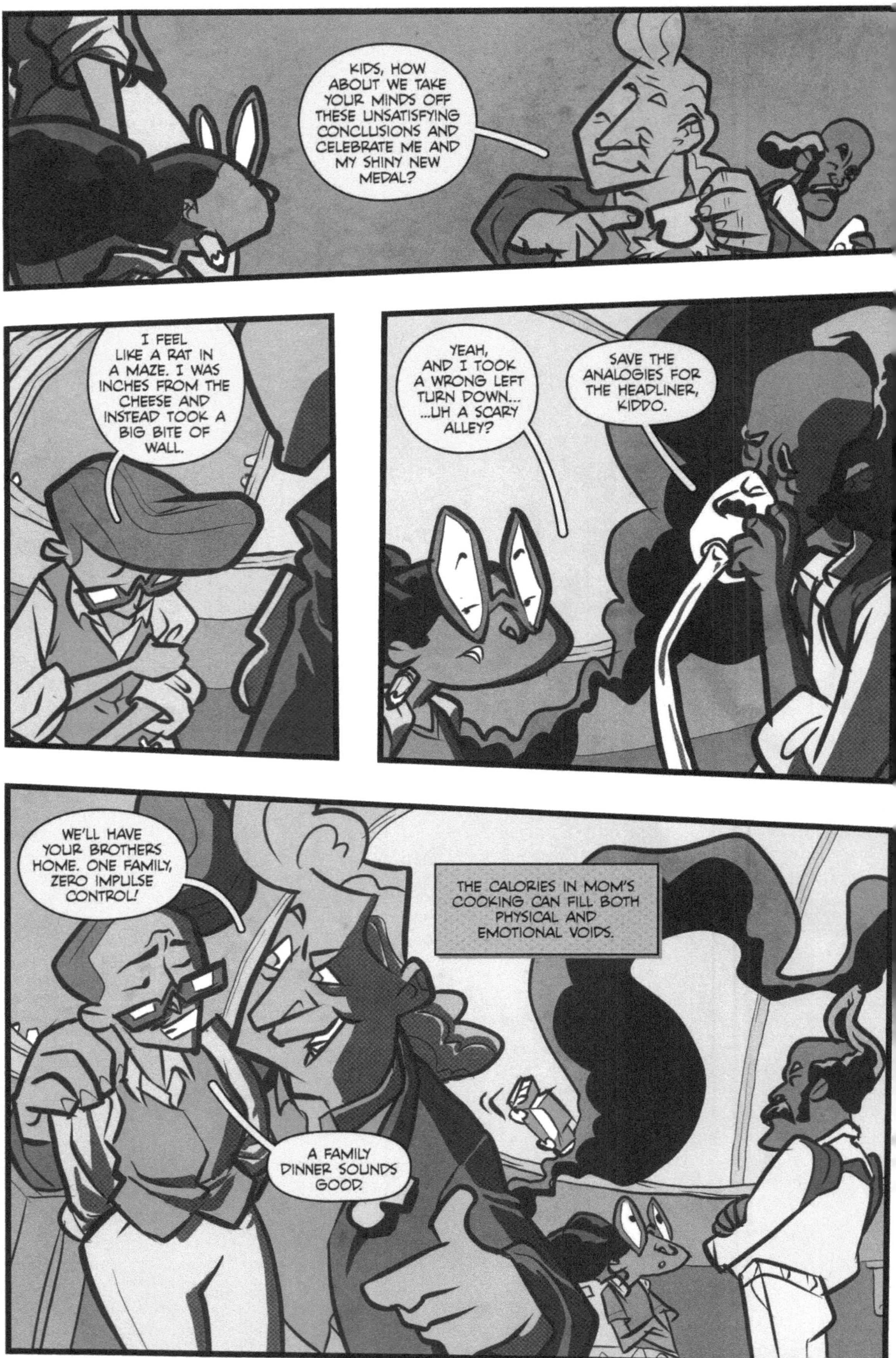
KIDS, HOW ABOUT WE TAKE YOUR MINDS OFF THESE UNSATISFYING CONCLUSIONS AND CELEBRATE ME AND MY SHINY NEW MEDAL?
I FEEL LIKE A RAT IN A MAZE. I WAS INCHES FROM THE CHEESE AND INSTEAD TOOK A BIG BITE OF WALL.
YEAH, AND I TOOK A WRONG LEFT TURN DOWN... ...UH A SCARY ALLEY?
SAVE THE ANALOGIES FOR THE HEADLINER, KIDDO.
WE'LL HAVE YOUR BROTHERS HOME. ONE FAMILY, ZERO IMPULSE CONTROL!
THE CALORIES IN MOM'S COOKING CAN FILL BOTH PHYSICAL AND EMOTIONAL VOIDS.
A FAMILY DINNER SOUNDS GOOD.

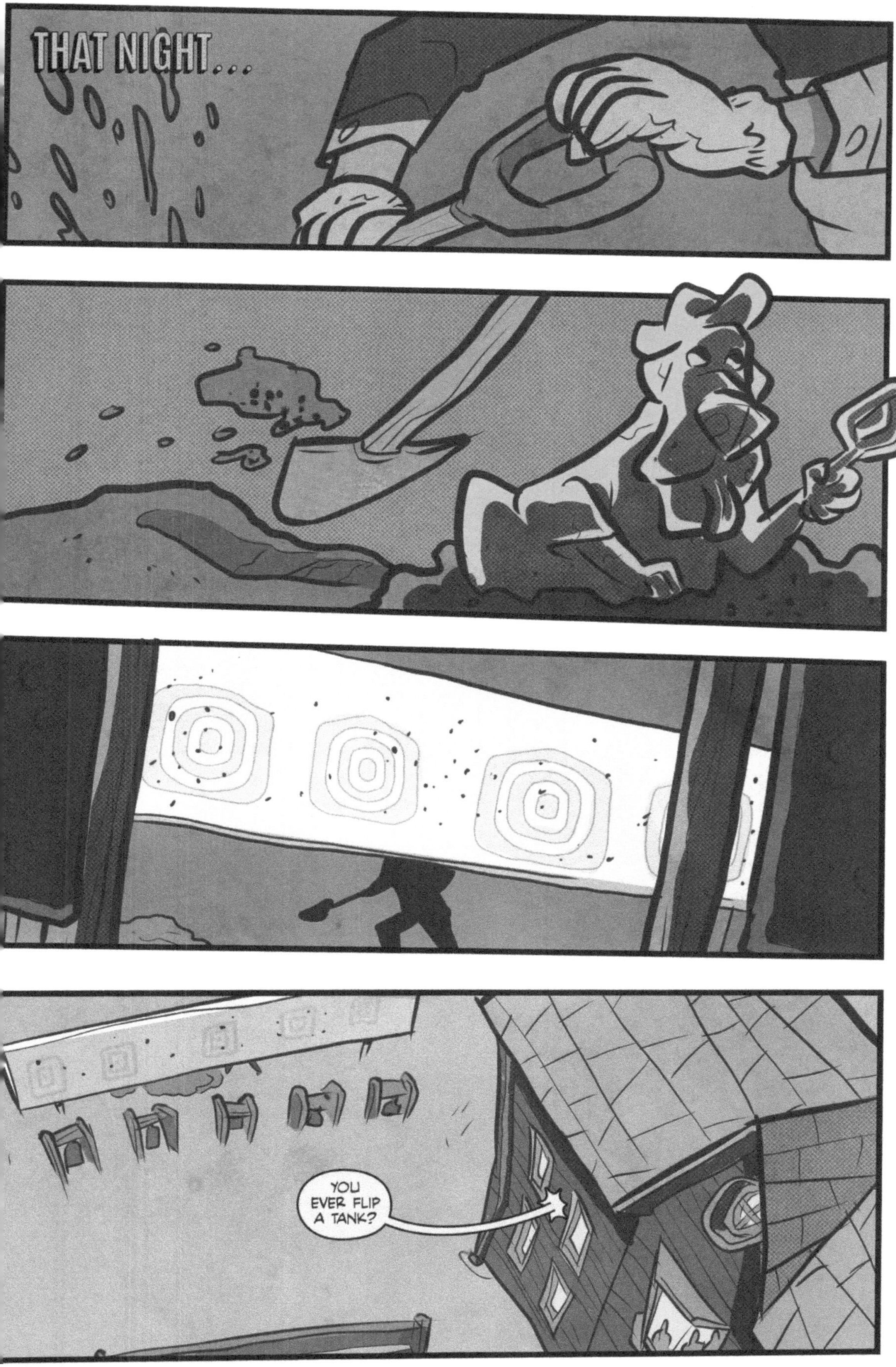
THAT NIGHT...
YOU EVER FLIP A TANK?

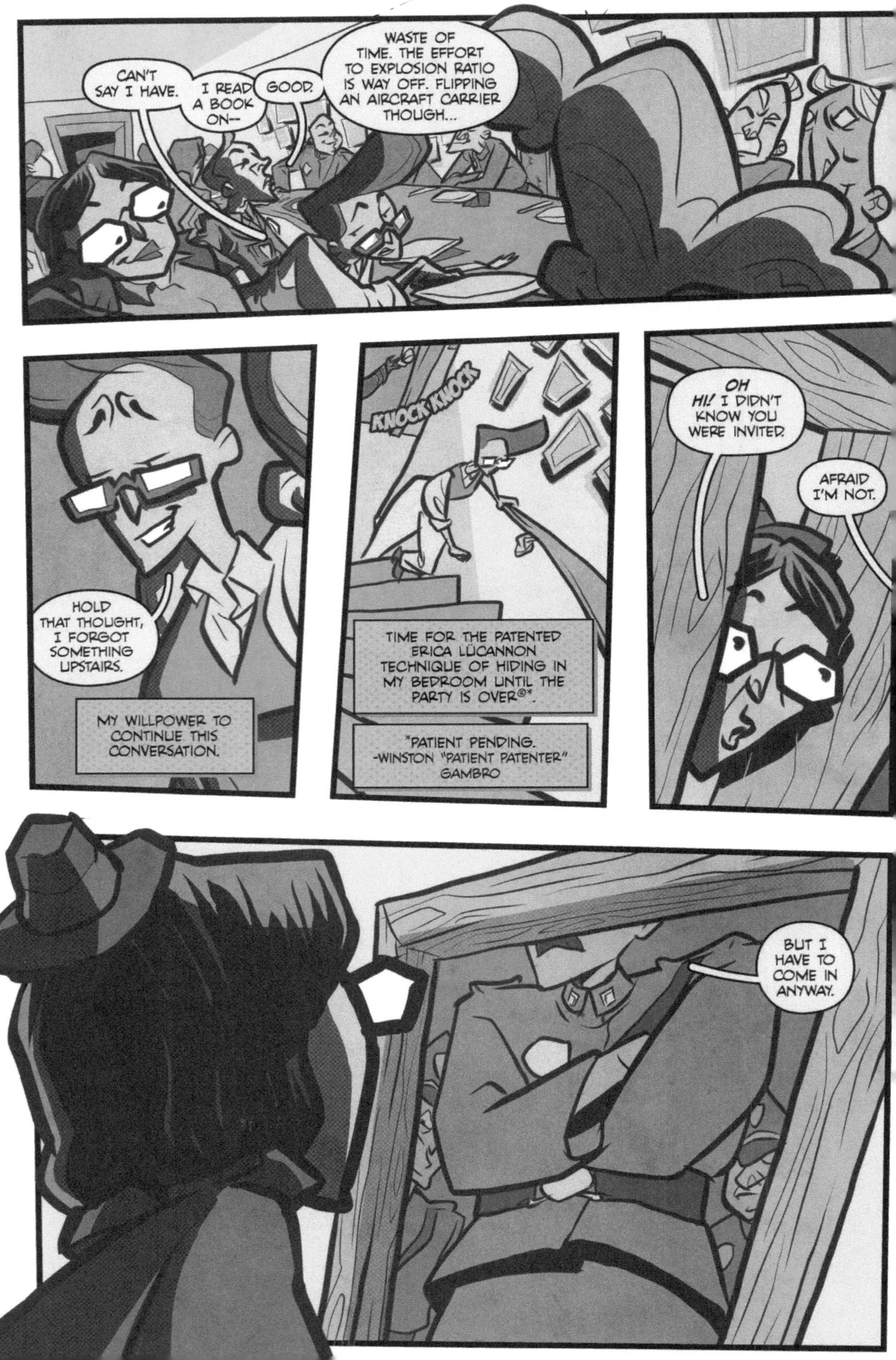
CAN'T SAY I HAVE.
I READ A BOOK ON--
GOOD.
WASTE OF TIME. THE EFFORT TO EXPLOSION RATIO IS WAY OFF. FLIPPING AN AIRCRAFT CARRIER THOUGH...
HOLD THAT THOUGHT, I FORGOT SOMETHING UPSTAIRS.
MY WILLPOWER TO CONTINUE THIS CONVERSATION.
KNOCK KNOCK
TIME FOR THE PATENTED ERICA LÜCANNON TECHNIQUE OF HIDING IN MY BEDROOM UNTIL THE PARTY IS OVER®*.
*PATIENT PENDING. -WINSTON "PATIENT PATENTER" GAMBRO
OH HI! I DIDN'T KNOW YOU WERE INVITED.
AFRAID I'M NOT.
BUT I HAVE TO COME IN ANYWAY.

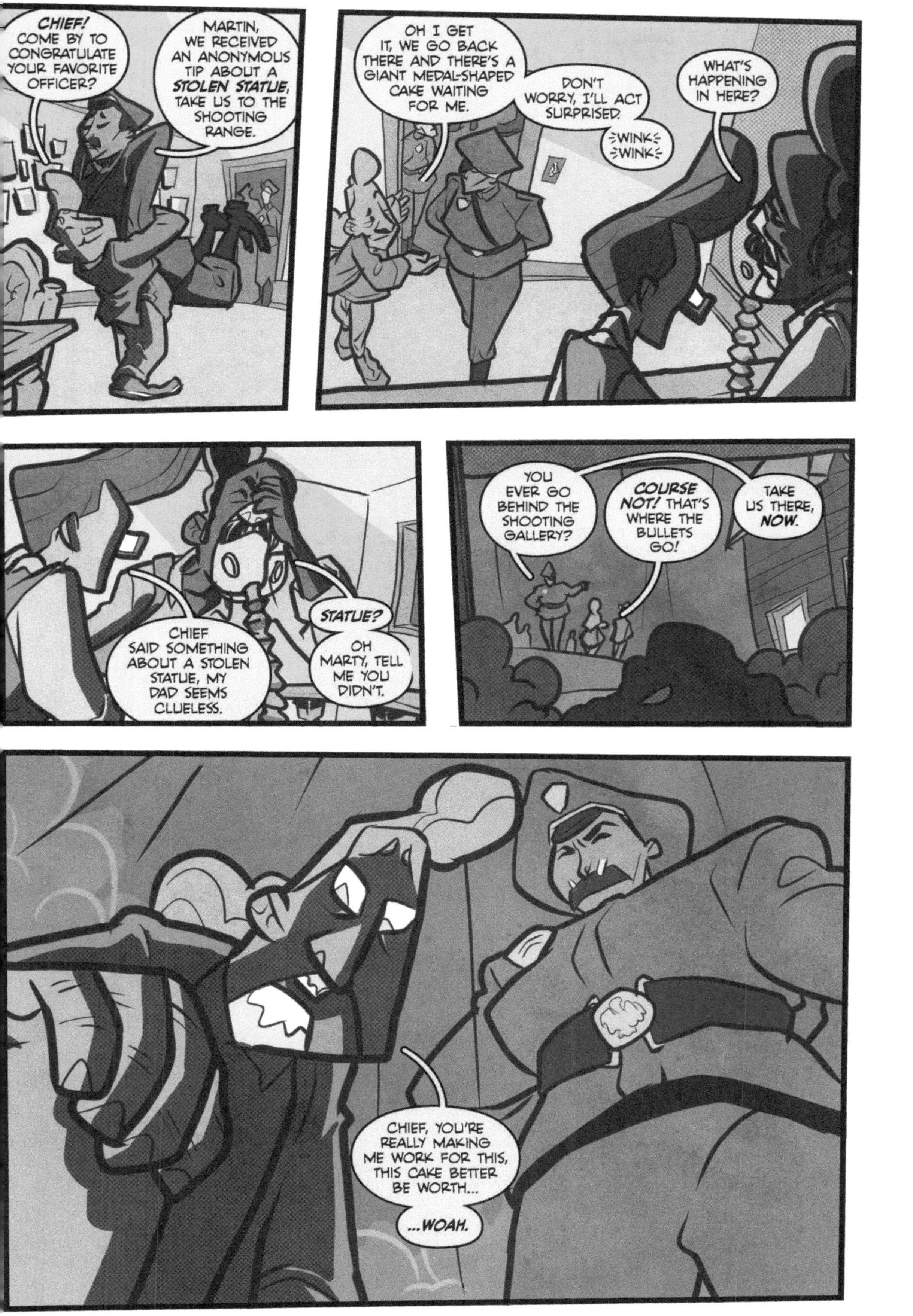

CHIEF! COME BY TO CONGRATULATE YOUR FAVORITE OFFICER?
MARTIN, WE RECEIVED AN ANONYMOUS TIP ABOUT A STOLEN STATUE, TAKE US TO THE SHOOTING RANGE.
OH I GET IT, WE GO BACK THERE AND THERE'S A GIANT MEDAL-SHAPED CAKE WAITING FOR ME.
DON'T WORRY, I'LL ACT SURPRISED.
WINK WINK
WHAT'S HAPPENING IN HERE?
CHIEF SAID SOMETHING ABOUT A STOLEN STATUE, MY DAD SEEMS CLUELESS.
STATUE?
OH MARTY, TELL ME YOU DIDN'T.
YOU EVER GO BEHIND THE SHOOTING GALLERY?
COURSE NOT! THAT'S WHERE THE BULLETS GO!
TAKE US THERE, NOW.
CHIEF, YOU'RE REALLY MAKING ME WORK FOR THIS, THIS CAKE BETTER BE WORTH...
...WOAH.

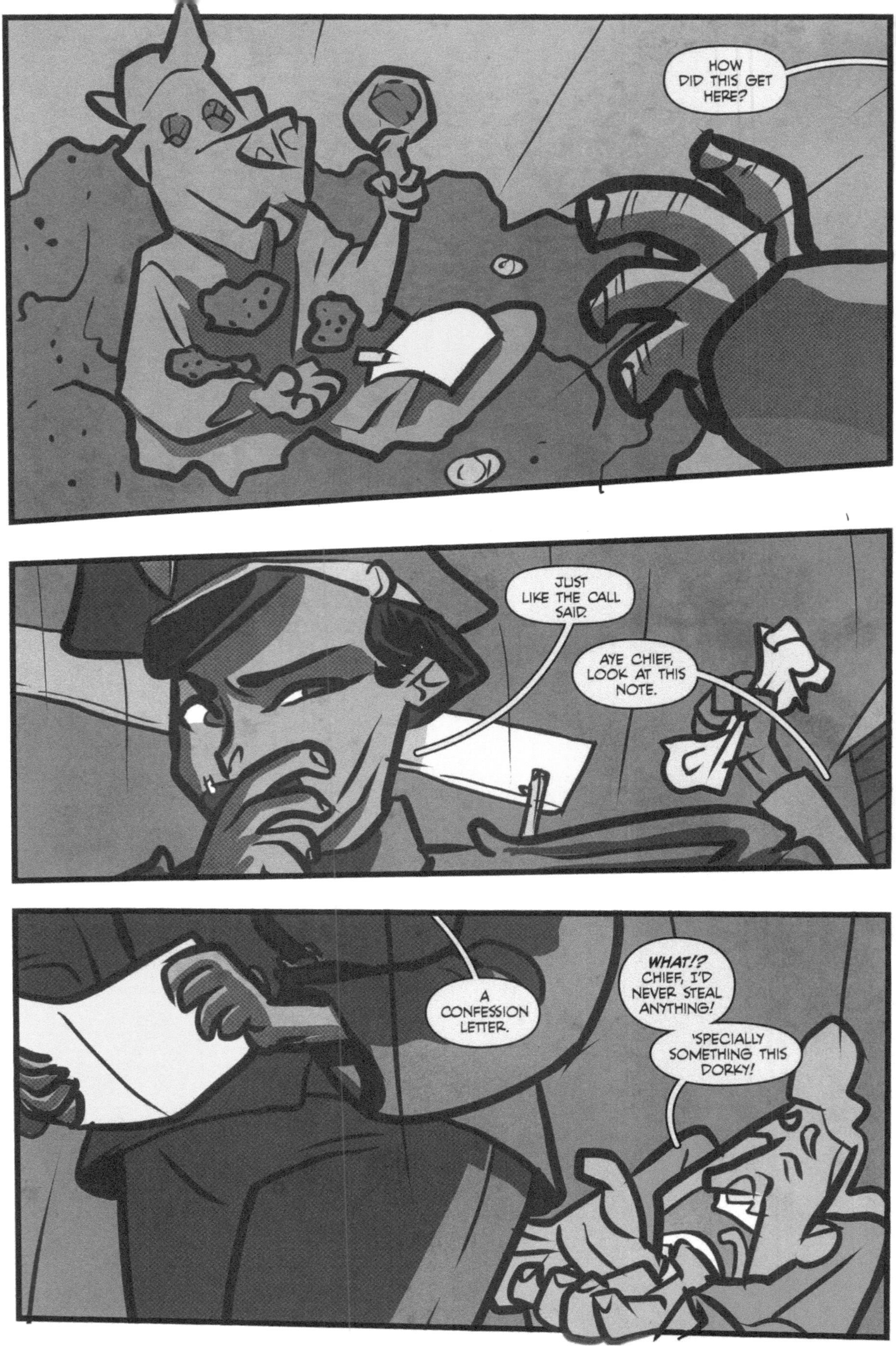
HOW DID THIS GET HERE?
JUST LIKE THE CALL SAID.
AYE CHIEF, LOOK AT THIS NOTE.
A CONFESSION LETTER.
WHAT!? CHIEF, I'D NEVER STEAL ANYTHING!
'SPECIALLY SOMETHING THIS DORKY!

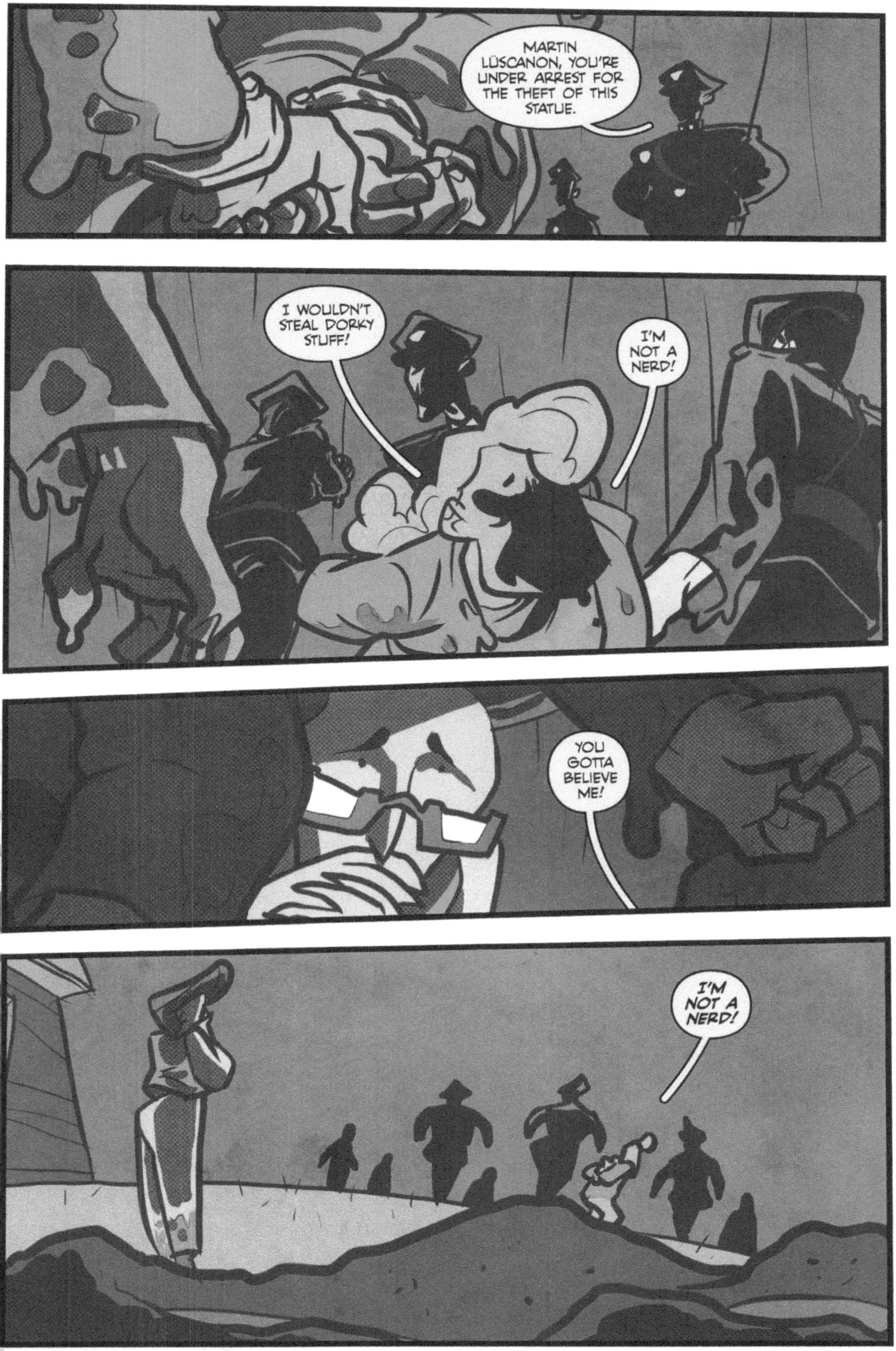
MARTIN LÜSCANON, YOU'RE UNDER ARREST FOR THE THEFT OF THIS STATUE.
I WOULDN'T STEAL DORKY STUFF!
I'M NOT A NERD!
YOU GOTTA BELIEVE ME!
I'M NOT A NERD!

CHAPTER EIGHT: THE MORNING AFTER YESTERDAY

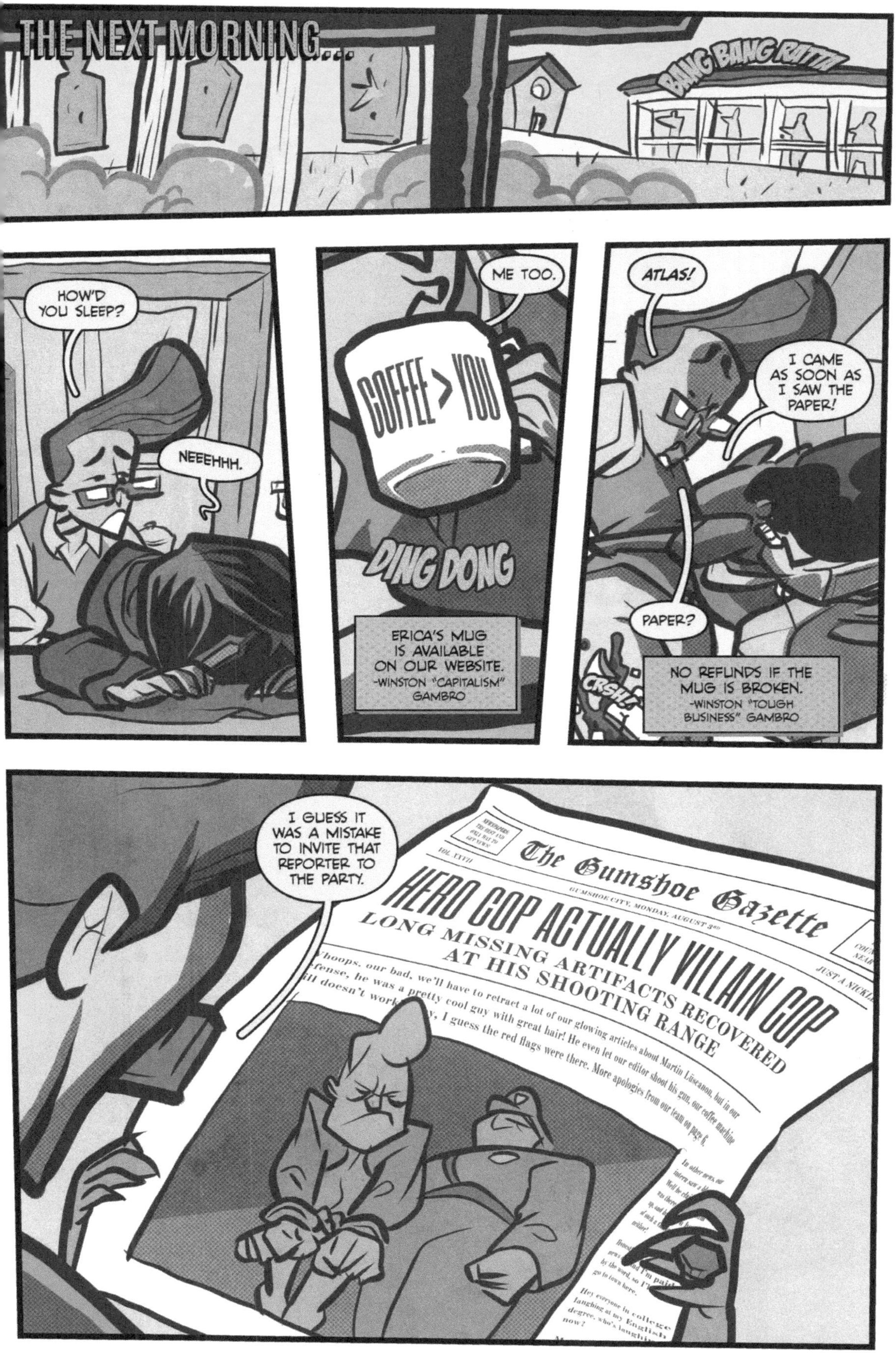
THE NEXT MORNING...
BANG BANG RATTA
HOW'D YOU SLEEP?
NEEEHHH.
ME TOO.
COFFEE > YOU
DING DONG
ERICA'S MUG IS AVAILABLE ON OUR WEBSITE. -WINSTON "CAPITALISM" GAMBRO
ATLAS!
I CAME AS SOON AS I SAW THE PAPER!
PAPER?
CRSH!
NO REFUNDS IF THE MUG IS BROKEN. -WINSTON "TOUGH BUSINESS" GAMBRO
I GUESS IT WAS A MISTAKE TO INVITE THAT REPORTER TO THE PARTY.
NEWSPAPERS: THE BEST AND ONLY WAY TO GET NEWS!
VOL. XVII
The Gumshoe Gazette
GUMSHOE CITY, MONDAY, AUGUST 3RD
JUST A NICKLE
HERO COP ACTUALLY VILLAIN COP
LONG MISSING ARTIFACTS RECOVERED AT HIS SHOOTING RANGE
Whoops, our bad, we'll have to retract a lot of our glowing articles about Martin Lüseanon, but in our
defense, he was a pretty cool guy with great hair! He even let our editor shoot his gun, our coffee machine
still doesn't work
I guess the red flags were there. More apologies from our team on page 6.
Hey everyone in college laughing at my English degree, who's laughing now?

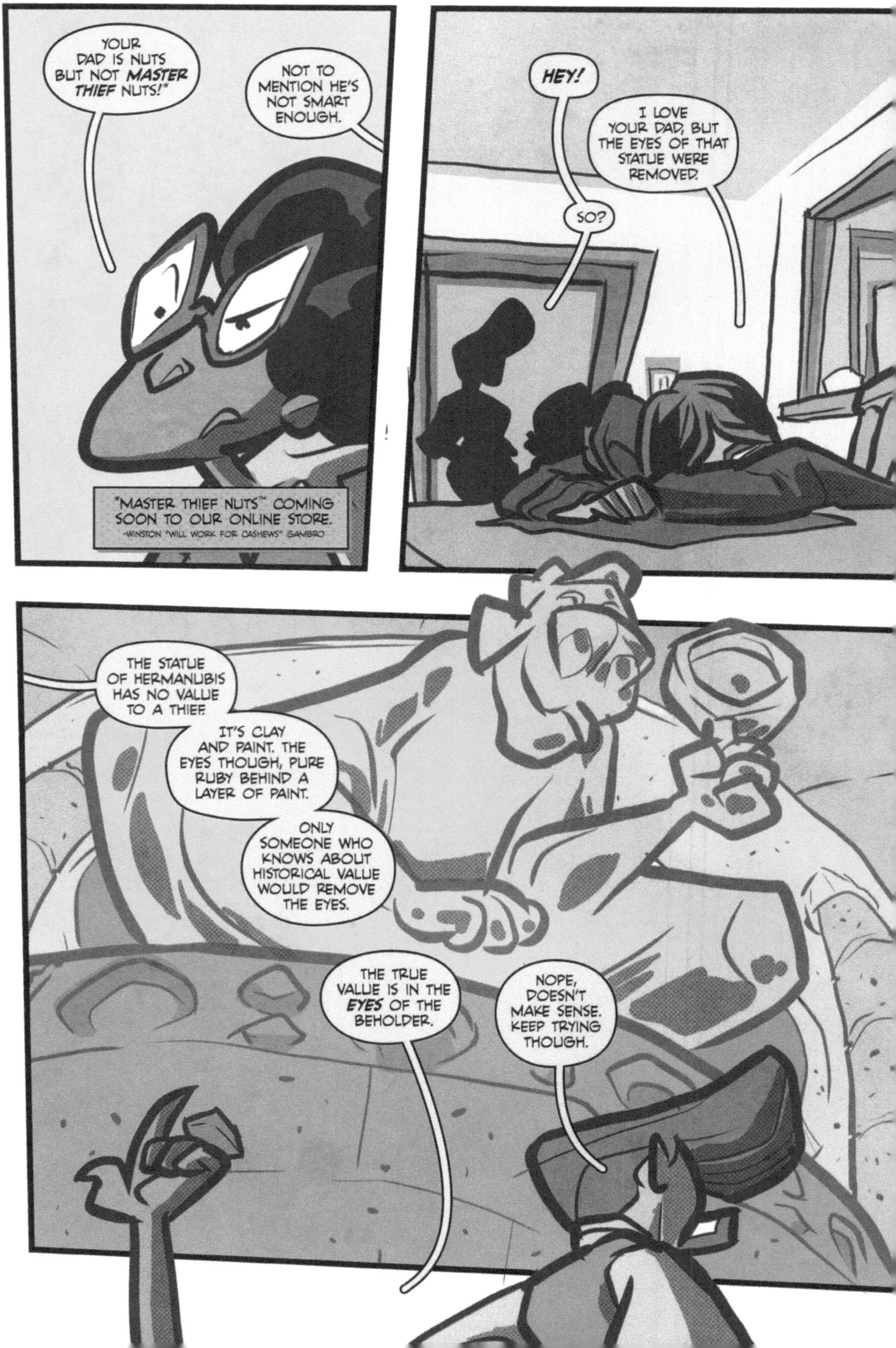
YOUR DAD IS NUTS BUT NOT *MASTER THIEF* NUTS!*
NOT TO MENTION HE'S NOT SMART ENOUGH.
*MASTER THIEF NUTS™ COMING SOON TO OUR ONLINE STORE.
-WINSTON "WILL WORK FOR CASHEWS" GAMBRO
HEY!
SO?
I LOVE YOUR DAD, BUT THE EYES OF THAT STATUE WERE REMOVED.
THE STATUE OF HERMANUBIS HAS NO VALUE TO A THIEF.
IT'S CLAY AND PAINT. THE EYES THOUGH, PURE RUBY BEHIND A LAYER OF PAINT.
ONLY SOMEONE WHO KNOWS ABOUT HISTORICAL VALUE WOULD REMOVE THE EYES.
THE TRUE VALUE IS IN THE *EYES* OF THE BEHOLDER.
NOPE, DOESN'T MAKE SENSE. KEEP TRYING THOUGH.

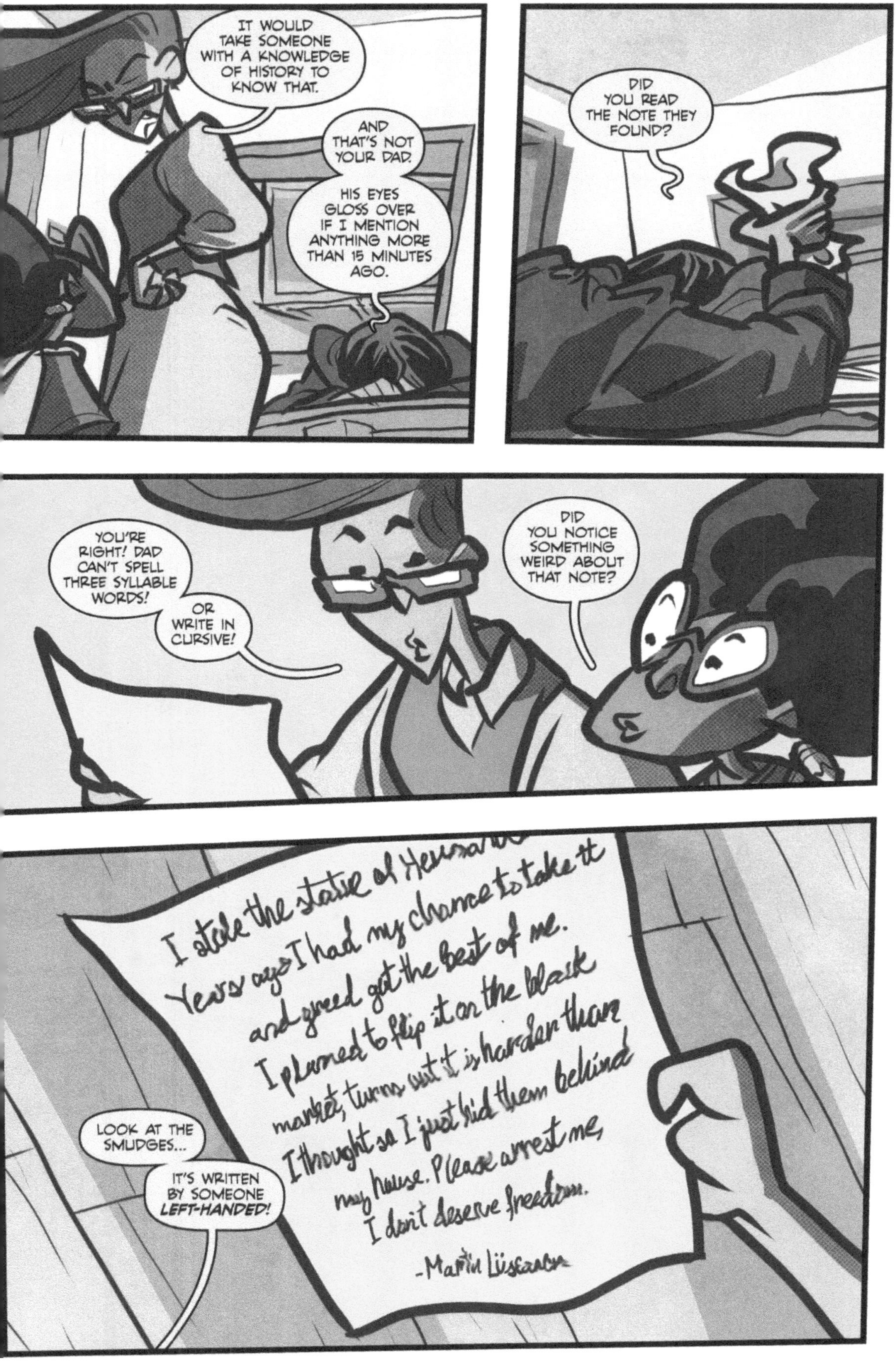
IT WOULD TAKE SOMEONE WITH A KNOWLEDGE OF HISTORY TO KNOW THAT.
AND THAT'S NOT YOUR DAD.
HIS EYES GLOSS OVER IF I MENTION ANYTHING MORE THAN 15 MINUTES AGO.
DID YOU READ THE NOTE THEY FOUND?
YOU'RE RIGHT! DAD CAN'T SPELL THREE SYLLABLE WORDS!
OR WRITE IN CURSIVE!
DID YOU NOTICE SOMETHING WEIRD ABOUT THAT NOTE?
I stole the statue of
Years ago I had my chance to take it
and greed got the best of me.
I planned to flip it on the black
market, turns out it is harder than
I thought so I just hid them behind
my house. Please arrest me,
I don't deserve freedom.
LOOK AT THE SMUDGES...
IT'S WRITTEN BY SOMEONE *LEFT-HANDED!*

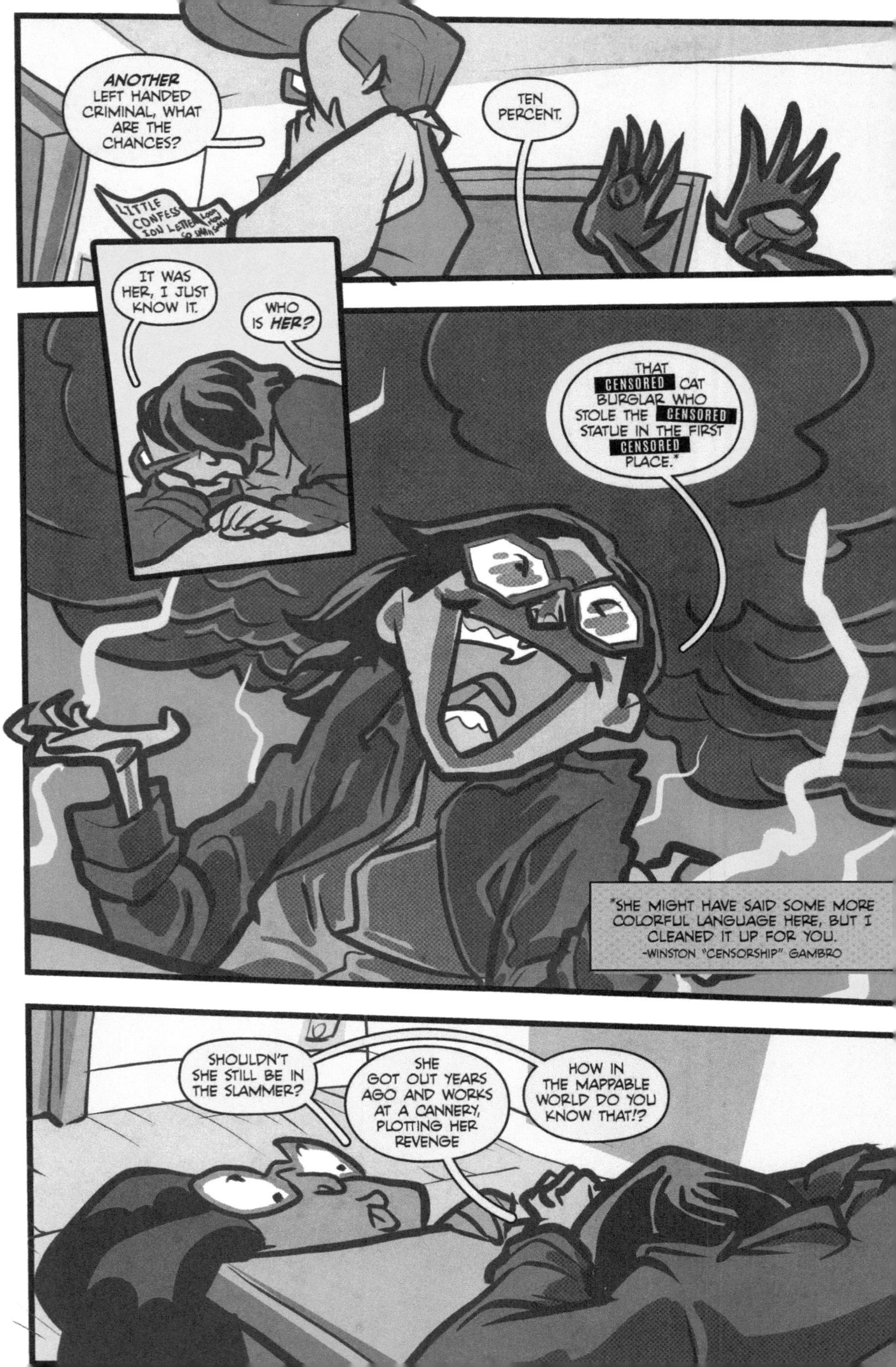

ANOTHER LEFT HANDED CRIMINAL, WHAT ARE THE CHANCES?
LITTLE CONFESSION LETTER
TEN PERCENT.
IT WAS HER, I JUST KNOW IT.
WHO IS HER?
THAT CENSORED CAT BURGLAR WHO STOLE THE CENSORED STATUE IN THE FIRST CENSORED PLACE.*
*SHE MIGHT HAVE SAID SOME MORE COLORFUL LANGUAGE HERE, BUT I CLEANED IT UP FOR YOU.
-WINSTON "CENSORSHIP" GAMBRO
SHOULDN'T SHE STILL BE IN THE SLAMMER?
SHE GOT OUT YEARS AGO AND WORKS AT A CANNERY, PLOTTING HER REVENGE
HOW IN THE MAPPABLE WORLD DO YOU KNOW THAT!?

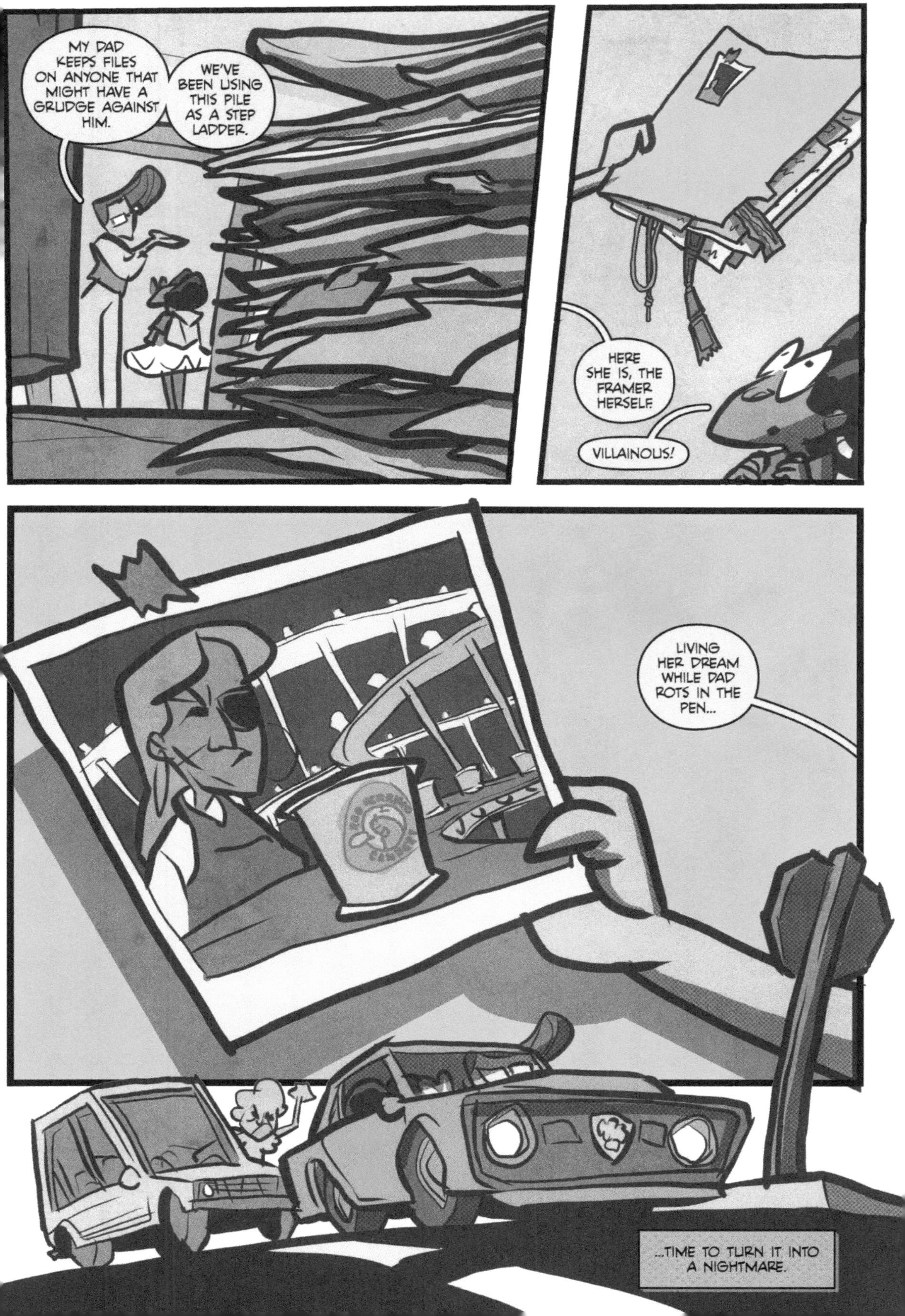
MY DAD KEEPS FILES ON ANYONE THAT MIGHT HAVE A GRUDGE AGAINST HIM.
WE'VE BEEN USING THIS PILE AS A STEP LADDER.
HERE SHE IS, THE FRAMER HERSELF.
VILLAINOUS!
LIVING HER DREAM WHILE DAD ROTS IN THE PEN...
...TIME TO TURN IT INTO A NIGHTMARE.

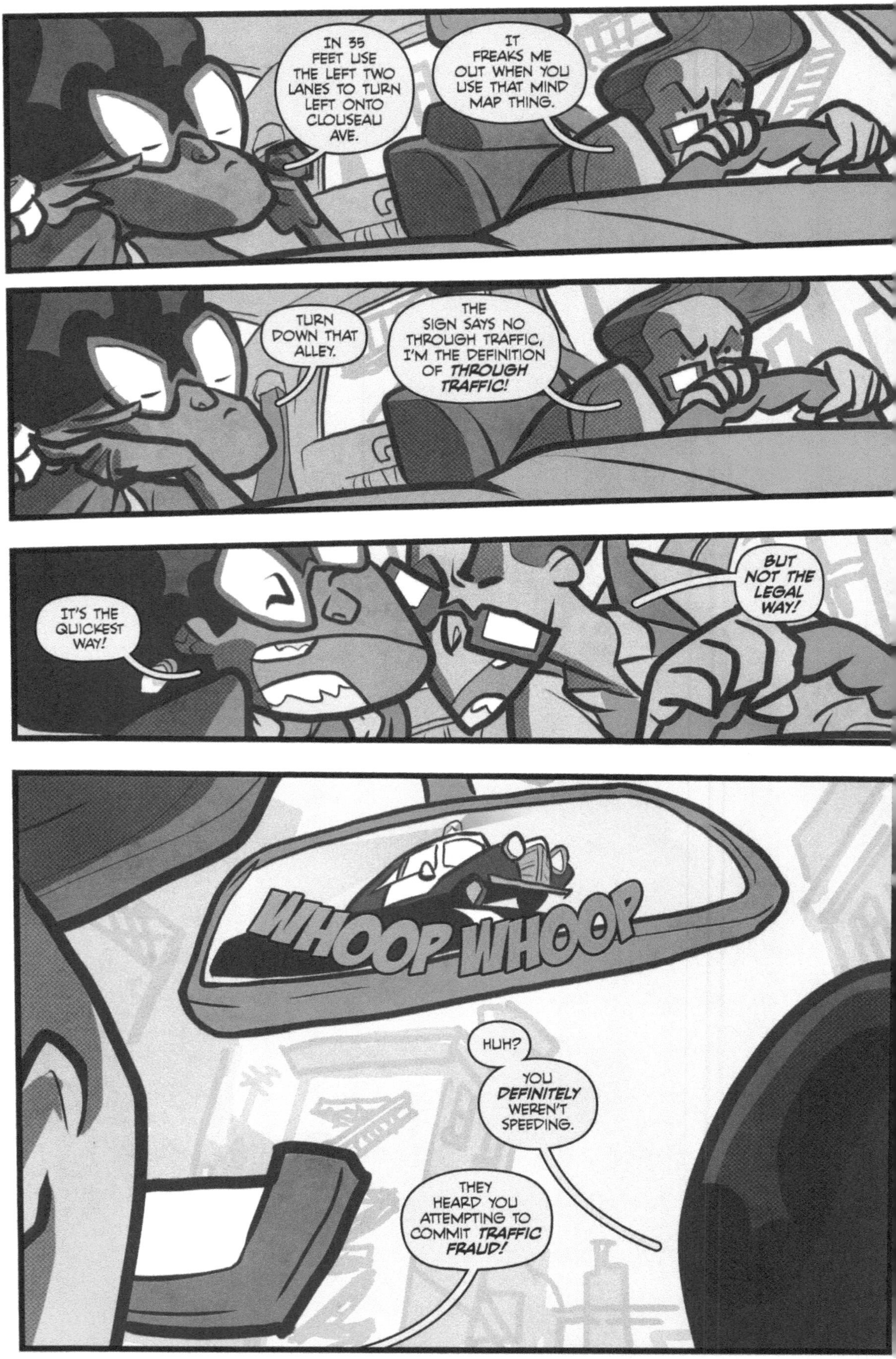
IN 35 FEET USE THE LEFT TWO LANES TO TURN LEFT ONTO CLOUSEAU AVE.
IT FREAKS ME OUT WHEN YOU USE THAT MIND MAP THING.
TURN DOWN THAT ALLEY.
THE SIGN SAYS NO THROUGH TRAFFIC, I'M THE DEFINITION OF *THROUGH TRAFFIC!*
IT'S THE QUICKEST WAY!
BUT NOT THE LEGAL WAY!
WHOOP WHOOP
HUH?
YOU *DEFINITELY* WEREN'T SPEEDING.
THEY HEARD YOU ATTEMPTING TO COMMIT *TRAFFIC FRAUD!*

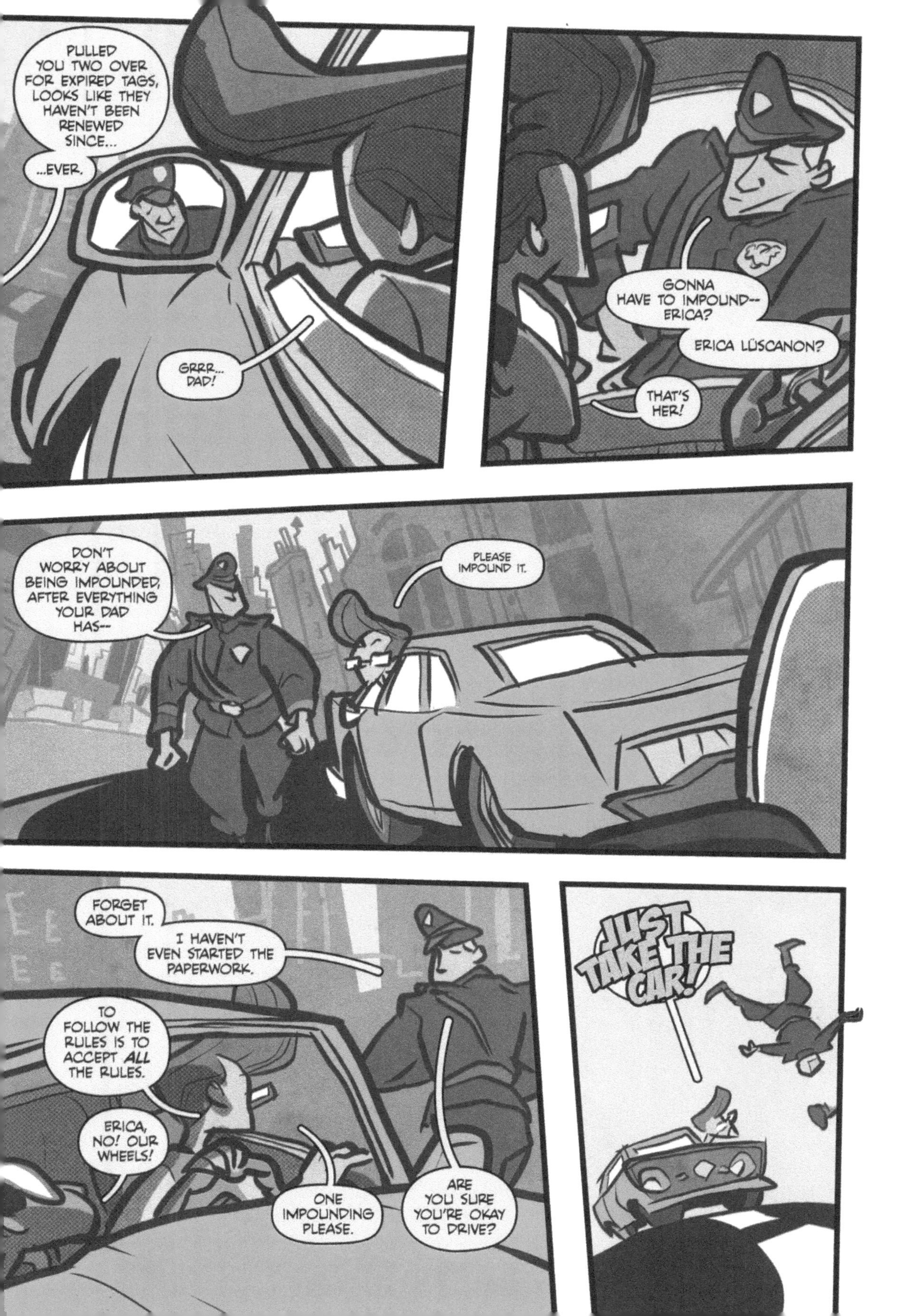
PULLED YOU TWO OVER FOR EXPIRED TAGS, LOOKS LIKE THEY HAVEN'T BEEN RENEWED SINCE...
...EVER.
GRRR... DAD!
GONNA HAVE TO IMPOUND-- ERICA?
ERICA LÜSCANON?
THAT'S HER!
DON'T WORRY ABOUT BEING IMPOUNDED, AFTER EVERYTHING YOUR DAD HAS--
PLEASE IMPOUND IT.
FORGET ABOUT IT.
I HAVEN'T EVEN STARTED THE PAPERWORK.
TO FOLLOW THE RULES IS TO ACCEPT ALL THE RULES.
ERICA, NO! OUR WHEELS!
ONE IMPOUNDING PLEASE.
ARE YOU SURE YOU'RE OKAY TO DRIVE?
JUST TAKE THE CAR!

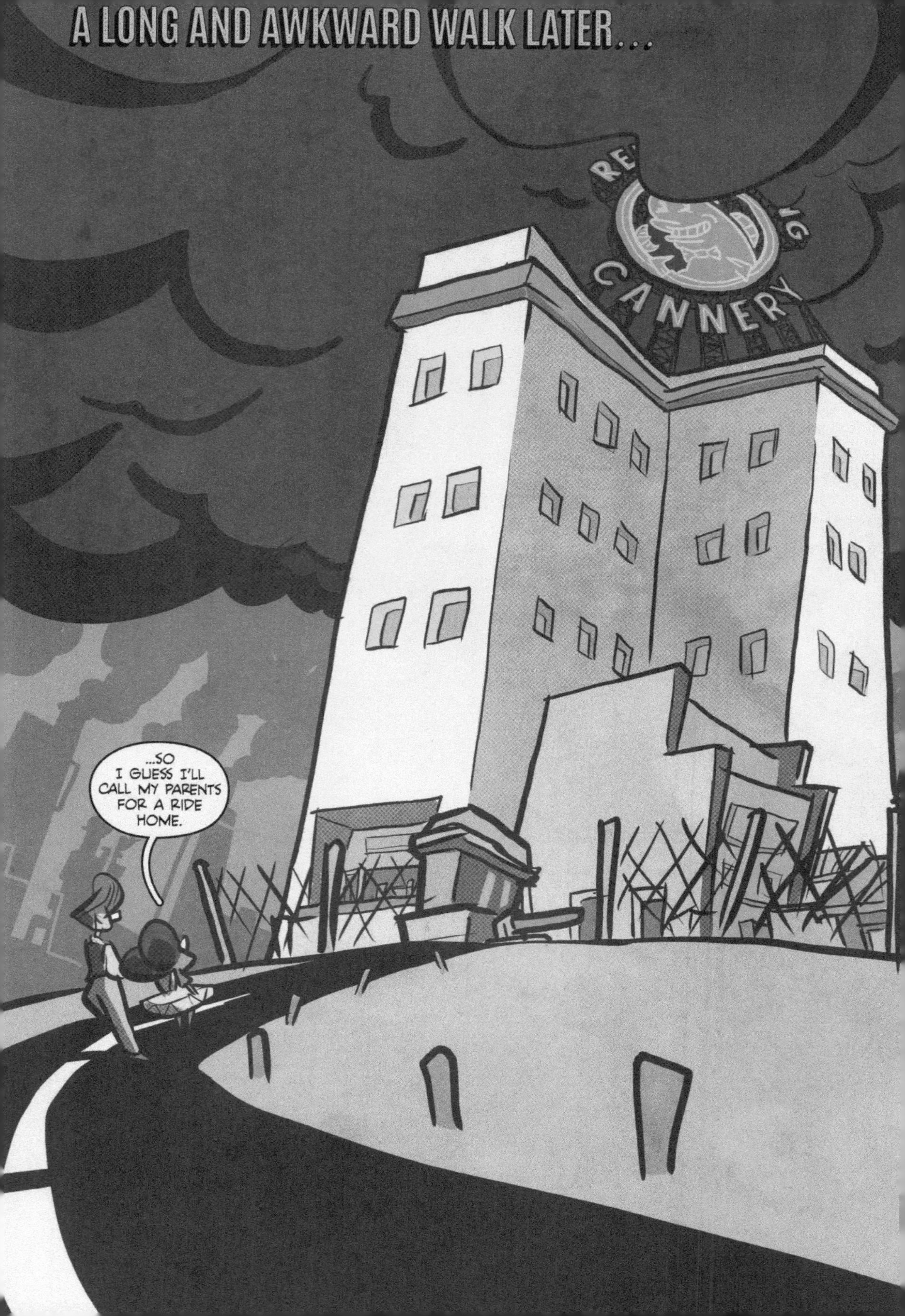
A LONG AND AWKWARD WALK LATER...
CANNERY
...SO I GUESS I'LL CALL MY PARENTS FOR A RIDE HOME.

CHAPTER NINE:

SOMETHING SMELLS FISHY at the CANNERY

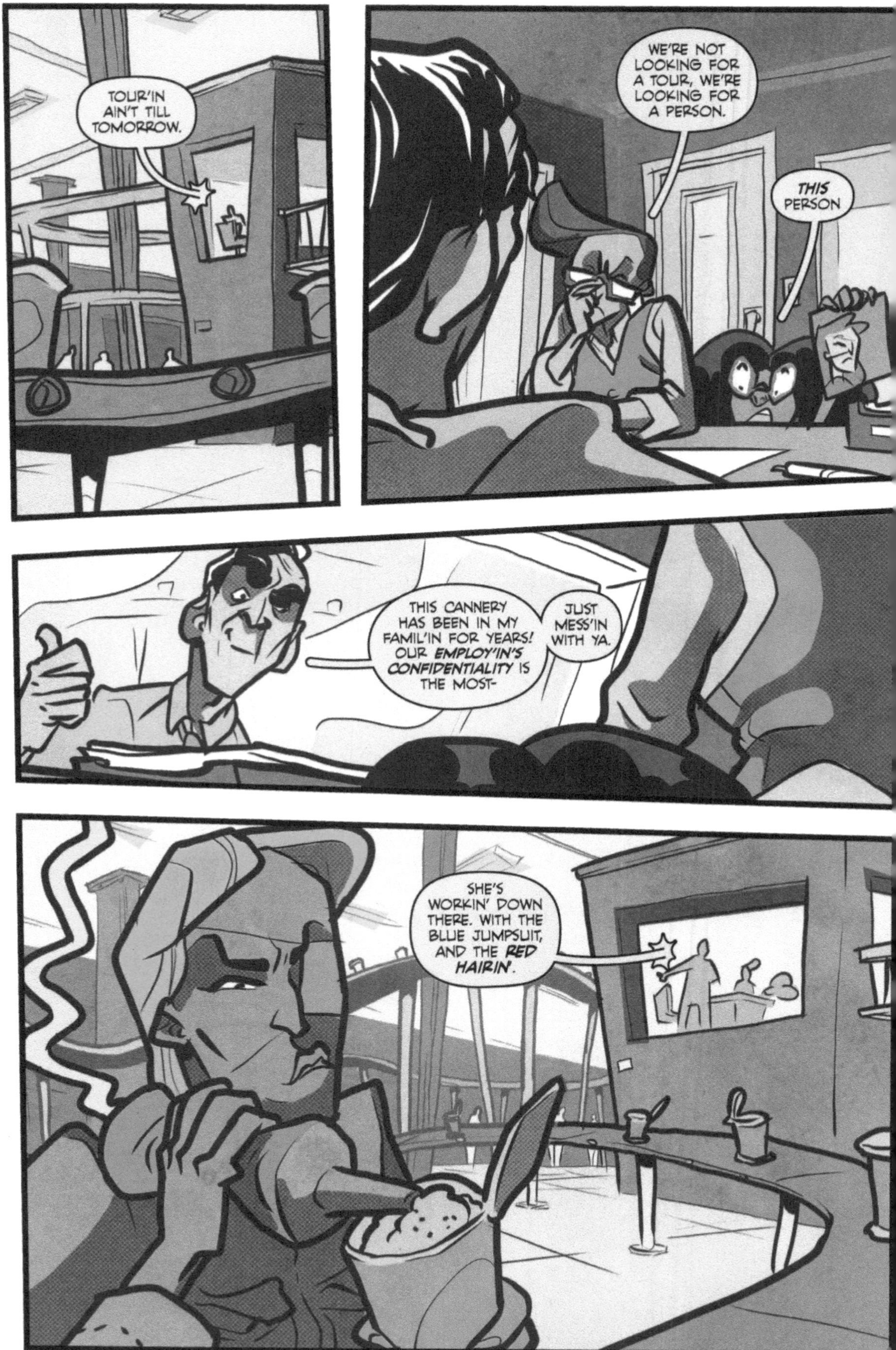
TOUR'IN AIN'T TILL TOMORROW.
WE'RE NOT LOOKING FOR A TOUR, WE'RE LOOKING FOR A PERSON.
THIS PERSON
THIS CANNERY HAS BEEN IN MY FAMIL'IN FOR YEARS! OUR EMPLOY'IN'S CONFIDENTIALITY IS THE MOST-
JUST MESS'IN WITH YA.
SHE'S WORKIN' DOWN THERE. WITH THE BLUE JUMPSUIT, AND THE RED HAIRIN'.

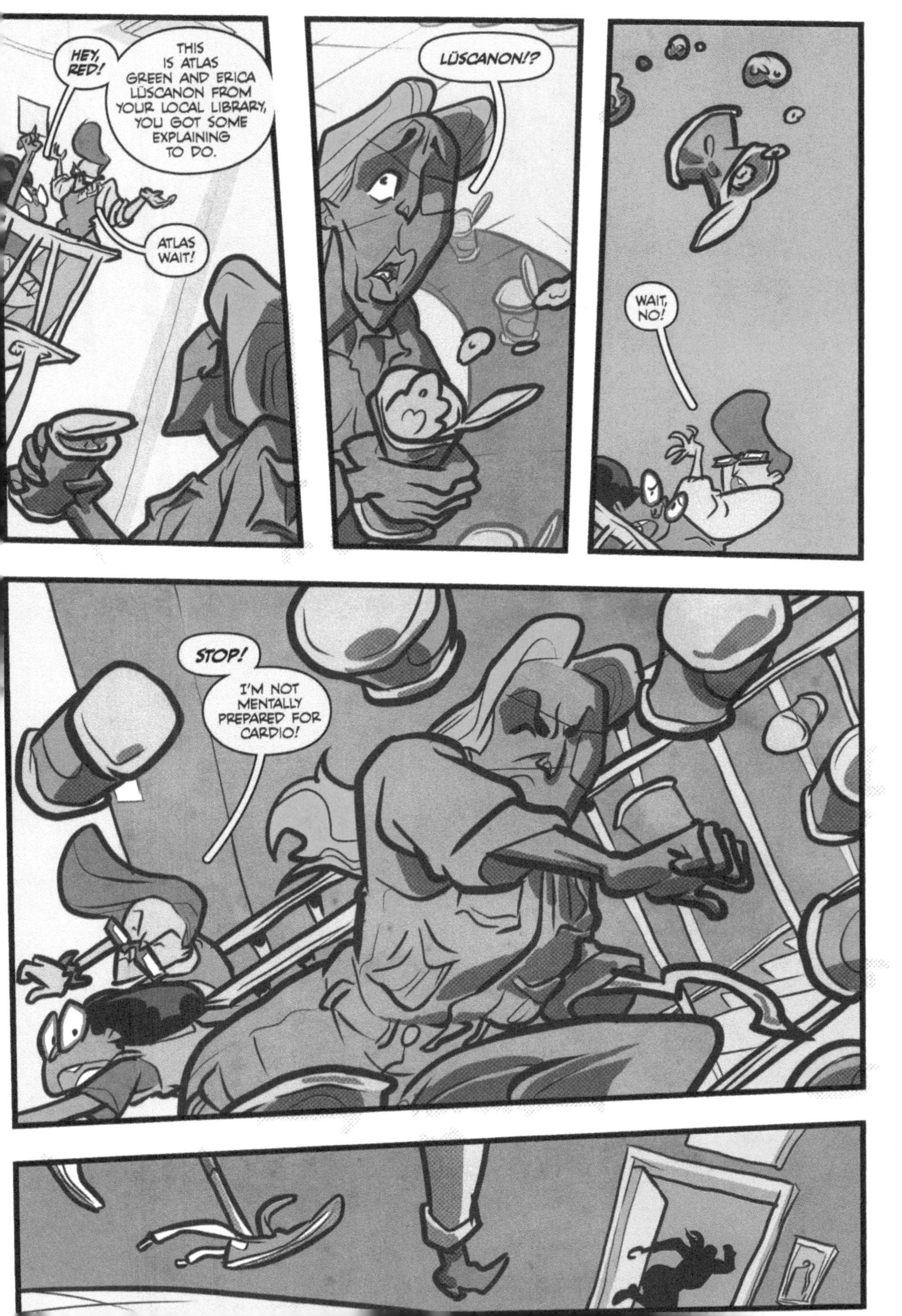
HEY, RED!
THIS IS ATLAS GREEN AND ERICA LÜSCANON FROM YOUR LOCAL LIBRARY, YOU GOT SOME EXPLAINING TO DO.
ATLAS WAIT!
LÜSCANON!?
WAIT, NO!
STOP!
I'M NOT MENTALLY PREPARED FOR CARDIO!

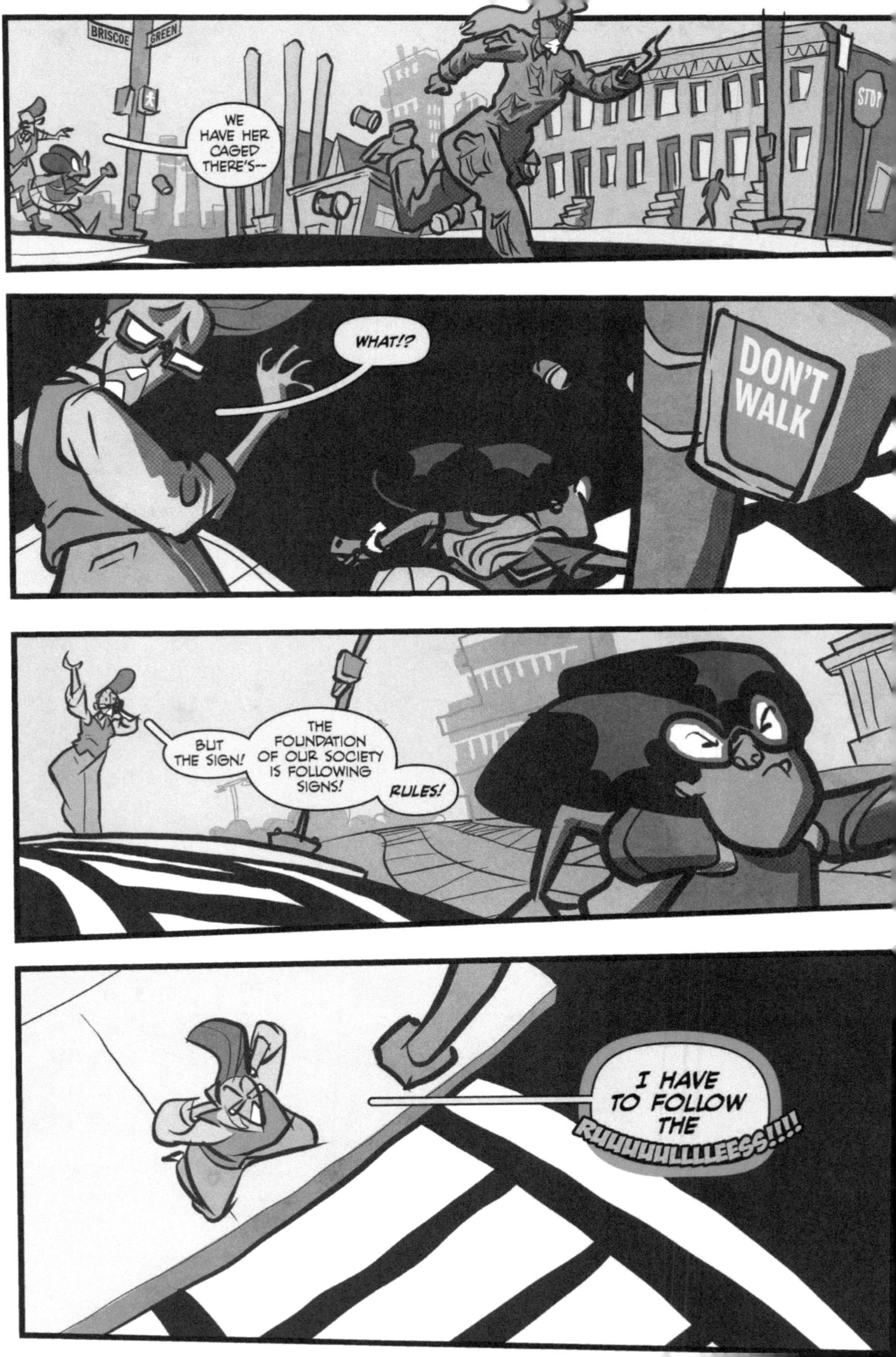
BRISCOE
GREEN
STOP
WE HAVE HER CAGED THERE'S--
WHAT!?
DON'T WALK
BUT THE SIGN!
THE FOUNDATION OF OUR SOCIETY IS FOLLOWING SIGNS!
RULES!
I HAVE TO FOLLOW THE RUUUUULLLLEESS!!!!

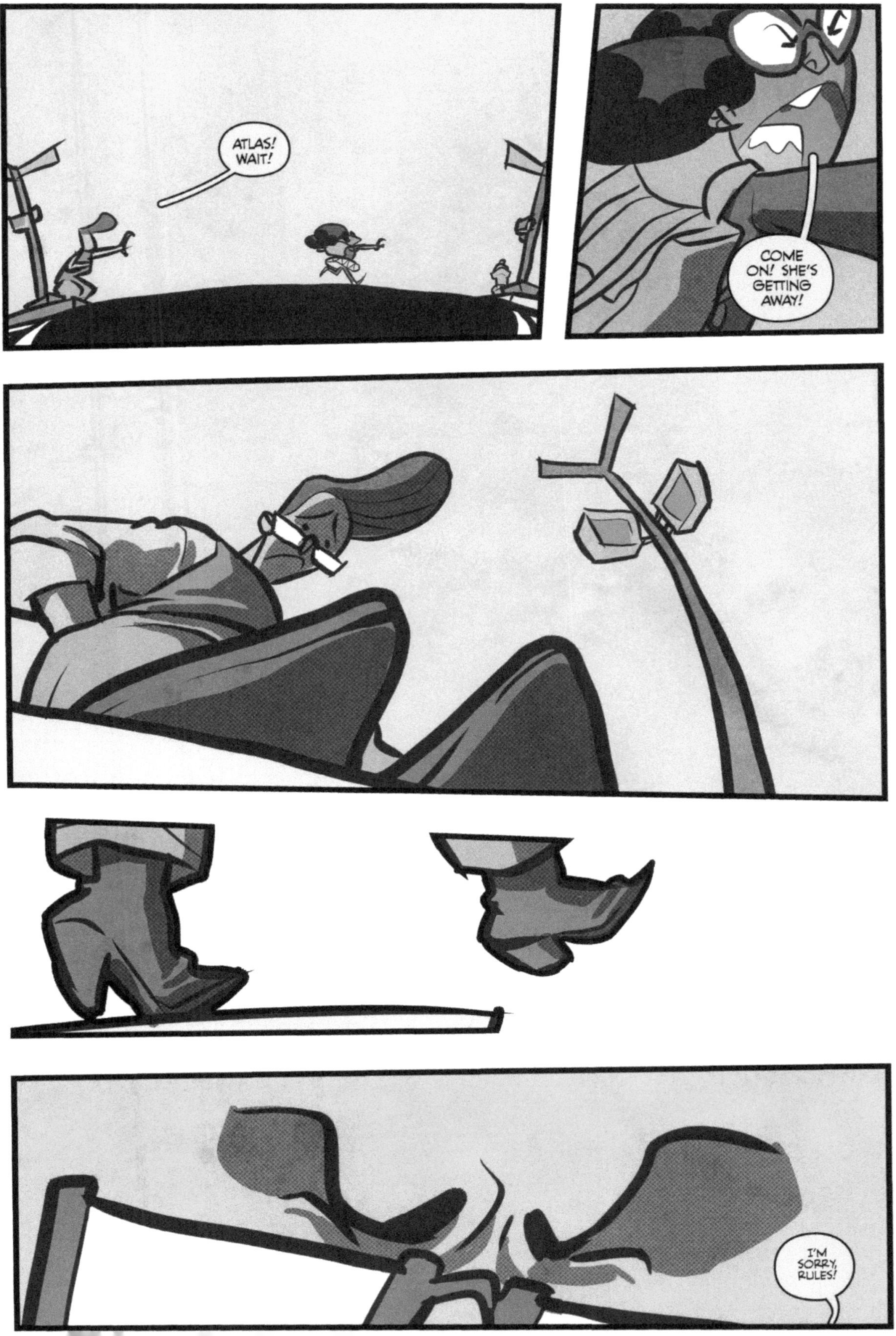
ATLAS! WAIT!
COME ON! SHE'S GETTING AWAY!
I'M SORRY, RULES!

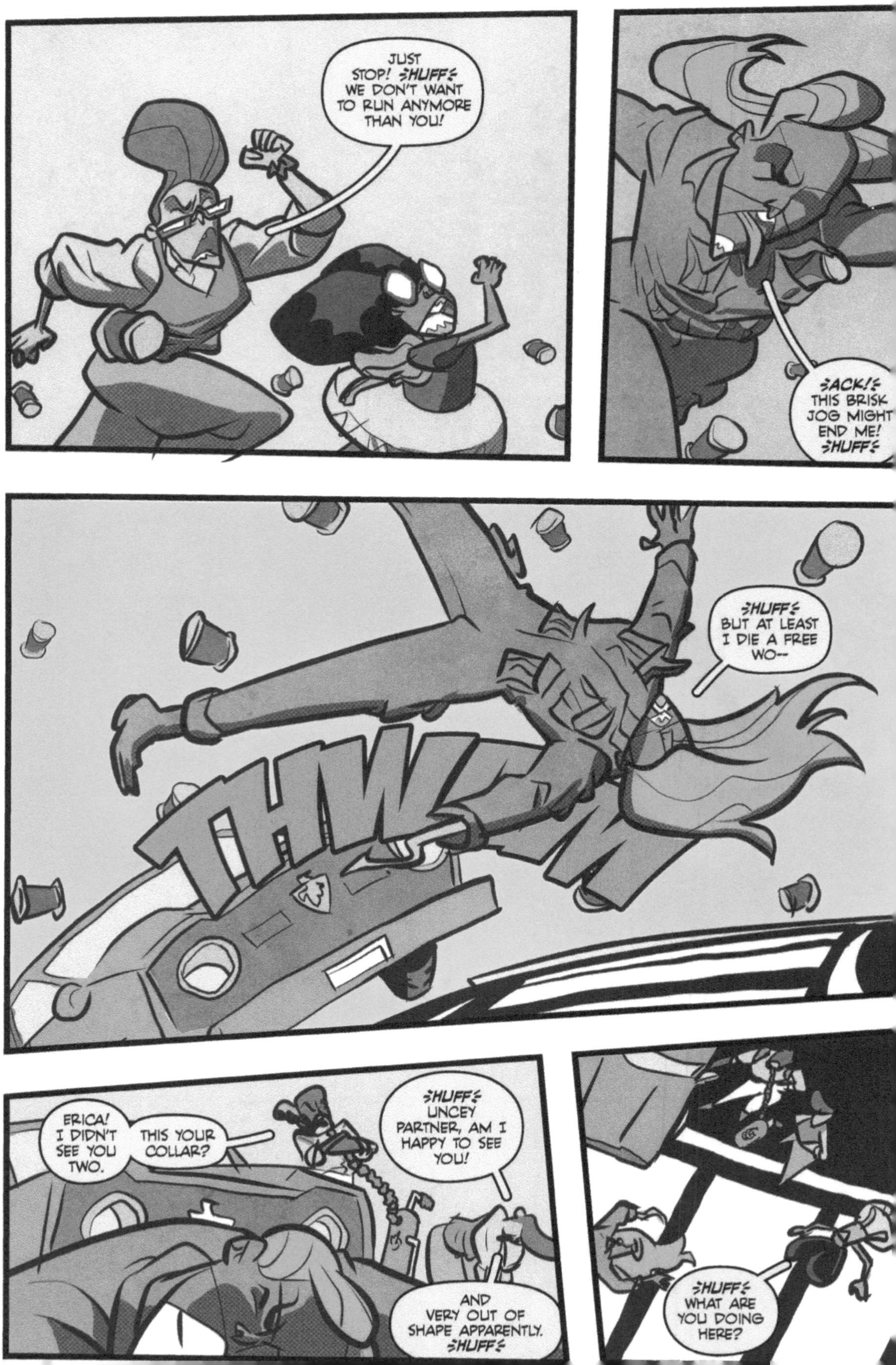
JUST STOP! HUFF WE DON'T WANT TO RUN ANYMORE THAN YOU!
ACK! THIS BRISK JOG MIGHT END ME! HUFF
HUFF BUT AT LEAST I DIE A FREE WO--
ERICA! I DIDN'T SEE YOU TWO.
THIS YOUR COLLAR?
HUFF UNCEY PARTNER, AM I HAPPY TO SEE YOU!
AND VERY OUT OF SHAPE APPARENTLY. HUFF
HUFF WHAT ARE YOU DOING HERE?

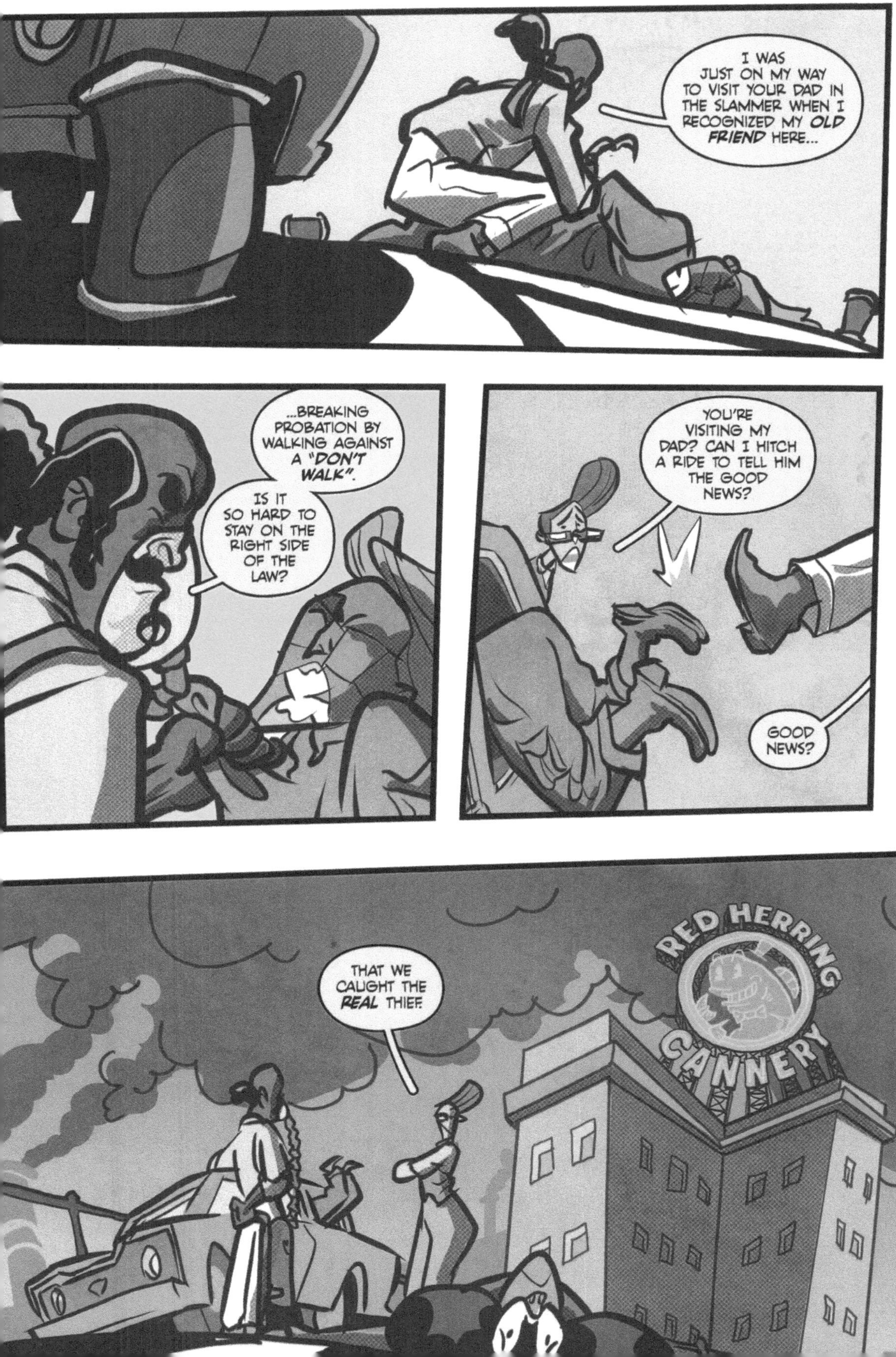
I WAS JUST ON MY WAY TO VISIT YOUR DAD IN THE SLAMMER WHEN I RECOGNIZED MY OLD FRIEND HERE...
...BREAKING PROBATION BY WALKING AGAINST A "DON'T WALK".
IS IT SO HARD TO STAY ON THE RIGHT SIDE OF THE LAW?
YOU'RE VISITING MY DAD? CAN I HITCH A RIDE TO TELL HIM THE GOOD NEWS?
GOOD NEWS?
THAT WE CAUGHT THE REAL THIEF.
RED HERRING
CANNERY

CHAPTER TEN
JAILHOUSE ROCK'EM SOCK'EM

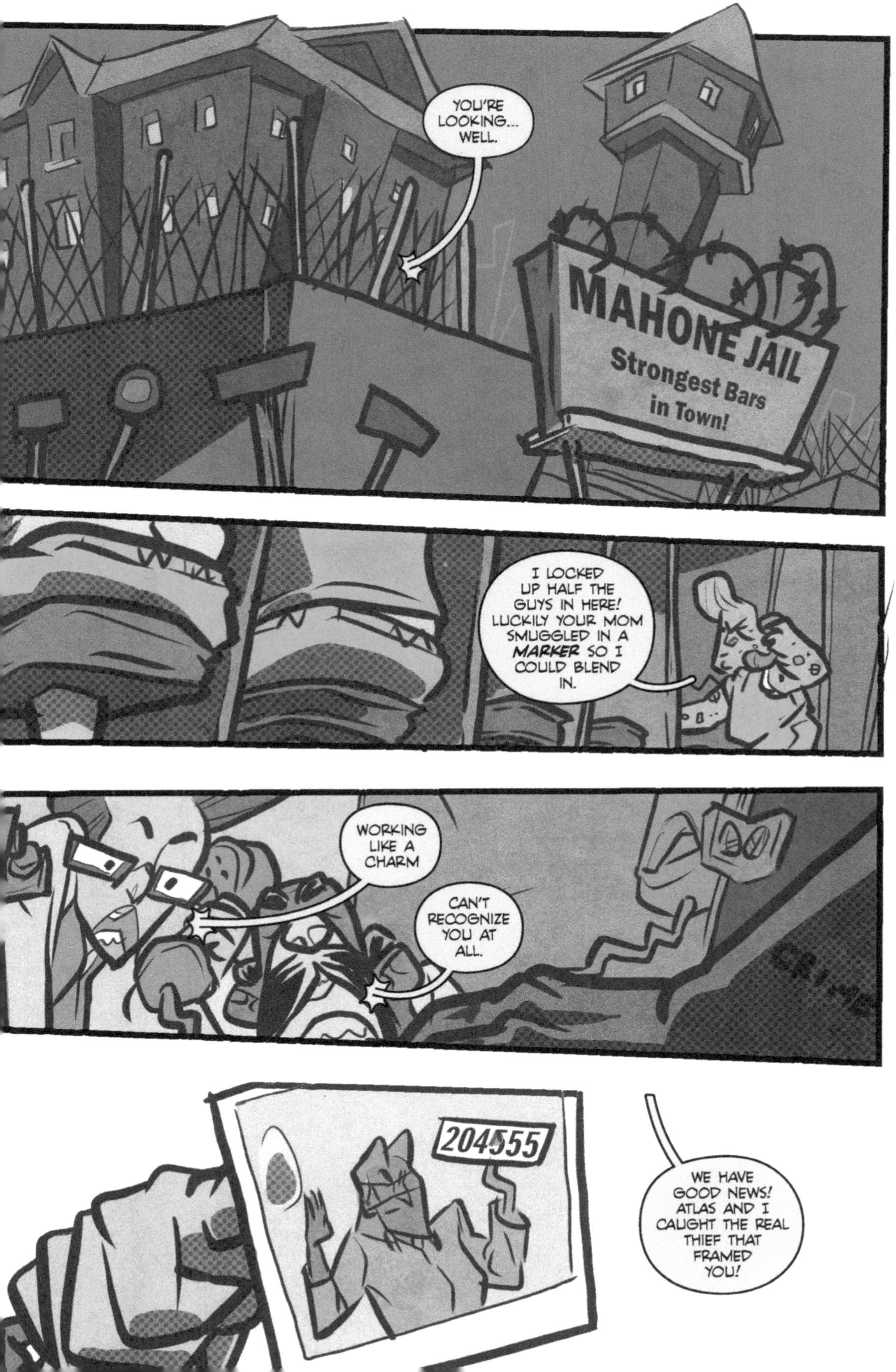
YOU'RE LOOKING... WELL.
MAHONE JAIL
Strongest Bars in Town!
I LOCKED UP HALF THE GUYS IN HERE! LUCKILY YOUR MOM SMUGGLED IN A MARKER SO I COULD BLEND IN.
WORKING LIKE A CHARM
CAN'T RECOGNIZE YOU AT ALL.
204555
WE HAVE GOOD NEWS! ATLAS AND I CAUGHT THE REAL THIEF THAT FRAMED YOU!

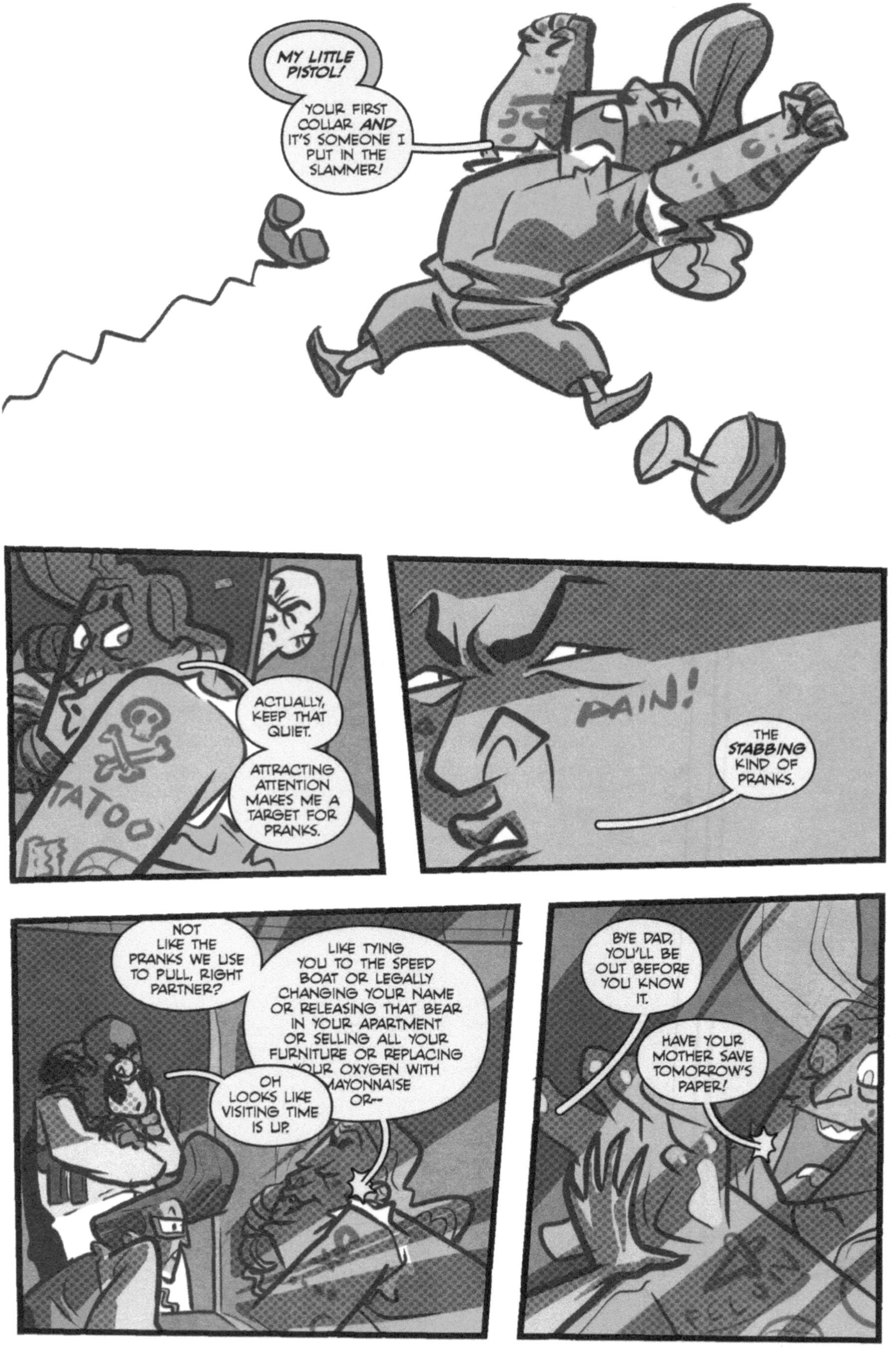
MY LITTLE PISTOL!
YOUR FIRST COLLAR AND IT'S SOMEONE I PUT IN THE SLAMMER!
TATOO
ACTUALLY, KEEP THAT QUIET.
ATTRACTING ATTENTION MAKES ME A TARGET FOR PRANKS.
PAIN!
THE STABBING KIND OF PRANKS.
NOT LIKE THE PRANKS WE USE TO PULL, RIGHT PARTNER?
LIKE TYING YOU TO THE SPEED BOAT OR LEGALLY CHANGING YOUR NAME OR RELEASING THAT BEAR IN YOUR APARTMENT OR SELLING ALL YOUR FURNITURE OR REPLACING YOUR OXYGEN WITH MAYONNAISE OR--
OH LOOKS LIKE VISITING TIME IS UP.
BYE DAD, YOU'LL BE OUT BEFORE YOU KNOW IT.
HAVE YOUR MOTHER SAVE TOMORROW'S PAPER!

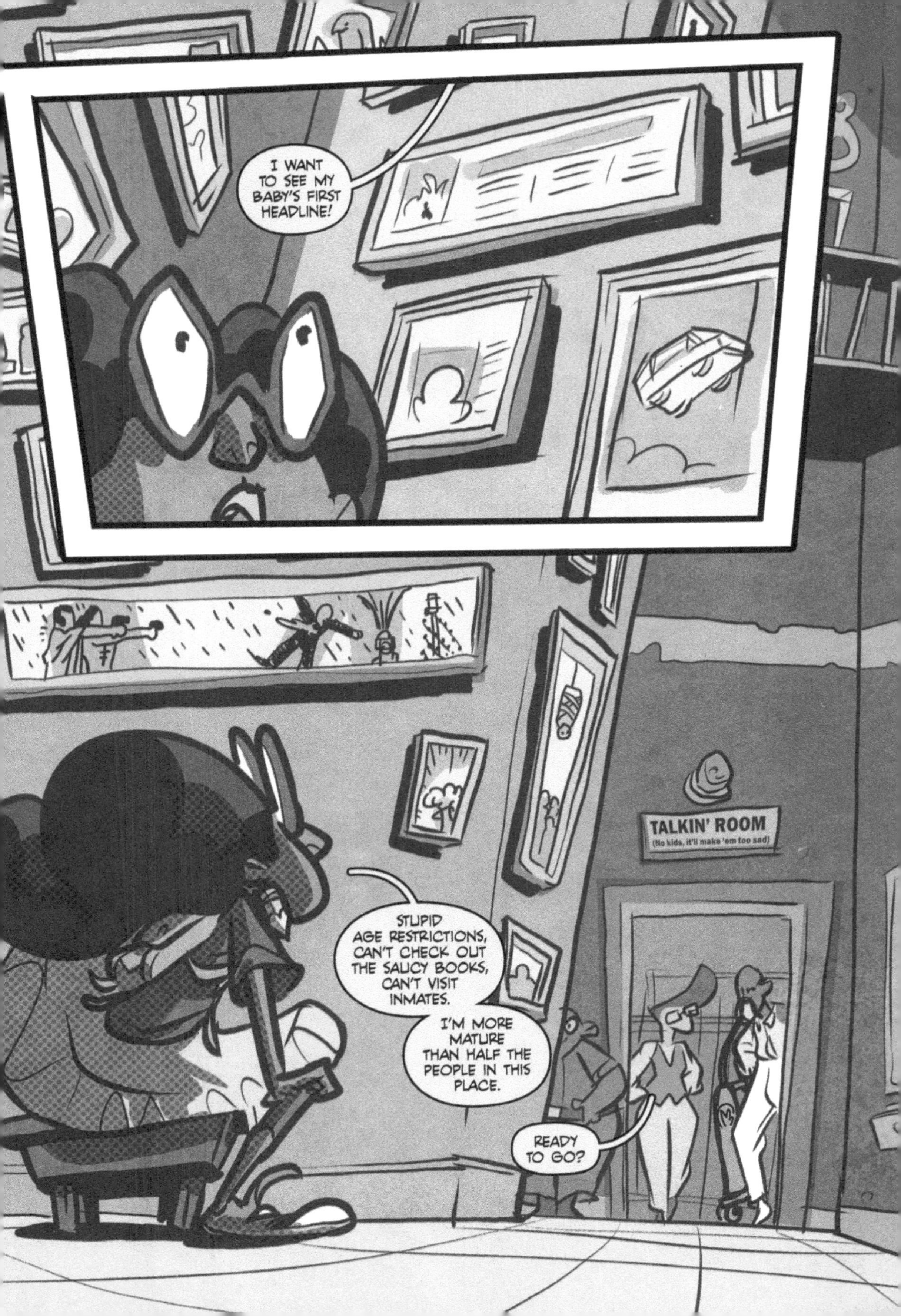
I WANT TO SEE MY BABY'S FIRST HEADLINE!
TALKIN' ROOM
(No kids, it'll make 'em too sad)
STUPID AGE RESTRICTIONS, CAN'T CHECK OUT THE SAUCY BOOKS, CAN'T VISIT INMATES.
I'M MORE MATURE THAN HALF THE PEOPLE IN THIS PLACE.
READY TO GO?

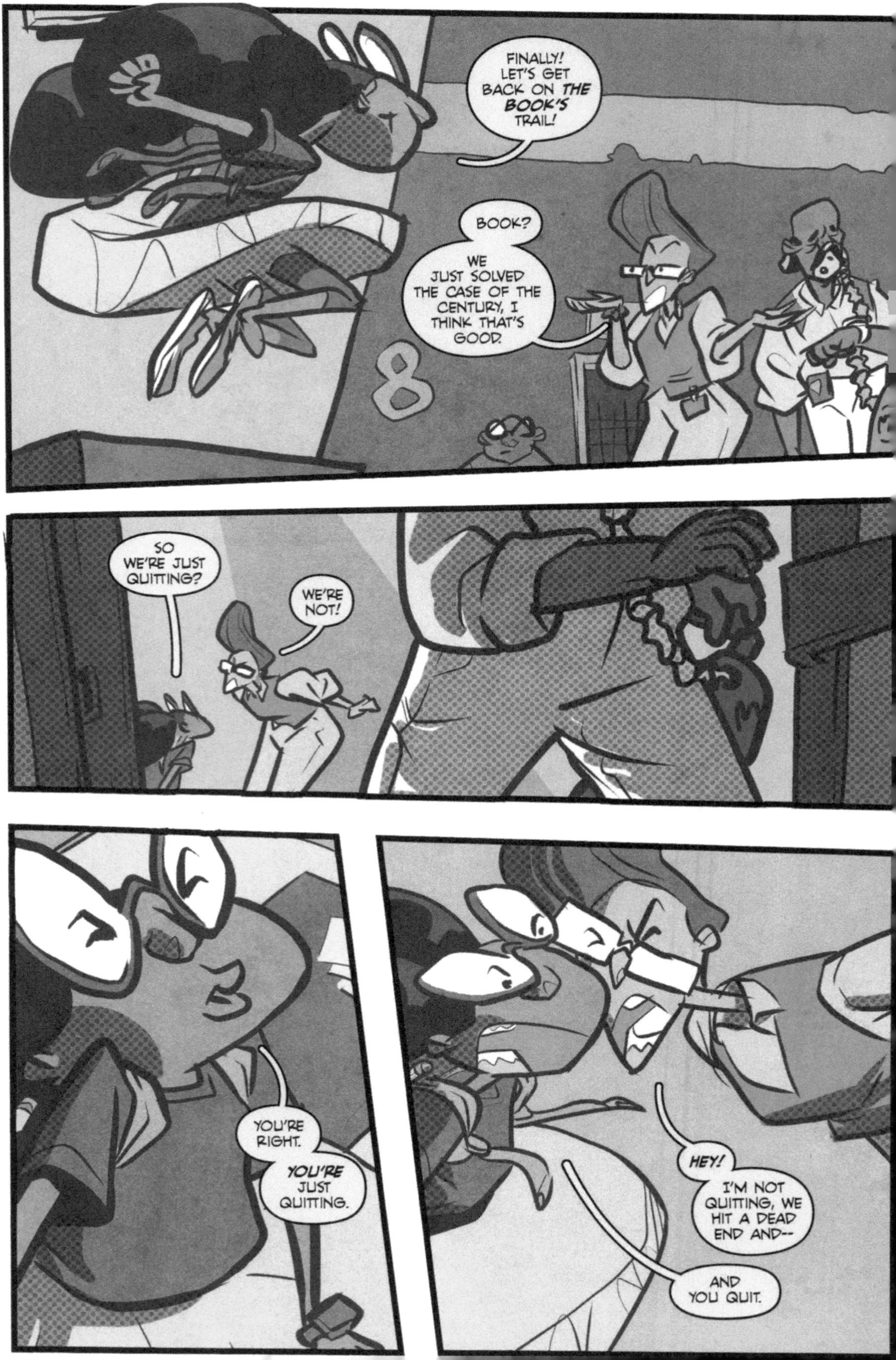
FINALLY! LET'S GET BACK ON THE BOOK'S TRAIL!
BOOK?
WE JUST SOLVED THE CASE OF THE CENTURY, I THINK THAT'S GOOD.
8
SO WE'RE JUST QUITTING?
WE'RE NOT!
YOU'RE RIGHT.
YOU'RE JUST QUITTING.
HEY!
I'M NOT QUITTING, WE HIT A DEAD END AND--
AND YOU QUIT.

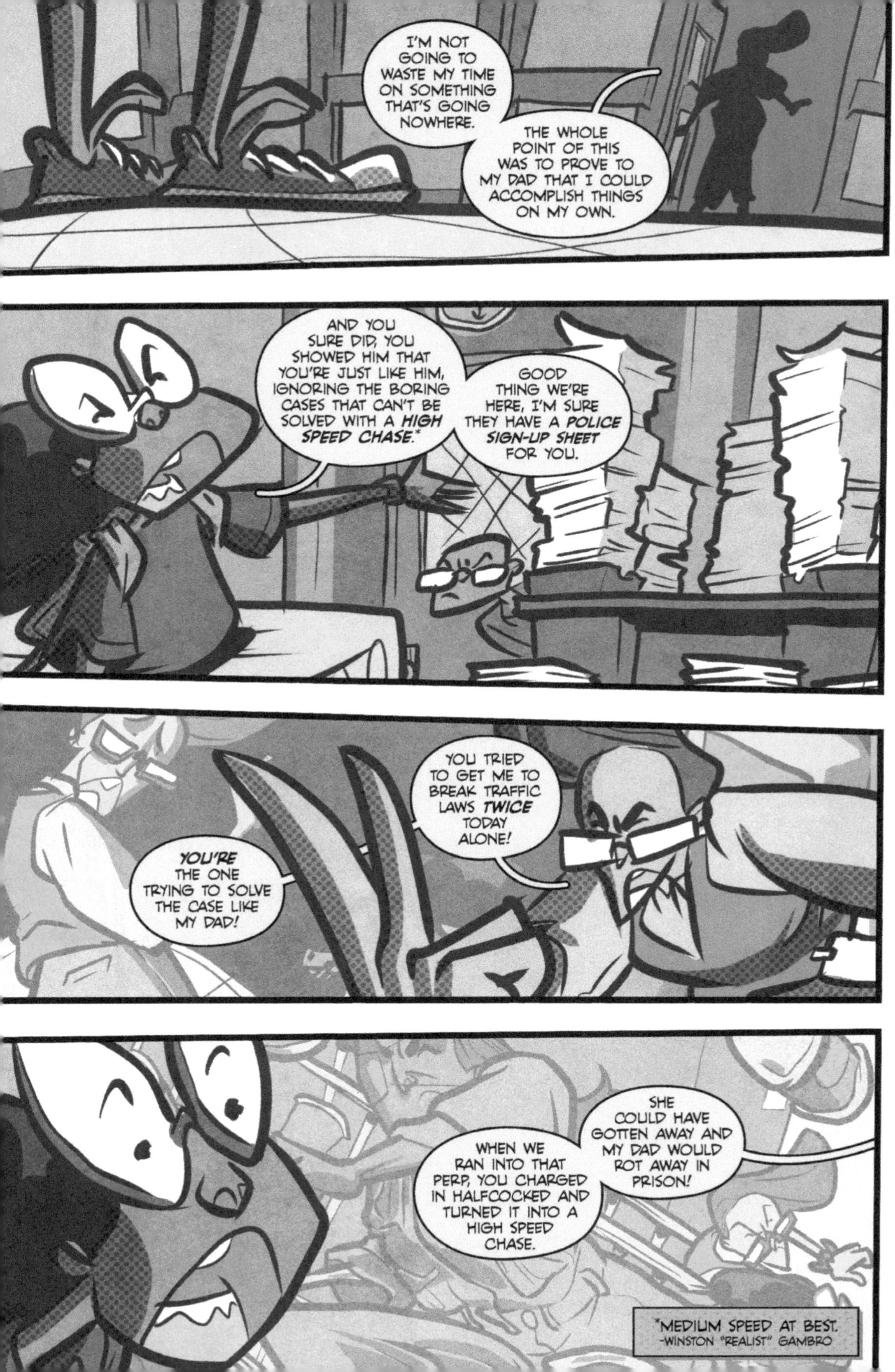
I'M NOT GOING TO WASTE MY TIME ON SOMETHING THAT'S GOING NOWHERE.
THE WHOLE POINT OF THIS WAS TO PROVE TO MY DAD THAT I COULD ACCOMPLISH THINGS ON MY OWN.
AND YOU SURE DID, YOU SHOWED HIM THAT YOU'RE JUST LIKE HIM, IGNORING THE BORING CASES THAT CAN'T BE SOLVED WITH A ***HIGH SPEED CHASE***.*
GOOD THING WE'RE HERE, I'M SURE THEY HAVE A ***POLICE SIGN-UP SHEET*** FOR YOU.
YOU'RE THE ONE TRYING TO SOLVE THE CASE LIKE MY DAD!
YOU TRIED TO GET ME TO BREAK TRAFFIC LAWS ***TWICE*** TODAY ALONE!
WHEN WE RAN INTO THAT PERP, YOU CHARGED IN HALFCOCKED AND TURNED IT INTO A HIGH SPEED CHASE.
SHE COULD HAVE GOTTEN AWAY AND MY DAD WOULD ROT AWAY IN PRISON!
*MEDIUM SPEED AT BEST.
-WINSTON "REALIST" GAMBRO

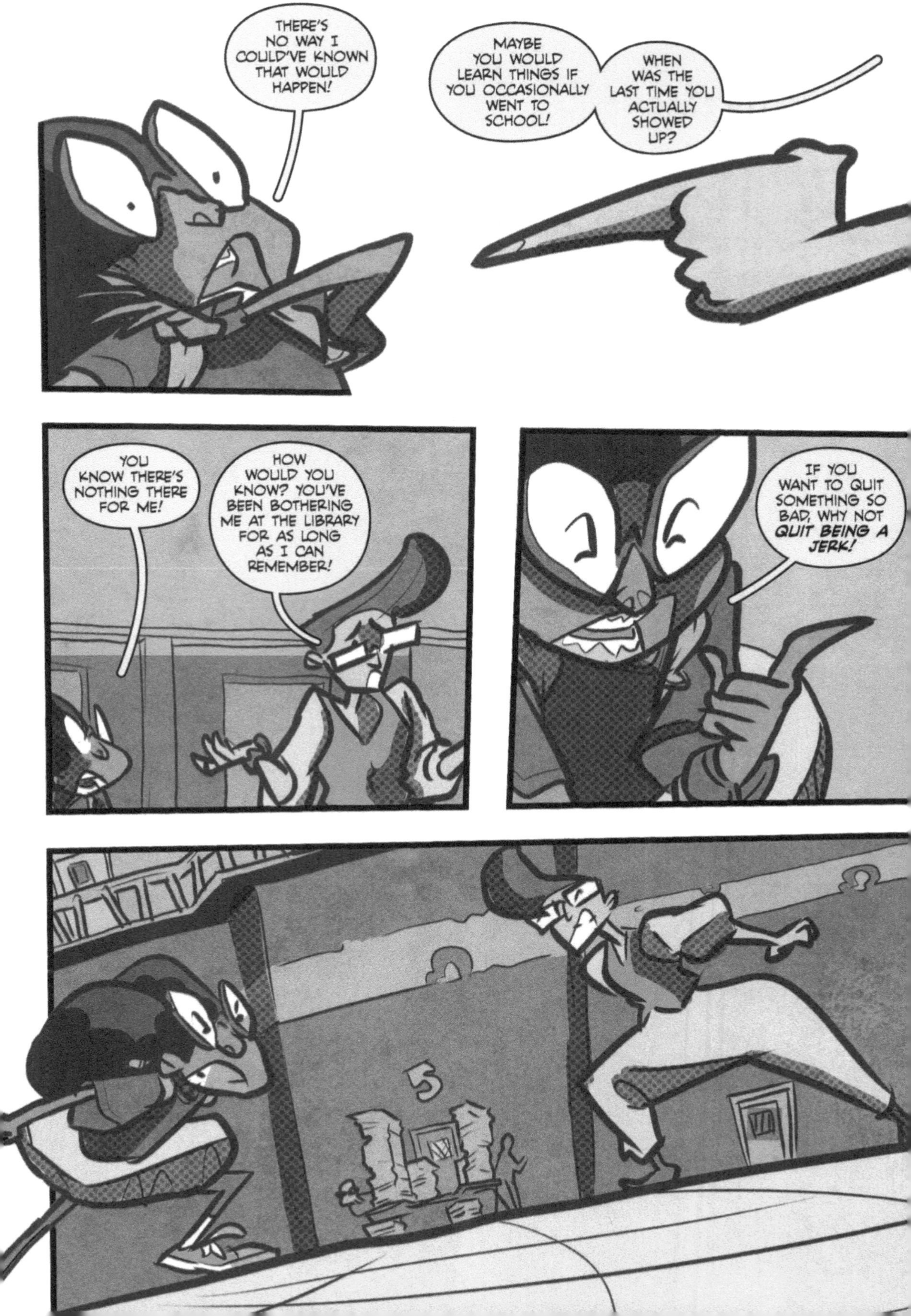
THERE'S NO WAY I COULD'VE KNOWN THAT WOULD HAPPEN!
MAYBE YOU WOULD LEARN THINGS IF YOU OCCASIONALLY WENT TO SCHOOL!
WHEN WAS THE LAST TIME YOU ACTUALLY SHOWED UP?
YOU KNOW THERE'S NOTHING THERE FOR ME!
HOW WOULD YOU KNOW? YOU'VE BEEN BOTHERING ME AT THE LIBRARY FOR AS LONG AS I CAN REMEMBER!
IF YOU WANT TO QUIT SOMETHING SO BAD, WHY NOT ***QUIT BEING A JERK!***
5

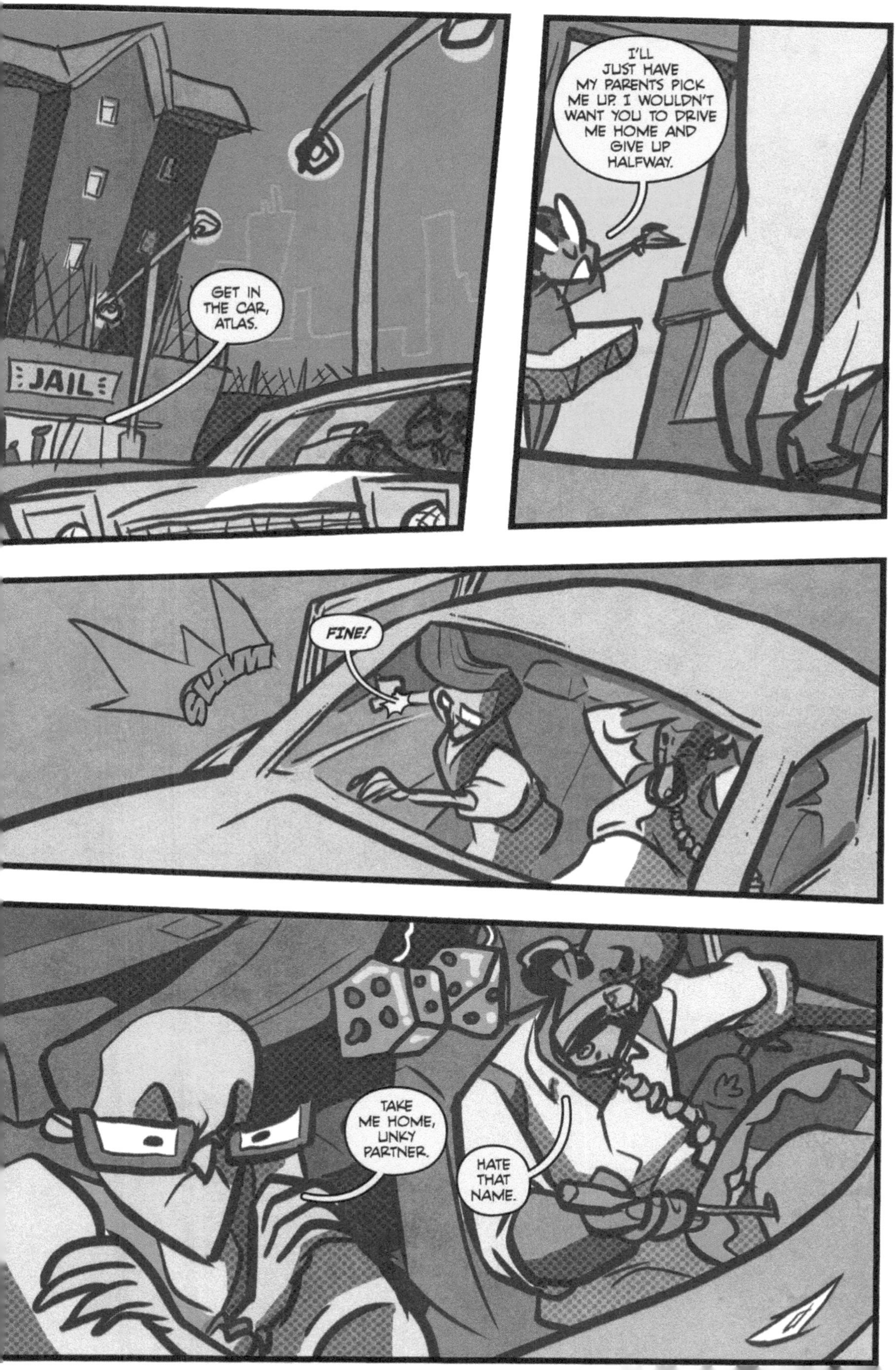
JAIL
GET IN THE CAR, ATLAS.
I'LL JUST HAVE MY PARENTS PICK ME UP. I WOULDN'T WANT YOU TO DRIVE ME HOME AND GIVE UP HALFWAY.
SLAM
FINE!
TAKE ME HOME, UNKY PARTNER.
HATE THAT NAME.

CHAPTER ELEVEN:

TURN TURN TURN

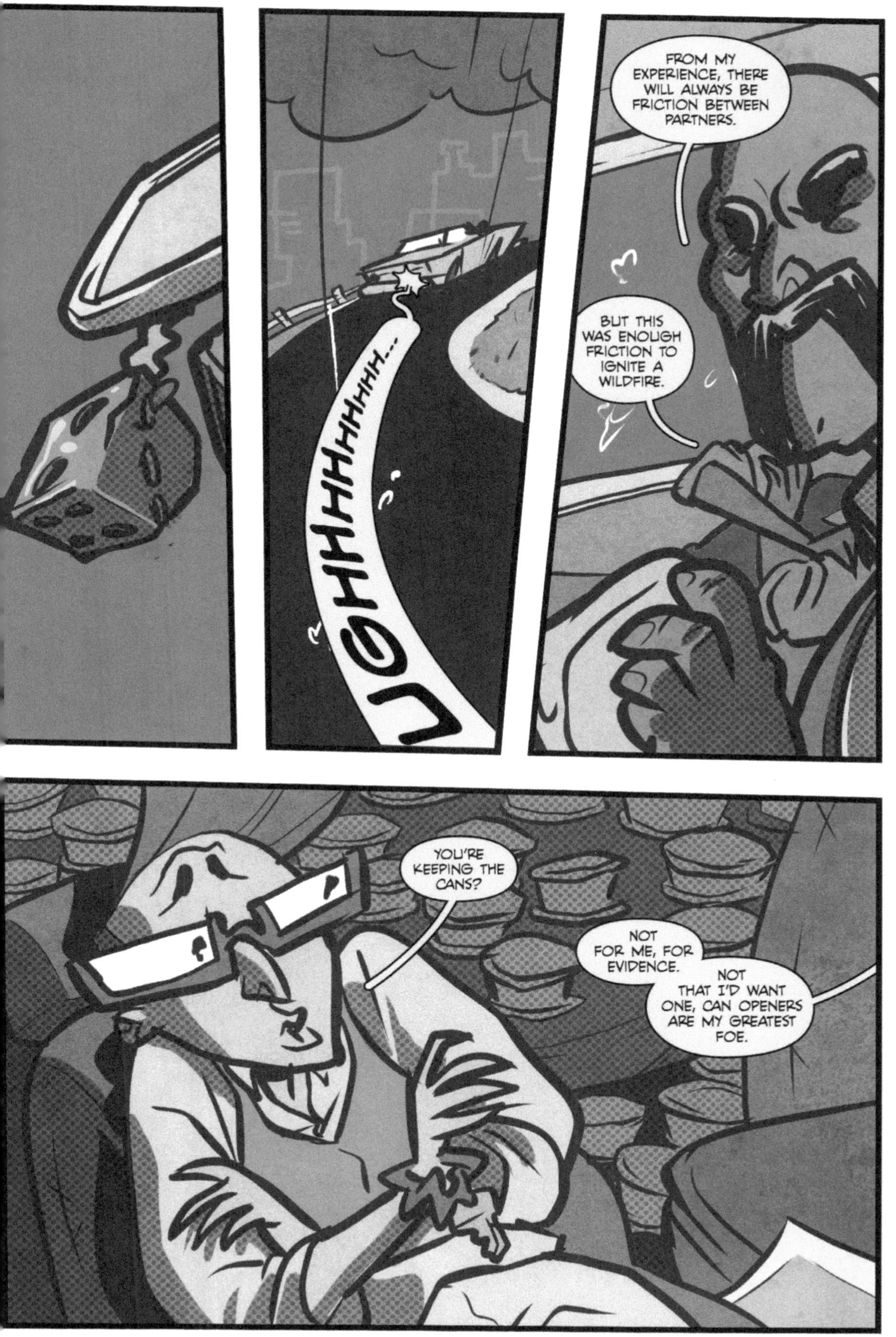
UGHHHHHHHHHHHH...
FROM MY EXPERIENCE, THERE WILL ALWAYS BE FRICTION BETWEEN PARTNERS.
BUT THIS WAS ENOUGH FRICTION TO IGNITE A WILDFIRE.
YOU'RE KEEPING THE CANS?
NOT FOR ME, FOR EVIDENCE.
NOT THAT I'D WANT ONE, CAN OPENERS ARE MY GREATEST FOE.

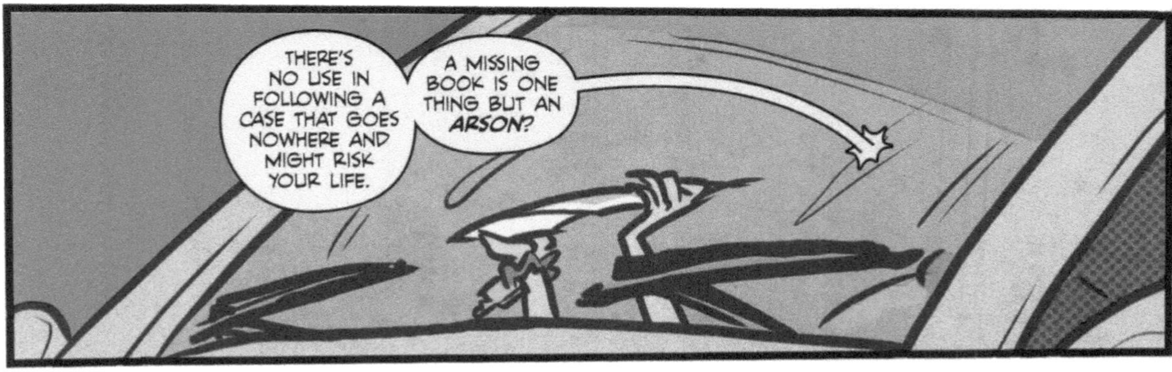
THERE'S NO USE IN FOLLOWING A CASE THAT GOES NOWHERE AND MIGHT RISK YOUR LIFE.
A MISSING BOOK IS ONE THING BUT AN *ARSON*?

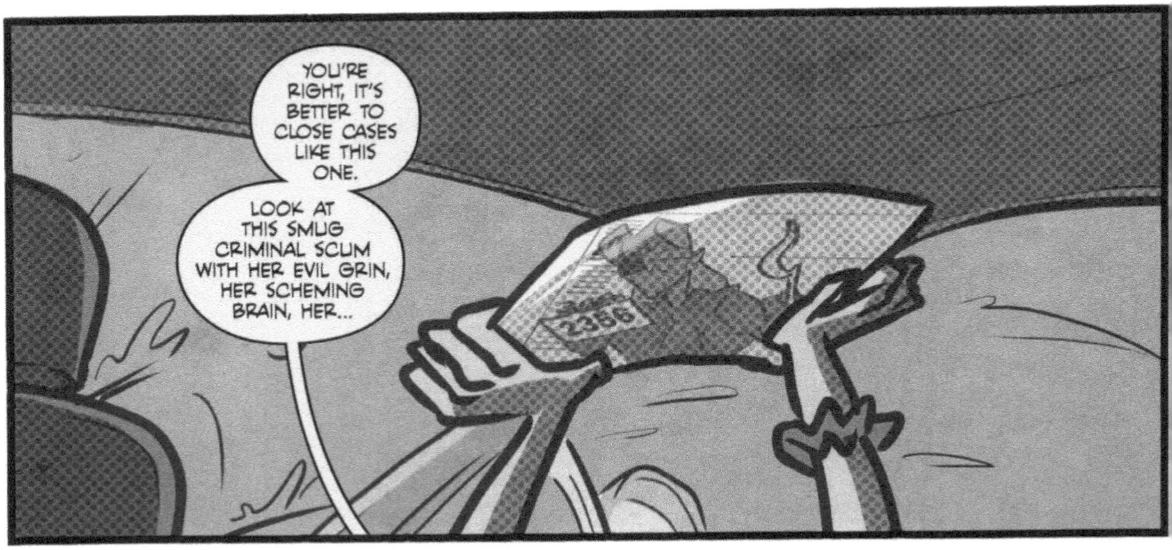
YOU'RE RIGHT, IT'S BETTER TO CLOSE CASES LIKE THIS ONE.
LOOK AT THIS SMUG CRIMINAL SCUM WITH HER EVIL GRIN, HER SCHEMING BRAIN, HER...
2356

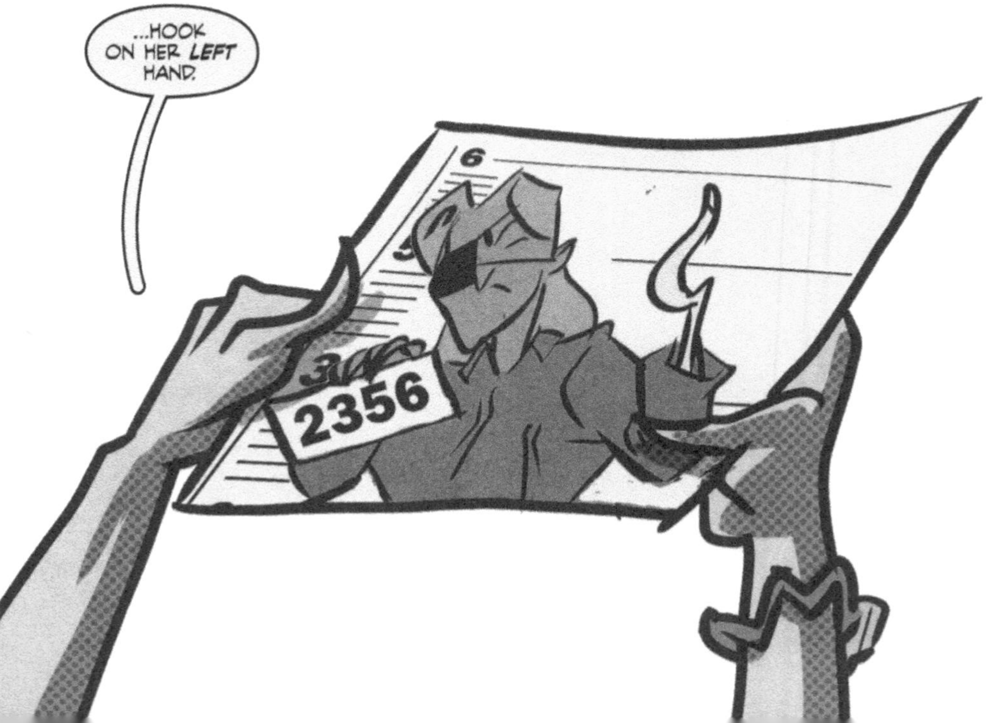
...HOOK ON HER *LEFT* HAND.
6
2356

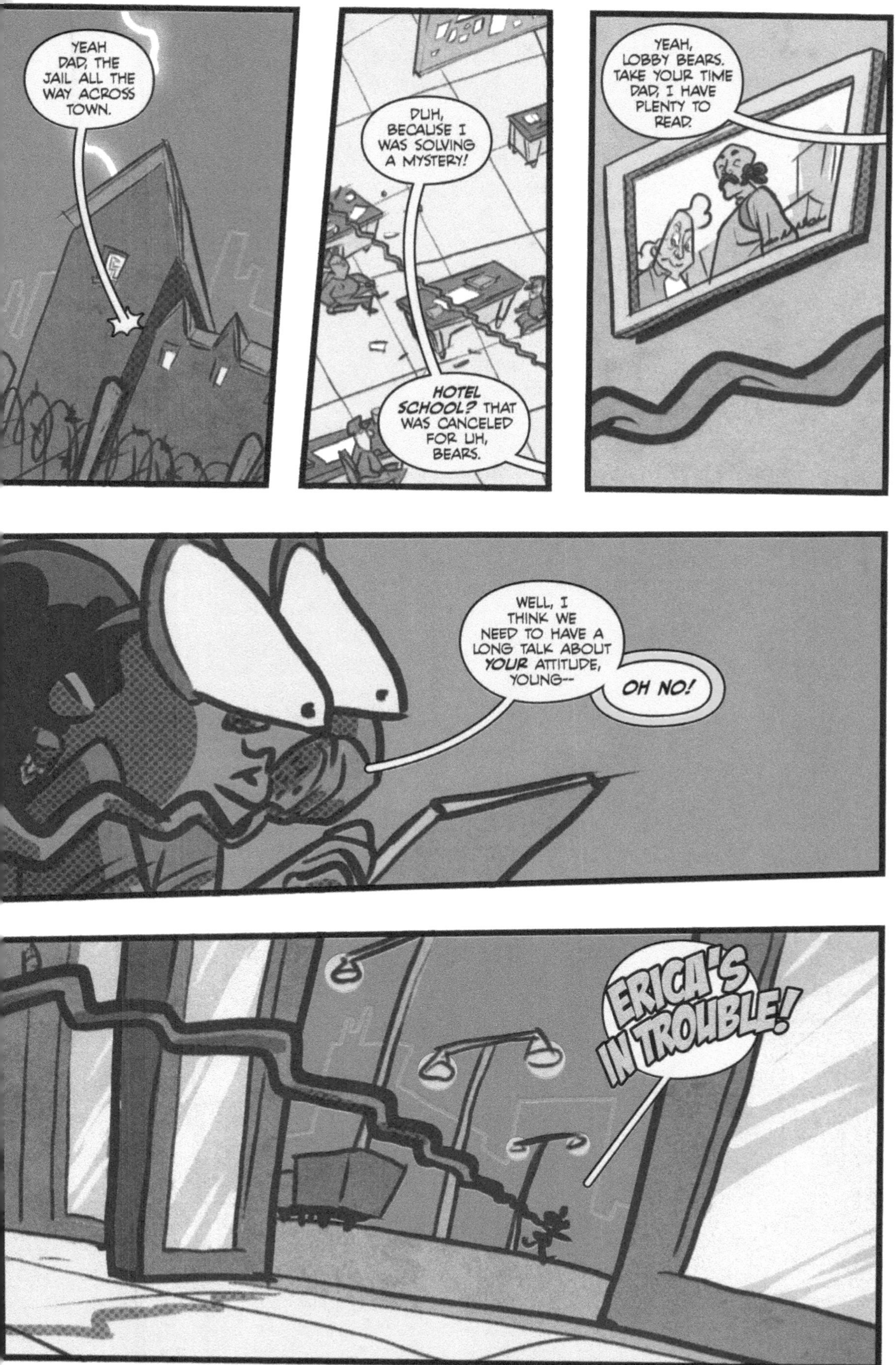
YEAH DAD, THE JAIL ALL THE WAY ACROSS TOWN.
DUH, BECAUSE I WAS SOLVING A MYSTERY!
HOTEL SCHOOL? THAT WAS CANCELED FOR UH, BEARS.
YEAH, LOBBY BEARS. TAKE YOUR TIME DAD, I HAVE PLENTY TO READ.
WELL, I THINK WE NEED TO HAVE A LONG TALK ABOUT YOUR ATTITUDE, YOUNG--
OH NO!
ERICA'S IN TROUBLE!

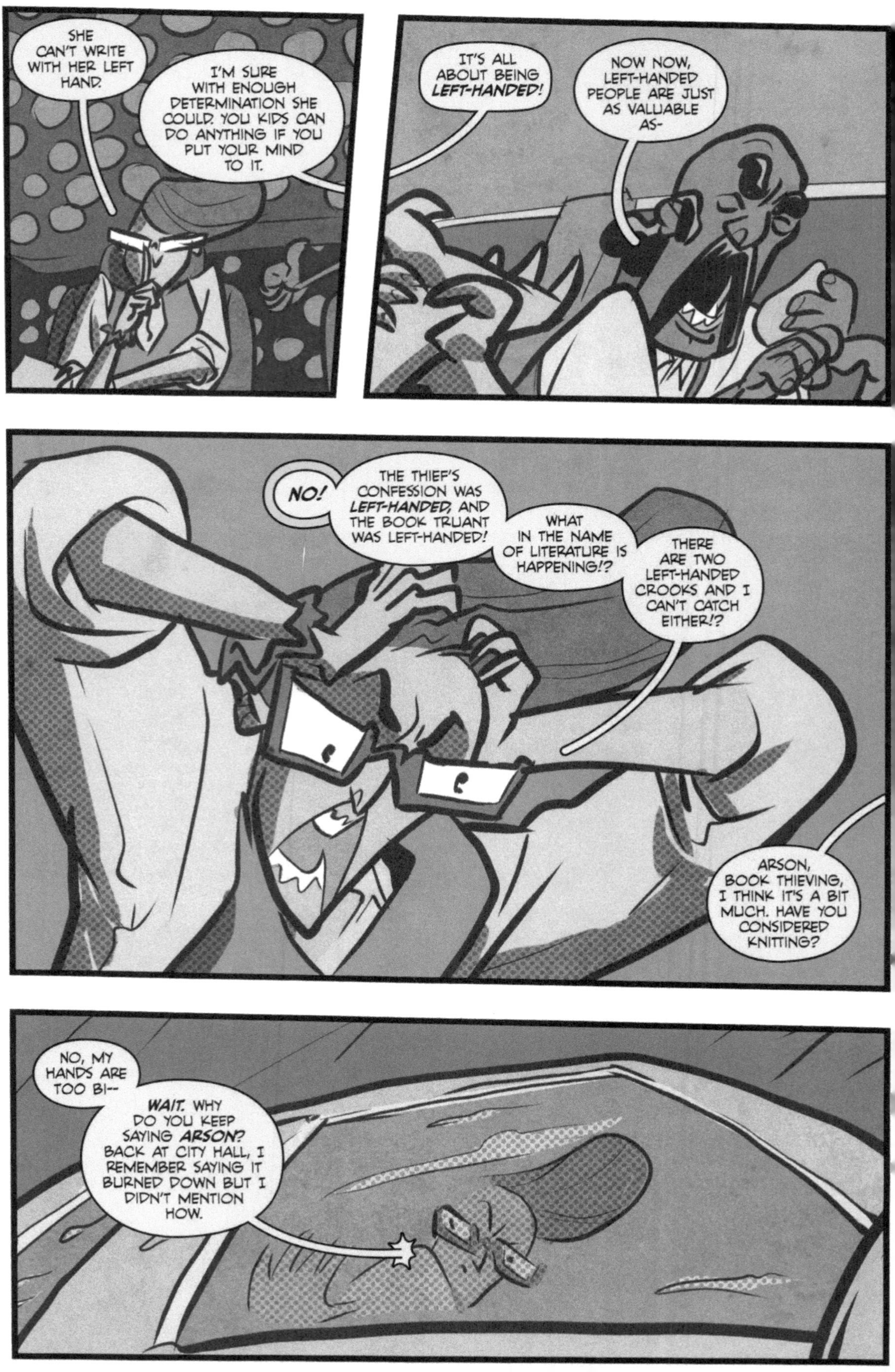
SHE CAN'T WRITE WITH HER LEFT HAND.
I'M SURE WITH ENOUGH DETERMINATION SHE COULD. YOU KIDS CAN DO ANYTHING IF YOU PUT YOUR MIND TO IT.
IT'S ALL ABOUT BEING LEFT-HANDED!
NOW NOW, LEFT-HANDED PEOPLE ARE JUST AS VALUABLE AS-
NO!
THE THIEF'S CONFESSION WAS LEFT-HANDED, AND THE BOOK TRUANT WAS LEFT-HANDED!
WHAT IN THE NAME OF LITERATURE IS HAPPENING!?
THERE ARE TWO LEFT-HANDED CROOKS AND I CAN'T CATCH EITHER!?
ARSON, BOOK THIEVING, I THINK IT'S A BIT MUCH. HAVE YOU CONSIDERED KNITTING?
NO, MY HANDS ARE TOO BI--
WAIT. WHY DO YOU KEEP SAYING ARSON? BACK AT CITY HALL, I REMEMBER SAYING IT BURNED DOWN BUT I DIDN'T MENTION HOW.

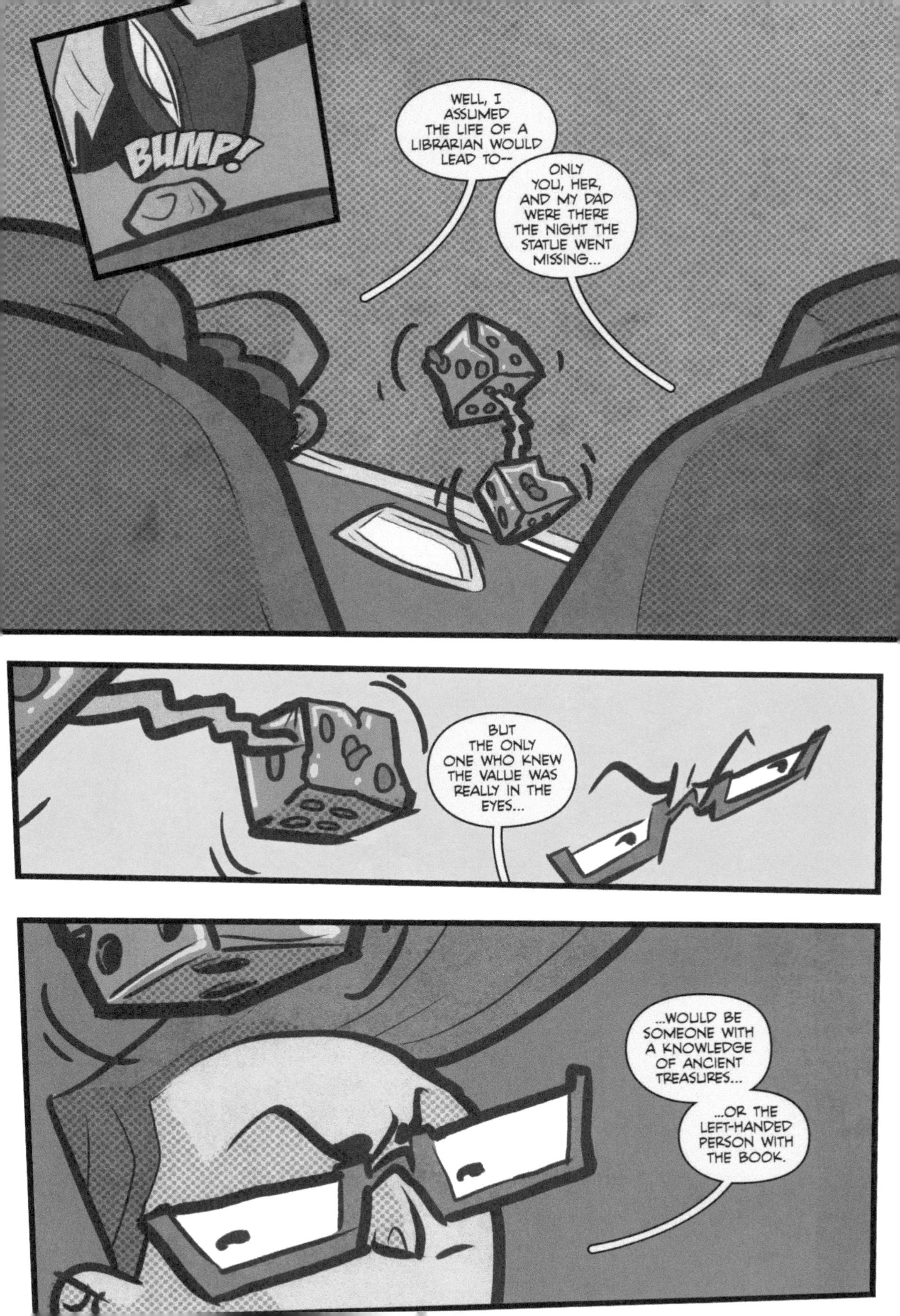
BUMP!
WELL, I ASSUMED THE LIFE OF A LIBRARIAN WOULD LEAD TO--
ONLY YOU, HER, AND MY DAD WERE THERE THE NIGHT THE STATUE WENT MISSING...
BUT THE ONLY ONE WHO KNEW THE VALUE WAS REALLY IN THE EYES...
...WOULD BE SOMEONE WITH A KNOWLEDGE OF ANCIENT TREASURES...
...OR THE LEFT-HANDED PERSON WITH THE BOOK.

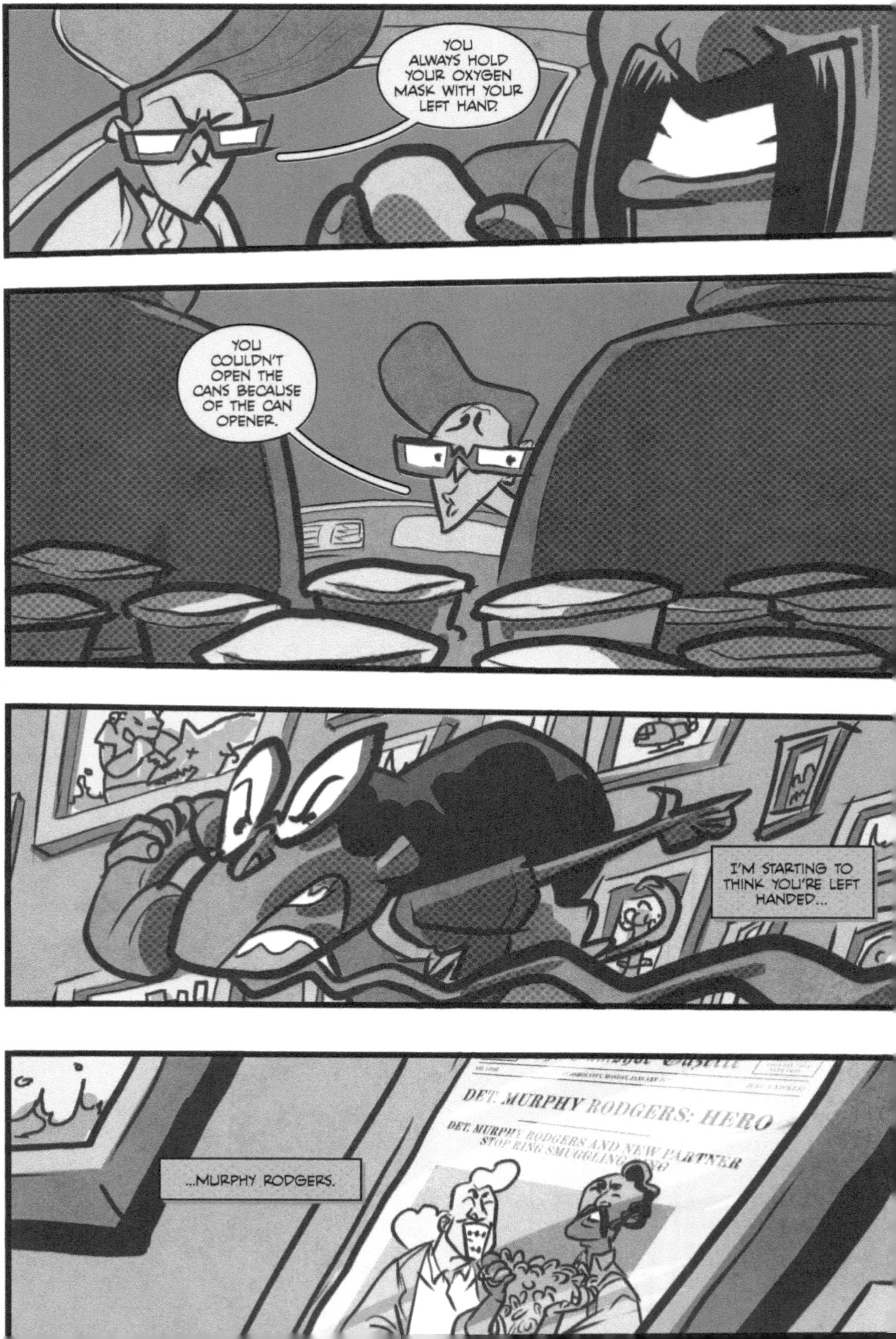
YOU ALWAYS HOLD YOUR OXYGEN MASK WITH YOUR LEFT HAND.
YOU COULDN'T OPEN THE CANS BECAUSE OF THE CAN OPENER.
I'M STARTING TO THINK YOU'RE LEFT HANDED...
...MURPHY RODGERS.
DET. MURPHY RODGERS: HERO
DET. MURPHY RODGERS AND NEW PARTNER STOP RING SMUGGLING

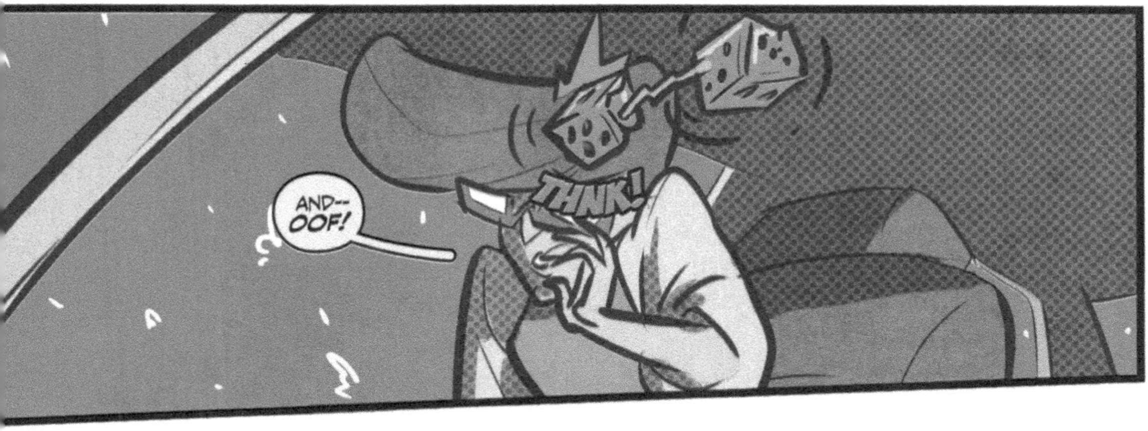
AND-- OOF!
THNK!

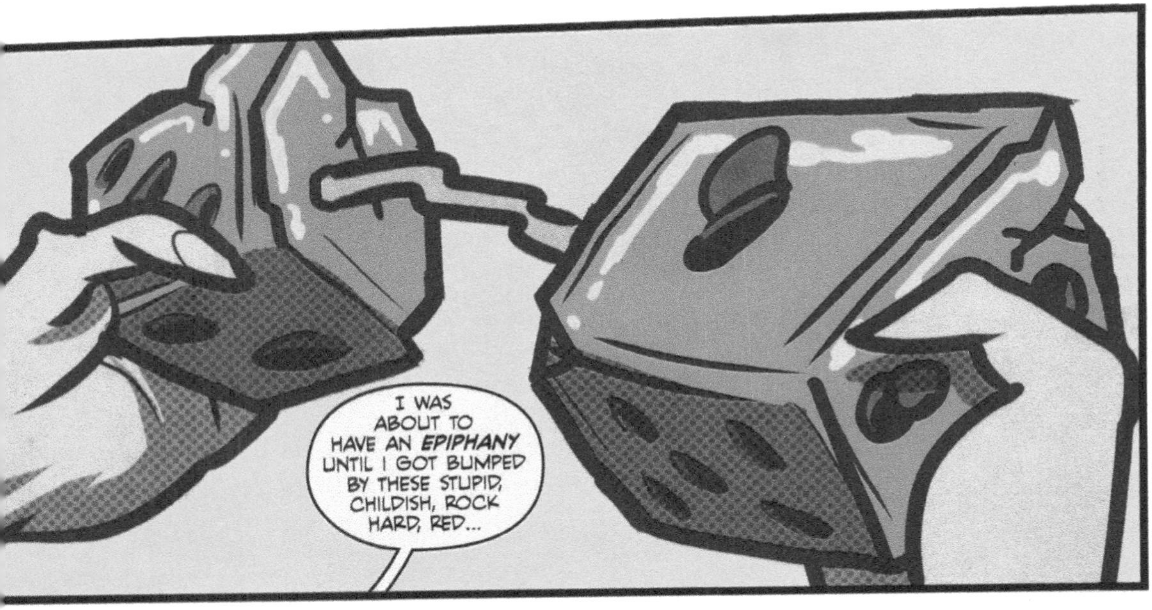
I WAS ABOUT TO HAVE AN *EPIPHANY* UNTIL I GOT BUMPED BY THESE STUPID, CHILDISH, ROCK HARD, RED...

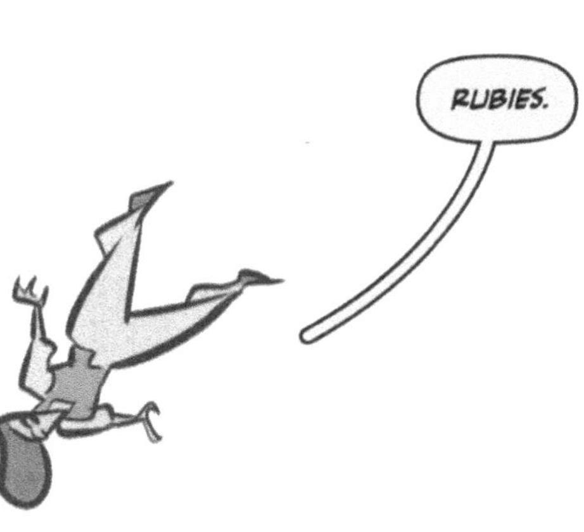
RUBIES.

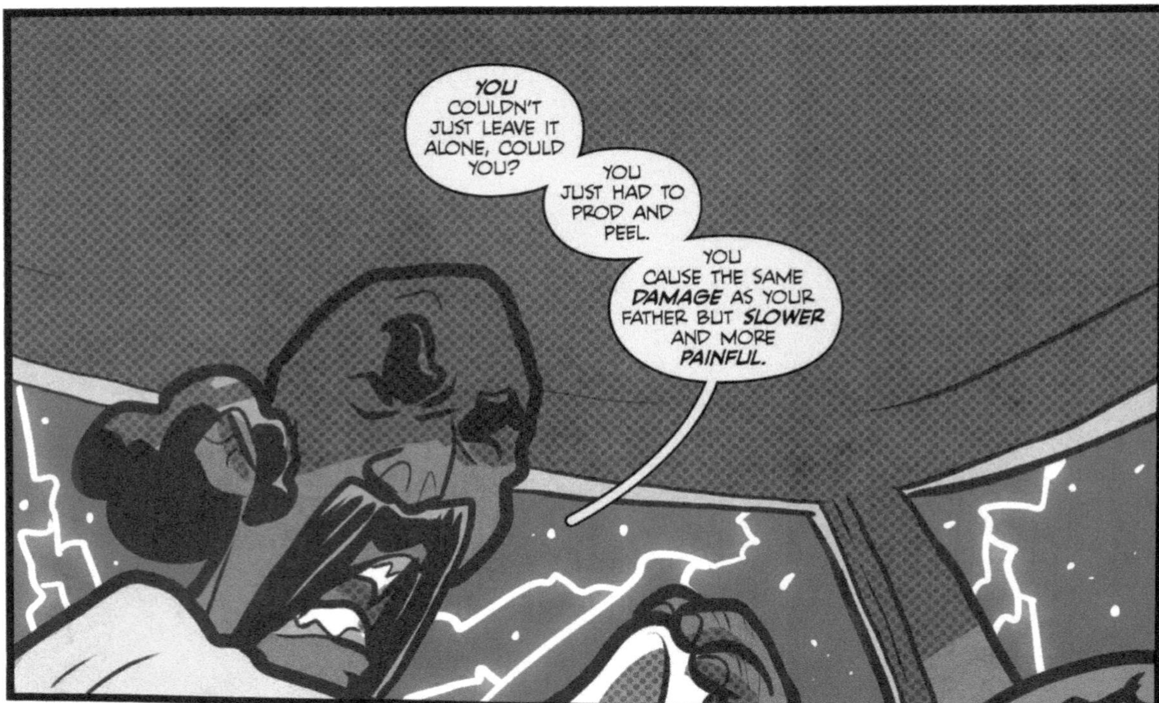
YOU COULDN'T JUST LEAVE IT ALONE, COULD YOU?
YOU JUST HAD TO PROD AND PEEL.
YOU CAUSE THE SAME DAMAGE AS YOUR FATHER BUT SLOWER AND MORE PAINFUL.

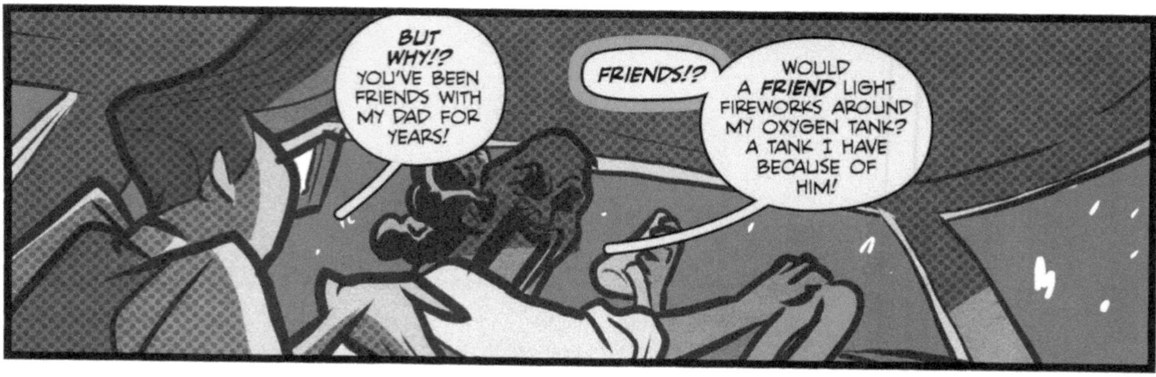
BUT WHY!? YOU'VE BEEN FRIENDS WITH MY DAD FOR YEARS!
FRIENDS!?
WOULD A FRIEND LIGHT FIREWORKS AROUND MY OXYGEN TANK? A TANK I HAVE BECAUSE OF HIM!

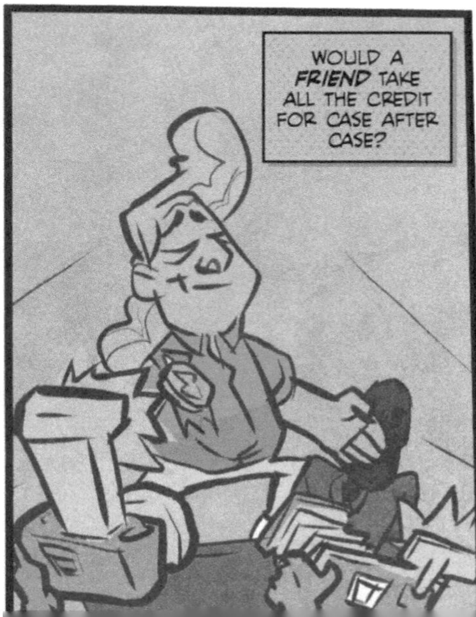
WOULD A FRIEND TAKE ALL THE CREDIT FOR CASE AFTER CASE?

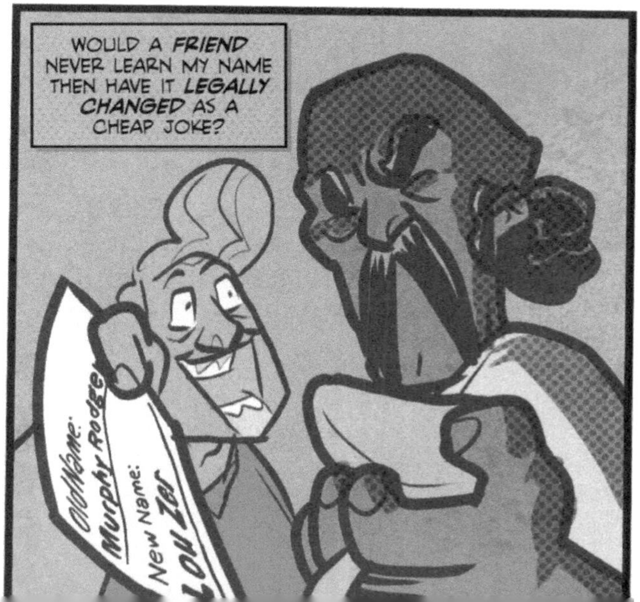
WOULD A FRIEND NEVER LEARN MY NAME THEN HAVE IT LEGALLY CHANGED AS A CHEAP JOKE?
Old Name:
Murphy Rodge
New Name:

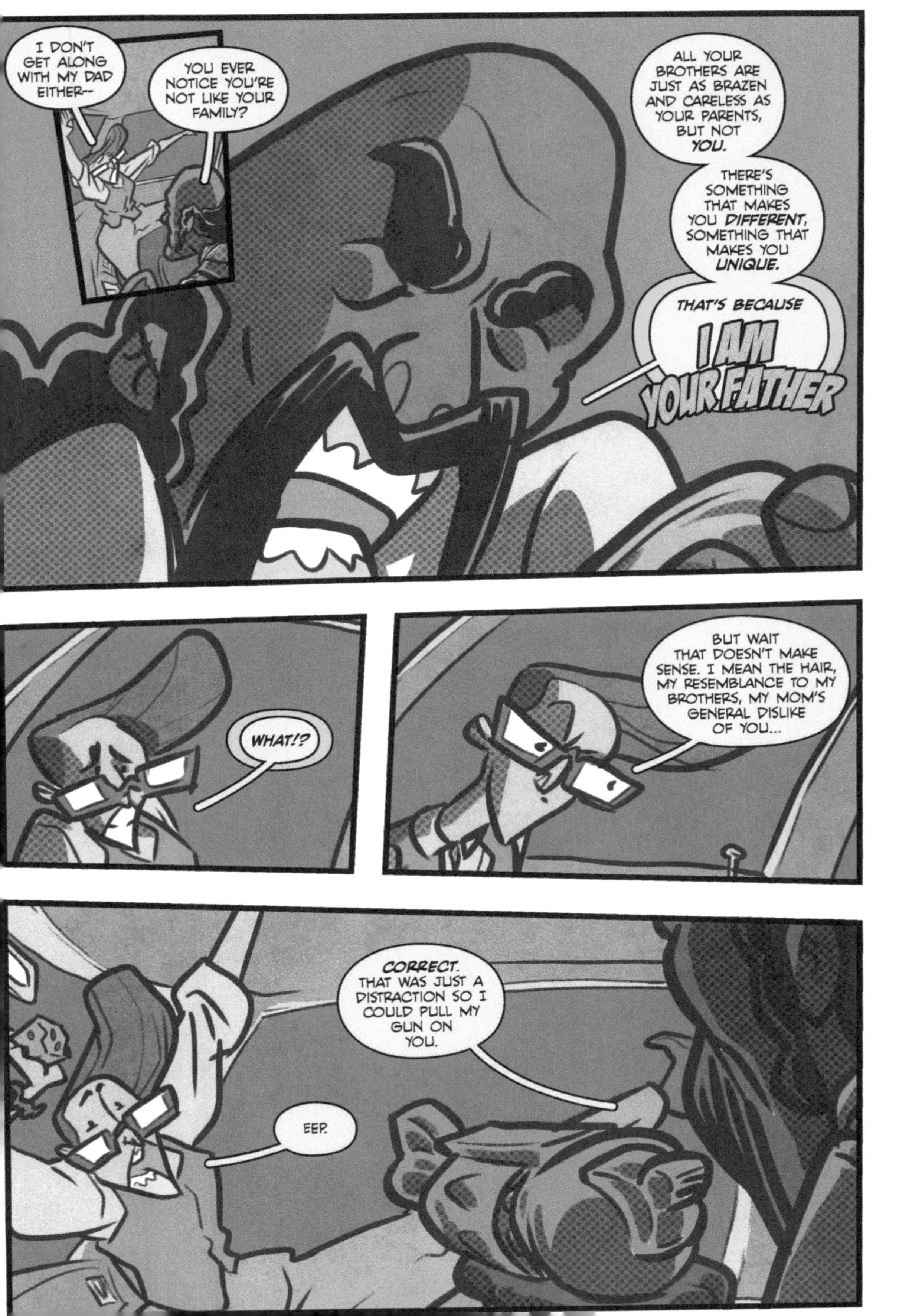

I DON'T GET ALONG WITH MY DAD EITHER--
YOU EVER NOTICE YOU'RE NOT LIKE YOUR FAMILY?
ALL YOUR BROTHERS ARE JUST AS BRAZEN AND CARELESS AS YOUR PARENTS, BUT NOT *YOU.*
THERE'S SOMETHING THAT MAKES YOU *DIFFERENT*, SOMETHING THAT MAKES YOU *UNIQUE.*
THAT'S BECAUSE I AM YOUR FATHER
WHAT!?
BUT WAIT THAT DOESN'T MAKE SENSE. I MEAN THE HAIR, MY RESEMBLANCE TO MY BROTHERS, MY MOM'S GENERAL DISLIKE OF YOU...
CORRECT. THAT WAS JUST A DISTRACTION SO I COULD PULL MY GUN ON YOU.
EEP.

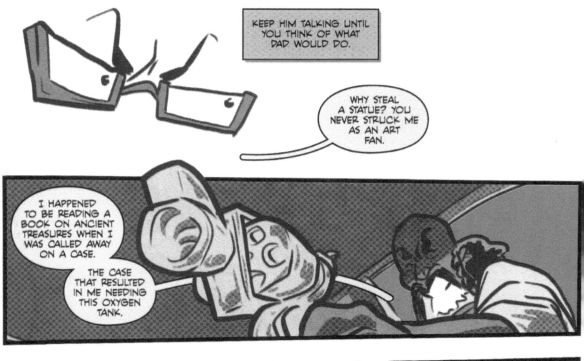

KEEP HIM TALKING UNTIL YOU THINK OF WHAT DAD WOULD DO.

WHY STEAL A STATUE? YOU NEVER STRUCK ME AS AN ART FAN.

I HAPPENED TO BE READING A BOOK ON ANCIENT TREASURES WHEN I WAS CALLED AWAY ON A CASE.

THE CASE THAT RESULTED IN ME NEEDING THIS OXYGEN TANK.

THE SAME EXPLOSION THAT INJURED ME, BLASTED ME TOWARD THE HIDING PLACE OF THE STATUE.

I TOOK IT AS A SIGN, YOUR DAD FINALLY WENT TOO FAR AND THE UNIVERSE SAID "WE'RE PAYING YOU FORWARD AND PAYING HIM BACK".

BUT OF COURSE, I COULDN'T LET ANYONE ELSE FIND THE STATUE!

IN THE CHAOS I STOWED IT IN A PLACE THAT WOULD HIDE IT FROM THE SEARCH AREA.

BUT OFFERED ME A WAY TO GET IT BACK LATER.

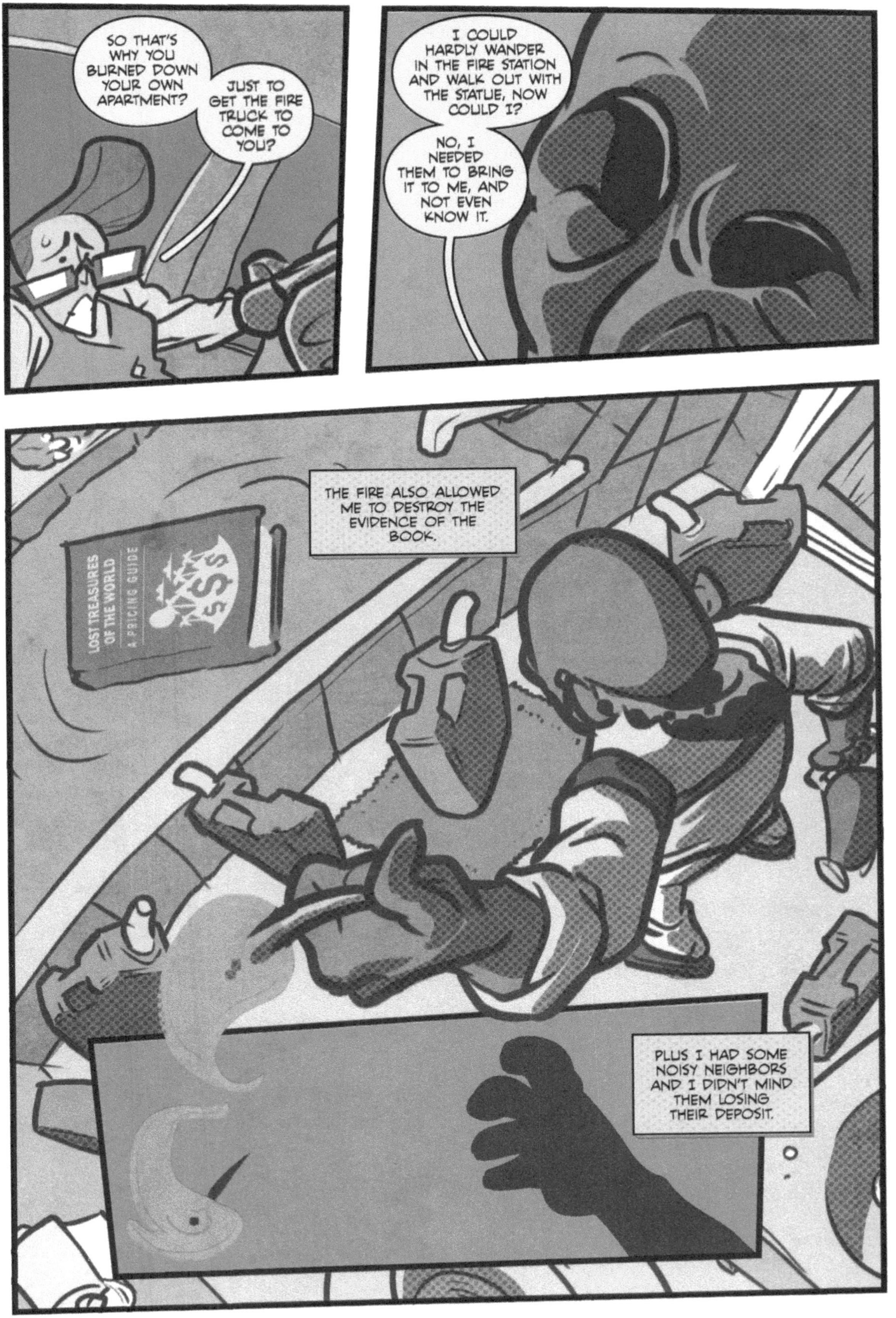
SO THAT'S WHY YOU BURNED DOWN YOUR OWN APARTMENT?
JUST TO GET THE FIRE TRUCK TO COME TO YOU?
I COULD HARDLY WANDER IN THE FIRE STATION AND WALK OUT WITH THE STATUE, NOW COULD I?
NO, I NEEDED THEM TO BRING IT TO ME, AND NOT EVEN KNOW IT.
THE FIRE ALSO ALLOWED ME TO DESTROY THE EVIDENCE OF THE BOOK.
LOST TREASURES OF THE WORLD
A PRICING GUIDE
PLUS I HAD SOME NOISY NEIGHBORS AND I DIDN'T MIND THEM LOSING THEIR DEPOSIT.

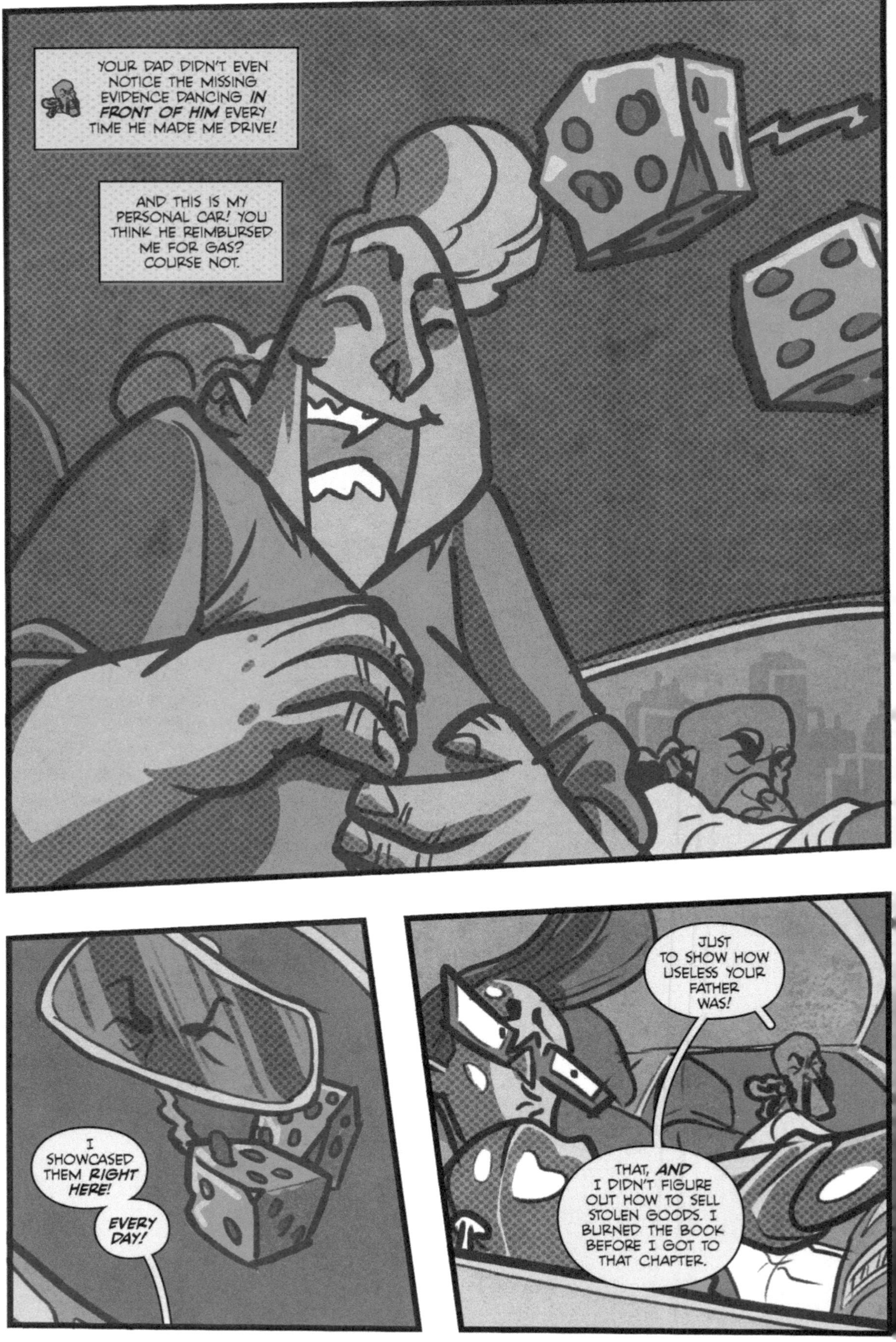
YOUR DAD DIDN'T EVEN NOTICE THE MISSING EVIDENCE DANCING *IN FRONT OF HIM* EVERY TIME HE MADE ME DRIVE!
AND THIS IS MY PERSONAL CAR! YOU THINK HE REIMBURSED ME FOR GAS? COURSE NOT.
I SHOWCASED THEM *RIGHT HERE!*
EVERY DAY!
JUST TO SHOW HOW USELESS YOUR FATHER WAS!
THAT, *AND* I DIDN'T FIGURE OUT HOW TO SELL STOLEN GOODS. I BURNED THE BOOK BEFORE I GOT TO THAT CHAPTER.

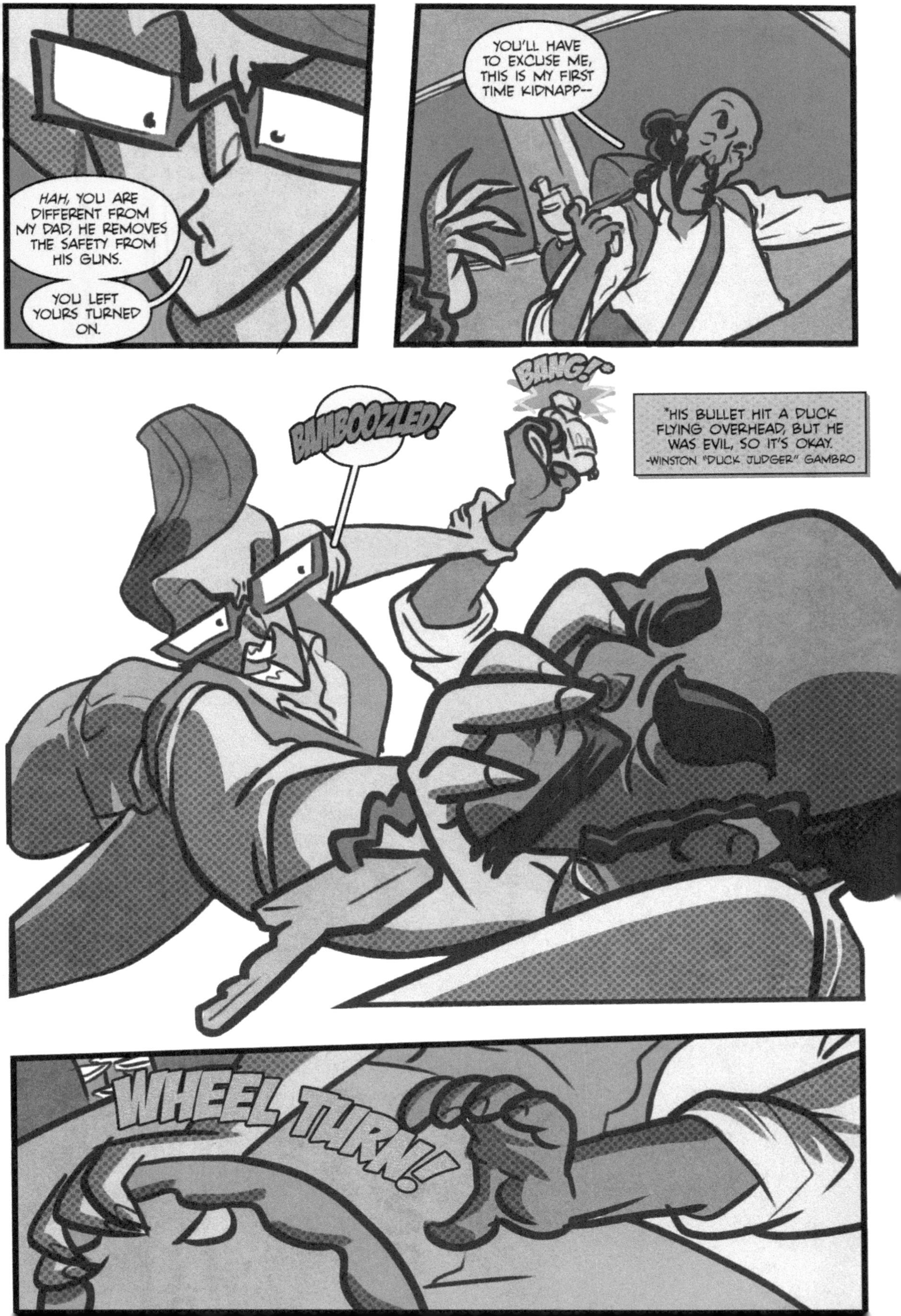

HAH, YOU ARE DIFFERENT FROM MY DAD, HE REMOVES THE SAFETY FROM HIS GUNS.
YOU LEFT YOURS TURNED ON.
YOU'LL HAVE TO EXCUSE ME, THIS IS MY FIRST TIME KIDNAPP--
BAMBOOZLED!
BANG!*
*HIS BULLET HIT A DUCK FLYING OVERHEAD, BUT HE WAS EVIL, SO IT'S OKAY. -WINSTON "DUCK JUDGER" GAMBRO
WHEEL TURN!

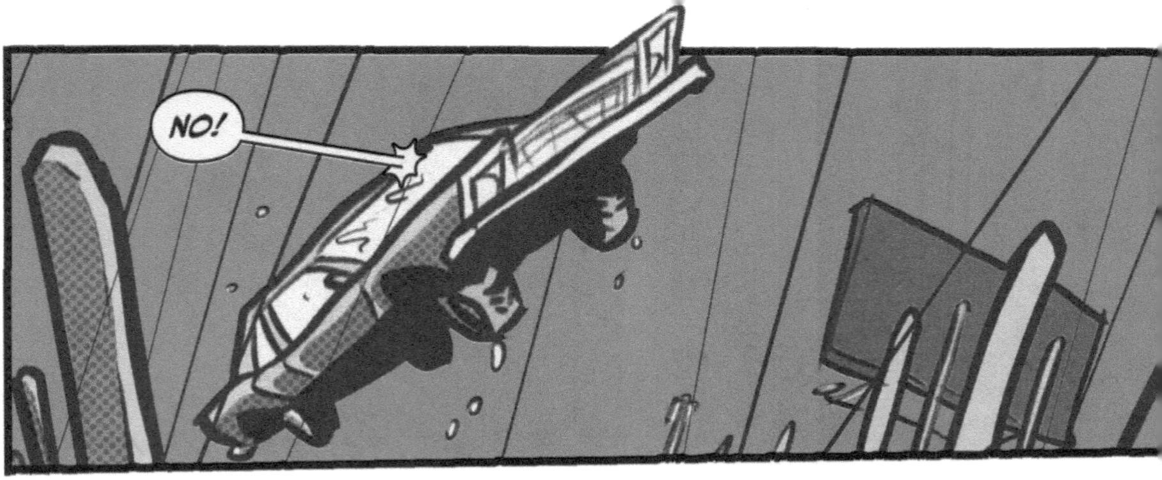
NO!
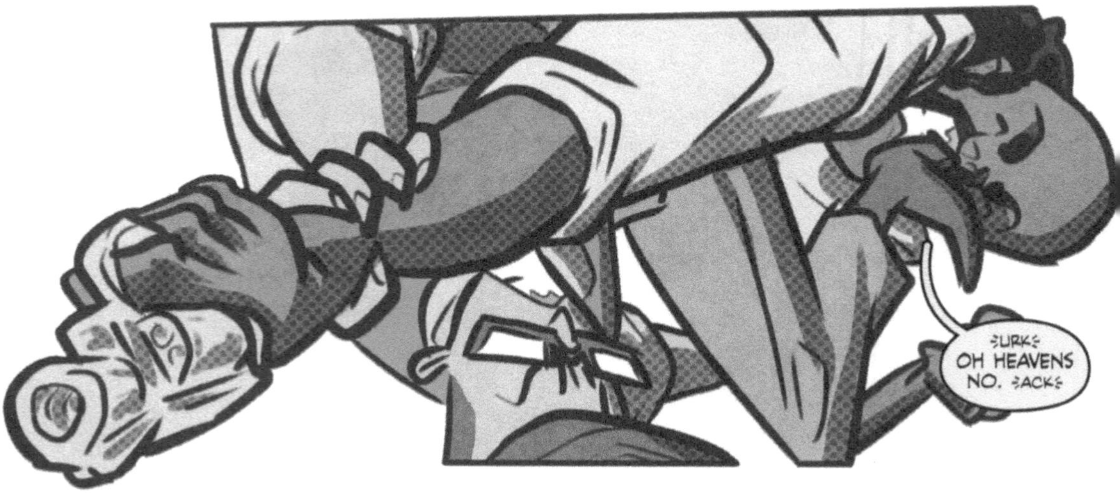
URK
OH HEAVENS NO. ACK
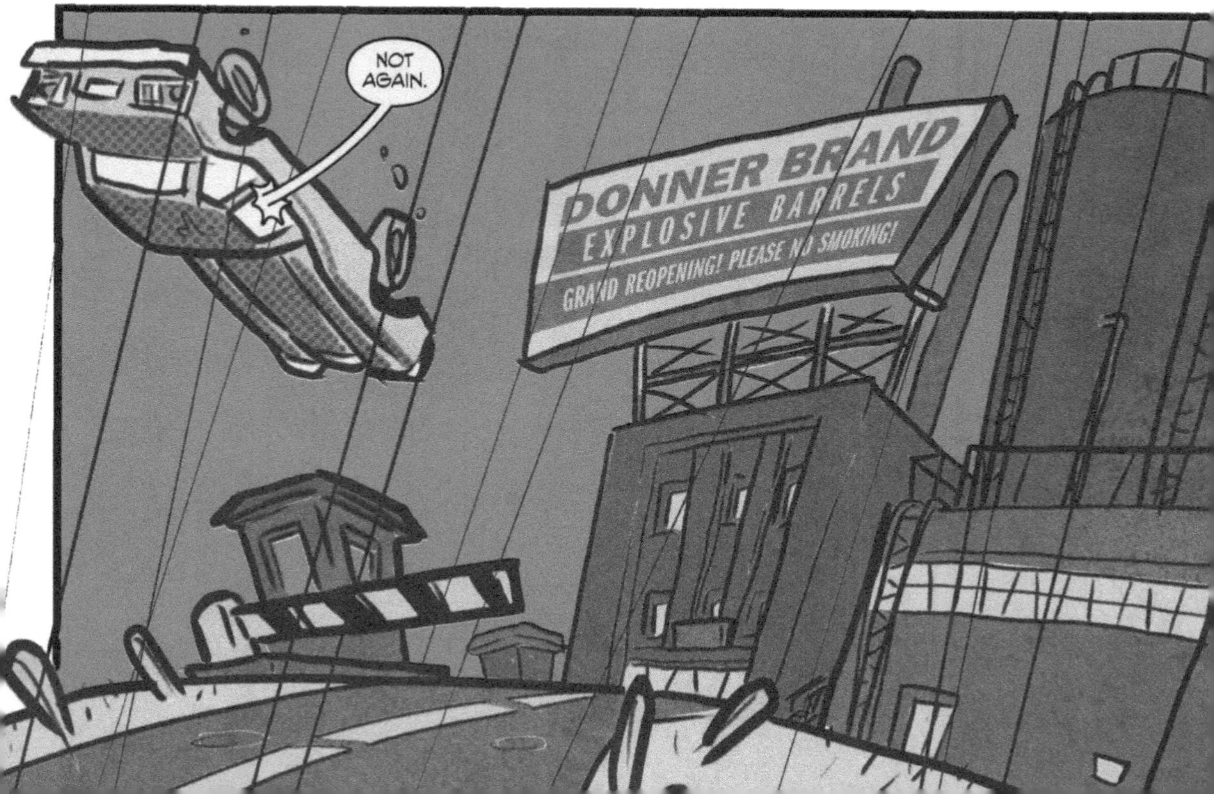
NOT AGAIN.
DONNER BRAND
EXPLOSIVE BARRELS
GRAND REOPENING! PLEASE NO SMOKING!

CHAPTER TWELVE:

THIS FACTORY ONLY PRODUCES CLIMAXES

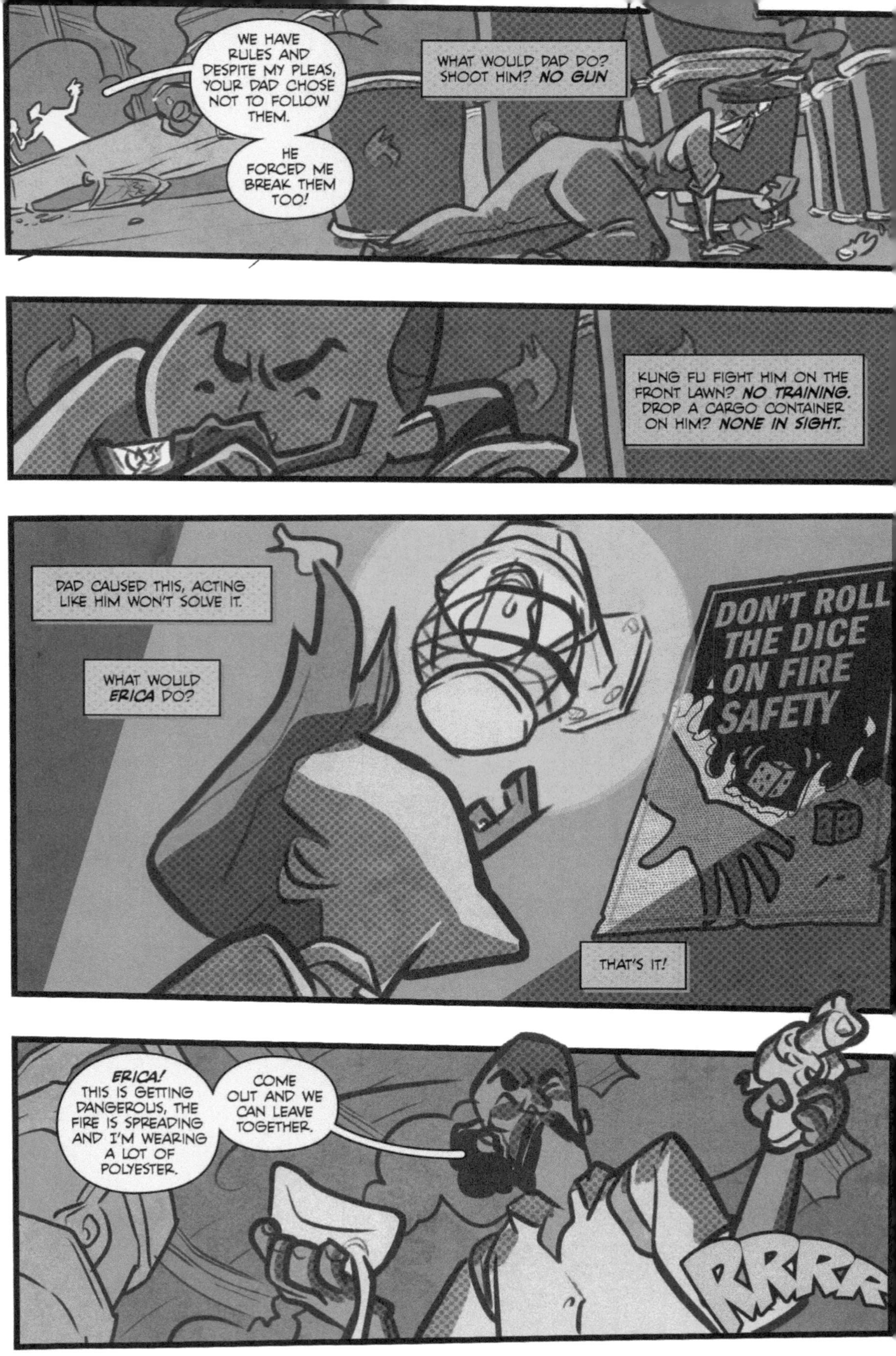
WE HAVE RULES AND DESPITE MY PLEAS, YOUR DAD CHOSE NOT TO FOLLOW THEM.
HE FORCED ME BREAK THEM TOO!
WHAT WOULD DAD DO? SHOOT HIM? NO GUN
KUNG FU FIGHT HIM ON THE FRONT LAWN? NO TRAINING. DROP A CARGO CONTAINER ON HIM? NONE IN SIGHT.
DAD CAUSED THIS, ACTING LIKE HIM WON'T SOLVE IT.
WHAT WOULD ERICA DO?
DON'T ROLL THE DICE ON FIRE SAFETY
THAT'S IT!
ERICA! THIS IS GETTING DANGEROUS, THE FIRE IS SPREADING AND I'M WEARING A LOT OF POLYESTER.
COME OUT AND WE CAN LEAVE TOGETHER.
RRRRR

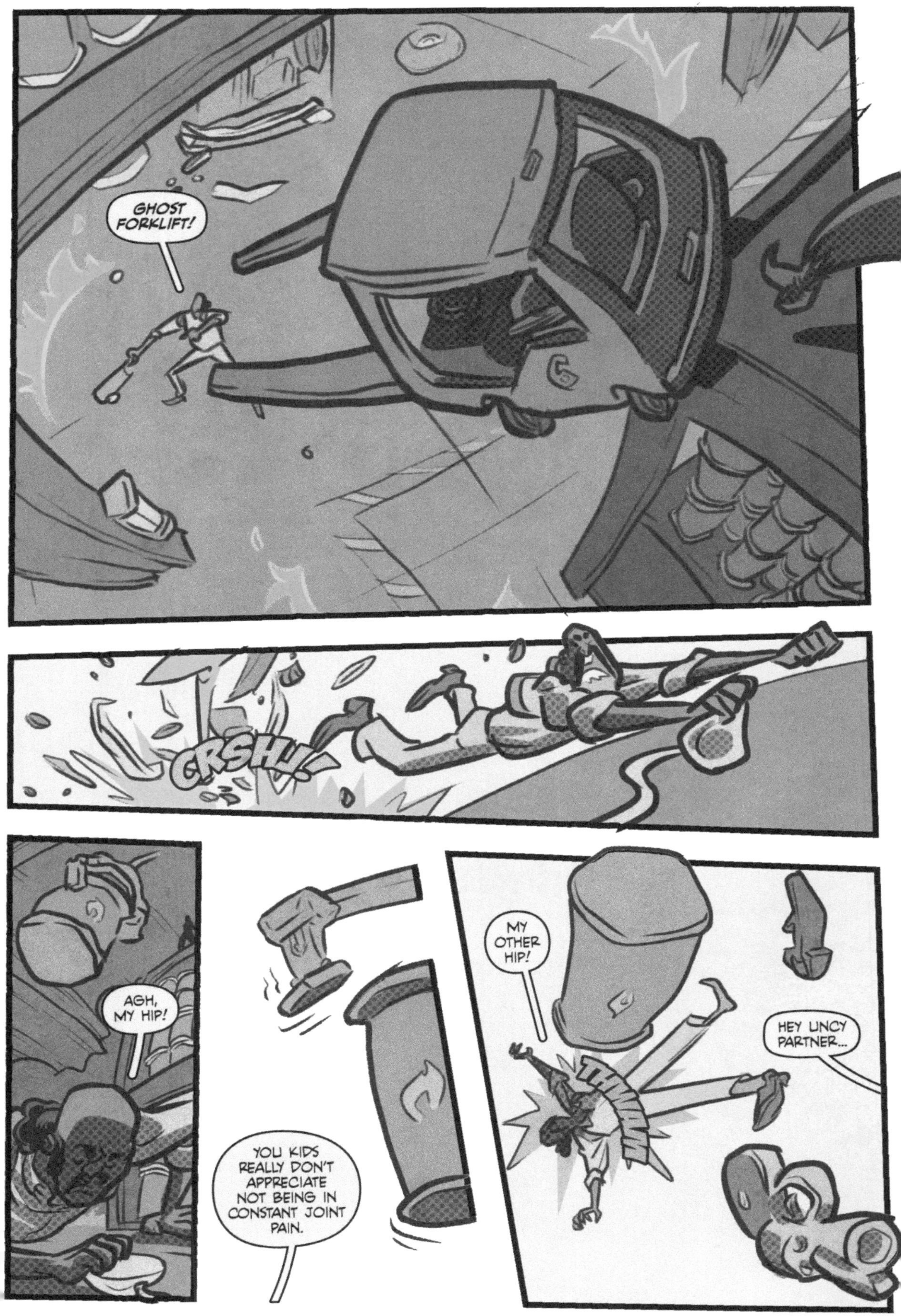
GHOST FORKLIFT!
CRSH!!
AGH, MY HIP!
YOU KIDS REALLY DON'T APPRECIATE NOT BEING IN CONSTANT JOINT PAIN.
MY OTHER HIP!
HEY UNCY PARTNER...

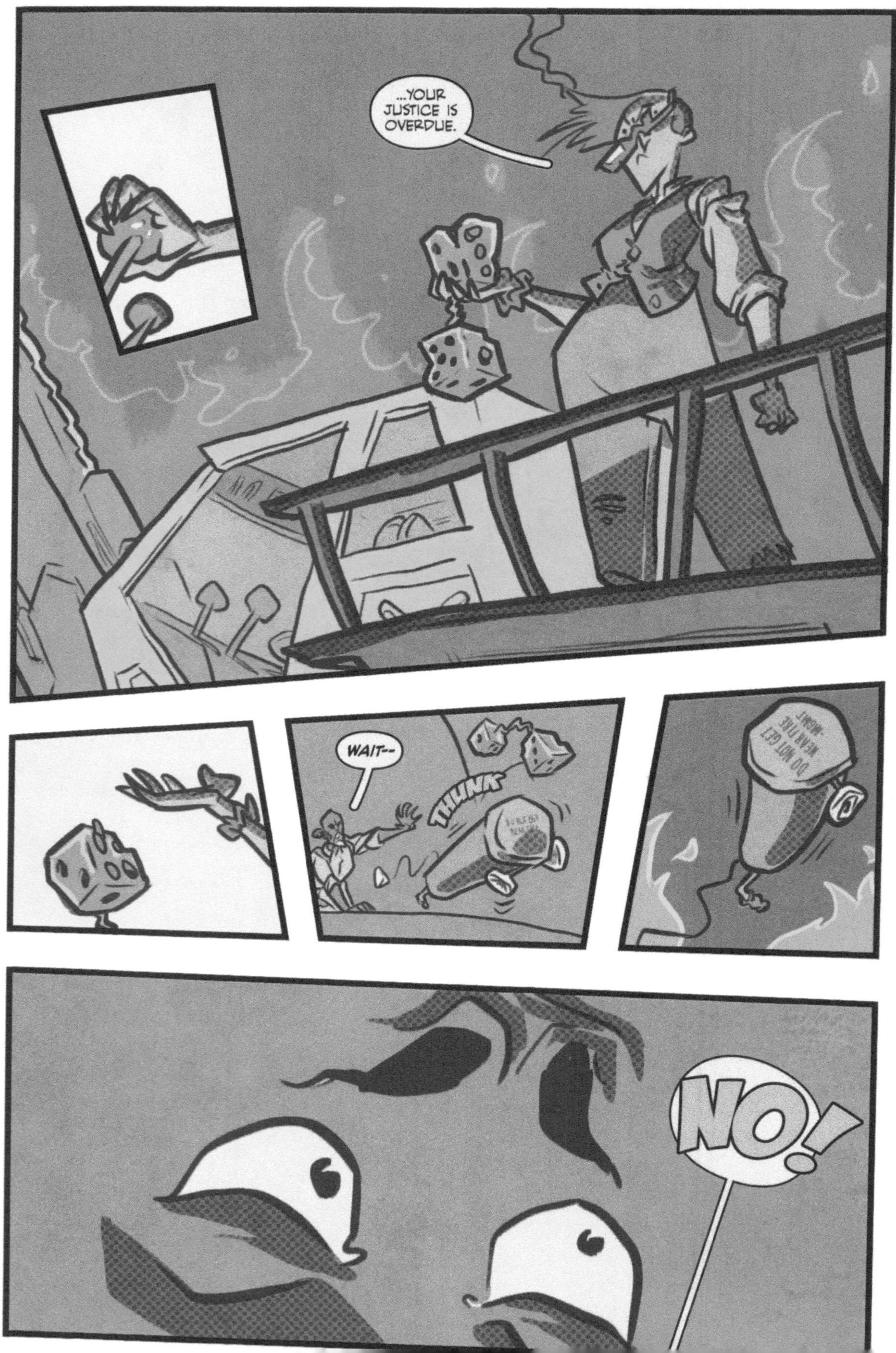
...YOUR JUSTICE IS OVERDUE.
WAIT--
THUNK
DO NOT GET NEAR FIRE -MGMT
NO!

CHAPTER THIRTEEN:
FALLING ACTION

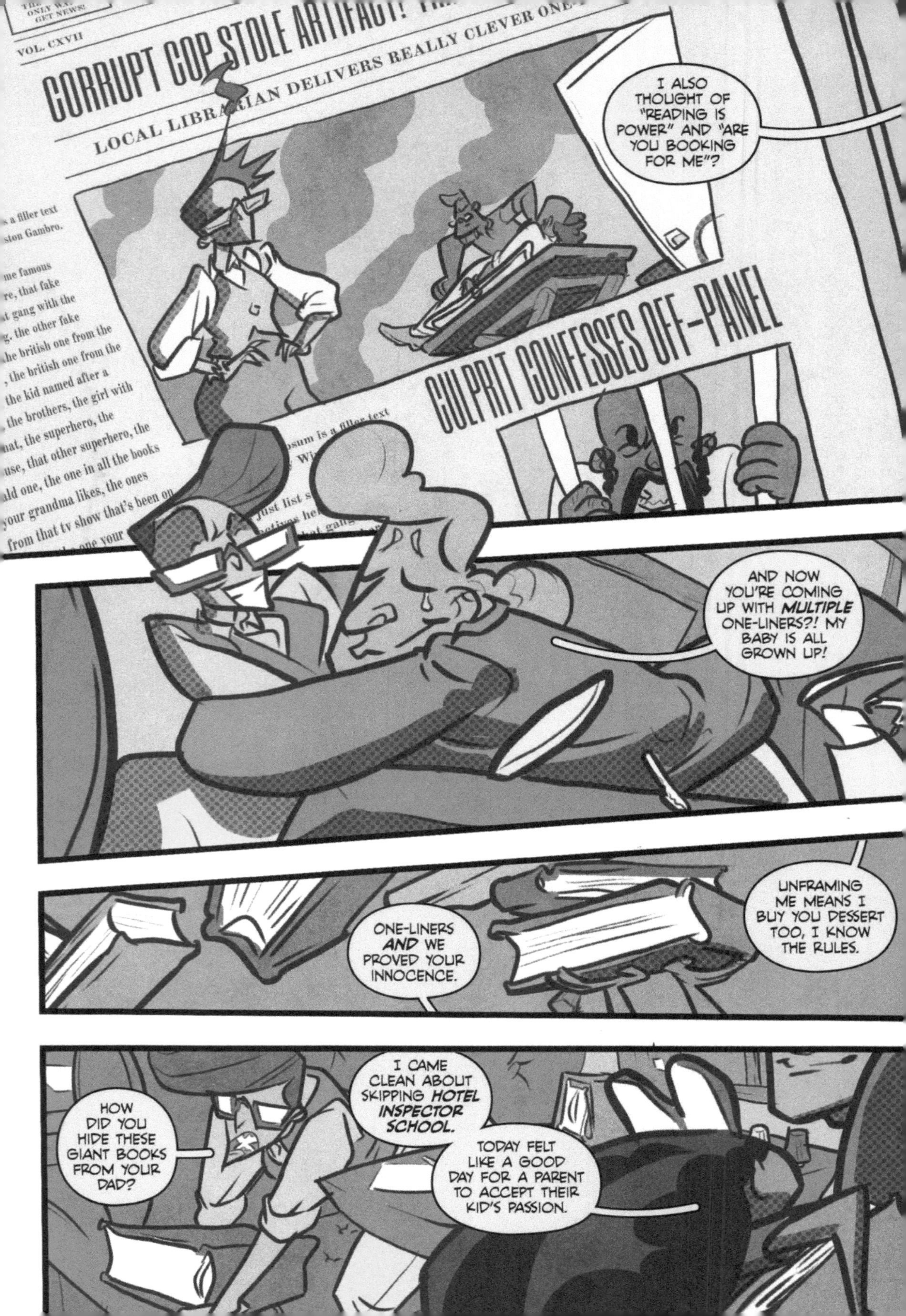

VOL. CXVII
CORRUPT COP STOLE ARTIFACT!
LOCAL LIBRARIAN DELIVERS REALLY CLEVER ONE
CULPRIT CONFESSES OFF-PANEL
I ALSO THOUGHT OF "READING IS POWER" AND "ARE YOU BOOKING FOR ME"?
AND NOW YOU'RE COMING UP WITH MULTIPLE ONE-LINERS?! MY BABY IS ALL GROWN UP!
ONE-LINERS AND WE PROVED YOUR INNOCENCE.
UNFRAMING ME MEANS I BUY YOU DESSERT TOO, I KNOW THE RULES.
HOW DID YOU HIDE THESE GIANT BOOKS FROM YOUR DAD?
I CAME CLEAN ABOUT SKIPPING HOTEL INSPECTOR SCHOOL.
TODAY FELT LIKE A GOOD DAY FOR A PARENT TO ACCEPT THEIR KID'S PASSION.

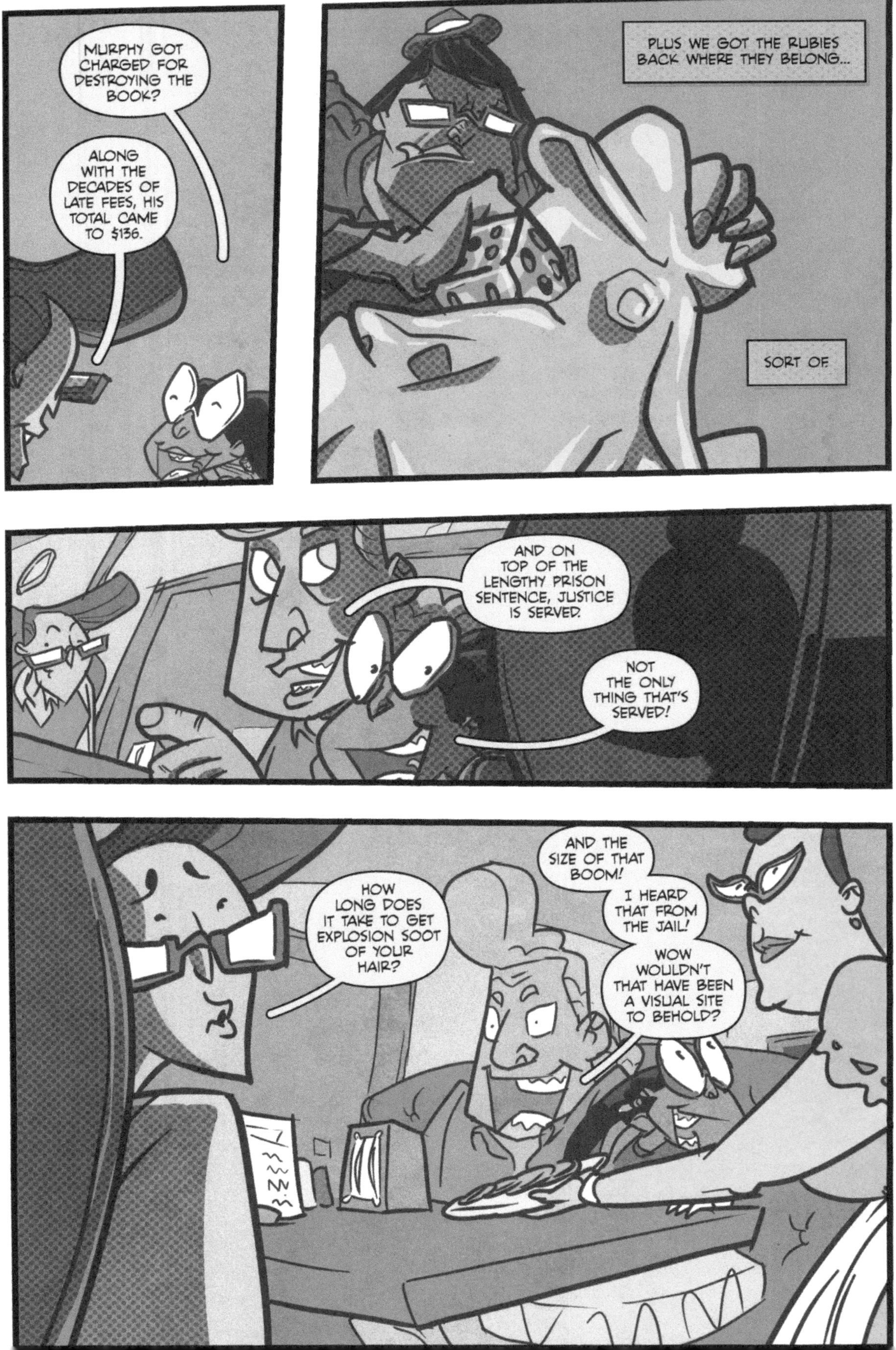
MURPHY GOT CHARGED FOR DESTROYING THE BOOK?
ALONG WITH THE DECADES OF LATE FEES, HIS TOTAL CAME TO $136.
PLUS WE GOT THE RUBIES BACK WHERE THEY BELONG...
SORT OF.
AND ON TOP OF THE LENGTHY PRISON SENTENCE, JUSTICE IS SERVED.
NOT THE ONLY THING THAT'S SERVED!
HOW LONG DOES IT TAKE TO GET EXPLOSION SOOT OF YOUR HAIR?
AND THE SIZE OF THAT BOOM!
I HEARD THAT FROM THE JAIL!
WOW WOULDN'T THAT HAVE BEEN A VISUAL SITE TO BEHOLD?

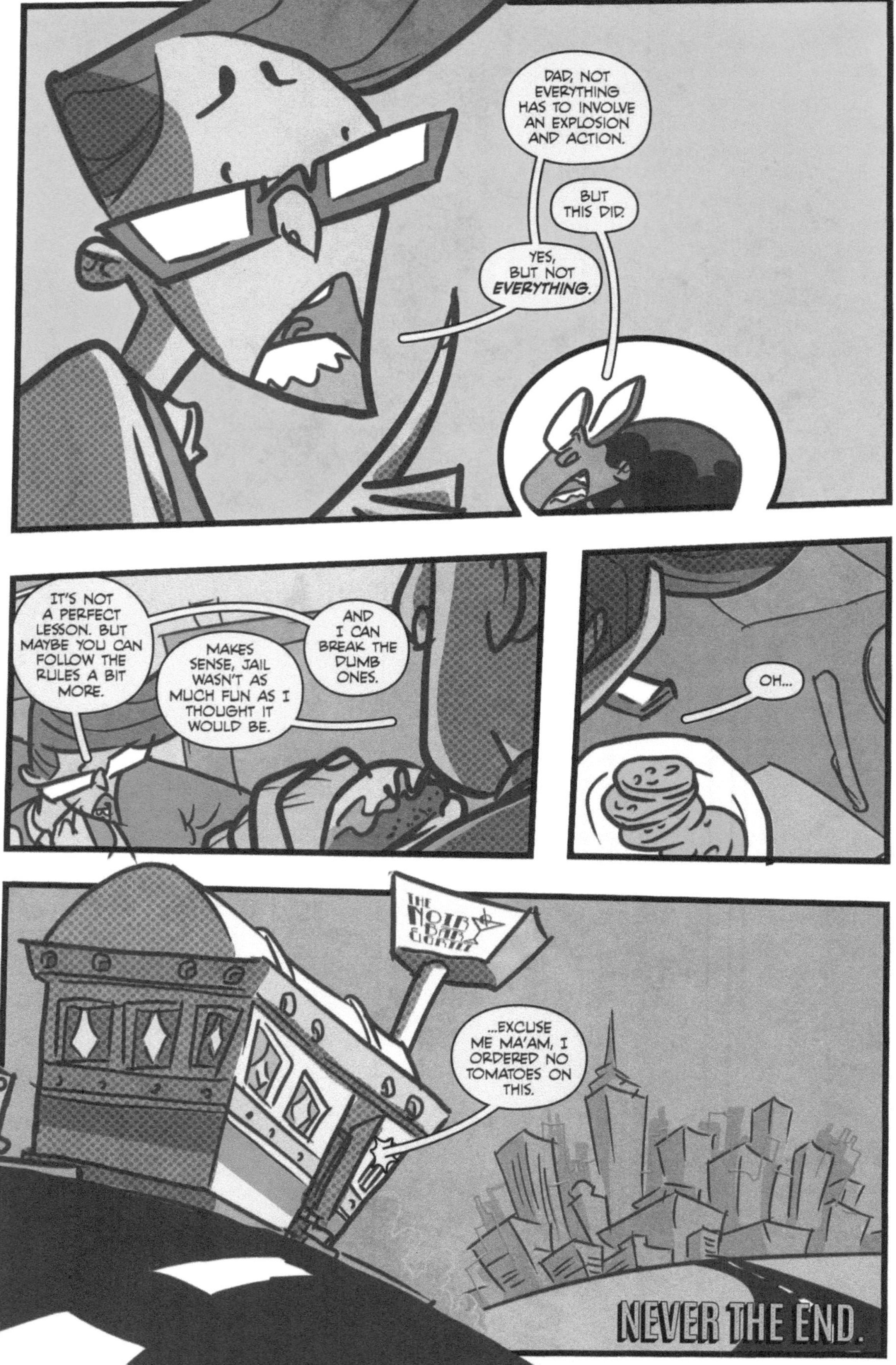
DAD, NOT EVERYTHING HAS TO INVOLVE AN EXPLOSION AND ACTION.
YES, BUT NOT *EVERYTHING*.
BUT THIS DID.
IT'S NOT A PERFECT LESSON. BUT MAYBE YOU CAN FOLLOW THE RULES A BIT MORE.
MAKES SENSE, JAIL WASN'T AS MUCH FUN AS I THOUGHT IT WOULD BE.
AND I CAN BREAK THE DUMB ONES.
OH...
...EXCUSE ME MA'AM, I ORDERED NO TOMATOES ON THIS.
NEVER THE END.

GUMSHOE CITY HALL OF FAME

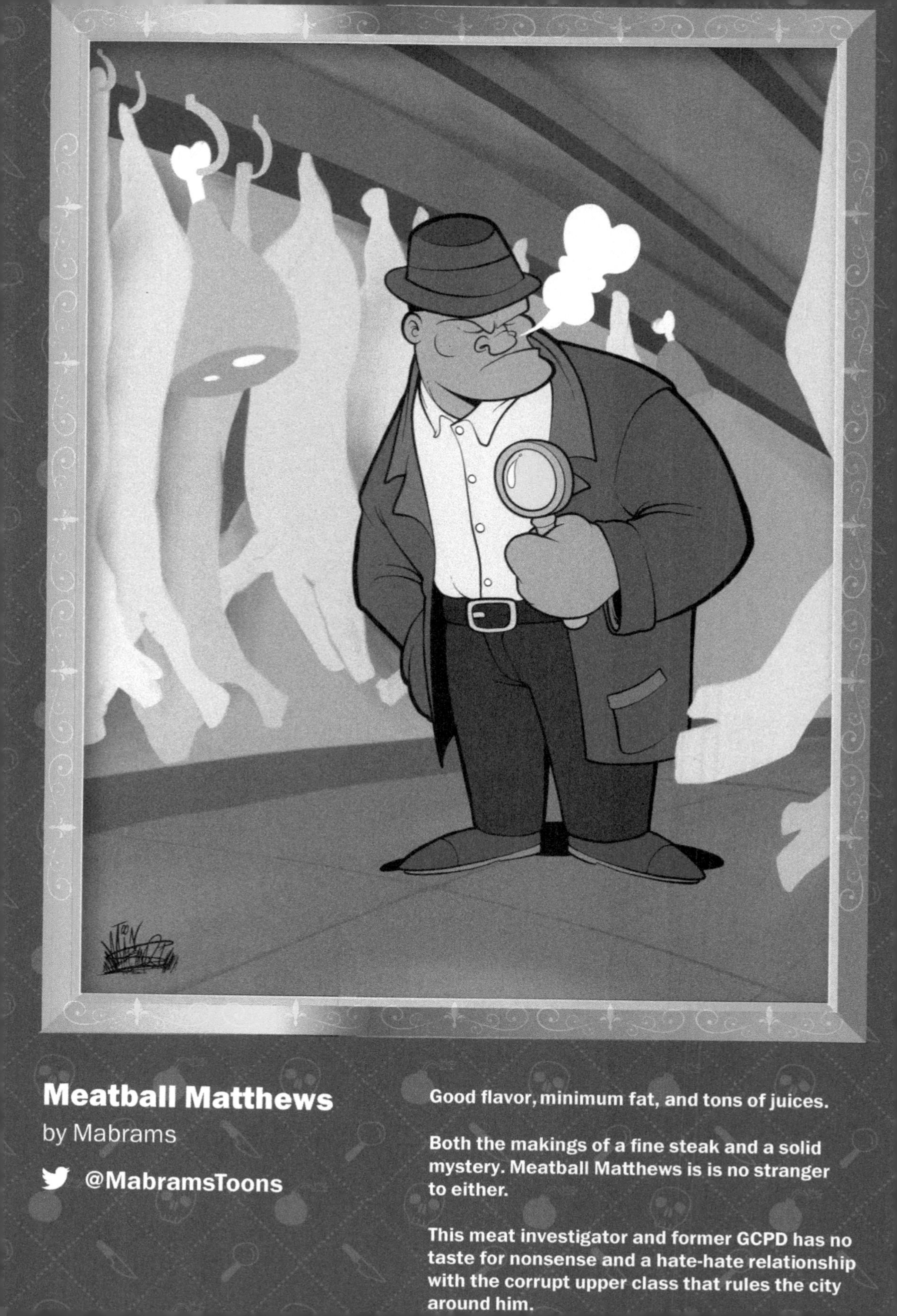

Meatball Matthews

by Mabrams

@MabramsToons

Good flavor, minimum fat, and tons of juices.

Both the makings of a fine steak and a solid mystery. Meatball Matthews is is no stranger to either.

This meat investigator and former GCPD has no taste for nonsense and a hate-hate relationship with the corrupt upper class that rules the city around him.

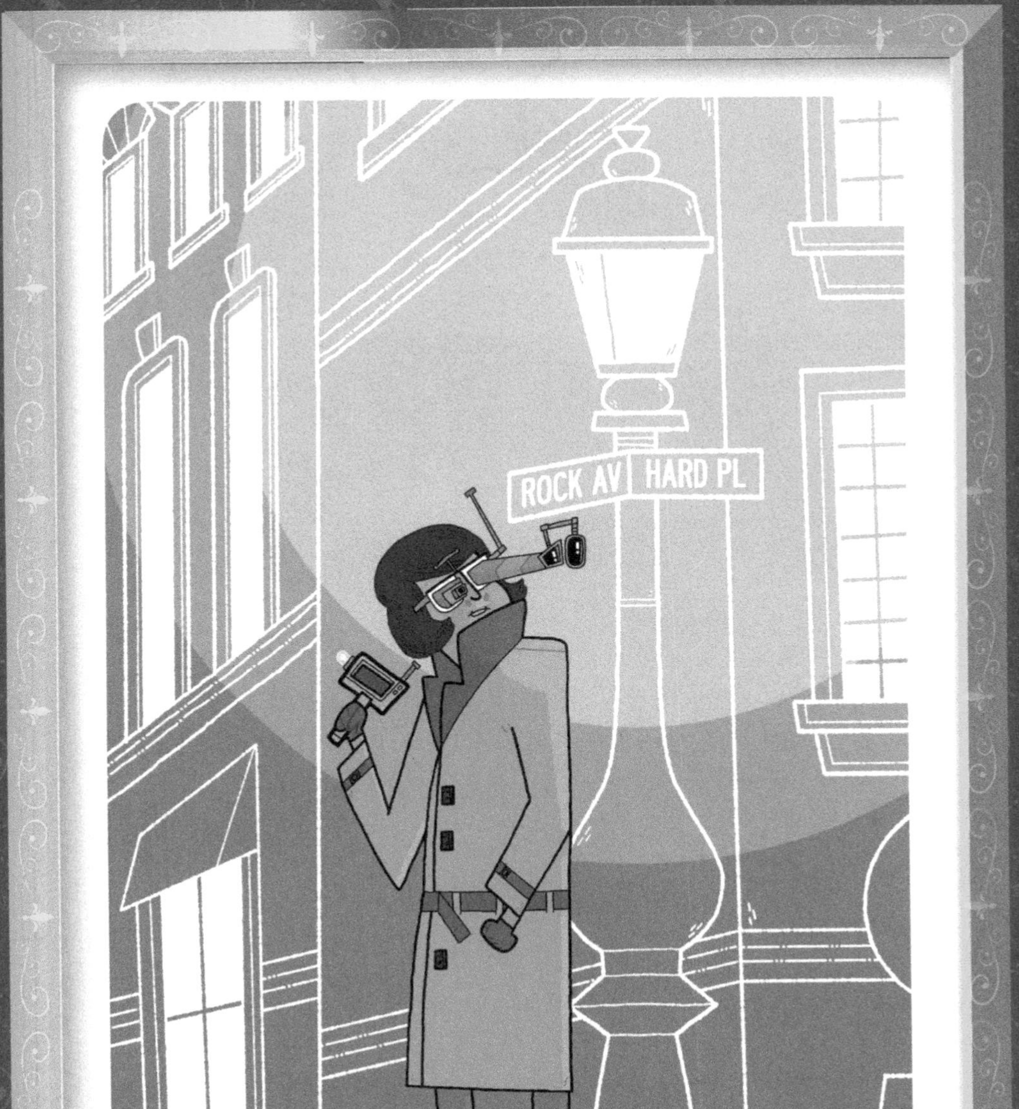
ROCK AV
HARD PL

Chief

by Reed Black

@reedblackcomics

You got a mystery, Chief's got a gadget for it (and sometimes two or three).

Forever torn between her duty to the law and those that think they live above it, Chief is forced to walk the narrow tightrope of justice in a corrupt city.

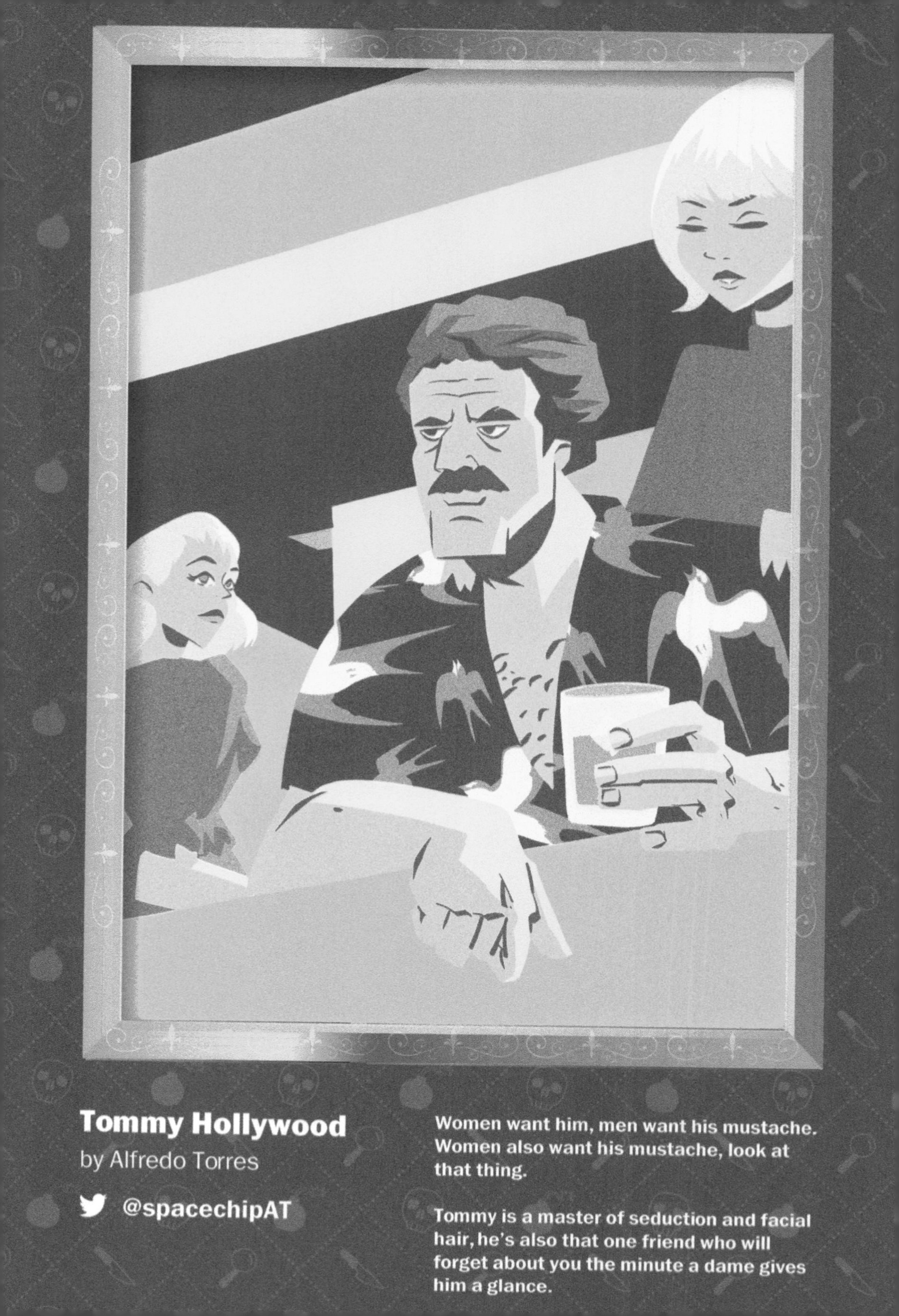

Tommy Hollywood
by Alfredo Torres

@spacechipAT

Women want him, men want his mustache. Women also want his mustache, look at that thing.

Tommy is a master of seduction and facial hair, he's also that one friend who will forget about you the minute a dame gives him a glance.

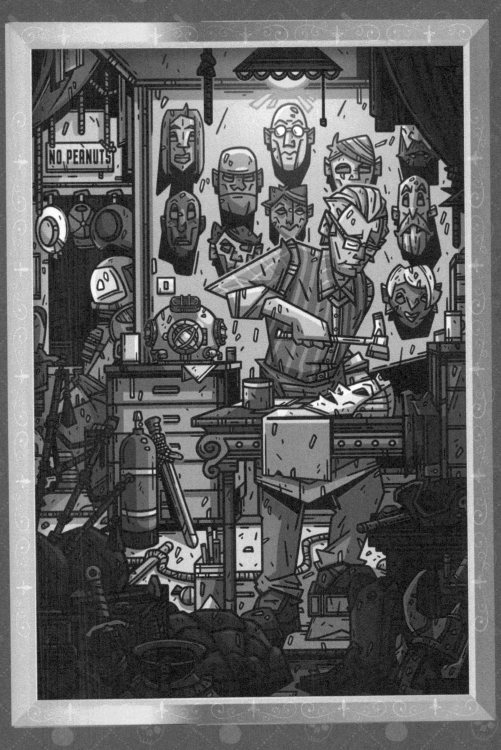

Snakeskin
by Approtis

@Approtis

Everyone wears metaphorical masks to get through the day, but Snakeskin (RIP) is the expert in it, truly a legally distinct master of disguise.

He is survived by his best pals, parrot, and countless wacky disguises.

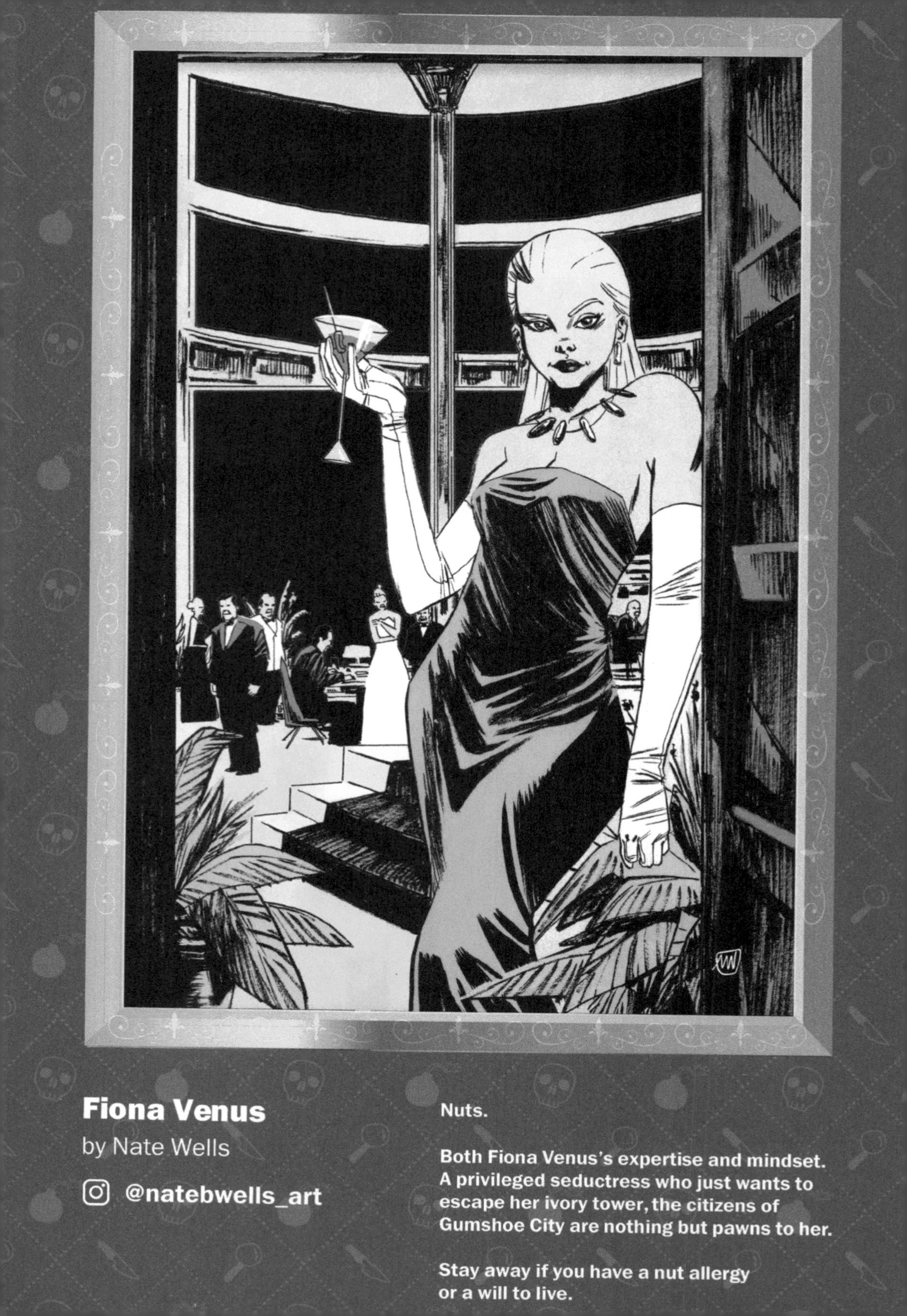

Fiona Venus

by Nate Wells

@natebwells_art

Nuts.

Both Fiona Venus's expertise and mindset. A privileged seductress who just wants to escape her ivory tower, the citizens of Gumshoe City are nothing but pawns to her.

Stay away if you have a nut allergy or a will to live.

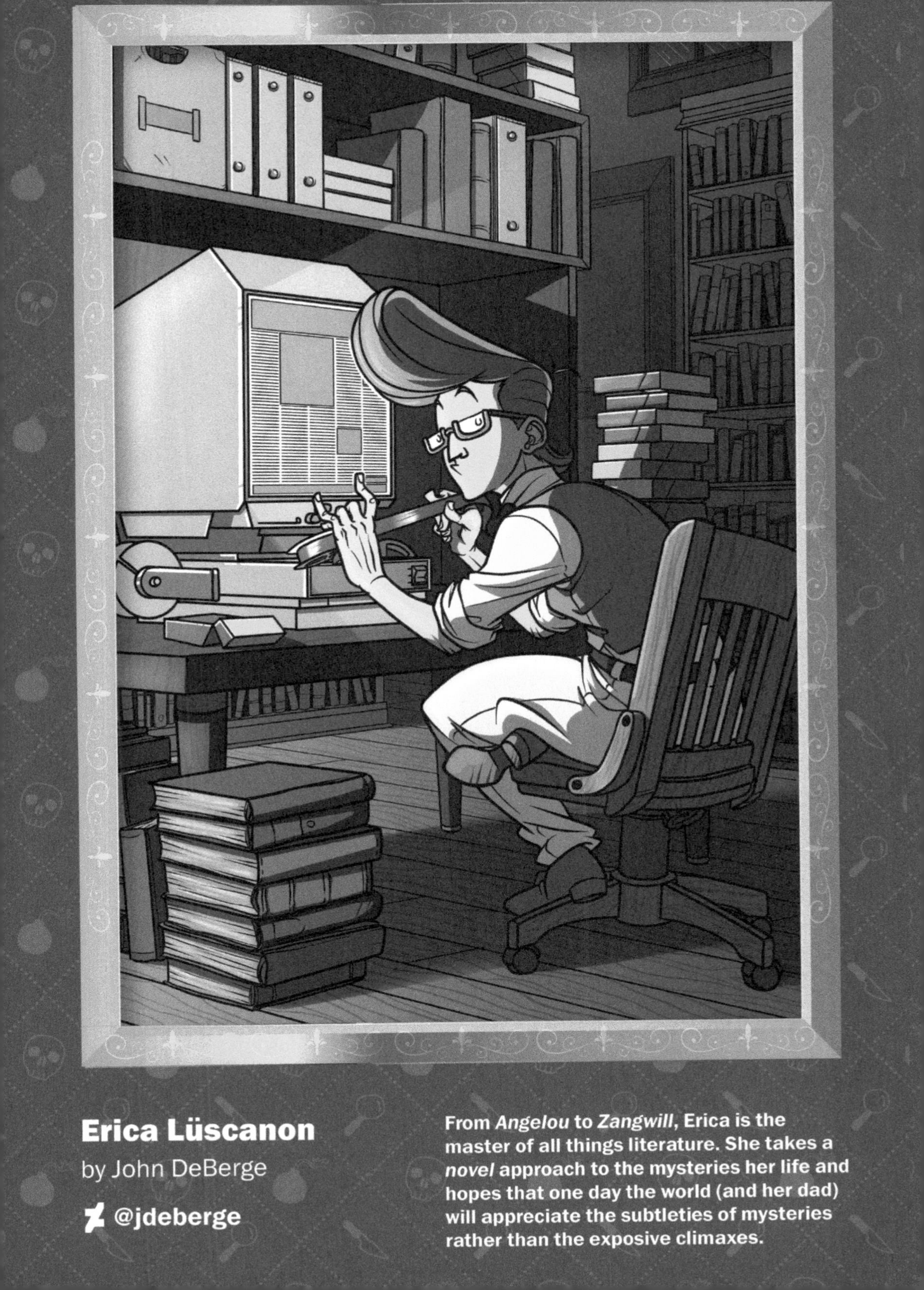

Erica Lüscanon

by John DeBerge

@jdeberge

From *Angelou* to *Zangwill*, Erica is the master of all things literature. She takes a *novel* approach to the mysteries her life and hopes that one day the world (and her dad) will appreciate the subtleties of mysteries rather than the exposive climaxes.

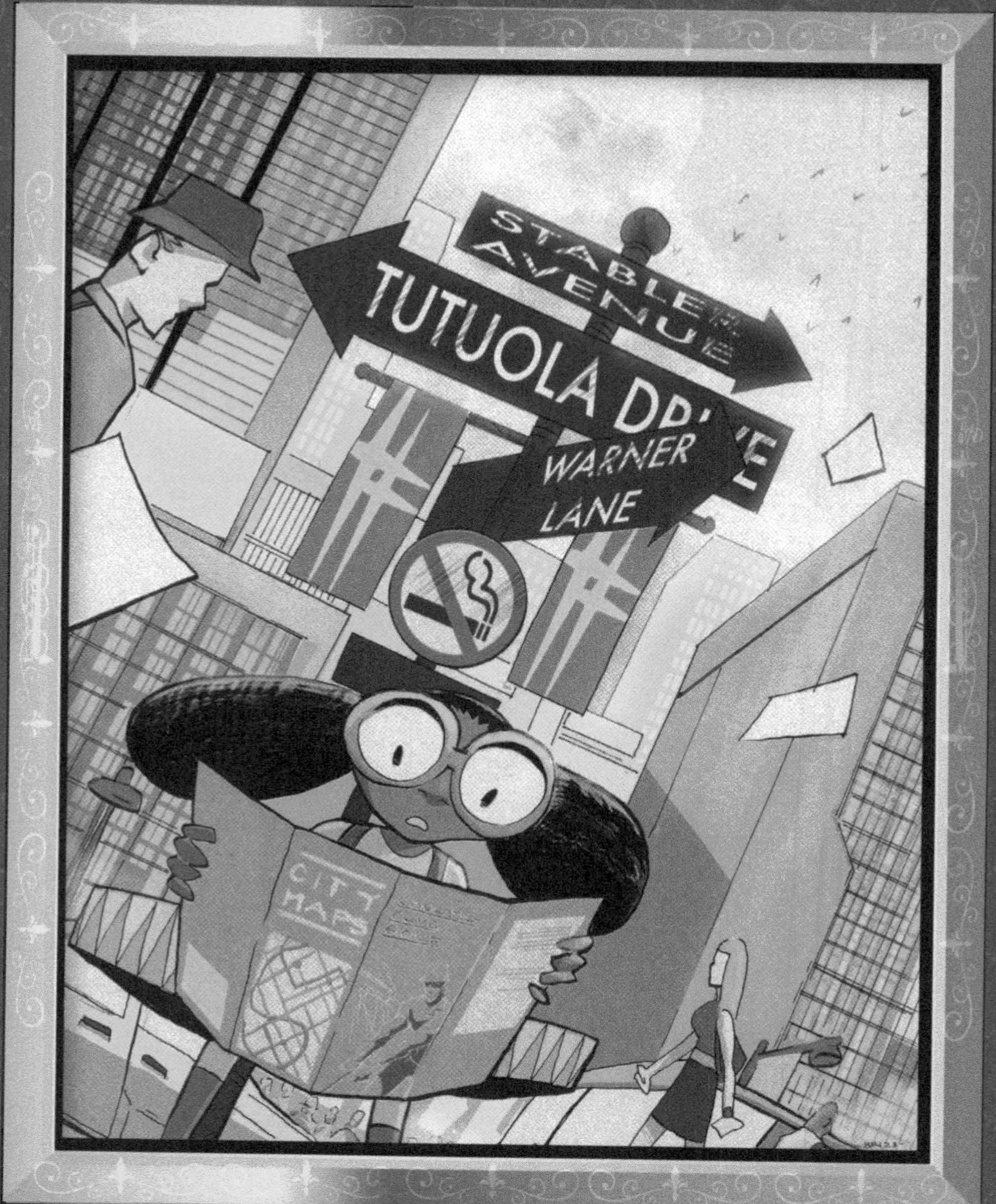
STABLER AVENUE
TUTUOLA DRIVE
WARNER LANE
CITY MAPS

Atlas Green

by Ray Briane Andan

@brianeandan06

If you're ever lost on the road trip of lfe, look for Atlas because she knows every turn. Literally at least, metaphorically she's still learning (but aren't we all?).

Rumor has it she can navigate from her home to any street on the continent blindfolded and deaf-folded.

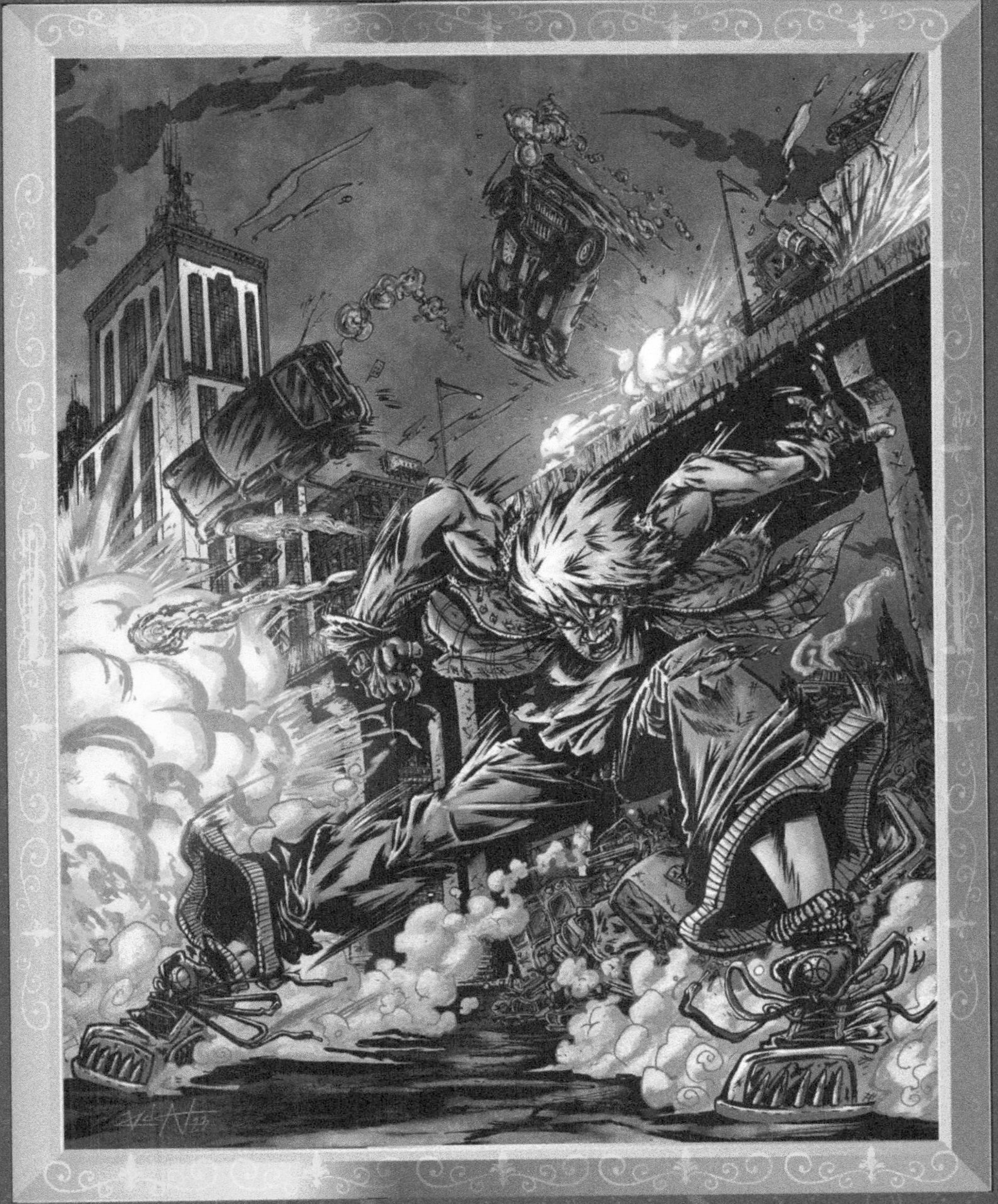

Marty "Dad" Lüscannon

by Jimmy Kucaj

@jimmykucaj

The public loves him!
Insurance companies do not.

Marty loves nothing more than closing cases, as long as closing means dropping a helicoptor on it. These adrenaline-fueled antics might make a good story, but will they be his undoing?

Debolina Lüscanon

by Matias Faggiani

:camera: @matias.faggiani

What's harder: dealing with snakes, vines, giant rolling boulders (how did they get those up there anyway?) or raising countless teenagers while married to a man who's having an affair (with explosions)?

Only Debolina can tell us!

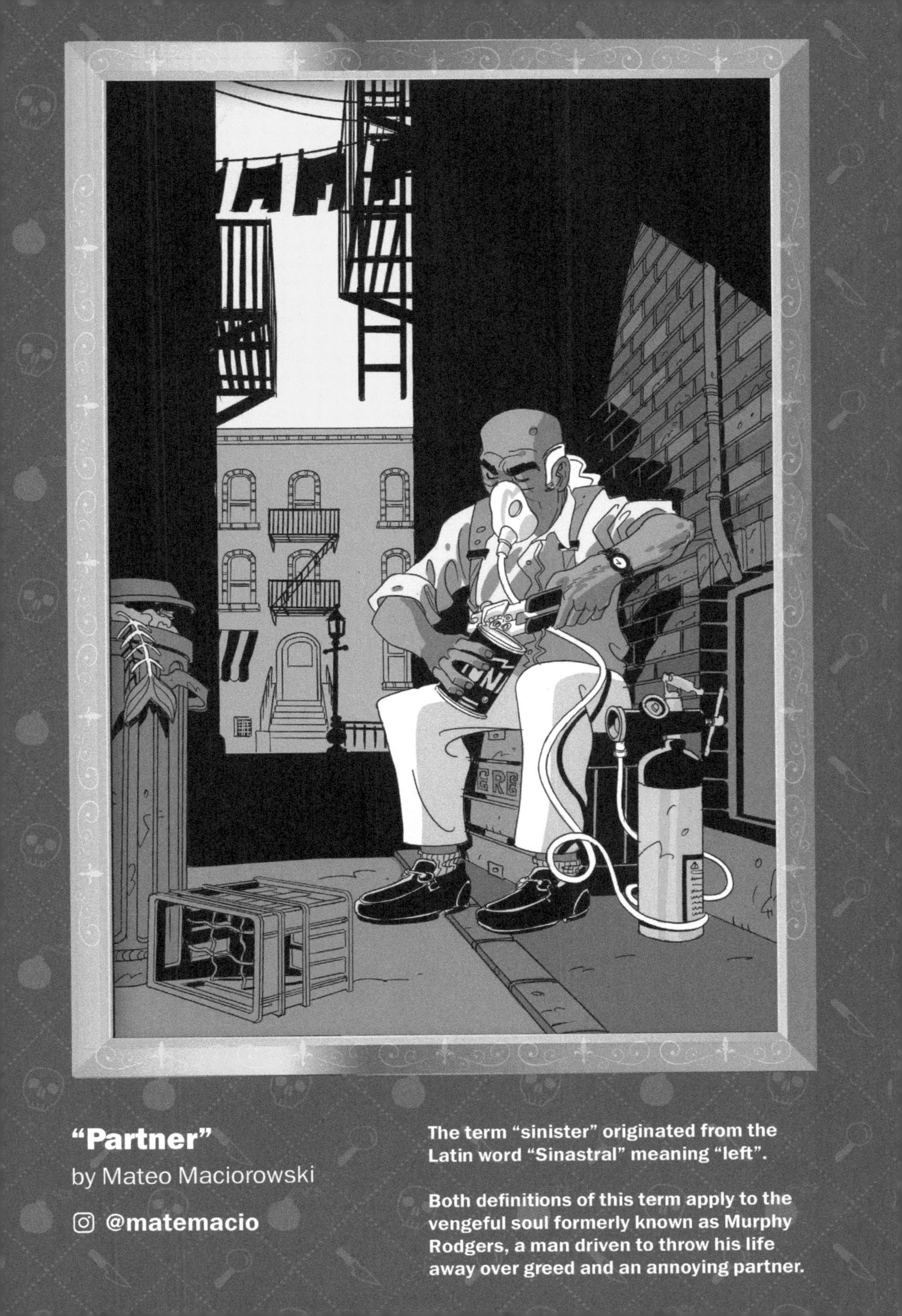

“Partner”

by Mateo Maciorowski

@matemacio

The term “sinister” originated from the Latin word “Sinastral” meaning “left”.

Both definitions of this term apply to the vengeful soul formerly known as Murphy Rodgers, a man driven to throw his life away over greed and an annoying partner.

MINI COMICS

Connections and Intersections
Words by Winston Gambro

Pictures by Brian Middleton

All Other Stories
Words and Pictures

by Winston Gambro

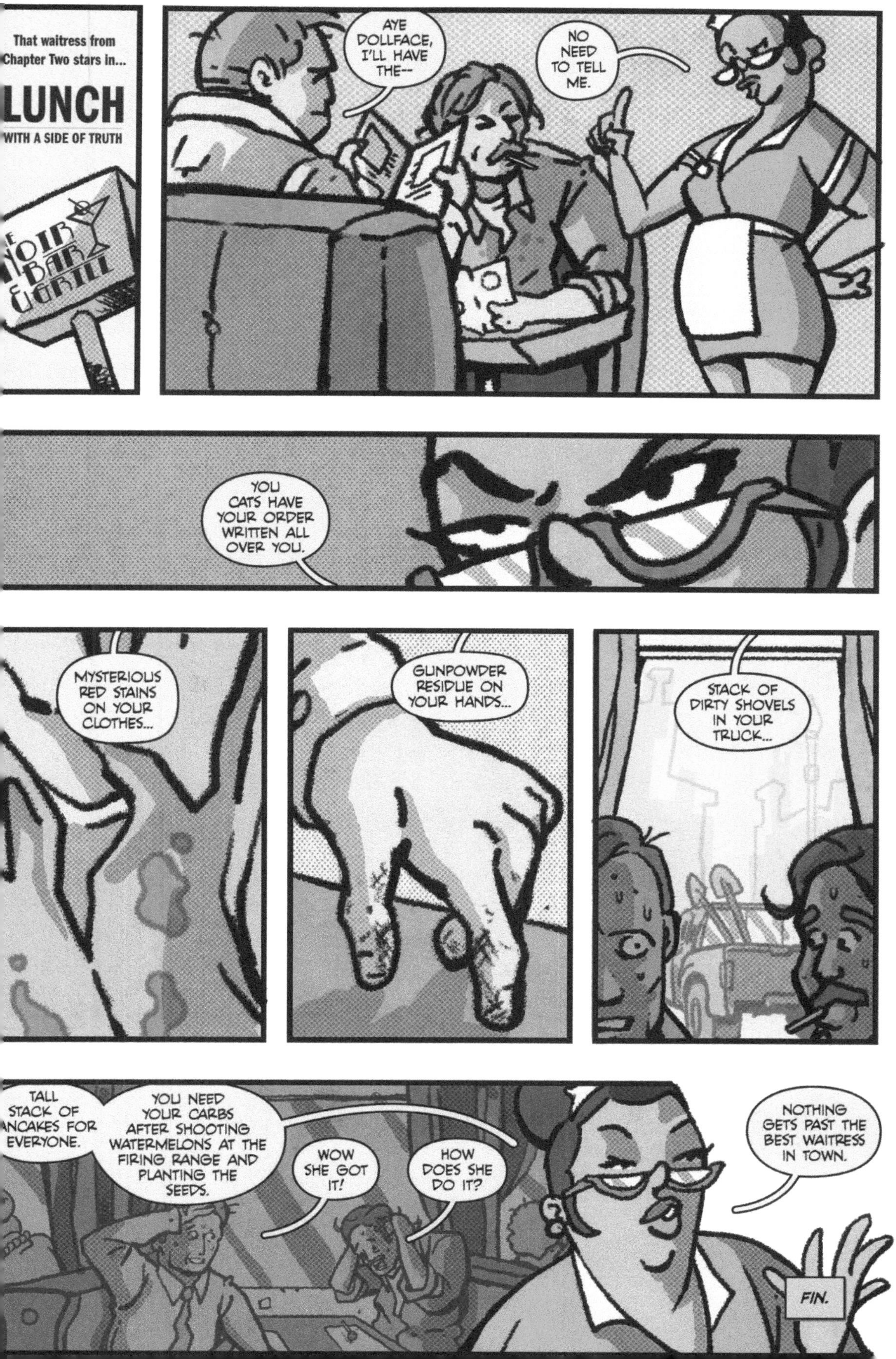
That waitress from Chapter Two stars in...
LUNCH
WITH A SIDE OF TRUTH
AYE DOLLFACE, I'LL HAVE THE--
NO NEED TO TELL ME.
YOU CATS HAVE YOUR ORDER WRITTEN ALL OVER YOU.
MYSTERIOUS RED STAINS ON YOUR CLOTHES...
GUNPOWDER RESIDUE ON YOUR HANDS...
STACK OF DIRTY SHOVELS IN YOUR TRUCK...
TALL STACK OF ANCAKES FOR EVERYONE.
YOU NEED YOUR CARBS AFTER SHOOTING WATERMELONS AT THE FIRING RANGE AND PLANTING THE SEEDS.
WOW SHE GOT IT!
HOW DOES SHE DO IT?
NOTHING GETS PAST THE BEST WAITRESS IN TOWN.
FIN.

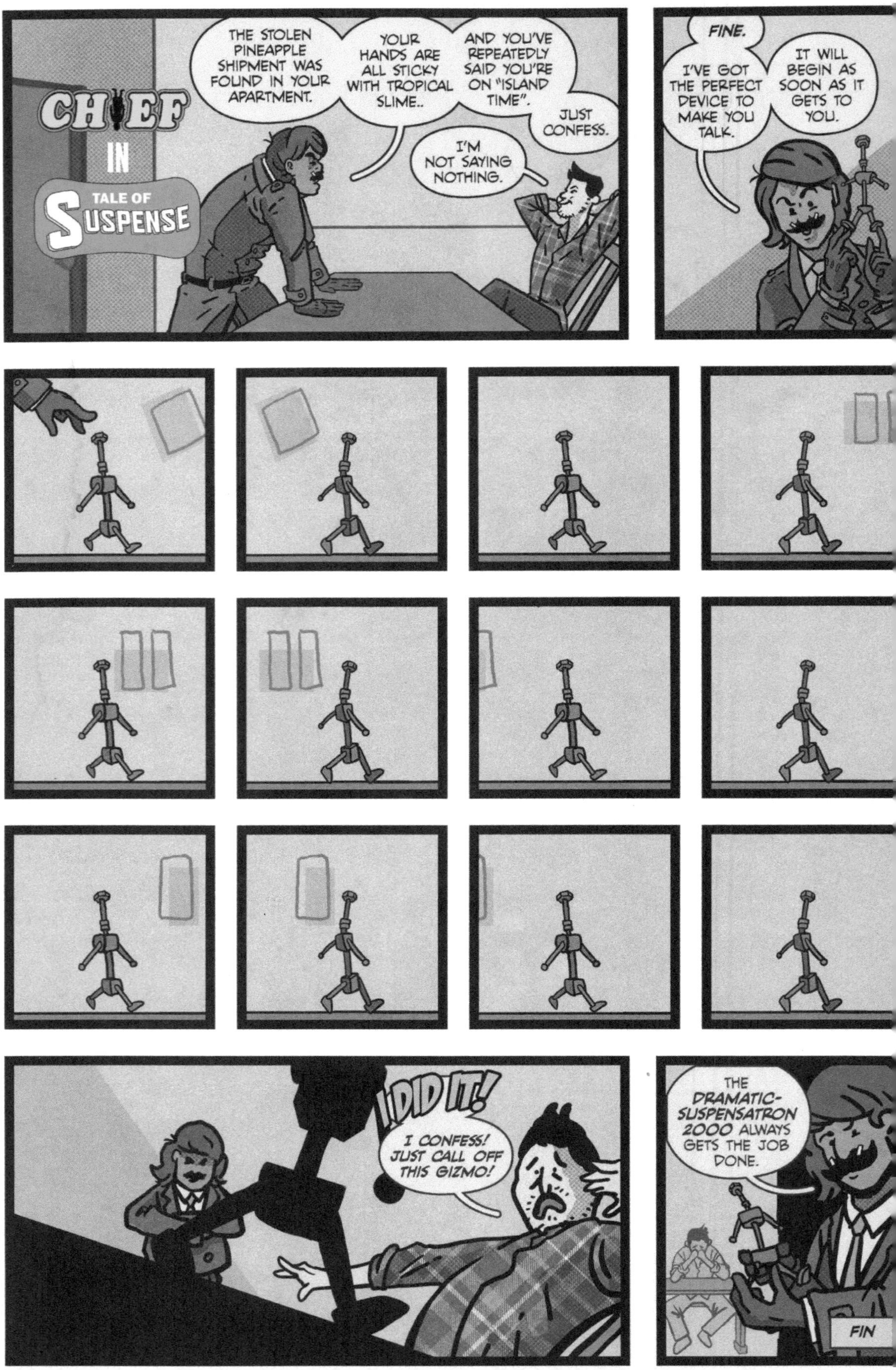
CHIEF
IN
TALE OF SUSPENSE
THE STOLEN PINEAPPLE SHIPMENT WAS FOUND IN YOUR APARTMENT.
YOUR HANDS ARE ALL STICKY WITH TROPICAL SLIME..
AND YOU'VE REPEATEDLY SAID YOU'RE ON "ISLAND TIME".
JUST CONFESS.
I'M NOT SAYING NOTHING.
FINE.
I'VE GOT THE PERFECT DEVICE TO MAKE YOU TALK.
IT WILL BEGIN AS SOON AS IT GETS TO YOU.
I DID IT!
I CONFESS! JUST CALL OFF THIS GIZMO!
THE DRAMATIC-SUSPENSATRON 2000 ALWAYS GETS THE JOB DONE.
FIN

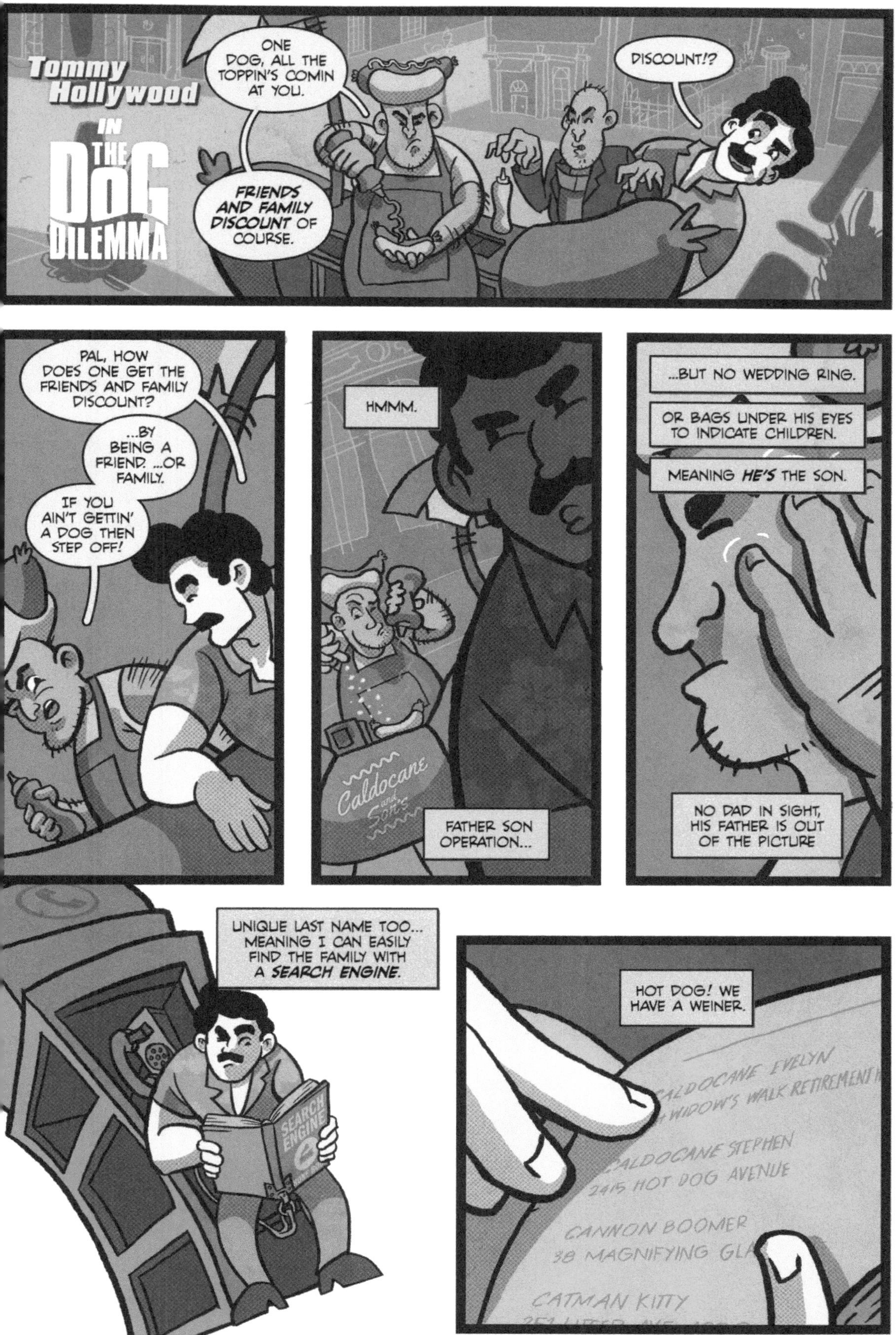
Tommy Hollywood
IN
THE DOG DILEMMA
ONE DOG, ALL THE TOPPIN'S COMIN AT YOU.
FRIENDS AND FAMILY DISCOUNT OF COURSE.
DISCOUNT!?
PAL, HOW DOES ONE GET THE FRIENDS AND FAMILY DISCOUNT?
...BY BEING A FRIEND. ...OR FAMILY.
IF YOU AIN'T GETTIN' A DOG THEN STEP OFF!
HMMM.
Caldocane and Son's
FATHER SON OPERATION...
...BUT NO WEDDING RING.
OR BAGS UNDER HIS EYES TO INDICATE CHILDREN.
MEANING HE'S THE SON.
NO DAD IN SIGHT, HIS FATHER IS OUT OF THE PICTURE
UNIQUE LAST NAME TOO... MEANING I CAN EASILY FIND THE FAMILY WITH A SEARCH ENGINE.
SEARCH ENGINE
HOT DOG! WE HAVE A WEINER.
CALDOCANE EVELYN
CALDOCANE STEPHEN
2415 HOT DOG AVENUE
CANNON BOOMER
CATMAN KITTY

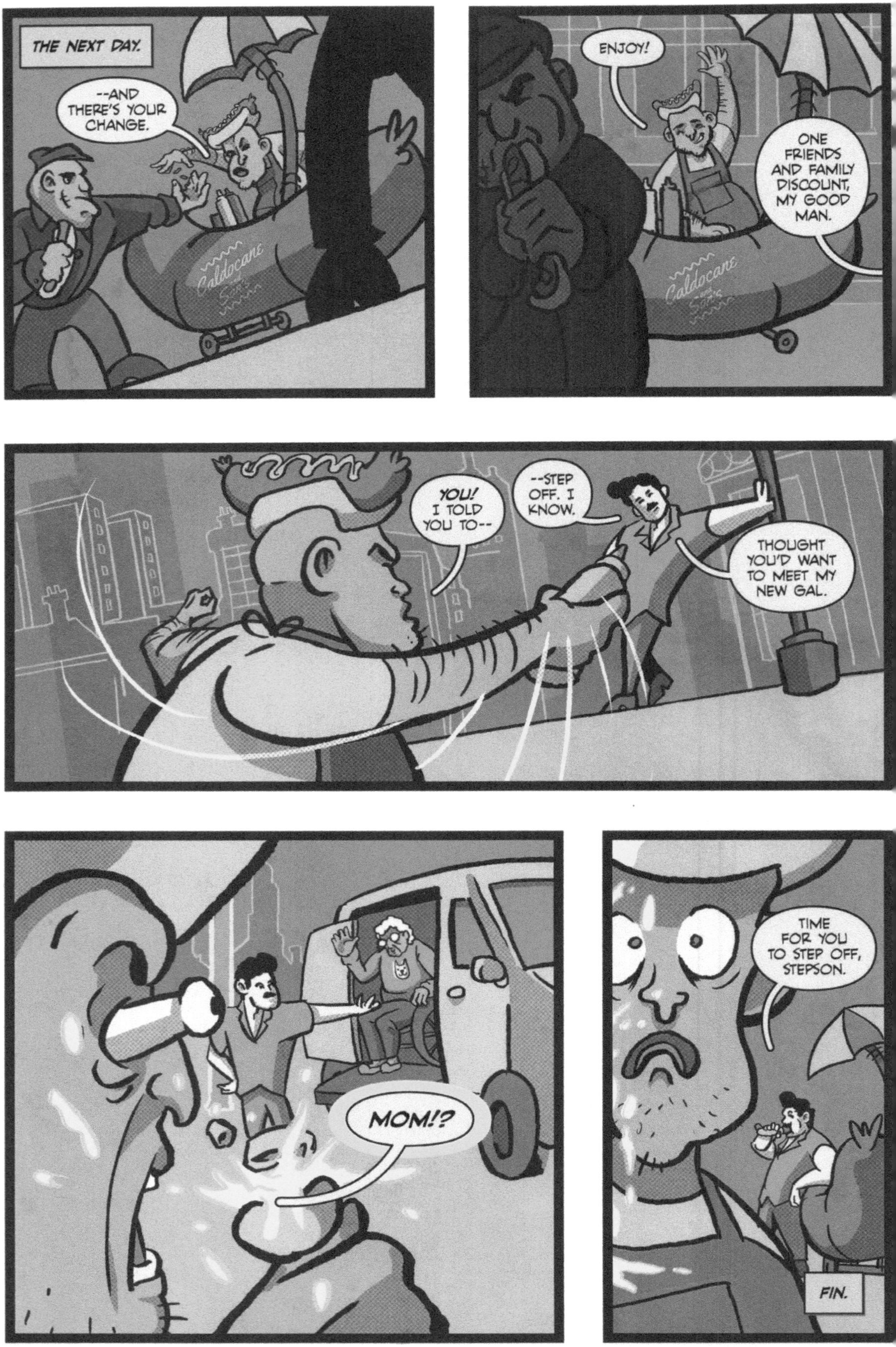
THE NEXT DAY.
--AND THERE'S YOUR CHANGE.
Caldocane and Sons
ENJOY!
ONE FRIENDS AND FAMILY DISCOUNT, MY GOOD MAN.
Caldocane and Sons
YOU! I TOLD YOU TO--
--STEP OFF. I KNOW.
THOUGHT YOU'D WANT TO MEET MY NEW GAL.
MOM!?
TIME FOR YOU TO STEP OFF, STEPSON.
FIN.

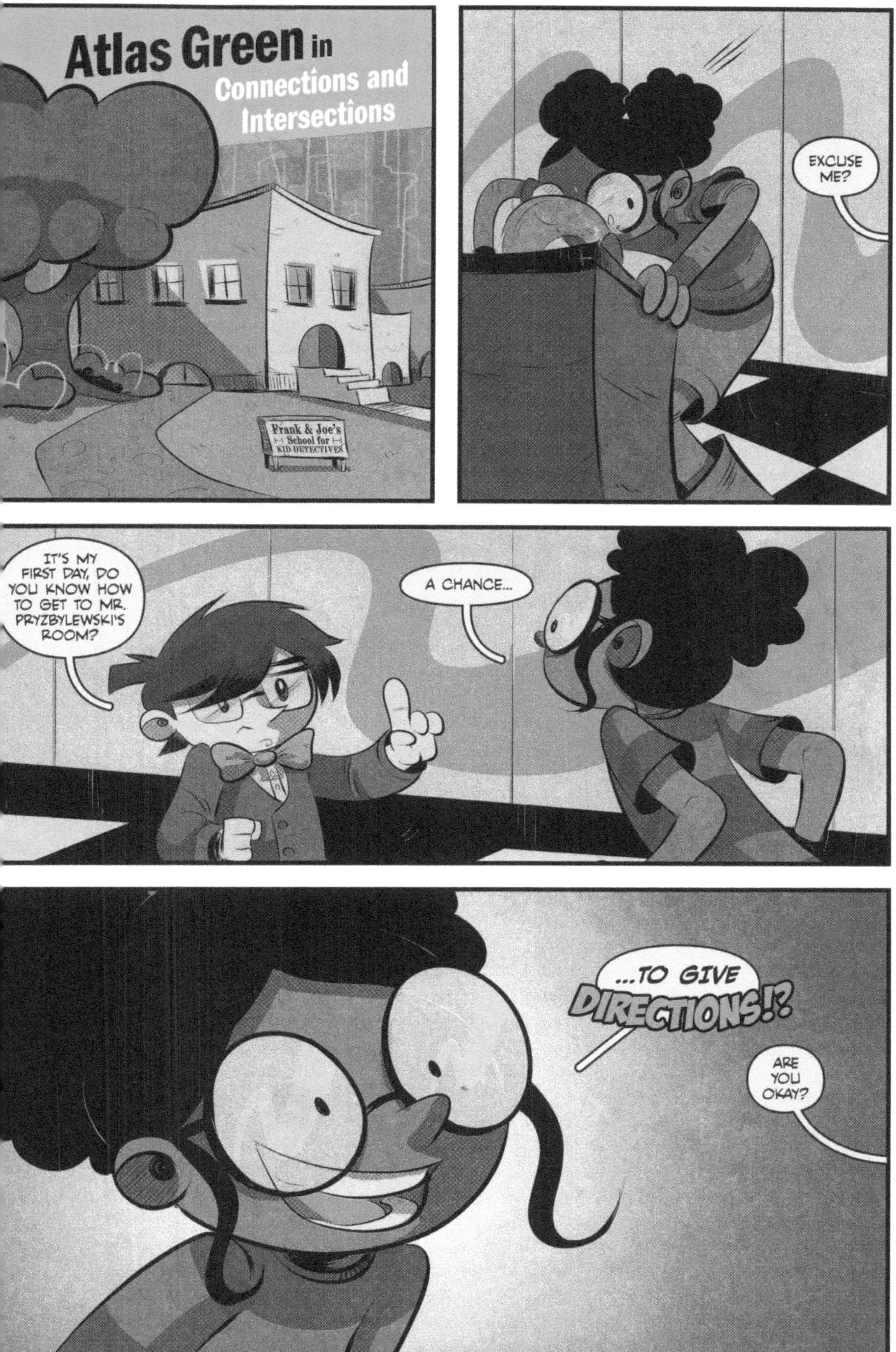
Atlas Green in
Connections and Intersections
Frank & Joe's School for KID DETECTIVES
EXCUSE ME?
IT'S MY FIRST DAY, DO YOU KNOW HOW TO GET TO MR. PRYZBYLEWSKI'S ROOM?
A CHANCE...
...TO GIVE DIRECTIONS!?
ARE YOU OKAY?

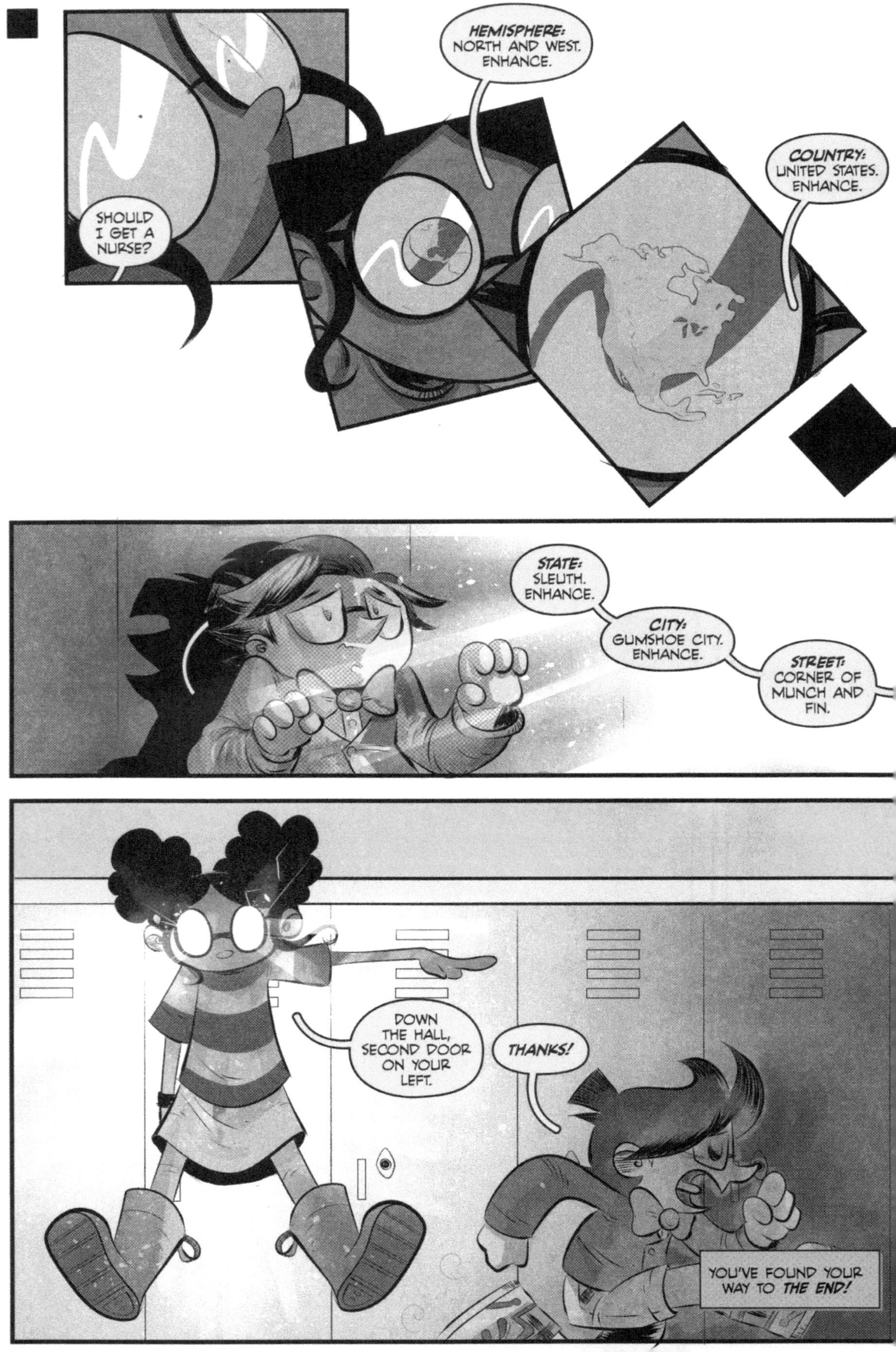
SHOULD I GET A NURSE?
HEMISPHERE: NORTH AND WEST. ENHANCE.
COUNTRY: UNITED STATES. ENHANCE.
STATE: SLEUTH. ENHANCE.
CITY: GUMSHOE CITY. ENHANCE.
STREET: CORNER OF MUNCH AND FIN.
DOWN THE HALL, SECOND DOOR ON YOUR LEFT.
THANKS!
YOU'VE FOUND YOUR WAY TO THE END!

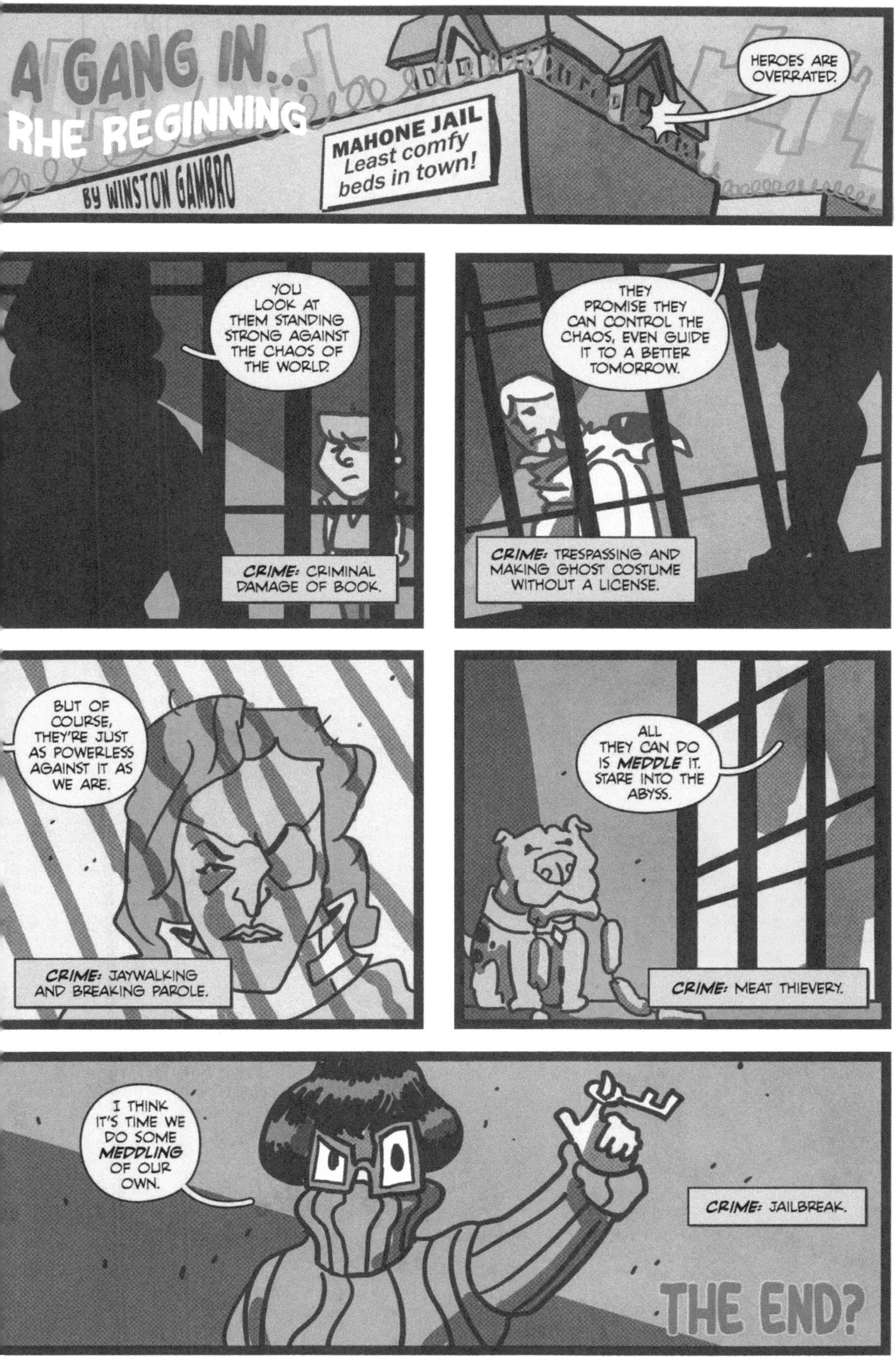
A GANG IN...
RHE REGINNING
BY WINSTON GAMBRO
MAHONE JAIL Least comfy beds in town!
HEROES ARE OVERRATED.
YOU LOOK AT THEM STANDING STRONG AGAINST THE CHAOS OF THE WORLD.
CRIME: CRIMINAL DAMAGE OF BOOK.
THEY PROMISE THEY CAN CONTROL THE CHAOS, EVEN GUIDE IT TO A BETTER TOMORROW.
CRIME: TRESPASSING AND MAKING GHOST COSTUME WITHOUT A LICENSE.
BUT OF COURSE, THEY'RE JUST AS POWERLESS AGAINST IT AS WE ARE.
CRIME: JAYWALKING AND BREAKING PAROLE.
ALL THEY CAN DO IS MEDDLE IT. STARE INTO THE ABYSS.
CRIME: MEAT THIEVERY.
I THINK IT'S TIME WE DO SOME MEDDLING OF OUR OWN.
CRIME: JAILBREAK.
THE END?

GUMSHOE CITY DECLASSIFIED

REFERENCE CITY

umshoe City is a city of mystery but also a city of references to ther detectives in fiction. Here's a list and explanation of the ubtle (and not so subtle) nods.

THE CASE OF THE ONGOING BEEF

Chief is a reference to *Inspector Gadget*, a detective that solved his cases with gizmos. She has a taped on mustache because Gadget had a mustache in his pilot episode, but was forced to shave by MGM due to his close resemblance to Inspector Clouseau.

Tommy Hollywood is a nod to Tom Selleck's Thomas Magnum in the series *Magnum P.I.*. He's known for his tropical adventures and glorious mustache. And no, I don't know why I have two mustache references in a row.

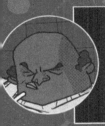

This chef is named Ross, a reference to *Gourmet Detective*. When the police are stumped, they turn to chef/blogger, Henry Ross, to solve food-based mysteries. You'd think they couldn't get a lot of material from that, but somehow there are eight books and five television movies.

Doc is a reference to Gregory House from *House M.D.*. Who himself is a reference to Sherlock Holmes.
House = Holmes, Wilson = Watson.
Pretty Clever right?
Yeah, that kind of subtly won like 50 awards.

This unnamed priest is a nod to *Father Brown*, the crime solving priest! His creator once said "I think it only fair to confess that I have myself written some of the worst mystery stories in the world." But I bet some were okay.

REFERENCE CITY

THESE
LIGHTA DO THE TRICK.

Snakeskin is a reference to the shockingly memorable film, *Master of Disguise*. A critical and box-office bomb starring Dana Carvey. Currently holding a 1% approval rating on Rotten Tomatoes, but we'll all remember "Am I turtley enough for the turtle club?" until we die.

Frank and Joe's School for Boy Detectives is named after the *Hardy Boys*, because obviously if you had that kind of childhood, you'd inflict it on other children in a learning environment.

Thorndyke Memorial Hospital is a nod to Dr. John Evelyn Thorndyke. One of the first forensic scientists, the author, R. Austin Freeman, even proved the character's methods were practical by doing them himself. I considered doing that for Gumshoe City, but realized I was too lazy.

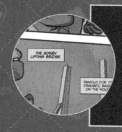

THE NORÉN LIFTING BRIDGE.

The Norén Lifting Bridge is named for Saga Norén, the main character of *The Bridge*, a Danish/Swedish television series.
I haven't seen it, but I assume it's about some hardboiled cops who investigate bridge crime.

THE CASE OF THE OVERDUE JUSTICE

Marty Lüscanon and "Partner" are inspired by the leads of *Lethal Weapon*, a series of movies and then television show about a pair of mismatched cops. The first one is worth seeing if only for the climax: a kung-fu fight on a suburban lawn while a fire hydrant rains on them.

REFERENCE CITY

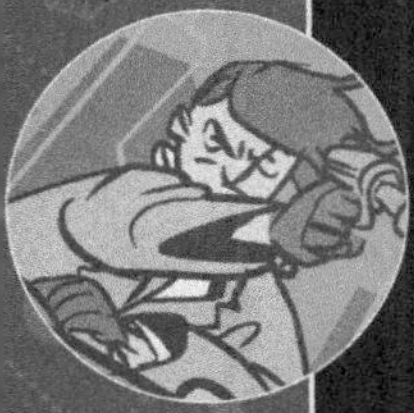

This unnamed villain is stylized after Goro Akechi. A fashionable boy detective from the video game, *Persona 5*. He loves pancakes almost as much as he loves justice.

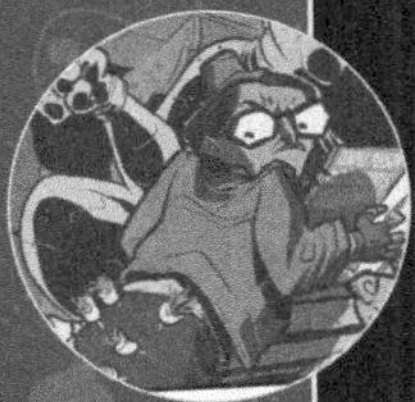

Debolina Lüscanon is a mixture of Indiana Jones and Kakababu, a Bengali adventurer specializing in archaeology. You might say that neither of those characters are technically "detectives" but to respond to that, I simply say, whoops I ran out of space!

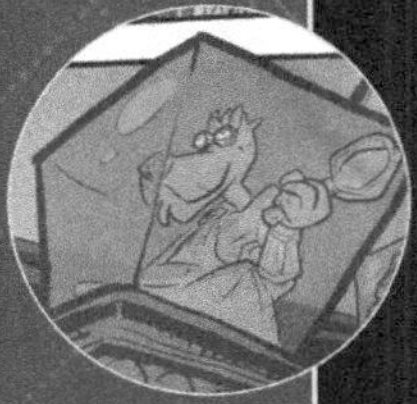

The macguffin of book two is a statue of Hermanubis. A god that was a combination of Hermes and Anubis. Along with various other god tasks, he "engaged in the investigation of truth" and that's as close as "god of detectives" as I could find.

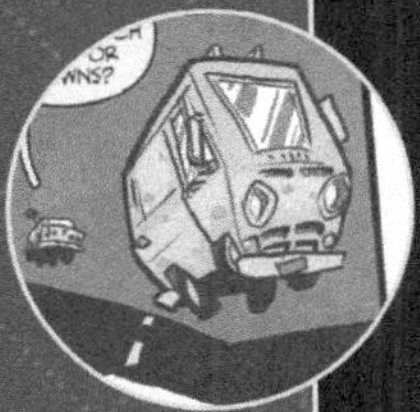

The criminal in the prologue is driving a green and blue van that references The Mystery Machine.

A vehicle from the obscure franchise, *Scooby-Doo*.

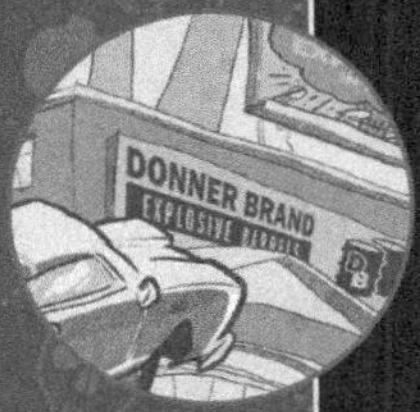
DONNER BRAND

Donner Brand Explosive Barrels are named after Richard Donner, director of the first four *Lethal Weapon* movies and countless other classics, including *Superman* and *Superman II: The Richard Donner Cut* (you probably could have guessed that one).

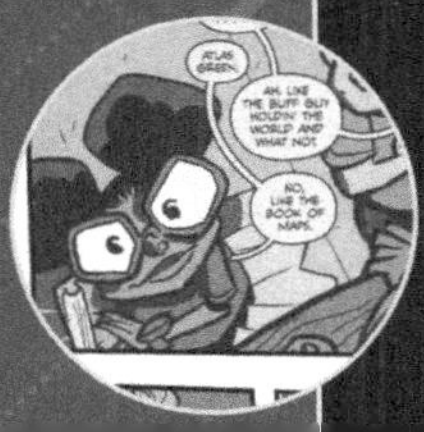

Atlas Green is loosely inspired by *Encyclopedia Brown*, a series of short stories about a boy genius that helps his police chief father solve mysteries. In hindsight, his dad must have been awful at his job if he relied on his 10-year old son so often.

REFERENCE CITY

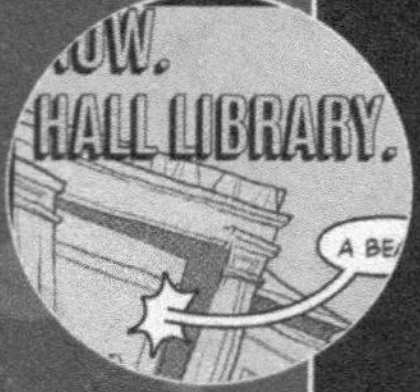
HALL LIBRARY.

Hall Library is named after Philip Baker Hall, renowned character actor known for playing Lt. Joe Bookman or "the library cop" on *Seinfeld*. Initially Erica had a boss parodying him, but my editor said "He seems redundant, also could you wear a shirt when you're in my office?".

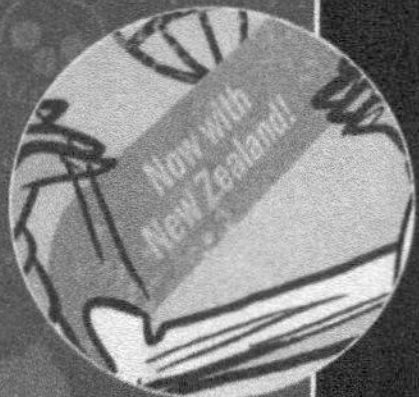
Now with New Zealand!

The Big Book of Maps's tagline "Now with New Zealand" is inspired by the scandal/conspiracy of New Zealand frequently being left off of maps.

No word on Old Zealand at this time.

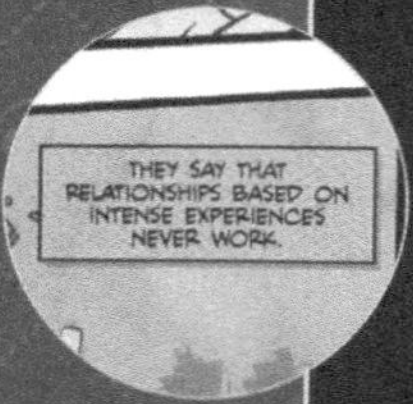
THEY SAY THAT RELATIONSHIPS BASED ON INTENSE EXPERIENCES NEVER WORK.

This line is based on a quote from the film *Speed.* I guess the line is accurate because Keanu didn't return for the sequel; *Speed 2: Cruise Control*.

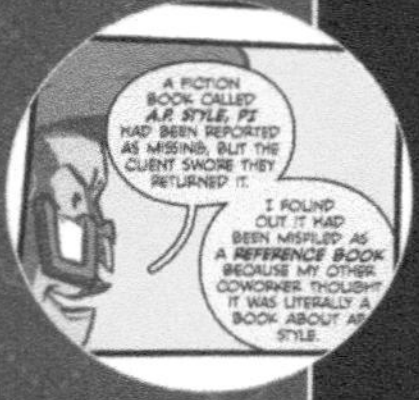
A FICTION BOOK CALLED A.P. STYLE, PI HAD BEEN REPORTED AS MISSING, BUT THE CLIENT SWORE THEY RETURNED IT.
I FOUND OUT IT HAD BEEN MISFILED AS A REFERENCE BOOK BECAUSE MY OTHER COWORKER THOUGHT IT WAS LITERALLY A BOOK ABOUT STYLE.

A.P. Style, PI is a reference to the *Associated Press Style*, better known as "I finished this essay on how islands can be used as metaphors, time to work another three hours while I use this incredibly outdated process to cite my sources so I don't get kicked out of school".

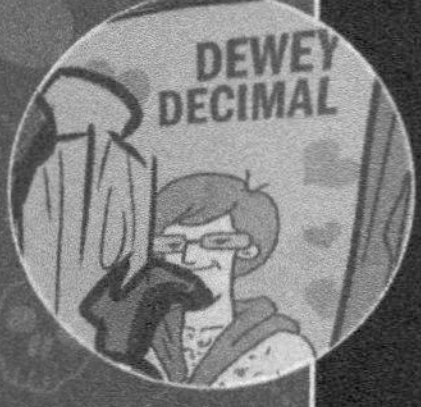
DEWEY DECIMAL

This is the background gag I'm most proud of, it's so funny I won't even make a joke here to overshadow it.

He's named after the Dewey Decimal Classification, aka how libraries sort books.

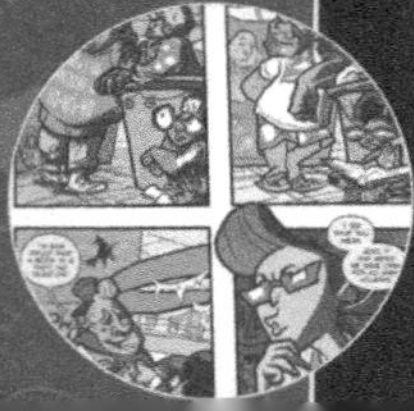

Dad's holiday shirt is a reference to *Die Hard*, which I'm sure he watches every year. On Halloween, he's dressed like Clint Eastwood from the *Good, the Bad and the Ugly.* Erica is Edgar Allen Poe and Atlas is Magellan (always a hit costume with the kids).

REFERENCE CITY

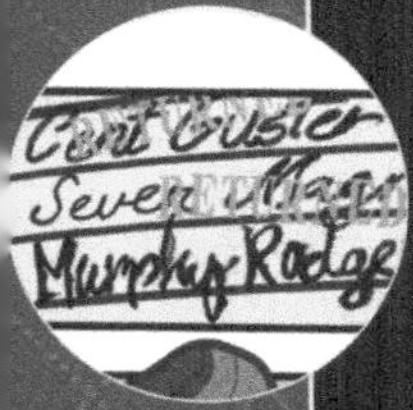

The previous library patrons to check out the missing book are "Cent Guster" and "Seven Magnum". These are the detective names of the writer and artist of this book. Want your own? Your detective name is just a couple pages away!

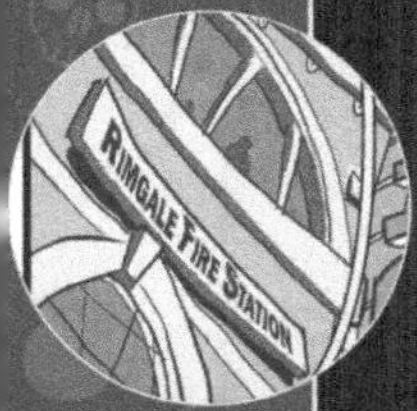
RIMGALE FIRE STATION

Rimgale Fire Station is named after Donald "Shadow" Rimgale, the arson investigator from the 1991 film *Backdraft*.

Spoiler alert: the fire was the villain the whole time.

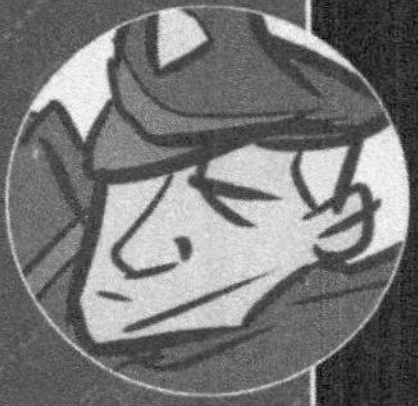

The unnamed traffic cop is loosely designed after detective Cole Phelps from the video game *L.A. Noire*.

The game is a masterpiece with no glaring issues.
ⓧ Doubt

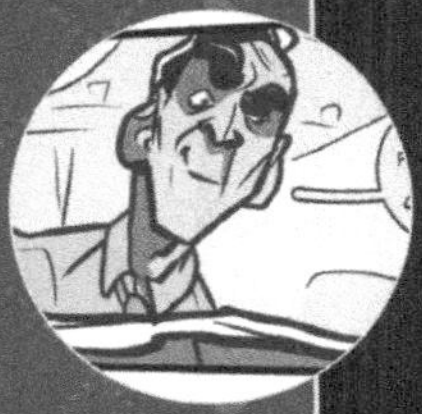

The cannery owner's look is based on Abe Vigoda's portrayal of Phil Fish from *Barney Miller* and the spin-off *Fish*.
Look, I know this is a stretch, but did you really want me to reference *Fish Police* instead?

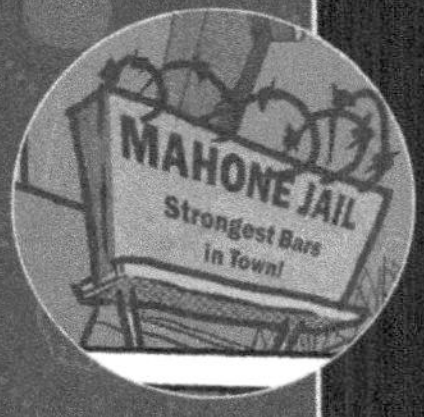
MAHONE JAIL
Strongest Bars in Town!

Mahone Jail is named after Agent Alexander Mahone from the television series, *Prison Break*. It's a great two season show, very smart and action packed! No, there weren't two more seasons, a tv movie, and a reboot, what do you mean?

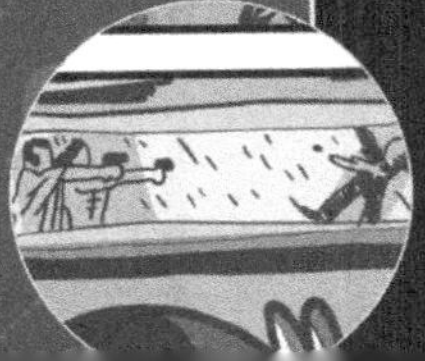

The framed photo above Atlas is the ending scene of *Lethal Weapon*. I just love the idea of a police photographer following around the most unhinged cops at the chance something bizarre happens.

REFERENCE CITY

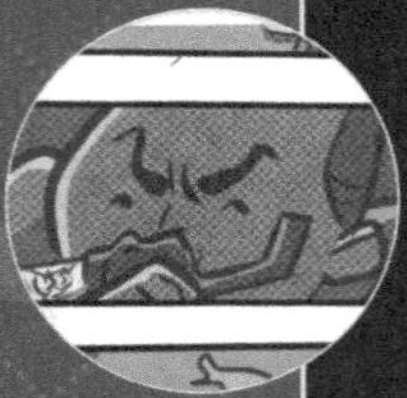

Erica's various idea on how to confront Partner are the climaxes of the first two *Lethal Weapon* films. Stay tuned for the next volume where she mentions shooting through a bulldozer blade or impaling with rebar.

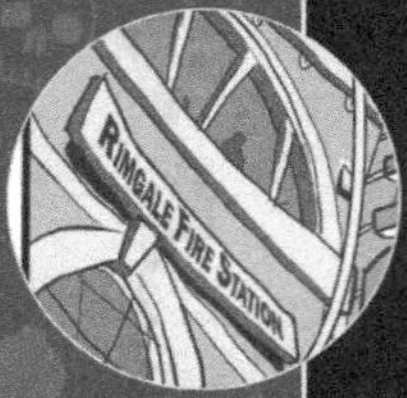
RINGALE FIRE STATION

The extremely low late fees are a reference to the low penalities offered by your local library. This isn't particularly funny, but libraries are awesome and you should support them more.
Especially if they've stocked this book.

MINI COMICS

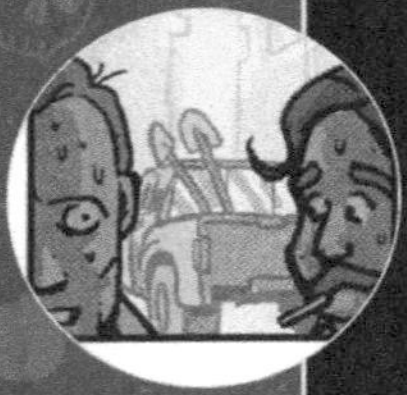

These two nervous nellies are inspired by the leads from the first season of *True Detective*. I unfortunately I haven't seen it all, but I got the gist of it after 15 minutes of the first episode, I assume there's a murder at some point.

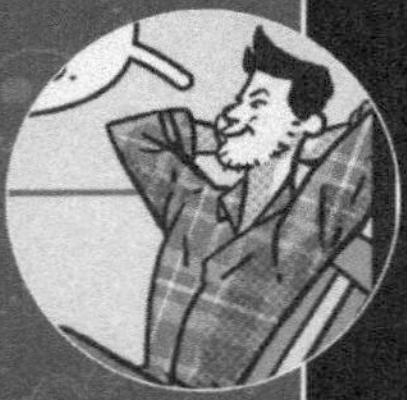

The interrogated man in this mini comic is a reference to Shawn Spencer of *Psych* fame. There was a pineapple hidden in every episode. Can you imagine that wasted effort? Who spends the time hiding pointless gags like that? Couldn't they be doing something productive?

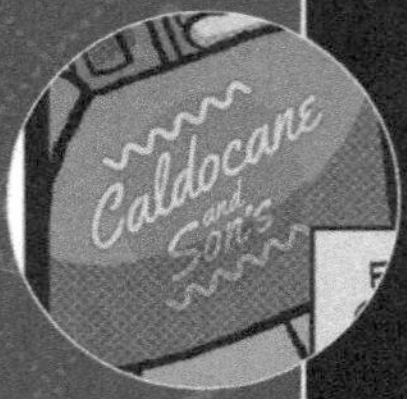
Caldocane and Son's

Caldocane is the literal translation of hot dog in Italian, I knew that off the top of my head because of my Italian heritage and didn't have to look it up at all.

REFERENCE CITY

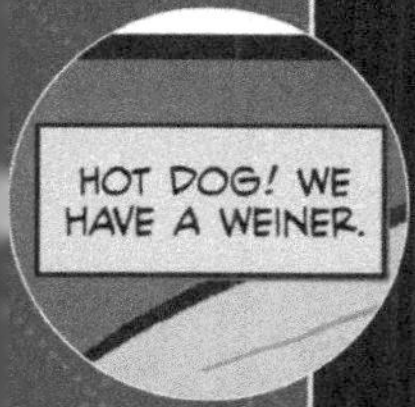
HOT DOG! WE HAVE A WEINER.

You know that annoying guy that relates everything to *The Simpsons*? Anyway, that's me.

This line is from that show.

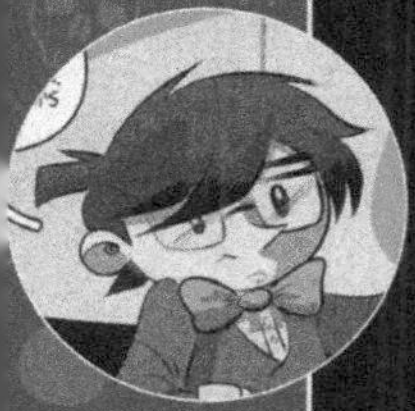

This precocious tyke is inspired by the manga/anime, *Case Closed*, specifically Detective Conan.

I considered writing him as a barbarian or red-headed talk-show host, but that would be only funny to me.

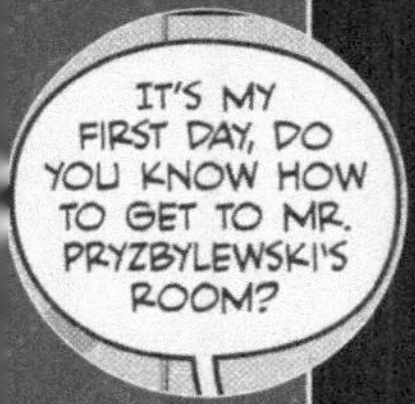
IT'S MY FIRST DAY, DO YOU KNOW HOW TO GET TO MR. PRYZBYLEWSKI'S ROOM?

Mr. Pryzbylewski is based on Roland "Prez" Pryzbylewski from *The Wire*, a detective turned teacher. *The Wire* is considered one of the greatest television shows of all time, and instead of watching it, I spent my time writing this joke-explanation section. You're welcome.

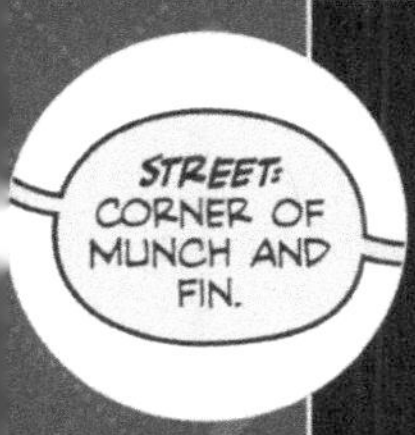
STREET: CORNER OF MUNCH AND FIN.

These streets are based off of two of the detectives from *Law & Order: SVU*. Fin Tutuola is the longest running prime-time live-action male character of all time with 400+ episodes, while John Munch is credited with 325, and appearing in 10 separate series.

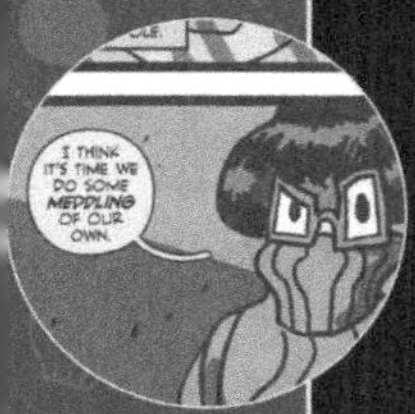
I THINK IT'S TIME WE DO SOME MEDDLING OF OUR OWN.

Not only is this gag a reference to the Scooby gang, but it's based upon the stinger at the end of the theatrical *Justice League* film. So much work to reference a scene that no one likes or remembers, that's the Winston Way®.

NEWSPAPER FULL STORIES

Each newspaper article in Gumshoe City is painstakingly written by me (Winston) even though it will often be printed at an unreadable size. Here's the full articles at a legible size so my work isn't for naught.

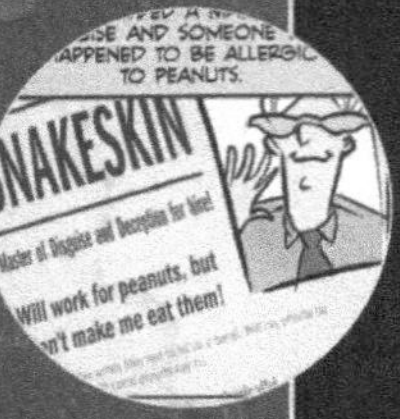
TO PEANUTS.
SNAKESKIN
Will work for peanuts, but

Snakeskin
Master of disguise and deception for hire!

Will Work for peanuts, but don't make me eat them!

--

Local writer writes filler text to fill up a panel. Will his efforts be noticed at all? Local experts say no.

HERO COP BLOWS UP (Metaphorically)

Noted hero cop, Martin Lüscanon was awarded the key to the city over the weekend for his takedown of a counterfeit ring ring. Lüscanon was quoted as saying "it was hard to work an explosion into that, but I pulled it off". A local youth seeing the explosion described it as "cool as heck."

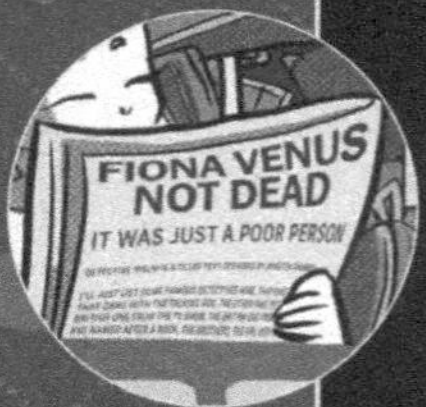
FIONA VENUS NOT DEAD
IT WAS JUST A POOR PERSON

Fiona Venus Not Dead
It was just a poor person

Detective Ipsum is a filler text designed by Winston Gambro.

I'll just list some famous detectives here, that fake psychic, that gang with the talking dog. the other fake psychic, the british one from the tv show, the british one from the movie, the kid named after a book, the brothers, the girl with the hat, the superhero, the mouse, that other superhero, the bald one, the one in all the books your grandma likes, the ones from that tv show that's been on forever, the one your mom had a crush on, the one your dad secretly had a crush on...

NEWSPAPER FULL STORIES

NEWSPAPERS: THE BEST AND ONLY WAY TO GET NEWS!

The Gumshoe Gazette

CITY EDITION
DON'T LET COUNTRY FOLK NEAR THIS!

VOL. CXVII   GUMSHOE CITY, MONDAY, FEBRUARY 13ᵀᴴ   JUST A NICKLE!

HERO COP MARTIN LÜSCANON FOILS ROBBERY

CAPTURES THIEF IN EXCITING EXPLOSION. ARTIFACTS LOST IN SAID AWESOME FIREBALL.

"More words to fill space!?" screamed the newspaper writer next to me. "I should have become an accountant, my mother was right!" she yelled into the void as she broke into tears. Spirits are low in the gazette's bullpen as we realized it was another day of writing pointless filler text to fill up blank space in a newspaper within a single comicbook page.

What am I doing with my life? Am I just telling someone's else story?? DO I EXIST!? HELP ME!

Luckily no one reads this very small text so I don't have to be funny or witty!

Noted department store owner and paparazzi hound, Theodore Venus, was ticketed today for harassing the paparazzi for photos.

"I just want to live my life in peace" said one unnamed cameraman. "He harasses me day and night asking for photos, telling me every intriciate part of his day! Who cares!?".

Theodore Venus offered his comment even though we didn't even ask. "Of course I offer my life to the world, it's give and take, they get to live in envy of my perfect life and I get attention!".

NEWSPAPER FULL STORIES

CONTINUED FROM PREVIOUS PAGE

"Newspapers will never die!" bellowed our editor as she jumped into an olympic-sized pool of caviar.

"Moving pictures? Those things that take months to make? No competition! Television? Never heard of it! A complicated series of electricity forming a pattern of 1s and 0s that creates any and all information that can be shared instantly across the world and will eventually be so simplified that it could fit into a wristwatch? Ha! I'd like to see that!" Quoted our editor as she rubbed a crystal ball and her eyes fogged over.

Hero Cop Actually Villain Cop
Long Missing Artifacts Recovered at his Shooting Range

Whoops, our bad, we'll have to retract a lot of our glowing articles about Martin Lüscanon, but in our defense, he was a pretty cool guy with great hair! He even let our editor shoot his gun, our coffee machine still doesn't work! Okay, I guess the red flags were there. More apologies from our team on page 6.

Honestly it's a slow news day and I'm paid by the word, so I'll just go to town here.

Hey everyone in college laughing at my English degree, who's laughing now?

Me! All the way to the bank! Take that Professor "no one wants to read your novel" Birch.

In other news, our intern saw a blue duck! Well he claims, no one was there to back him up, and have you heard of such a thing? Me neither!

LOGO COLLECTION

I love to fill the world of Gumshoe City with various designs and logos.

It makes the city feel more lived in, as well as offering an easy marketing opportunity if anyone wants a shirt with "Sim's Brims" on it.

CHAPTER 1
THE DEAD DAME IN THE DOMICILE

CHAPTER 2
Last Supper

CHAPTER 0
IT HAPPENED AT THE DOCKS!

CHAPTER 4
WITH FRIENDS LIKE THESE...

CHAPTER 5
MONEY, CASH, AND OTHER TERRIBLE THINGS

Chapter Six
Heartbreakers & Lifetakers

CHAPTER SEVEN:
CRUEL DAZE OF SCHOOL DAYS

chapter 8:
a most UNSUSPICIOUS request.

A DAME WORTH
CHAPTER NINE:
BEING FRAMED FOR

CHAPTER TEN
BIRDS-EYE'S VIEW TO A KILL

CHAPTER 11
ROCK BOTTOM BLUES

CHAPTER TWELVE
SURRENDERING 1½ REVELATIONS

CHAPTER 13
NOW ARRIVING... TO CONCLUSIONS

CRIME-SCENE APARTMENTS
"For the most Desperate"

Frank and Joe's
School for
BOY DETECTIVES

GASHES AND ASHES
FUNERAL HOME

GUMSHOE CITY
GOLDEN GALA
THIS WEEKEND ONLY. ABOARD THE SHYSTER DIRIGIBLE
POOR NEED NOT APPLY.

MAYOR & SON'S
SHIPPING

THE NOIRY BAR & GRILL

Sim's BRIMS

LOGO COLLECTION

THICK AL'S STRUCTURES
Hardest ceilings and walls in town!

CHIEF

THE DOG DILEMMA

Tommy Hollywood

SEARCH ENGINE
PHONE BOOK

Caldocane and Son's

POLICE DEPARTMENT'S APARTMENTS

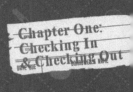

Chapter One: Checking In & Checking Out
DATE DUE BORROWER'S NAME

CHAPTER 2 ~~Last~~ SECOND TO Supper

CHAPTER THREE
BATTLE ON THE HOMEFRONT

CHAPTER FOUR: A CALL TO MYSTERY
1 2 3 4 5 6 7 8 9 0

CHAPTER FIVE: BOOKING FOR TROUBLE

CHAPTER SIX: PLANNING FOR TROUBLE

CHAPTER SEVEN: Reunions: Family & Otherwise

CHAPTER EIGHT: THE MORNING AFTER YESTERDAY

CHAPTER NINE: SOMETHING SMELLS FISHY AT THE CANNERY

CHAPTER TEN
JAILHOUSE ROCK'EM SOCK'EM

TURN TURN TURN
CHAPTER ELEVEN:

CHAPTER TWELVE: THIS FACTORY ONLY PRODUCES CLIMAXES

CHAPTER THIRTEEN: FALLING ACTION

PROLOGUE
FATAL HARDWARE

THE BIG BOOK OF MAPS
Now with Zealand!

DB

TALE OF SUSPENSE

WHAT'S YOUR
DETECTIVE NAME?

Have you dreamt about being a resident of Gumshoe City?

NOW'S YOUR CHANCE!

Use the **first letter** of your **first name**
to determine your new **first name**!

A - Flatfoot
B - Popeye
C - Kick
D - Gizmo
E - Boom
F - Sleuth
G - Ace
H - Bulldog
I - Hook

J - Steak Sauce
K - Boston
L - Cam
M - Seven
N - Soap
O - P.I.
P - Thorn
Q - Dutch
R - Ice

S - Brass
T - Cabbage
U - Tec
V - Sour
W - Cent
X - Bit
Y - Scratch
Z - Sawbuck

Use the **last letter** of your **last name**
to determine your new **last name**!

A - Monk
B - Hardy
C - Lockhart
D - Marple
E - Gently
F - Marlowe
G - Spade
H - Wimsey
I - Poirot

J - Dinkley
K - Bones
L - Castle
M - Tracy
N - Spencer
O - Guster
P - House
Q - Monaghan
R - Brown

S - Magnum
T - Steele
U - Boxer
V - Gray
W - Drew
X - Finger
Y - Mars
Z - Angel

WELCOME TO THE CITY! I'M THEODORE VENUS AND I'LL BE YOUR MAYOR!

TAXES ARE DUE ON THE 20TH!

ABOUT THE CREATORS

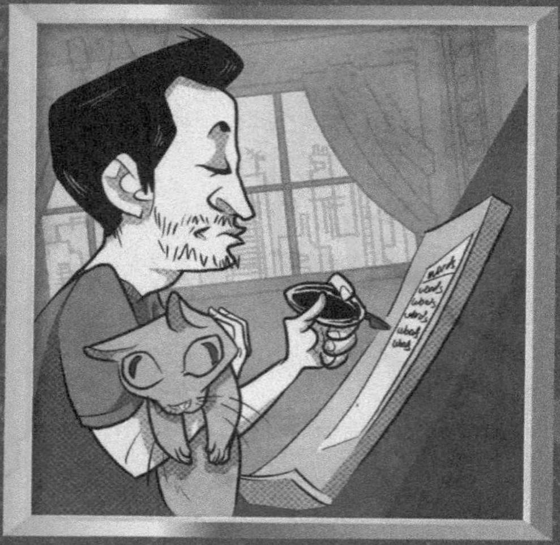

Work
words
words
words
about
words

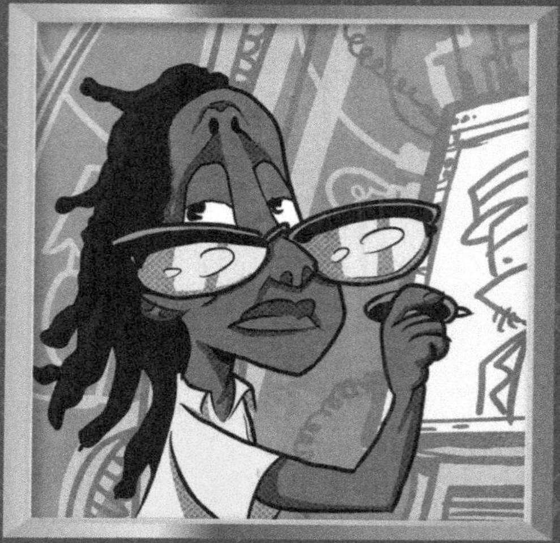

Winston Gambro is a Chicago based comic creator and designer.

He's created the cyberpunk mystery, *Overflow*, the all-ages action comic *Rex Radley: Boy Adventurer*, the horror-romance, *Haunted House: A Love Story* and is currently drawing *Lights in the Sky*.

He currently lives with his cat, Hazel.

Michael Lee Harris is a comic artist and illustrator based in Savannah, Georgia.

He has worked on titles such as *Choco Leche*, *Gumshoe City*, and *The Most Important Comic Book on Earth*, and contributed to several anthologies.

He enjoys writing, drawing comics, storyboarding, illustrating children's books, and talking about himself in the third person.

Milton Keynes UK
Ingram Content Group UK Ltd.
UKHW050654040324
438876UK00005B/53